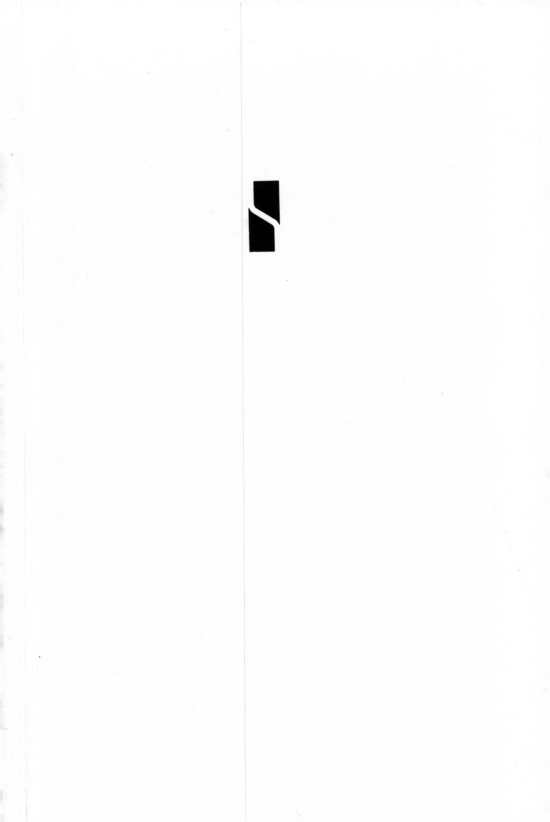

Composition/Rhetoric
A Synthesis

W. ROSS WINTEROWD

Southern Illinois University Press
Carbondale and Edwardsville

90 89 88 87 86   5 4 3 2 1

Permission to quote from the following copyright sources is gratefully
acknowledged:

From *Verses from 1929 On* by Ogden Nash. Copyright © 1935 by the
Curtis Publishing Company. Originally appeared in the *Saturday Evening Post*
May 25, 1935. By permission of Little, Brown and Company

"The Red Wheelbarrow" is reprinted from William Carlos Williams, *Collected
Earlier Poems*. Copyright 1938 by New Directions Publishing Corporation.
Reprinted by permission of New Directions.

"Colloquy in Black Rock": from *Lord Weary's Castle*, copyright 1946, 1974 by
Robert Lowell. Reprinted by permission of Harcourt Brace Jovanovich, Inc.

From "The Love Song of J. Alfred Prufrock" in *Collected Poems 1909–1962* by T. S.
Eliot, copyright 1936 by Harcourt Brace Jovanovich, Inc.; copyright © 1963,
1964 by T. S. Eliot. Reprinted by permission of the publisher.

Library of Congress Cataloging in Publication Data

Winterowd, W. Ross.
   Composition/rhetoric.
   Bibliography: p.
   Includes index.
   1. English language—Composition and exercises—
Study and teaching. 2. English language—Rhetoric—
Study and teaching. I. Title.
PE1404.W55 1986   808'.042'071173   85-2073
ISBN 0-8093-1237-9
ISBN 0-8093-1238-7 (pbk.)

For Al Kitzhaber

Contents

Form and Style

Reading

Teaching Composition

The Profession

Preface

The nine chapters in the first section of this book constitute a state-of-the-art essay which is synoptic, but not encyclopedic, and which approaches its subject from the attitudinal slant of the author.

The five chapters of Section II—"Essays on Composition/Rhetoric"—relate obviously to the first section, supplementing it and rounding out some of the discussions. Though cross referencing is frequent, the first section is independent of the second, and the second section is as attitudinal as the first.

The book, then, is unified by attitude as well as by subject matter. As Kenneth Burke (1968) has said, "an *attitude* towards a body of topics has a unifying force. In effect its unitary nature as a response 'sums up' the conglomerate of particulars towards which the attitude is directed" ("The Anaesthetic Revelation of Herone Liddell," p. 290).

In the first chapter, "From Brain to Ballpoint," I discuss Janet Emig's classic 1971 study of the composing process and the more recent work of Flower and Hayes. I then suggest that "thick description," though "unscientific," provides understanding of what it means to compose. Particularly I argue in behalf of writers' accounts of their own composing processes.

Chapter 2, "Gene and Scene," explores the decidedly unstartling proposition that writing is controlled by—or results from—one's cerebral organization and one's particular "scene." In other words, writing and literacy in general are contingent on one's genetic endowment, but also on the society that one inherits or chooses.

The current-traditional "model" for composition is based on *process*, most commonly prewriting, writing, and rewriting, or some variation of these terms. The model and the shibboleth derived from it ("Process, not product") have been useful, but in either ignoring or simply doing away with text and reader(s) have in a sense short-circuited theory, research, and teaching. Chapter 3, "From Process to Transaction," argues for a *transactional* model as the basis for composition/rhetoric studies and teaching.

Probably no aspect of composition/rhetoric is less understood and more misunderstood than invention, which is, of course, the first among equal "departments" of the field (the others being style and form). In chapter 4, I attempt to clarify some murky and commonly held notions about invention and to untangle the snarl of myth and opinion concerning heuristics and their use.

Chapters 5 and 6 deal with style, the first one with syntactic fluency, including the inevitable "sentence combining," and the second one with accessibility (that is, the ease with which a text can be read). Chapter 6 also gives a summary of the main principles of "document design."

Chapter 7, "Form," has little to say about the five-paragraph essay and a lot about what makes for *cohesion* and *coherence* in a text.

Chapter 8, "Home Base: the English Department," faces the fact that compositionist/rhetoricians are almost invariably members of English departments and thus should think carefully about the lie of the land. Ideally, the chapter is a report on current events.

The final chapter, "On Teaching Composition," is not as arrogant as it might seem. That is, I wouldn't attempt to tell anyone *how to* teach writing, but assume that my colleagues might be interested in how I do it, or how I would do it in the best of all possible situations.

As I said above, the book is unified in subject matter and through attitude. The essays in Part II "flesh out" the ideas in Part I. This being the case, a guide to relationships should be useful to readers. If I were using *Composition/Rhetoric: A Synthesis* as a textbook, I would "chunk" it as follows in my assignments:

Chapter 1 "From Brain to Ballpoint"
Related essay: "Brain, Rhetoric, and Style," pp. 129–57.
Chapter 2 "Gene and Scene" and Chapter 3 "From Process to Transaction"
Related essays: "The Rhetoric of Beneficence, Authority, Ethical Commitment, and the Negative," pp. 159–74; "Speech Acts and the Reader-Writer Transaction," pp. 175–93; "The Three R's: Reading, Reading, and Rhetoric," pp. 253–63; "The Rhetorical Transaction of Reading," pp. 265–72.
Chapter 4 "Rhetorical Invention"
Related essays: "Creativity and the Comp Class," pp. 205–18; "The Realms of Meaning: Text-Centered Criticism," pp. 273–80.
Chapter 5 "Style: Syntactic Fluency" and Chapter 6 "Style: Accessibility"
Chapter 7 "Form"
Related essays: "Dramatism in Themes and Poems," pp. 195–203; "The Grammar of Coherence," pp. 229–44; "Beyond Style," pp. 221–28; "*Dispositio*: The Concept of Form in Discourse," pp. 245–52.
Chapter 8 "Home Base: The English Department"
Related essays: "The Paradox of the Humanities," pp. 323–27; "Getting It Together in the English Department," pp. 329–35.
Chapter 9 "On Teaching Composition"
Related essays: "Developing a Composition Program," pp. 281–97; "From

Classroom Practice into Psycholinguistic Theory," pp. 299–306; "Black Holes, Indeterminacy, and Paulo Freire," pp. 307–13; "Teaching Composing Across the Curriculum," pp. 315–22.

Over the last couple of decades, I have regularly published essays in a wide range of journals, from *College Composition and Communication* and *College English* to *Philosophy and Rhetoric*, *Quarterly Journal of Speech*, and many others. Until now, this body of work has been difficult to get at, dispersed as it has been. I am gratified that now the essays I consider significant are collected and published, though I must admit some trepidation about inviting judgment on what amounts to my whole career.

In 1968, Holt, Rinehart and Winston published my first theoretical book, *Rhetoric: A Synthesis*. My editor then was Kenney Withers. I am gratified to say that my editor now is also Kenney Withers. Hence, I think that the title of this book, echoing that of the 1968 volume, is particularly apt. I thank Kenney for his unfailing good sense, for his impeccable taste, and for his encouragement and patience.

Dan Gunter of Southern Illinois University Press has been helpful and forebearing. Through a most inclement Illinois winter, he cheerfully tolerated my repeated malicious questions regarding the weather and has willingly used his skills to make this a much better book.

Finally, thanks to Deborah Hayward for her expert work on graphics.

Acknowledgments

Grateful acknowledgment is made to the original publishers for permission to reprint the following:

"From Process to Transaction": Portions of this chapter appeared originally in "Syntax, Readability, Intention, and the Real World," *Journal of English Teaching Techniques* (Summer 1980).

"Style: Syntactic Fluency" and "Style: Accessibility": Portions of these chapters were adapted from "Prolegomenon to Pedagogical Stylistics," *College Composition and Communication*, 34:1 (Feb. 1983), 80–90. Reprinted with the permission of the National Council of Teachers of English.

"Home Base: The English Department": This chapter appeared originally in *Pre/Text* (Spring 1983) as "Post–Structuralism and Composition" and is reprinted here, in a slightly altered form, by permission of the editors of *Pre/Text*.

"Brain, Rhetoric, and Style": This essay appeared originally in *Linguistics, Stylistics, and the Teaching of Composition*, ed. Donald A. McQuade (Akron: University of Akron, 1979).

"The Rhetoric of Beneficence, Authority, Ethical Commitment, and the Negative": Reprinted from *Philosophy and Rhetoric* (Spring 1976), by permission of The Pennsylvania State University Press, University Park, PA.

"Speech Acts and the Reader-Writer Transaction": From *Convergences*, ed. B. Petersen (NCTE forthcoming). Reprinted with the permission of the National Council of Teachers of English.

"Dramatism in Themes and Poems": This essay appeared originally in *College English* (Oct. 1983). Reprinted with the permission of the National Council of Teachers of English.

"Creativity and the Comp Class": This essay appeared originally in *Freshman English News* (Fall 1978). It is reprinted here with the permission of the editors.

"The Grammar of Coherence": This essay appeared originally in *College English* (May 1970). Reprinted with the permission of the National Council of Teachers of English.

"Beyond Style": Reprinted from *Philosophy and Rhetoric* (Spring 1972), by permission of The Pennsylvania State University Press, University Park, PA.

"*Dispositio*: The Concept of Form in Discourse": This essay appeared originally in *College Composition and Communication* (Feb. 1971). Reprinted with the permission of the National Council of Teachers of English.

"The Three R's: Reading, Reading, and Rhetoric": This essay appeared originally in *Rhetoric and Change*, ed. William E. Tanner and J. Dean Bishop (Mesquite, Tex.: Ide House, 1982). Reprinted by permission.

"The Rhetorical Transaction of Reading": This essay appeared originally in *College Composition and Communication* (May 1976). Reprinted with the permission of the National Council of Teachers of English.

"The Realms of Meaning: Text-Centered Criticism": This essay appeared originally in *College Composition and Communication* (Dec. 1972). Reprinted with the permission of the National Council of Teachers of English.

"Developing a Composition Program": Reprinted from *Reinventing the Rhetorical Tradition* edited by Aviva Freedman and Ian Pringle (Conway, AR, for the CCTE, 1980), copyright by the Canadian Council of Teachers of English, and reprinted by permission.

"From Classroom Practice into Psycholinguistic Theory": This essay appeared originally in *Learning to Write: First Language/Second Language*, edited by Aviva Freedman, Ian Pringle, and Janice Yalden (London and New York: Longman, 1983). Reprinted by permission.

"Black Holes, Indeterminacy, and Paulo Freire": This essay appeared originally in *Rhetoric Review* (Sept. 1983). Reprinted by permission.

"Teaching Composing across the Curriculum": This essay appeared originally in *The Writing Instructor* (Winter/Spring 1982). Reprinted by permission.

"The Paradox of the Humanities": Reprinted by permission of the Modern Language Association of America from *ADE Bulletin* (May 1980), copyright 1977 by the Association of Departments of English.

"Getting it Together in the English Department": Reprinted by permission of the Modern Language Association of America from *ADE Bulletin* (Nov. 1977), copyright 1977 by the Association of Departments of English.

"The Politics of Meaning": This essay appeared originally in *Written Communication*, 2:3 (July 1985). Reprinted by permission of Sage Publications, Inc.

Selections from "The Love Song of J. Alfred Prufrock" are reprinted by permission of Faber and Faber Ltd. from *Collected Poems 1909–1962* by T. S. Eliot.

Part I

The Field of Composition/Rhetoric

1. From Brain to Ballpoint

The current shibboleth in composition, "Process, not product," reflects a significant change in attitudes and teaching methods. Under the aegis of the New Criticism, the Old Compositionists reacted to finished texts, pointing out to students where they had gone wrong and sometimes where they had succeeded; the Old Composition was a correctionist discipline. The New Composition takes as its province the composing process, not the finished text, and the composition teacher seeks ways to intervene in the process, to teach students to *do* something more proficiently. The composition teacher is more like a mathematics teacher, a violin teacher, or oil painting instructor than a teacher of the history of science, music appreciation, or art history.

STUDIES OF THE COMPOSING PROCESS

Suppose we wanted to learn what writers do and think when they compose. The most direct method of finding out would be to watch them and to question them about their methods. If that statement seems reasonable, then the following should be astounding: it was not until the late 1960s that a composition researcher actually did observe and ask questions. That person was, of course, Janet Emig, whose monograph *The Composing Processes of Twelfth Graders* was published in 1971.

Janet Emig did not initiate the New Composition, but her 1971 monograph is the first significant document in modern attempts to study the composing process. It is a remarkably rich piece of work, carried out by an intelligent researcher whose own prose is graceful, a quality that is becoming increasingly rare in empirical studies in composition, the grittiness of which constitutes a sad paradox.

Emig advanced four hypotheses:

1. Twelfth-grade writers engage in two modes of composing—reflexive and extensive[1]—characterized by processes of different lengths with different clustering of components.

---

1. "The terms *reflexive* and *extensive* have the virtue of relative unfamiliarity in discussions of modes of discourse. Second, they suggest two general kinds of relations between the writing

3

2. These differences can be ascertained and characterized through having twelfth-grade writers compose aloud—that is, attempting to externalize their processes of composing.

3. . . . An implied or an explicit set of stylistic principles governs the selection and arrangement of components—lexical, syntactic, rhetorical, imagaic.

4. . . . Extensive writing occurs chiefly as a school-sponsored activity; reflexive, as a self-sponsored activity.

(P. 3)

Emig's many contributions to our understanding are well known, but worth rethinking now, more than a decade after her study was first published. In the first place, more than any other theorist or researcher, she helped establish the "process model" in the field. Another contribution, this one stunningly simple: we can observe and question to learn about the composing process, i.e., use an empirical rather than a rationalistic methodology. Emig is *the* pioneer in case studies of composing.

Her findings as a whole are not surprising, but in the context of the product-oriented Old Composition, they are revolutionary. In my own summary: (1) For the eight students in the study, extensive writing was mainly school-sponsored. (2) Reflexive writing took more time and was a more complex activity (a finding that runs counter to much textbook wisdom). (3) The teacher is the audience for school-sponsored writing, but more able students also aim at their peers. (4) Students do little prewriting in the extensive mode. (Do they have algorithms or formulas that enable them to produce the expected sorts of texts? Have they ever been taught prewriting strategies?) (5) Students are more likely to revise self-sponsored than school-sponsored writing. Finally, in Emig's own language, this supremely important point:

(6) Most of the criteria by which students' school-sponsored writing is evaluated concerns the accidents rather than the essences of discourse—that is, spelling, punctuation, penmanship, and length rather than thematic development, rhetorical and thematic sophistication, and fulfillment of intent. (P. 93)

One can fault the Emig study for the relative poverty of the discourse model on which it was based, lamenting the author's failure to use available resources, especially the richness that a dramatistic view would have provided, but that criticism is largely offset by the first chapter, an excellent review of extant literature on the composing process and by the marvelous heuristic that the following list of questions provides:

If the context of student writing—that is, community milieu, school, family—affects the composing process, in what ways does it do so, and why?

---

self and the field of discourse—the *reflexive*, a basically contemplative role: 'What does this experience mean?'; the *extensive*, a basically active role: 'How, because of this experience, do I interact with my environment?'" (p. 37).

What are the resources students bring to the act of writing? If there are specifiable elements, moments, and stages in the composing process of students, what are these? If they can be differentiated, how? Can certain portions be usefully designated by traditional nomenclature, such as planning, writing, and revising? Are elements organized linearly in the writing process? Recursively? In some other manner? How do these elements, moments, and stages in the composing process relate to one another? If there is a phenomenon "prewriting," how can it be characterized? What is a plan for a piece of writing? Under what conditions—physical, psychic—do students start to write?

If writing is essentially a selection among certain sorts of options—lexical, syntactic, rhetorical—what governs the choices students make?

What psychological factors affect or accompany portions of the writing process? What effects do they have? What is a block in writing (other than dysgraphia)?[2] When and why do students have blocks? How can they be overcome? Under what conditions do students stop work on a given piece of writing?

If all, or certain kinds of, writing within schools differs from all, or certain kinds of, writing outside schools, how do they differ and why?

If there are modes of school writing, how can these be differentiated? If the mode in which the piece is written affects the process of writing, or the process the mode, how?

What is the press of such variables as the reading of others' writing and the personal intervention of others upon any portion or upon the totality of the writing process? (Pp. 7–8)

It is extremely interesting to me that concentrated, systematic interest in the process that we supposedly teach began only a bit more than a decade ago. We are, as a matter of fact, members of a young discipline.

Linda Flower and John Hayes have used *protocols* to investigate the composing process. As they explain in *A Process Model of Composition* (1979), a protocol is "a description of the activities, ordered in time, which a subject engages in while performing a task" (p. 2). This description deals with the events in sequence, not merely with outcomes or goals; thus, a protocol is intended to capture the moment-by-moment actions that lead to a result. "When we collect protocols of people solving problems, we are interested not just in the answers they give us, but, also and more importantly, in the sequence of things they do to get those answers" (p. 3).

The great problem with protocols, of course, is the suspicion that delivering them skews the process they are intended to report on and describe. Can one generate a complex piece of writing and report on the process simultaneously?

In *The Mind's Best Work*, D. N. Perkins (1981, pp. 24–32) argues plausibly that mere reporting of an activity is not disruptive, though thinking about thinking undoubtedly is. But even though reports on an activity such as

2. See Mike Rose, *Writer's Block: The Cognitive Dimension* (Carbondale and Edwardsville: Southern Illinois Univ. Pr., 1984).

composing might not disrupt the process, research through protocols entails significant problems. In the first place,

Not even the most ardent introspectionist expects reports to reveal everything, certainly not the firing of neurons in the nervous system but not even necessarily such things as what clue triggered an insight. In fact, a little experience with think-aloud techniques quickly teaches that people simply do not have time to report everything that happens consciously if they are to get on with the task. (Perkins, 1981, p. 31)

It seems to me that metalinguistic knowledge could be the most important factor in think-aloud protocols regarding the composing process. To use a somewhat far-fetched analogy: I play the harmonica by ear, never having learned to read music. If I were to report on my harmonica playing—and I am quite skilled—I would be severely handicapped by my lack of metalinguistic knowledge: I simply lack the vocabulary to talk about music. More sophisticated subjects are capable of giving more richly textured reports because initiates have the vocabulary. In two or three instances at least, Flower and Hayes obtained protocols from postdoctoral fellows who were attending a year-long seminar at Carnegie-Mellon, and certainly these people could give a more richly embroidered account than, say, Emig's Lynn.

Both Lynn and the postdoctoral fellows, however, did provide insightful reports. Might it be the case that Lynn's was more reliable than were the postdoctoral fellows'? With the proper vocabulary at their disposal, and with all of the composition lore at their fingertips, the fellows were in a much better position to fabricate than was Lynn.

In any case, these are considerations when we look at data obtained from protocols.

The process model that Flower and Hayes derived from their protocols divides the "writer's world" into (1) the task environment, (2) the writer's long-term memory, and (3) the writing process. The task environment includes every influence outside the writer's skin. An aspect of long-term memory might be writing plans, such as the journalist's questions. And the writing process has the following components:

Planning
   Generating
   Organizing
   Goal Setting
Translating
Reviewing
   Reading
   Editing

In generating, the writer retrieves information from long-term memory. "Because each retrieved item is used as the new memory probe, items are re-

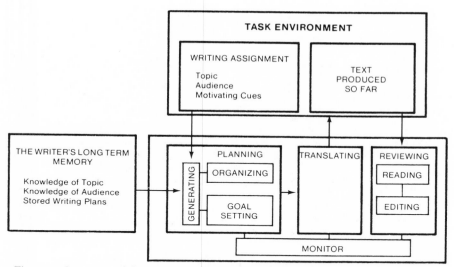

Figure 1. Structure of the writing model (from Linda S. Flower and John R. Hayes, *A Process Model of Composition* [1979]).

trieved from memory in associated chains" (p. 17). Irrelevant items, however, break the chain, sometimes the first one, but at most, the third.

Translating—the actual writing of the text—must involve such factors as syntactic fluency, paragraph sense, preference for appositional or propositional strategies (to be discussed later; see "Brain, Rhetoric, and Style," pp. 129–57, and "Dramatism in Themes and Poems," pp. 195–203), and so on, but Flower and Hayes have nothing to say about these operations. They boil their model down into the diagram shown in figure 1.

Notice that the model includes a *monitor*, which the authors explain thus: editing and generating "may interrupt other processes" (p. 28), taking priority over goal setting. By "monitor," Flower and Hayes seem to intend the control a writer has over the process. This aspect of the model relates interestingly to the work of Stephen Krashen (1976, 1978; see also "Developing a Composition Program," pp. 281–97). Humes (n.d.) bases an instructional model on the work of Flower and Hayes.

"THICK DESCRIPTION"

Though the Flower and Hayes model is clearcut and direct, providing a basis for interesting research, one criticism is that it sacrifices the texture which "phenomenological" research provides in abundance.

In *The Interpretation of Cultures*, Clifford Geertz (1973) takes a Burkean view of the anthropologist's task and debunks the "scientism" of methodologies which, for the sake of objectivity and empiricism, give "thin" descriptions of human phenomena:

> Once human behavior is seen as (most of the time; there *are* true twitches) symbolic action—action which, like phonation in speech, pigment in painting, line in writing, or sonance in music, signifies—the question as to whether culture is patterned conduct or a frame of mind, or even the two somehow mixed together, loses sense. The thing to ask about a burlesqued wink or a mock sheep raid is not what their ontological status is. It is the same as that of the rocks on the one hand and dreams on the other—they are things of the world. The thing to ask is what their import is: What it is, ridicule or challenge, irony or anger, snobbery or pride, that, in their occurrence and through their agency, is getting said. (P. 10)

For at least ten years, I have been asking both my graduate students and my freshmen to write accounts of their own composing processes, and my colleagues in the public schools have used the same assignment, *mutatis mutandis*. Whereas protocols have all the validity of eyewitness accounts—and we know how notoriously unreliable such accounts can be—the phenomenological papers that my students write have all the richness of fiction—and since Aristotle first told us, we have all known how veracious fiction is. It has become perfectly clear, as Geertz argues in *The Interpretation of Cultures*, that so-called ethnomethodological studies are very much like fiction, or at the very least like biography, which is, of course, very much like fiction.

In the composing process papers, I ask students to do enthnomethodology on themselves, and such research demands hermeneutics, not mere eyewitness reporting. One content that is typical of the composing process papers is discussion of attitudes toward writing.

> This morning I had a half-idea about how I might make this a paper about writing this paper. My prewriting stage has involved preparing myself for an intuitive leap. (I keep wanting to turn this paper into one about me and writing instead of about my composing process. That's what I'm really interested in.) That is, in prepping lit crit papers, I've tended to read and reread a text, waiting for ideas while making notes. SP kept giving me grief about the distance of my voice. I've already talked about this—mentioning it again was a way of trying to get at something else—got it. I feel uncomfortable about the fact that I feel uncomfortable about writing, that I feel I don't know enough to say anthing about X—except, of course, there are all those articles in professional journals which have made me say, "Why didn't I write this? I've already figured it out for myself." (Student number 307)

Intimidation and fear are the attitudes most commonly expressed by graduate students:

> To begin with, I have a fear—something ridiculous and crippling—of saying the obvious. This means worrying at length about what I will say. This worry is the first stage of the whole process. (Student number 136)

"The Composing Process Theme" . . . Shudder . . . I had heard of this famous as-signment two weeks before our class began and even then the thought of writing it made me cringe. My sense of dread was even stronger than what I usually felt when faced with a writing task. The subject was painful to me: I had been pleased with very little of the writing I'd done in graduate school so far, and I didn't want to think about the reasons why. Yet if there's anything I'm learning in my seemingly never-ending trek through academia, it is that the truth, once discovered, feels good. In this spirit and buoyed by the anonymity my social security number so humanely provides me, I am finding the courage and even a certain enthusiasm to write this paper—truthfully.

I will reluctantly begin by admitting that most of the critiques, interpretations, and sundry essays I've written for graduate school were not products of "my best," but products of fear and even, at times, panic. This leads me on to an ever more soul-shattering evaluation: my ability to teach. How could I propose to instruct others in something I didn't enjoy myself? The more I painfully introspected, the more I realized that an examination of my composing process was essential if I wanted to gain insights that might liberate my "hung-up" writing style and generate firsthand composing ad-vice I could pass on to my students. (Student number 457)

One of my students, working with a collaborator, had some success with television scripts. In her paper, she reported the Eureka phenomenon:

Working on a boring, non-spontaneous scene physically and mentally exhausted us, so we decided it was time to take a break. We took off to Marie Callender's Restaurant—our favorite change of environment. Of course, we took our legal pad with us in case we came up with any ideas for Scene Two. Suddenly inspiration struck over the straw-berry pie. Gags started pouring out our mouths faster than we could shovel in the pie. Unlike the first scene, we didn't feel straightjacketed by the plot, and our imaginations were able to wander freely. We stayed at the restaurant until we had worked out the entire scene, and we were quite pleased to find it up to our usual standards of wit and ingenuity, albeit with a few coffee stains. (Student number 152)

A typical statement in regard to prewriting:

I generally try to let my mind play with my subject for a time before I actually begin writing. Sometimes this involves a period of concentration with pencil and paper; other times it involves keeping a page or series of pages on which I make notes as ideas occur to me, often while I am working on something else. Frequently, both are in-volved. At some point in that process, there usually emerges a notion about the shape in which I can cast what I have to say. I jot that down as well. (Student number 307)

The following themes repeatedly arise in papers by graduate students:

attitude
easy and hard writing (Easy writing usually involves some kind of algorithm.)
the Eureka phenomenon
heuristics (Students report having developed their own before studying composition/rhetorical theory.)

instruction in writing (high school and undergraduate college)

the journal (Though I have not done a count, I have the impression that more than half of my graduate students keep some sort of journal.)

notes (on slips of paper or cards that can be arranged and rearranged)

pauses (to read over what is already written)

planning (Very few students use formal outlines; many use informal scratch outlines.)

prewriting

process (The two general categories might be called "inch-by-inch" and "all-at-once.")

purpose ("This dynamic [the writer-reader relationship] changes depending on my purpose and motives for writing. I write for three reasons—I have to, I want to, I need to. Although these are not mutually exclusive categories, they are motivations that produce different kinds of writing, and writing processes."—Student number 442)

rewriting (Some of my students, like D. H. Lawrence, rewrite by starting afresh from the beginning. Others make changes almost sentence by sentence.)

rituals (Such as elaborate preparations, using music to get in the mood, and so on.)

scene (Many students report that they work best in a given scene; others are unable to work outside the proper scenes. "Every writer, playwrite or prose essayist, serves his idiosyncracies. I have several. First, I demand a familiar, comfortable place. Only two places work: at my desk at home or at a long wooden table in a library reading room. Home can be almost anywhere; I once wrote the better part of a play in a series of bed-and-breakfast places on Scotland's east coast. I was only in each place a week, but I felt settled."—Student number 469)

starting

structure

talk-write

time (morning, afternoon, evening, late night)

typing versus handwriting

At the very least, the "thick description" of the composing process paper is a useful supplement to the protocol method of gaining knowledge about the composing process. In some ways, the thick description is better, for the subject has time to think about his or her thinking and thus give an interpretation, something which is not possible with protocols.

An exquisitely simple fact about composition is that every teacher can be—should be—a researcher. Before us in every class are the data: the composing processes of the students we teach. If we are observant, we can learn worlds about what happens when writers are successful and unsuccessful. We should rely more heavily on what we can discover for ourselves and less heavily on the dogma of the composition textbooks.

2. Gene and Scene

If we are to follow the language transaction as far into its source as possible, we must take account of the individual genetic endowment functioning in a given place and age; we must be aware of the gene-scene dialectic that creates mind.

Those among us who are not technologically inclined find the takeoff of a 747 miraculous, and even scientific sophisticates are awed by black holes and antimatter. No less glamorous are the revelations about humankind's dual brain, a growing body of knowledge that is fascinating in itself and that helps us understand the language transaction.

The basic story is simple enough. In order to alleviate life-threatening and intractible epilepsy, neurosurgeon Joseph Bogen cut the *corpus callosum*—the large bundle of neurons that connects the left and right hemispheres (hereafter LH and RH) of the brain. Imagine one-half of a whole walnut; the two lobes equal the brain's hemispheres, and the bridge between the lobes is the corpus callosum. Since this massive coaxial cable of nerves is the line of communication between the cerebral continents, *commissurotomy* (the procedure that cuts the cable) creates, if you will, two functioning brains within one skull.

Roger Sperry of the California Institute of Technology, a collaborator with Bogen, realized that commissurotomized (hereafter "split-brain") patients gave neuropsychologists the opportunity to explore the functions of the hemispheres. As long as the LH and the RH can communicate through the corpus callosum, behavior and cognition must be taken as a mix; in split-brain subjects, volition, behavior, and cognition can be certainly attributed to one or the other hemisphere.[1]

1. See Caplan and Kinsbourne (1981); Caramazza, Gordon, Zuriff, and DeLuca (1976); Chall and Mirsky (1976); Day and Ultowska (1979); Dimond and Beaumont (1974); Emig (1978); Freed (1981); Friederici, Schoenle, and Goodglass (1981); Gazzaniga (1972); Glassner (1980, 1981); Globus, Maxwell, and Savodnik (1976); Klein and Armitage (1979); Lake and Bryden (1976); Levy (1980); Levy and Reid (1976); Ley and Bryden (1979); Luria (1973); MacLean (1978); McKeever and Dixon (1981); Miner (1976); Moscovitch (1976); Obler, Zatorre, Galloway, and Vaid (1982); Ornstein (1975); Pirozzolo and Rayner (1977); Rose (1976); Schmuller and Goodman (1979); Schnitzer (1978); Segalowitz and Hansson (1979); Sperry

There are, of course, other ways to isolate brain function. Wilder Penfield began mapping by applying electrical probes to the brains of conscious subjects, a painless procedure (once the skull has been opened) since the brain itself is without pain sensoria. Furthermore, one or the other hemisphere can be anesthetized, and, grotesquely, some conditions necessitate removal of one hemisphere in infants (hemidecortication), allowing the study of language development in individuals with only the RH or the LH intact. The following abstract is worth quoting in full:

The language development of three 9- and 10-year-old children possessing only a right or left hemisphere was studied. Surgical removal of one brain half antedated the beginning of speech, so each child has acquired speech and language with only one hemisphere. Different configurations of language have developed in the two isolated hemispheres: phonemic and semantic abilities are similarly developed but syntactic competence has been asymmetrically acquired. In relation to the left, the right brain half is deficient in understanding auditory language, especially when meaning is conveyed by syntactic diversity; detecting and correcting errors of surface syntactic structure; repeating stylistically permuted sentences; producing tag questions which match the grammatical features of a heard statement; determining sentence implication; integrating semantic and syntactic information to replace missing pronouns; and performing judgments of word relationships in sentences. Language development in an isolated right hemisphere, even under seizure-free conditions, results in incomplete language acquisition. (Dennis and Whitaker, 1976)

The human organism operates on a strange crossover principle, whereby the LH controls right-side functions and the RH controls the left, an important fact if we are to understand brain function. For example, the visual field in each eye is split, data from the right field feeding into the LH and vice versa. The LH controls the right hand, and the RH controls the left. Without the corpus callosum, the left hand does not know what the right hand is doing.

All of this appears enormously prosaic.

An ordinary, everyday 727 weighs 84 tons when it takes to the air after a 51-second run to reach approximately 180 miles per hour. We can experience this technological thrill.

A black hole is the result of a gravitational field so intense that even light cannot escape. We can fantasize about this scientific fugue.

But the mere flick of a scalpel severing a bundle of nerves? So what else is new?

The answer: two brains in one skull, two minds in one body. Nor will I go on to mention soul.

Except to say in advance that as mind is not tissue, so soul is not mind.

(1976); Ten Houten and Kaplan (1973); *UCLA Educator* (1975); Vaid and Lambert (1979); Vonnegut (1976); Wapner and Gardner (1981); Wapner, Hamby, and Gardner (1981); Winterowd (1979); Wittrock (1977, 1980a).

(Where is our physiology taking us? Perhaps—just perhaps—back to language: to an immensely disturbing middle-ground. We can convince ourselves that mind cannot be reduced to brain tissue, but can we convince ourselves that soul cannot be reduced to mind? Is mind a function of brain, is language a creation of mind, and is soul the product of language?)

In summary, the *left hemisphere* is the logician, the arithmetician, working deductively from whole to part. Language is an LH function, as is the temporal sense. (When we listen to music, the LH processes tempi.) The *right hemisphere* is largely without language; it is excellent at gestalt recognition. (With our RHs anesthetized, you and I would not be able to recognize familiar faces.) RH is the inductive hemisphere, moving readily from part to whole. When we read, apparently the RH identifies gross forms, the gestalts of letters and words; the LH picks out the features that, for instance, differentiate O and Q. Furthermore, the RH works well with images.

Henceforth in this discussion, the family of terms that includes "LH," "RH," and "hemisphericity" will be taken metaphorically since the geography of brain functions is irrelevant to our concerns whereas the nature of those functions, as they reveal themselves in language, is crucial.

LH, RH, AND LITERACY

For genetic and cultural reasons—because of the gene-scene dialectic—humans have various mixes of RH and LH functions, that is, of lateralization. By and large, literate people in the Occident are predominantly left hemispheric, comfortable with the LH mode of cognition: logical, highly verbal, abstract thinkers. But a significant minority, perhaps for genetic reasons, are RH dominant. And cerebral dominance bears directly on our understanding of both reading and writing.

Presumably the LH writer should work easily with the accepted Western forms of explanation and argumentation, which might be summarized (as in virtually all composition instruction) thus: "State a general thesis, and support it with appropriate logic or details or both"—in other words, move from the general to the specific, from the whole to the part. The cardinal injunction in our school writing might be paraphrased, then, as "Use LH methods to convey your ideas." And since we products of Western technological society are largely LH dominant (Ten Houten and Kaplan, 1973), the injunction has an intrinsic rightness for the vast majority. We tend to be at home with deduction.

Yet there is another and equally powerful mode of thought, the one that seems to be genetically programmed into the RH. The RH thinker is likely to use the specific example, not the general thesis, as a pivot and to work from the instance to its import, inductively.

Notice how a typical paragraph states a general idea, a topic, and then supports it with examples, in classic deductive fashion:

We live in an age when the eye is feasted and the ear, if not starved, is kept on short rations.

Special merit is accorded to the cartoon which makes its effect without a caption. In the theater we expect a higher standard of scenic design, aided by elaborate lighting, than playgoers have ever known. It is not uncommon for a stage setting, at the rise of the curtain, to be greeted with a round of applause. But how long is it since you have heard an actor applauded because he had delivered a fine speech particularly well? This calls attention to our comparative indifference to fine speech; it is not altogether lacking, but we do not insist upon it as we insist on the gratification of the eye. But how do the books you read reach your consciousness? By words which you hear, or pictures which you see?—Robertson Davies, *A Voice from the Attic*

We are not here speaking merely of writing strategies, but of characteristic modes of thought that are genetically and culturally determined.

We in the West are conditioned to believe that the inexorable march of the syllogism—from the general statement to the specific conclusion—and the equally inevitable leap from the "statistically" valid sample to the general conclusion are the only valid modes of thought. But even our vaunted scientific method, the ideal example of induction, is covertly deductive, in that the scientist works from hypothesis (a general statement that controls the selection of data), not simply at random. The successful hypothesis becomes a theory that allows random data to be organized.

May scientists ever continue with their covert deductivism, particularly since we are unwilling to trust our 747s, our errantly cancerous cells, and our fragile environment to the poets. Yet we will argue that Western "logic" is only one mode of thought, and we should take advantage of the fact that the "logical" West (LH) has access to the "mystic" East (RH) via the corpus callosum.

Brilliantly, Joseph Bogen, who must be something of a poetic neurosurgeon, has called the two modes of thought *propositional* and *appositional*. Our propositionalists are experts at dealing with the neatly-laid-out, but the appositionalists can make sense of the montage.

Take the problem of problem-solving, which is certainly a major problem in itself. In class A uniform, with burnished brass and spit-shined boots, the LH can name the parts of this one without any trouble:

> Supply the last sentence for the following:
> All dictatorships are undemocratic.
> All undemocratic governments are unstable.
> All unstable governments are cruel.
> All cruel governments are objects of hate.
> . . . .
> (Cohen and Nagel, 1962, p. 94)

But our spit-and-polish LHer will sweat and struggle with the next one, unless he or she is willing to get out of uniform and don the artist's besmeared smock and (inevitable) beret.

One morning, exactly at sunrise, a Buddhist monk began to climb a tall mountain. A narrow path, no more than foot or two wide, spiraled around the mountain to a glittering temple at the summit. The monk ascended at varying rates of speed, stopping many times along the way to rest and eat dried fruit he carried with him. He reached the temple shortly before sunset. After several days of fasting and meditation he began his journey back along the same path, starting at sunrise and again walking at variable speeds with many pauses along the way. His average speed descending was, of course, greater than his average climbing speed. Prove that there is a *spot* along the path that the monk will occupy on both trips at precisely the same time of day. (Adams, 1979, p. 4; from Koestler, 1967)

The solution to the second problem involves the typically RH ability to use images, not language or arithmetic. If you *imagine* one monk going down the mountain while, simultaneously, his identical twin trudges upward, you will have the solution, for, at some point, they will meet.

In a study of the relationship of hemisphericity to problem solving, Virginia Fultz (1978) found that LH subjects are less versatile than are RH subjects. However, it does seem to be the case that regardless of the nature of the problem, subjects choose characteristic solution strategies, depending on lateralization.

It is a well established fact that both schizophrenia and certain forms of aphasia cause radical dislocations of language function. Some victims seem to retreat or are forced into the kind of language that we might characterize as totally propositional: the ghost of coherence without the body of specificity. Others produce all palpability, a montage with no apparent guiding idea, no generality. (For further discussion and examples, see "Brain, Rhetoric, and Style," pp. 129–57.)

Writing that we accept as "normal" is a mix of propositionality and appositionality, a generality supported by the specific. When teachers ask a highly propositional student to use examples, they are asking him or her not only to adopt a writing strategy, but to change the basic mode of cognition. And the highly appositional student begins—and sometimes ends—with the specific instance.

All of this is profoundly clear to your author, a congenital appositionalist. The pivots for my thought are specific instances, anecdotes, images, and I move from them to my conclusions—a method of cognition that is less than acceptable in our propositional society. My characteristic (inevitable) ploy in an intellectual conversation is "That reminds me of. . . ." At which point, I encounter, frequently, either ennui or hostility. I *am* trying to get on with the subject (in the way that my genetic-scenic heritage has determined for me), but my gambit is frequently viewed as a diversionary tactic or an irrelevance.

Now the methods and motives of poetry should be somewhat clearer to us. Most poems are mixtures of statements

Had we but world enough, and time,
This coyness, lady, were no crime.

Let us go, then, you and I. . . .

metaphors

Time's winged chariot hurrying near. . . .

When the evening is spread out against the sky. . . .

similes

    The youthful hue
Sits on thy skin like morning dew. . . .

and images

Restless nights in one-night cheap hotels
And sawdust restaurants with oyster shells. . . .

Thou by Indian Ganges' side should rubies find. . . .

As we have seen, each hemisphere has its own kind of knowledge: that of the LH is largely verbal, the kind that we convey through exposition; that of the RH is, in the jargon of psychology, *episodic* or experiential (Tulving, 1972), conveyed inadequately by language. Poetry is the attempt to convey episodic, RH knowledge through language and is thus a marvelous and endlessly fascinating subject. Indeed, imagist poems contain no statements in the logical sense, but they are definitely not meaningless.

If we use a broad definition of "poetry," so that we can include certain prose writings, then we can say that one difference between exposition and poetry is the relative mix of LH and RH knowledge that we get from it. The point is nicely illustrated by the following two passages about trout fishing:

1. It was a beautiful stretch of water, either to a fisherman or to a photographer, although each would have focused his equipment on a different point. It was a barely submerged waterfall. The reef of rock was about two feet under the water, so the whole river rose into one wave, shook itself into spray, then fell back on itself and turned blue. After it recovered from the shock, it came back to see how it had fallen.

No fish could live out there where the river exploded into colors and curves that would attract photographers. The fish were in that slow backwash, right in the dirty foam, with the dirt being one of their chief attractions. Part of the speckles would be pollen from pine trees, but most of the dirt was edible insect life that had not survived the waterfall.—Norman MacLean, *A River Runs through It*

2. The Clark Fork, which is open the year around, is probably the most underrated trout fishing stream in Montana. The lower part starts at Bonner Dam 6 miles

east of Missoula, passes through Missoula, Superior, St. Regis, and Thompson Falls, and leaves the state about 15 miles west of Noxon. With all factors considered, it could be rated as one of the best trout streams in the northwest. It has Rainbow, Bull Trout, Native Eastern Brook, and an inexhaustible supply of whitefish. The Rainbow are probably predominant. Being a rather large body of water, you will find the holes are large and deep with long stretches of quiet water.—*Montanan's Fishing Guide*

We have seen, of course, that we usually need the specific—examples, images—to understand even the most prosaic prose, and we know also that most poems contain a declarative element. Successful writing gives us the correct proportions.

METAPHOR

The metaphor is a key to our understanding of literacy. The metaphor has the form X *is* Y, X being the literal term (I. A. Richards' "tenor") and Y being the figurative term (Richards' "vehicle"). But common metaphors do not appear to have this form: "Deserts of vast eternity," "Time's winged chariot." Notice, however, that these latter two mean "Eternity is a vast desert" and, by a more complex process, "Time is a passenger in a winged chariot." Or this from Shakespeare: "Sheathe thy impatience." Since we know that the verb "sheathe" applies to "sword," we can rephrase the metaphor thus: "Impatience (X) is a sword (Y)."

Since the metaphor is a logical predication (X is Y), we should expect it to be a function of the LH, but since it also presents an image—something that we can picture mentally or with a camera or a brush—we should also expect it to be a function of RH. (See "Brain, Rhetoric, and Style," pp. 129–57; Gardner and Winner, 1979.)

Could it be that poetry is "practical," giving writers and readers essential abilities—as well as a particularly humanizing and intense pleasure? Studies are now under way to determine the relationship of metaphoric ability to literacy. In this age of getting "back to basics," it would be especially satisfying to many of us if poetry turned out to be one of them.

GENE AND FRESHMAN ENGLISH

Just one more thought about the genetic endowment for literacy. Reading and writing depend on neurology, the "wiring" of the human brain. There are intelligent human beings, capable of profound thought and intricate learning, who are simply miswired—some portion, undoubtedly, of those diagnosed as dyslexic or aphasic. Our public education at every level provides massive opportunities for most of the disabled, special programs for the blind and paraplegics, but, especially in higher education, we have carefully designed the system to eliminate those with literacy problems, whatever their source. The typical freshman English program at virtually every university is an obstacle course that students with literacy problems find impossible. There *are* alternative learning methods, and while a bright freshman with reading and writing problems might be ill advised to enter such a book-bound field as history, he or she could well become a skilled surgeon or mathematician. Illiteracy simply does not correlate inevitably with lack of intelligence.

SCENE AND LITERACY

The infant with a given genetic endowment is born into a scene—a family, a community, a culture—and this scene has as much to do with literacy as does gene. (For example, see Taylor, 1983.) In fact, we are interested in the gene-scene dialectic. The argument is an old one: environment versus heredity. Our twist is to eliminate the "versus," to explore the relationships between the two.

A prime document is *Literacy: Writing, Reading, and Social Organization*, by John Oxenham (1980). In this book, the author outlines the motives for literacy, all of them essentially scenic—and enormously instructive for those who are concerned about some children's failure to gain the skills of literacy.

Oxenham makes three critical points about reading and writing. First, "they are means to various ends" (p. 6). If the child does not see the ends or finds them unimportant, he or she will never become "basically" literate. In other words—and unsurprisingly—motivation is crucial to learning, and it is axiomatic that motives for gaining language skills fall into two categories: *integrative* and *instrumental*. One person works diligently to lose his Brooklyn accent and the social stigma that it carries in certain groups, and another gives up evenings and weekends to study Russian so that she can read scientific materials in that language—the one person having an integrative motive and the other an instrumental motive.[2]

Second, the importance of literacy depends on the nature of the society in question. The hunter-gatherers of the Kalahari have no practical use for literacy, and one would be hard put to teach children of those tribes to read and write.

Third, in addition to its purposive nature, "literacy is nearly always associated with some notion of education, enlightenment and mental expansion" (p. 7). Aside from specific ends, literacy gives the user access to realms and modes of thought that are impossible in speaking and hearing.

The social (scenic) forces that have created the enormous drive for literacy are commerce, printing, the needs of government, and religion. (Pp. 9–10)

The Phoenicians, who invented the alphabet from which ours derives, were a commercial people, seafaring traders. Like all good businesspeople,

2. For an excellent study of motivation among college composition students, see J. D. Williams and Scott D. Alden, "Motivation in the Composition Class," *Research in the Teaching of English*, 17:2 (May 1983), 101–12.

Table 1. Book production in the world (number of titles published)

	1955	(%)	1965	(%)	1976	(%)
World	269,000	(100)	426,000	(158)	591,000	(219)
Africa	3,000	(100)	7,000	(233)	11,000	(366)
Asia	54,000	(100)	61,000	(113)	100,000	(185)
Europe	131,000	(100)	200,000	(152)	269,000	(205)
North America	14,000	(100)	58,000	(414)	91,000	(650)
Oceania	1,000	(100)	5,000	(500)	5,000	(500)
South America	11,000	(100)	19,000	(172)	31,000	(281)
USSR	55,000	(100)	76,000	(138)	84,000	(152)

Adapted from John Oxenham, *Literacy: Writing, Reading, and Social Organization* (1980).

they needed to keep their records—not to mention their navigation—straight, and their writing system was the result of this need. Earlier than the Phoenicians even, the Sumerians were writing, but the *Gilgamesh* epic is only a brief interlude among the commercial records of the Sumerian clay tablets. Romantics by inclination, we would like to believe that writing developed from the needs to express humankind's more sublime aspirations in poetry and philosophy; but realists by necessity, we are ready to accept the fact that historically, writing had the purpose of making a complex economic system possible.

In the fifteenth century, Gutenberg started the democratization of literacy with his invention of movable type. Before Gutenberg, of course, each book was one-of-a-kind, laboriously inscribed on vellum by the legendary monks. Table 1 gives some idea of the flood that Guttenberg loosed.

Movable type, cheap paperbacks, offset rotary printing, computerized typesetting—these technologies of the word created some of our most familiar scenes: the paperback racks in supermarkets (Harlequin romances prominently displayed), Brentano's, the Carnegie free public library. (Andy was a steelmaker, an industrialist, but he chose to memorialize himself through bookishness.)

Martin Luther takes his place in our pantheon, alongside Gutenberg, McGuffey of reader fame, and Noah Webster, who compiled his dictionary and concocted his ubiquitous Blueback Speller on the patriotic assumption that members of a unified democratic society needed a standard common language. When Christianity was one, authority having devolved from Christ through Peter to a succession of earthly vicars and thence to the priesthood, the laity had no need for direct access to the Bible, for interpretation came through the hierarchy. However, Luther in effect said to the masses, "See for yourselves!" and the ability to read became a religious duty. (Legend has it that John Bunyan had read no book other than the Bible.)

Finally, the state. Nicolai Lenin said, "An illiterate man is nonpolitical; first he must be taught how to read." And in 1974, the government of Iraq published the following:

The high rate of illiteracy among citizens, particularly in rural areas, is considered to be the most serious and dangerous constraint impeding political, economic and social progression of the country. With the present rate of illiteracy, it is impossible to raise the standard of the masses, build up an advanced revolutionary society capable of confronting the problems of the age and its complicated requisites. It is also not possible for our country to contribute to the building up of a united socialist Arab nation. Therefore, the fight against illiteracy within the shortest possible time is considered the most important sphere of our struggle and activities.

Literacy serves the ends of government.

The scene must be right for literacy. An excellent rough-and-ready test for the literacy potential of children is the number of books and magazines around a household. Children who grow up in a family that demonstrates the values of literacy will be literate; the children of readers and writers become readers and writers, naturally and without coercion, sometimes even in spite of their school experience.

Three most instructive and readable documents in this regard are *GNYS AT WRK*, by Glenda Bissex (1980), a case study of her son's preschool acquisition of reading and writing; *Family Literacy*, by Denny Taylor (1983), a case study of the children in six families; and *The Foundations of Literacy*, by Don Holdaway (1979), which argues that direct teaching is ineffective, whereas creating the appropriate scene gives children the opportunity and the desire to acquire literacy.

The concept of scene has both temporal and spatial dimensions, and as if with a camera, our focus on scene can be broadened or narrowed. Thus we can do a closeup of one home or one year, and then we can adjust the lens to capture a panorama of America in the 1980s—one of the attempts of this discussion—or of the age of electronics. We would then ask about the values and uses of literacy in our nation, with its complex economic, political, and social systems.

Example: one of the most important scenes for literacy is the classroom in which writing is taught. What happens there? What are the attitudes, methods, and materials that appear to be successful or unsuccessful? We know precious little about these important questions, and we should be attempting to learn more. The late Mina Shaughnessy, whose *Errors and Expectations* (1977) is a landmark in our understanding of written composition, once said, "The classroom is like a bedroom. The participants enter and close the door. An hour later, they emerge to assure you that great things have happened." But no one observes, and we have only a hazy notion of what actually did happen. We need to know a great deal more about the classroom scene.

Example: revision is a tedious process, for it involves taking a manuscript apart and putting it together again, and yet all successful writers know that revision is an essential process. When it involves tedious recopying with pen or typewriter, the author is likely to compromise, but word processors

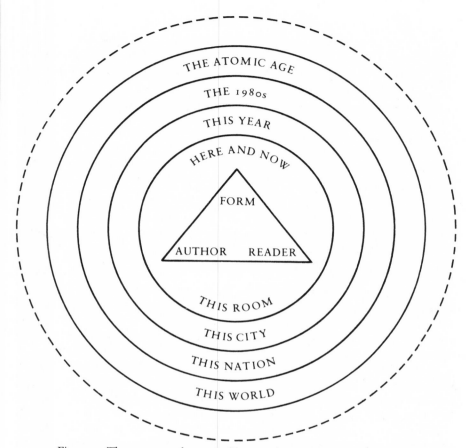

Figure 2. The concept of scene in literacy (from W. Ross Winterowd,
The Contemporary Writer [2nd ed.; 1981]).

make revision relatively painless—the mere flicking of two or three keys. In a study at the University of Southern California, Mark Olson, a graduate student, found that students who compose on a word processor revise freely and with great success. And this homely instance does not even take into account the undoubtedly massive influence that electronic media such as television have on attitudes toward reading and writing and, indeed, on cognitive patterns.[3]

Figure 2 summarizes the concept of scene in literacy.

3. *The Writing Instructor*, 2:4 (Summer 1983) gives an excellent introduction to the uses of the computer in composition instruction.

ATTITUDE

Throughout his long career, our mentor Kenneth Burke has been concerned about *attitude*, which he equates with the speech act theorists' *illocutionary force*, the purpose embodied in a locution regardless of the propositional content. In fact, Burke subsumes illocutionary force under attitude. It is the preparation for an act, a state of mind that may or may not lead to an act. (*A Grammar of Motives*, p. 20) "It may be either an incipient act or the substitute for an act" (*A Grammar of Motives*, p. 476).

An attitude towards a body of topics has a unifying force. In effect its unitary nature as a response "sums up" the conglomerate of particulars toward which the attitude is directed. . . .

Attitudes, in this respect, are a kind of censorial entitling, reduced to terms of behaviour. They are an implicit charade, a way of "acting out" a situation. Or they are like a highly generalized term of classification, a broad logical category—for in effect they classify under one head all the many different particular situations that call forth the same attitude. ("The Anaesthetic Revelation of Herone Liddell," p. 290)

With his notion of attitude, Burke has made a significant contribution to speech act theory, hence to our understanding of composition/rhetoric. In standard theory, the *perlocutionary act* (the effect of the utterance) has no apparent delimitations. I issue a command (illocution): "Stop!" You stop in the middle of the street, look about, see that a car is coming, jump out of the way, fall down a manhole. . . . If we define perlocution as "uptake," which is merely a way of saying that it is the perception of intention, then we can say that illocution and perlocution are identical in the happy speech act: I intend to warn, and you take my utterance as a warning; I intend to promise, and you take my utterance as a promise. And it hardly needs to be said that in the vast majority of cases, the illocution-perlocution transaction is tacit for both parties; unless there is some kind of breakdown or hitch in our dialogue, we are no more focally aware of intentions than we are of our musculature when we type.

If I say, "I hereby order you to leave the United States and never come back," it will be a true order only if you believe that I believe that you believe I am warranted.) The belief structure that underlies speech acts is seldom in consciousness, though it can always be brought into focus.

Each illocutionary act, then, contains or inevitably implies its corresponding perlocution, and if it did not, it would not be an illocutionary act. This is precisely the point that Burke makes in "Epilogue: Prologue in Heaven," from *The Rhetoric of Religion*. Introductory to this masque, the impressario tells us,

. . . imagine such intuitive expression as a dialogue between two persons that are somehow fused with each other in a communicative bond whereby each question is its own answer, or is answered without being asked.

Such is the formal paradox underlying the discourse between The Lord and Satan [in the masque which follows]. (P. 273)

In the dialogue, Satan asks, "Is it true that in these new creatures you shall have solved a basic logical contradiction, making it possible for them to disobey your all-powerful authority?"

The answer (pp. 277–78) is this: When the command and the obedience are one, we have a unilateral speech act, as when I give an order to you, believing (as I must) that you believe that I believe the giving is warranted. This is to say, the unilateral speech act is the utterance viewed only from the perspective of the addresser. The addressee may be incapable of receiving the message—may, for instance, be deaf or defunct. Nonetheless, the addresser has performed a real speech act.

To use Burkean terminology, we might rename the unilateral speech act, calling it henceforth the "pure" speech act. And the name for the other kind—that in which there is a happy transaction between addresser and addressee—is clearly the "temporal" speech act, the sort studied by Austin (1962) and Searle (1969).

In "The Prologue in Heaven," we learn that God is capable of pure speech acts, but what about mortals? In a sense, from the point of view of the addresser, every speech act is pure, else it would not count as a true speech act. We might also assume that some mentally deranged persons are capable of pure speech acts or perhaps are incapable of any other, carrying on dialogues with themselves, never emerging from their autism. (We wonder about the nature of text written by such a godlike creature.) By its very nature, the temporal speech act must involve an other, in our jargon, an addressee.

Cultural values are nothing more than prevalent attitudes; conceivably attitudes create political values as surely as political commitments create attitudes. (Which came first, conservative economic policy or the attitudes that accompany it, the "back to basics" movement in literacy or the attitudes toward learning and culture of its adherents?)

Here, from William Labov's *The Study of Nonstandard English* (1969), is a superb example of the effects of attitude on language learning and use:

In high stratified situations, where society is divided into two major groups, the values associated with the dominant group are assigned to the dominant language by all. Lambert and his colleagues at McGill University have shown how regular are such unconscious evaluations in the French-English situation in Quebec, in the Arabic-Hebrew confrontations in Israel, and in other areas as well. When English-Canadians heard the same person speaking Canadian French, on the one hand, and English, on the other, they unhesitatingly judged him to be more intelligent, more dependable, kinder, more ambitious, better looking, and taller—when he spoke English. Common sense would tell us that French-Canadians would react in the opposite manner, but in fact they do not. Their judgments reflect almost the same set of unconscious values as the English-Canadians show. This overwhelmingly negative evaluation of Canadian

French is a property of the society as a whole. It is an omnipresent stigma which has a strong effect on what happens in school as well as in other social contexts. (P. 31)

The destructive power of negative attitude is almost so obvious as to require no discussion. There is, for example, the classic study in which teachers were informed that one group of students was gifted and another below average, when actually the two groups were evenly matched. The "gifted" students outperformed the others, apparently because of teacher attitude.

It is perhaps not so obvious that our general and specific attitudes are the wellsprings of intentions and that intentions result in actions. Quite literally, we live by attitudes.

3. From Process to Transaction

Among others, Louise Wetherbee Phelps points out that the "process" view of composition eliminates too much from the focus. In *Acts, Texts, and the Teaching Context* (1980), she looks at composing as an *act* in Kenneth Burke's sense. The primary acts in the domain of composition, according to Phelps, are (1) the productive act of composing, (2) the speech act performed by the discourse, and (3) the receptive or interpretive act of the reader. (The transactive paradigm is developed in "Speech Acts and the Reader-Writer Transaction," pp. 175–93.)

Roman Jakobson (1960) proposed a model of the discourse act that I have used repeatedly and have always found particularly illuminating.

$$\begin{array}{c} \text{Context} \\ \text{Message} \\ \text{Addresser} \text{——————————} \text{Addressee} \\ \text{Contact} \\ \text{Code} \end{array}$$

Each of the six factors in this model strongly implies not only a process, but a transaction.

The *addresser* projects a semantic intention to the *addressee*, an act of faith whether the message is written or spoken, and the *addressee* must reconstruct (or simply construct) the intention that he or she believes the addresser has projected.

This transaction—this elegantly intricate ballet of intention and response—goes on automatically, the participants normally unaware of the interpretive task, attempting with greater or lesser commitment to construct or reconstruct the "drift" of the discourse.

Another factor in the Jakobsonian schema is *context*, the information

---

1. Portions of this chapter appeared originally in "Syntax, Readability, Intention, and the Real World," *Journal of English Teaching Techniques* (Summer 1980).

about other-than-text that can be derived by means of the text. (Note that I do not say *from* the text.) However, to derive information by means of the text, the reader must bring massive knowledge to the text.

Cambourne (1981) discusses some of the problems that researchers in artificial intelligent face. For example, take a fairly simple problem (as the conundrums faced by those who would construct a "thinking machine" go). To interpret the following two sentences, a machine (or human being) must know quite a great deal about both cats and roofs:

1. Because it was slanted, the cat fell off the roof.
2. Because it was injured, the cat fell off the roof.

Cambourne summarizes:

The message from artificial intelligence appears to be that the utterance never provides all the information one needs for understanding. Neither the computer nor the human being, it seems, can be merely a language parser, sorting out information in the incoming signal. Both also need to be constructors of meaning. Understanding is a constructive process which involves using the linguistic cues provided by other speakers as a basis on which to build up a more elaborate and informative meaning representation. This construction can only take place if the appropriate scenarios and linguistic patterns are already part of the comprehender's knowledge. (Cambourne, pp. 91–92)

The *message* as a structure and *code* as style—which might seem to be inscribed givens—are inevitably part of the negotiation between the addresser and the addressee. That is, the structure of the message is realized in the memory of the reader (e.g., Kintsch, 1974; Frye, 1963), and the style of the code is just as certainly a response in the reader as it is quantifiable on the page. (More about style and form hereafter, pp. 47–65 and 67–81.)

Suppose the Jakobson schema (p. 25) to be a large neon sign. Each of the six elements—addresser, context, message, contact, code, addressee—can be made brighter or dimmer, but none of the six can be totally extinguished. In an ordinary reading of the daily newspaper, *context* glows brightly while the others are barely perceptible; ordinarily we read the newspaper to learn the news. In reading a poem by a familiar author, the neon sign is perhaps lambent. Knowing the poem is by Coleridge, for the moment we hear the *addresser* speaking, but the brightness of that factor is modulated as we begin to pay attention to language itself, and *code* glows brightly, only to be outshone by *addressee* as we attend to the personal effect the poem is having on us.

This metaphoric interpretation of Jakobsen's framework is, I think, a particularly apt way of viewing the writing-reading transaction. As readers, we can attend to the "voice" of the writer (addresser), to the information obtainable through the text (context), to the structure of the piece (message), to the "medium" (contact), to the style (code), or to the effects upon ourselves (addressee). The reading act is a "mix" of these factors.

Two more angles on the transactive paradigm of composition. First, we can view the text as *a set of instructions for the gaining of meaning*. The writer inscribes them, and the reader follows them.

The "instructions" that constitute a text fall into two categories: *exophoric*, referring "outward", and *endophoric*, referring "inward." Take a sample text:

The Purist

I give you now Professor Twist,
A conscientious scientist.
Trustees exclaimed, "He never bungles!"
And sent him off to distant jungles.
Camped on a tropic riverside,
One day he missed his loving bride.
She had, the guide informed him later,
Been eaten by an alligator.
Professor Twist could not but smile.
"You mean," he said, "a crocodile."

—Ogden Nash

The first word, the pronoun "I," has an exophoric thrust, calling attention to a speaker who, of course, turns out to be fictive, a persona. On the other hand, if we take "The Purist" to be a fiction, the thrust of "Professor Twist" is endophoric. We assume there is no such person, but that we will gain requisite information about him from the text itself. (Of course, the title "professor" is exophoric in thrust, for the reader's world knowledge gives the term meaning.)

Notice that short stories "invite" readers to attend endophorically whereas expository essays normally invite exophoric attention.

The white man, leaning with both arms over the roof of the little house in the stern of the boat, said to the steersman:
"We will pass the night in Arsat's clearing. It is late."

—Joseph Conrad, "The Lagoon"

The reader does not know who the "white man" might be or anything about Arsat, but the tale itself will fill in the details, or, to stick to our jargon, will provide the context. On the other hand, the typical expository essay does not invite this kind of endophoric attention:

President Reagan has indicated he will sign the landmark immigration legislation passed by Congress, but the measure has caused lawmakers such election-year anxiety that one of the bill's sponsors worries that it may never reach the president's desk.
"This baby is hanging by a thread," says Republican Sen. Alan K. Simpson of Wyoming, sponsor of the Senate immigration bill that was passed more than a year ago.—Margaret Shapiro and David Hoffman, in *The Washington Post National Weekly Edition* (July 23, 1984)

The assumption here is that readers can identify "President Reagan"; Alan K. Simpson is identified immediately, the assumption being that most readers will not know of him.

Finally, a point that has already been implied: to account for the meaning that a reader gains from a text, he or she must take into consideration the text itself, the context (scene), and his or her perceiving mind.

INTENTIONS

Each language act is a complex web of intentions, seldom directly expressed, but always present. For example, I can give you an order without directly stating my intention:

1. Stop drumming your fingers on the table.

Or I can state my intention:

2. I hereby order you to stop drumming your fingers on the table.

In either case, the intention is the same, and the utterances are essentially identical—provided the contexts (scenes) are identical. (And, of course, "A Modest Proposal" is not a *proposal* at all.)

Just what are we doing when we speak or write a sentence? In the first place, we are creating noises or marks, meaningless in themselves. Second, we are creating propositions, and these propositions consist of predication and reference. In

3. Mary adores John.

the nouns *Mary* and *John* refer, and the verb predicates. Other versions of the sentence have the same predication and reference:

3a. John is adored by Mary.
3b. John—Mary adores him.
3c. Whom Mary adores is John.

Third, we are projecting intentions, as in the following classification by Searle (1975):

Representatives, which convey belief in a statement (i.e., are intended to inform). Mary adores John.
Directives, which are intended to get the addressee to do something.
Stop drumming your fingers on the table.
Commissives, through which the addresser commits himself or herself to some future course of action.
I'll buy you a lollipop tomorrow.

Expressives, through which the addresser expresses a psychological state. I'm sorry that you dropped your lollipop.

Declarations, through which the addresser brings about a new state of affairs. I pronounce you man and wife.
I hereby resign.
I hereby declare this session ended.

Fourth, we are anticipating results. At the very least, we expect the hearer or reader to understand the sentence and its intention.

Consider the dance of discourse. I say to an attractive young woman, "You're looking lovely today." To which she responds, "What do you mean by that?" She is not inquiring about predication and reference or word meaning, but about intention, and she might well have inquired, "What was the intention behind the statement?" But this kind of breakdown seldom occurs, and if it did, language would be impossible, for participants would everlastingly be working at the snarl of misunderstood intentions, and the fabric of conversation or writing would never get woven.

What this amounts to (as we have seen) is that the addresser predicts the addressee's response, and the addressee reconstructs the addresser's intention—instantaneously, almost never pausing to question intention. And that, if you'll think about it, is one of the most glamorous of language's mysteries.

LANGUAGE VALUES

In "The Rhetoric of Beneficence, Authority, Ethical Commitment, and the Negative" (pp. 159–74), I argue that three values fuel language, but what I don't say—and should have said—is that these values are scenic. Beneficence, authority, and commitment—these are the values that fuel language.

The argument is a bit tricky, but it is worth following.

Here are two sentences which, uttered in the proper circumstances (e.g., scene) by the appropriate person, might be taken as valid:

4. I sentence you to fifteen years at hard labor in the state penitentiary.
5. The Finnish alphabet is almost perfectly phonetic.

Sentence 4 is valid if and only if the speaker has the civil (societal, legal, social) authority to pronounce sentences (and then only if the scene is appropriate, i.e., a court of law). Sentence 5 will be taken as valid if and only if we believe the speaker has requisite knowledge of the subject, i.e., if the speaker has epistemic authority. The value of authority, then, comes from scenic and epistemic sources. Authority is conferred by institutions or assumed by the individual through knowledge. Of course, the two sources of language power overlap; we might grant more credence to a state-of-the-union report by the president—with his doublebarrelled civil and epistemic authority—than to the same report by a professor of government at Harvard. (On the other hand, depending on our politics, our feelings about academia, and other factors, the situation might be reversed.)

And to complicate matters further. If a private orders a general, "Forward march!" it is a real order if the private *believes* that he has the authority to give orders, and the general will take it as an order if he believes that the private believes in his (the private's) authority—though, of course, the general probably will not obey. The value of authority gives some language transactions their force.

Take another class of speech acts: vows, promises, and such (commissives). For example:

> 6. I hereby vow that I will remain on the grapefruit diet for four days.
> 7. I won't drink a martini until Saturday.
> 8. I hereby promise to fix the screen door on Sunday.
> 9. I'll scrub the floor also.

The first two sentences, 6 and 7, can be taken as vows, the second two, 8 and 9, as promises. Now, in vows and promises, authority plays little role, but another value becomes crucial: commitment. For a hearer to take these sentences as vows or promises, he or she must believe that the speaker is committed to the courses of action stipulated. Without commitment, no vow or promise.

We have all experienced the "promise" that we take to be evasive and hence as no promise at all: "I'll fix the screen door later"; or the vow: "Some day I'll give up martinis." Our skepticism arises from our inability to attribute the value of commitment to the statement.

Finally, beneficence fuels language. For instance, I cannot *advise* you to do something that I think will not benefit you. If I want harm or any other unfavorable result to be the consequence of my statement, it is not advice:

> 10. I advise you to go jump in the lake.

This principle explains the strangeness of the following:

> 11. I hereby *will* you my ugliest necktie.
> 12. I *wish* you a married life of feuding and fighting.
> 13. I *donate* all of my worthless stocks to the university.

We normally think of wills, wishes, and donations as conferring benefits.

The principle of negativity turns these values upside down:

> 14. A student (jokingly) to a teacher: "I'll flunk you if you come to class late."
> (The student does not have the authority to flunk the teacher.)
> 15. A child (evasively) to a parent: "I'll do the dishes after the baseball game."
> (The child is not committed to the course of action.)

16. An employer to an employee: "If you're late again, I'll give you a permanent vacation." (The "gift" of a permanent vacation is not beneficial to the employee.)

So far, so good. But now the trail of intention becomes increasingly difficult to follow, though the panorama of insights that lies at the end of the tortuous path is worth the struggle.

We have seen that some sentences state intentions directly with verbs:

17. I *state* that only males have been elected president of the local Rotary Club. (a statement)
18. I *promise* that I'll vote for a woman in the next election. (a promise)
19. I *command* you to pay attention. (a command)
20. I *apologize* for having ignored you. (an apology)

Some sentences, however, do not state intentions, but imply them.

21. Only mules can negotiate the trails in the Grand Canyon. (a statement)
22. I'll feed your mule tonight. (a promise)
23. Pay the bill. (a command)
24. I've been thoughtless. (an apology)

The verbs that directly state intentions are, of course, *performatives*, and there must be a verb for every intention. Since every verb has a noun equivalent, every intention has a name, for example:

Verb	*Noun*
I ACCEPT your apology.	Your ACCEPTANCE is most gracious.
I BEG you to forgive me.	Your BEGGING is abject.
I CHARGE you with arson.	Your CHARGE is absurd.
I DEFY your threats.	Your DEFIANCE is foolish.

Whereas attitude is not readily conveyed in one word, the intention of a sentence can always be made explicit with either a verb or a noun. If, then, a discourse is controlled by an enthymeme, the intention of the discourse can be made explicit.

SPEECH AND WRITING

We have followed the language act from its source in the gene-scene dialectic through attitude to specific intention, and we have discovered that every intention can be expressed with a verb or named with a noun. We can call the whole meaning of any language act its *semantic intention*, which includes predication, reference, illocutionary force, attitude, and so on. Finally, this total semantic intention must be "mapped" onto structures that are either spoken or written.[1]

The most obvious—and perhaps the most important—difference between speech and writing is this: *speech is an array in time; writing is an array in space.* You can look back at writing, or glance forward; you can skim a book; you can set your own pace for reading.

In "Subvocalization during Writing" (1981), two of my students, James Williams and Micky Riggs, raise a great many of the crucial problems regarding the speech-writing relationship. (The study was ultimately published by Williams [1983] as "Covert Language Behavior during Writing.")

It is well known that subvocalization increases as reading becomes more difficult. (Gibson and Levin, 1975, pp. 340–50.) If all reading is difficult, as it is for some children and adults, then the amount of subvocalization will always be high, but "mature" readers increase their subvocalization only when texts become more difficult because of content or the structure of the message. (See the discussion of readability on pp. 55–65.) In any case, here is the Williams and Riggs abstract:

The purpose of this study was to investigate the interaction between covert linguistic behavior, rhetorical modes, and the reading and writing processes. We measured the change in muscle action potentials in the articulatory musculature during linguistic tasks—reading and writing—that shifted from the concrete to the abstract.

Five voluntary subjects were selected from the University of Southern California Freshman Writing Program and given a reading test to determine individual reading levels. Under Condition I, the subject read selections that varied in abstraction; under Condition II, the subject composed short essays that varied in abstraction. Subvocalization was measured continuously by four electromyographs and analyzed via computer to determine physiological changes across rhetorical modes under both conditions.

In each case, subjects demonstrated a definite increase in subvocalization as the linguistic task became more abstract. This suggests not only that reading and writing are closely associated on a psychological level but that rhetorical modes are more than arbitrary categories, indeed, that they have a cognitive reality that can be measured. In addition, the psychophysiological processes involved in reflective thought during that portion of the study in which the subjects were not actually writing was much more active than in the concrete mode.

It is risky, but sometimes useful, to schematize, if one does not take the schematic too seriously. The following sums up the main idea that we have been pursuing, but, of course, in its neatness distorts that very idea. Nonetheless,

2. In regard to the speaking-writing relationship, see Barritt and Kroll (1978); Cayer and Sacks (1979); Collins and Williamson (1981); Cooper and Odell (1976); Higgins (1973); Keenan and Bennett (1977); Kroll and Vann (1981); Lord (1960); Newman and Horowitz (1965); Radcliffe (1972); Schafer (1981); Shaughnessy (1977); Sokolov (1969); Sternglass (1980); Williams (1983); Williams and Riggs (1981); Zoellner (1969).

Attitude ─────────────→ Intention ─────────────→ (Speech or Writing)

From the general "attitude toward history" is distilled a specific semantic intention which the addresser must map onto structures, for

> *Every act of discourse, written or spoken, is the projection of a SEMANTIC IN-TENTION through STRUCTURES to an AUDIENCE in a SCENE.*

The structures of written and spoken discourse are different. For example, Bennett (Keenan and Bennett, 1977) compared written and oral versions of narratives and found that first person occurred more frequently in the written version; that the oral narratives contained more "progressive-like verbs" than the written; and that passives occurred more frequently in the written.

Keenan (Keenan and Bennett, 1977) makes the distinction between *planned* and *unplanned* discourse and says that "*when speakers have not planned the form of their discourse, they rely more heavily on morpho-syntactic and discourse skills acquired in the first three to four years of life*" (p. 4; emphasis hers). Kroll (Keenan and Bennett, 1977) finds that in unplanned discourse "speech production is carried forward by heavy reliance on the use of 'and.'"

Not only are structural conventions different in speech and writing, but "The Writer's Audience Is Always Fiction" (Ong, 1977).

To sense more fully the writer's problem with his so-called audience let us envision a class of students asked to write on the subject to which schoolteachers, jaded by summer, return compulsively every autumn: "How I Spent My Summer Vacation." The teacher makes the easy assumption, inviting and plausible but false, that the chief problem of a boy or a girl in writing is finding a subject actually part of his or her real life. In-close subject matter is supposed to solve the problem of invention. Of course it does not. The problem is not simply what to say but also whom to say it to. Say? The student is not talking. He is writing. No one is listening. There is no feedback. Where does he find his "audience"? He has to make his readers up, fictionalize them. (Pp. 58–59)

Writing takes place in a bracketed area that has only tenuous connections with any real scene. In conversation one can gesture toward the corner and nod toward the window, but in writing, there are no gestures or nods; there is no scene, except that which the author provides in the text.

Obviously, the advice "write like you talk" is dangerous, for it implies that written language is, or can be, simply a transcription of unplanned oral language. That, in fact, seems to be one of the problems that "basic writers" bring with them to the composition class. Shaughnessy (1977) said, "*the beginning writer does not know how writers behave*. Unaware of the ways in which writing is different from speaking, he imposes the conditions of speech upon writing" (p. 79).

Basic writers, then, need to learn "writerly" behavior, and they obviously do this by reading and writing—but more about teaching hereafter.

Piaget had outlined the growth of cognition and language from autistic through egocentric to logical. Vygotsky (1962) disagreed. From his point of view, "Egocentric speech is a transitional stage in the evolution from vocal to inner speech" (p. 17). The process is analogous to that of drawing: "A small child draws first, then decides what it is that he has drawn; at a slightly older age, he names his drawing when it is half done; and finally he decides beforehand what he will draw" (p. 17). Inner speech—predicate heavy—is an adult's instrument of thought. The early development of speech is just a biological fact. However, verbal thought "is not an innate, natural form of behavior but is determined by a historical-cultural process and has specific properties and laws that cannot be found in the natural forms of thought and speech" (p. 51). Gene and Scene. Which is where we came in.

4. Rhetorical Invention

In *The Philosophy of Composition* (1977), E. D. Hirsch, Jr. argued that composition and rhetoric are separate fields, and it was this argument that led Hirsch into what I have called neo-Ramism, the exclusion of invention from composition. In fact, Hirsch's "philosophy" reduced composition to stylistics. But as practitioners, we know positively that style is not all, not even our central concern when we teach composition.

Favorable or unfavorable, each of our responses to student texts falls into one of four categories: content, organization, style, or editing. We react to logic, semantic intention, development of ideas; to the order in which the ideas are presented; to sentence structure, figurative language, tone; and to "mechanics" such as punctuation and verb agreement. If this spectrum does represent what we can say about a text, then we must have methods for teaching *invention, arrangement, style,* and *mechanics.*

The traditional departments of rhetoric are invention, arrangement, style, delivery, and memory, but since we are dealing with written discourse, not spoken, delivery and memory become irrelevant.

Obviously, then, composition and rhetoric are *not* identical, in just the same way that cardiology and medicine are not: one is a branch of the other. Just as a cardiologist must be a physician, so a compositionist must be a rhetorician. Aristotle and his successors wrought better than they could have imagined. Much better.

A schematic of the field of composition/rhetoric appears on page 36. I will use the diagram—which captures something of the elegance of rhetoric, either traditional or modern—as the basis for this and the two subsequent chapters.

Rhetorical invention concerns the generation of subject matter: any process—conscious or subconscious, heuristic or algorithmic—that yields something to say about a subject, arguments for or against a case. Inartificial arguments are simply the facts of the "case," discoverable through research if they are not immediately obvious. (Aristotle lists such evidence as contracts, testimony of witnesses, statements under torture, and so on.) Artificial arguments

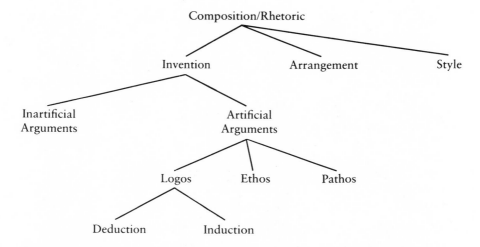

are more subtle, arising from the character of the speaker (*ethos*), the nature of the audience (*pathos*), or the integrity of the argument itself (*logos*). And, of course, logical arguments can be either deductive or inductive.

"Brain, Rhetoric, and Style" (pp. 129–57) is, in fact, a contemporary reaction to the deduction-induction dichotomy in rhetoric and logic. It is perhaps dangerous to boil the argument down to its simplest terms, but for the sake of clarity: the left hemisphere of the brain works deductively, and the right hemisphere works inductively. Western rationalist that he was, Aristotle had little to say about induction, the mode of reasoning most congenial to the "intuitive" right hemisphere, and rhetoric throughout its history has not paid attention to the alternative, right hemispheric processes of logos. Currently, however, the situation is changing: a great deal of work in rhetoric proper, linguistics, psychology, neurophysiology, anthropology, and other fields is concerned with cognitive and discourse modes of the right hemisphere, and certainly this work will be a major influence on composition theory and teaching in the next decades. (See Benderly, 1981; Emig, 1978; Freed, 1981; Glassner, 1981; Miner, 1976.)

It is a useful oversimplification to point out that in literary criticism, mimetic theories focus on "truth" value (logos); expressive, on the poet (ethos); pragmatic, on the reader (pathos); and objective, on the text itself (arrangement and style). However, as chapters 2 and 3 should have demonstrated, a theory of language, a hermeneutic method, or a set of evaluative criteria will be unsatisfactory unless it squares with the classical theory of rhetoric, dealing with all factors as they interrelate. Thus, it can be argued that a literary theory (or any other theory of discourse) will be adequate just to the degree that it squares with the classical theory of rhetoric. (See "The Three R's: Reading, Reading, and Rhetoric," pp. 253–63.) I am not claiming that modern rhetoric is simply a new application of the same old stuff, though I would argue strongly that modern work in linguistics, psycho-

linguistics, speech act theory, anthropology, and other fields gives a more penetrating conception of the triad ethos-pathos-logos, but does not supersede it.

INVENTION, LOST AND FOUND

As composition became a massive, if not respectable, enterprise in American
schools and universities, the emphasis was squarely on style and structure, to
the virtual exclusion of invention. (See Berlin, 1984.)

Inside the front cover of my edition of *The Foundations of Rhetoric*, by
Adams Sherman Hill, Boylston Professor of Rhetoric and Oratory in Harvard
University (Harper and Brothers Publishers, 1897)—owned once by Julian U.
Siegel of Baltimore—are these ghostly wisps of humor: "Shake well before
using!" and "Take in small doses!" This, from the preface:

Differ as good writers may in other respects, they are all distinguished by the judicious
and the skilful placing of words. They all aim (1) to use no word that is not established
as a part of the language in the sense in which they use it, and no word that does not
say what they wish it to say so clearly as to be understood at once, and either so
strongly as to command attention or so agreeably as to win attention; (2) to put every
word in the place fixed for it by the idiom of the language, and by the principles which
govern communication between man and man—the place which gives the word its exact value in itself and in its relations with other words; (3) to use no more words than
are necessary to effect the purpose in hand. If it be true that these simple principles
underlie all good writing, they may properly be called *The Foundations of Rhetoric*.

In short, for A. S. Hill as for E. D. Hirsch, Jr., almost a century later, stylistics
was virtually the all.

The Foundations of Rhetoric is by no means a bad book; it is not schlock
mindlessly and quickly produced to capitalize on a G. I. Bill or a Baby Boom
or a Sputnik. For our purposes, it is merely a typical book, and the highest
praise we can give it is to say it is an admirable example of an era that stretched
from the latter part of the nineteenth century to, roughly, 1964, when Rohman
and Wlecke published their landmark study of invention: *Pre-Writing: The
Construction and Application of Models for Concept Formation in Writing*.
It was the genius of these scholars to understand that the compositionist must
deal with substance, for a composition has meaning as well as style and structure. No doubt Adams Sherman Hill would have agreed, but he was caught in
a rhetorical paradigm which implied that his colleagues in the substantive
fields had a corner on the content market, Brothers Hunt who, in the educational marketplace, controlled logos: "Save the fuss; leave the thinking to us."

A kind of antiquarian passion leads me from one old composition text to
another, those solidly bound, magisterial books with now-fading notations of
students from generations ago; the ignominy of the old texts—none of them
classics, all of them forgotten—is a melancholy but salubrious commentary
on the profession that we share. Our best works, composition texts that do
give students the ability to write (and hence a powerful tool of cognition), are

as doomed as is *Composition and Rhetoric,* by Alfred M. Hitchcock (Henry Holt, 1923; copyright 1906, 1908, 1909, 1913, 1914, 1917). In the margin on page 270 (chapter 21 "Adjectives and Adverbs"), the penciled enigmatic word "Lymerick." What drowsy lecture inspired Rina White, 849 Genesee Ave. (telephone Wasatch 7079), to make the inscription? We can be certain that on that day in the 1910s or 1920s—in Salt Lake City—there was a lecture in the composition class, and probably some exercises on adjectives and adverbs. And looming somewhere was a theme for Rina to compose; when it was turned in, the lecturer would become a correcter. (A Saturday afternoon in May. The trees are lacy green, and the peonies are almost ready for their Memorial Day duty. The lecturer-correcter sits at her dining-room table, "marking" papers. She is unmarried, necessarily so, lest students in her high school think of—fantasize about—her libido, thus losing respect for the virginal purity of her nunlike mediation between the doctrine according to Saint Alfred Hitchcock—presumably no relation—and their imperfect attempts to achieve correctness.) No doubt this digression is invidious, but let it stand. As a corrective, assume that Hitchcock, lecturer-correcter, and Rina were decent, intelligent folk doing the best they knew how within the paradigm and educational system that they inherited. Assume the same about us and our students. With this healthier, at least more charitable, attitude, let us proceed with our delineation of the enlightened present, hoping that our successors will be at least as mellow as we.)

After a long, disastrous hiatus, composition once again became rhetorical, starting, as I have said, in about 1964 with the Rohman Wlecke study. (*Writing Instruction in Nineteenth-Century American Colleges,* by James A. Berlin [1984], is essential reading.) In 1965, Edward P. J. Corbett reintroduced students and teachers to the tradition with *Classical Rhetoric for the Modern Student,* and second and third editions of even the most conservative texts began to include sections on prewriting and invention. William Irmscher's enormously successful *Holt Guide to English* (1972) included an extensive introduction to Kenneth Burke's Pentad.

In his important essay "Invention: A Topographical Survey" (1976), Richard Young outlines current "methodologies": neo-classical invention, adapted from the classical tradition, as in Corbett (1965); Burke's dramatism, as in Irmscher (1972); prewriting (Rohman and Wlecke, 1964); and tagmemic invention, as in Young, Becker, and Pike (1970); to which I would subjoin the variety of heuristics to be found in the second edition of my own textbook (1981).

HEURISTICS

In " 'Topics' and Levels in the Composing Process" (1973), I have explained a system for classifying and evaluating heuristics; however, my purpose now is to discuss their usefulness for composition teachers.

We find ourselves uncomfortably on the spot when we claim that we're

trying to teach people to think or to think creatively, for we are hardly philosophers or psychologists, and yet we find ourselves equally in an uncomfortable
position (since being on the spot whether we are standing or sitting is not
an optimum sort of repose) when we must respond to student texts with
"You need to develop your ideas" or "Your ideas are unoriginal"—though, of
course, in more tactful ways, less scarifying terms, for we attempt to give sym-
pathetically helpful reactions to texts that we must, as teachers, take seriously.
As teachers! What are we to advise students? "Think, and you'll discover
ideas!" "Be original, and you'll be original!" We are constrained, in fact, to
teaching thinking or methods thereof.

The fashionable word "heuristics" is broad enough to cover the field of
methods available to the comp teacher faced with the problem of a student
who either seems unable to generate ideas concerning a topic or inscribes
platitudes—and my dour tone here simply obscures my respect for every student's potential to write amply and originally, though I find myself, for the
strategic purposes of this essay, too often assuming the negative stance, which,
of course, is always disastrous in teaching: the sort of attitude that implies
bare tolerance of the acne-essays submitted by our composition students, the
bubble-gum writings of juveniles who will never mature to the suave literacy
and keen thinking of their mentors. As mentors, nonetheless, we must respect
our charges enough to believe that maturity and a healthy diet will cure the
acne and that our guidance will overcome the taste for bubble gum.

In his 1976 essay, Richard Young provides an apposite account of
heuristics:

It is important to distinguish between rule-governed procedures (i.e., algorithms) and
heuristic procedures lest we make the error of thinking that because invention is a systematic activity it is necessarily a mechanical one. A rule-governed procedure specifies
a finite series of steps which can be carried out consciously and mechanically without
the aid of intuition or special ability and, if properly carried out, infallibly produces a
correct result—for example, the procedure for making valid inferences in syllogistic
reasoning. A heuristic procedure provides a series of questions or operations whose
results are provisional; it helps us guess more effectively—for example, the procedure
used by journalists for gathering information for an article, the familiar who? what?
when? where? how? and why? It does not infallibly lead to a comprehensive and useful
account but it makes data gathering more efficient and increases the likelihood that
the account will be adequate. Although systemtic, heuristic search is neither purely
conscious nor mechanical, intuition, relevant experience and skill are necessary for
effective use. The use of heuristic procedures is, by implication, an acknowledgment
that the psychological processes involved in invention are too unpredictable to be controlled by rule-governed procedures. (P. 2)

In more homely terms, heuristics are procedures that encourage the writer
to "walk around" his or her subjects, viewing them from different angles—
the problem with invention frequently being the head-on, unwavering approach that the writer takes.

The subject of heuristics is properly a branch of creativity theory, the literature of which is massive, fascinating and sometimes fatuous, often commonsensical but frequently outlandish, useful to some degree though often just plain esoteric. "Creativity and the Comp Class" (pp. 205–20) provides an entry into the field and a bibliography.

If I were asked to recommend the single best discussion of heuristics in general, I would unhesitatingly cite Chapter 7, "Plans Up Front," from *The Mind's Best Work*, by D. N. Perkins (1981). In three propositions, Perkins sums up his points regarding heuristics:

The broad organization of behavior does not necessarily take care of itself once contributing performances are mastered. Both particular heuristic advice and the more general heuristics of managerial strategies may be helpful. Most of all, one's big plans for conducting various activities deserve critical scrutiny and creative revision. (P. 200)

People often modify considerably the heuristics they are taught. But they may gain anyway, by improving poor heuristics, leaning to think about how they think, and in many other roundabout ways. (P. 206)

Of course, one needs particular knowledge and experience to function at all in a field. But beyond that, knowing the informal rules of the game is more important than knowing very general heuristics.(P. 213)

The "translation" of these propositions for composition teachers yields productive advice and an understanding of what heuristics can be expected to do (or not to do).

Heuristics are obviously prompts, aids to "natural" cognitive processes in problem solving. We would expect, then, that various procedures—such as brainstorming, clustering, the Pentad, the tagmemic grid—would have differing appeal and utility for various writers working on various topics. In other words, we have strong reason to believe that some writers prefer and are more successful with some heuristics than with others, and we know for a fact that heuristics function well or poorly, depending on the subject matter. (See Adams, 1979, pp. 83–101.) And, of course, hemisphericity is a factor. In discussing cerebral organization and function, Jerry Levy (in Wittrock, ed., 1980) might well have been presenting an argument in favor of heuristics:

Neither the nature of stimuli, choices, nor responses, or even actual hemispheric capacity, determines hemispheric dominance. Rather a hemisphere's propensity to control behavior seems to be a function of how it perceives the cognitive requirements for a given task. If those requirements call for literal encoding of sensory information or visualization of spatial relations, the right hemisphere assumes and maintains control, even if it turns out that the particular task is poorly processed by the controlling hemisphere. If there appears to be a requirement for speaking, phonetic analysis, semantic decoding of words, or for the derivation of conceptual categories, the left hemisphere assumes and maintains control, even if on the particular task, the right hemisphere is as competent as the left. (P. 258)

We are, of course, interested in teaching skills—for instance, those of syntactic fluency and accessibility in style. The Christensen (1967) free modifiers (illustrated on pp. 52–53) are a heuristic for the development of style, giving students possibilities to elaborate their sentences; in Perkins' terms, the system of free modifiers constitutes "particular heuristic advice." However, the ability to elaborate sentences is one thing, and knowing when to do so is quite another, a decision that might be facilitated by "the more general heuristics of managerial strategy"—for instance, Roman Jakobson's schema for the discourse act, which places style in relation to purpose (emotive, referential, phatic, and conative), which imply various relationships with audiences. (Jakobson, 1960; see Winterowd, 1981, pp. 86–93.)

In a sense, heuristics such as the Jakobson schema, the Pentad, and the tagmemic procedure are what Kenneth Burke calls "terministic screens." If you view the world through the Pentad, all acts are dramas—scenes, purposes, agents, and agencies being foregrounded—whereas tagmemics brings one to look at features, contrasts, processes, organizations. It seems obvious that the Pentad is more useful as an instrument for understanding literature but that tagmemics could be valuable for developing a critique of, say, an organization such as a college cafeteria.

When Perkins talks about "knowing the informal rules of the game," he is getting at one of the central points of language skills learning. By and large, we acquire those skills—i.e., do not learn them through conscious effort—and our knowledge of them is tacit. (See pp. 95–101; also "Developing a Composition Program," pp. 281–97; and "From Classroom Practice to Psycholinguistic Theory," pp. 299–306.) Heuristics can help us acquire them by calling them to our attention, and can help us bring them into performance once acquired. You could never teach students to write expository essays by using heuristics alone; writers gain a sense of genre only through immersion in it, acquiring the informal rules of the game, but once some acquisition has taken place, heuristics can be extremely useful as teaching methods. For instance, I find the Jakobson schema helpful when I am attempting to help a student create a satisfactory essay. Using the schema as a guide, I can teach the student to ask questions about *audience*, the *writer* and his or her intentions, the *content* of the piece, its *structure*, its *format*, and its *style*. In Chapter 9 (pp. 104–6), I give an extended example of how this heuristic works.

These sets of questions are no panacea, but they do provide useful points of departure for instruction, and they do make students aware of the manifold problems involved in producing a successful text. The heuristic itself is of no value, however, if students have not at least partially internalized the informal rules of the game. Perkins summarizes:

This might seem to say that general heuristics are useless. Indeed to a degree it says just that. There is no substitute for knowledge—experience, familiarity with a field, knowing the ins and outs, the rules of the game, whether explicit or tacit. Yet for all that, general heuristics have their place. When genre-specific principles are used, general strategies can add to their power. Moreover, we do not always operate in familiar problem domains. In fact, we encounter new kinds of problems constantly not only as we explore novel subject areas but as we go further in a familiar field. General strategies provide an initial approach that will give way to genre-specific understanding as experience accumulates. Finally, remember that the deliberate search for and use of genre-specific strategies can itself be a potent general strategy. (P. 213)

It is important to realize, however, that Perkins is talking about heuristics in specialized fields such as mathematics or botany. In composition, we are concerned with those areas of knowledge that constitute liberal education; the thinking and writing that we are interested in is nonspecialist; we attempt to create *bricoleurs*, not engineers. Perkins deals with the use of heuristics for "engineers"; we are concerned about the analytic and inventive abilities of "bricoleurs." (Obviously, I am not talking about specialized composition courses, such as technical writing or proposal writing.) In fact, I completely agree with George Dillon (1981) when he says,

The expository essay as here understood has a rhetorical purpose beyond 'conveying information'; it attempts to convince the reader that its model of experience or the world is valid. It does not seek to engage the reader in a course of action, however, but rather in the process of reflection, and its means of convincing are accordingly limited to the use of evidence [including, from my point of view, the non-logical proofs that I characterize as "appositional"] and logical proof and the posture of openmindedness. These methods are also associated with the liberally educated person, who is meditative, reflective, clear-headed, unbiased, always seeking to understand experience freshly and to find things of interest in the world. (P. 23)

EUREKA, THE TEXTBOOKS

Among textbooks, we can take *Forming, Thinking, Writing: The Composing Imagination*, by Ann E. Berthoff (1978), as the Alpha in regard to heuristics and Young, Becker, and Pike's *Rhetoric: Discovery and Change* (1970) as the Omega.

Berthoff is enormously suspicious of "recipes" such as the tagmemic grid, believing that composition is an organic process which begins with

. . . meaning, not with thought ("Think of what you want to say . . .") or language ("Choose the words which you feel would fit your idea best . . ."); we will never get the two together unless we begin with them together. The making of meaning is the work of the active mind, or what used to be called the *imagination*—that power to create, to discover, to respond to form of all kinds. My guiding philosophical principle is that this form-finding and form-creating is a natural activity; the book's central pedagogical principle is that we teach our students *how* to form by teaching them *that* they form. Man is the forming animal, the *animal symbolicum*, as the philosopher Ernst Cassirer puts it. (P. 2)

Berthoff's claim seems to be that in the discovery of meaning, students will find the forms to embody it (provided, I assume that the substratum of competence, gained from reading, is there). We must enthusiastically grant the premise that form follows purpose (see Shuy, 1981), and we know painfully that "dry-run" exercises are the bane of composition classes.

In regard to tagmemic heuristics, I can do no better than quote from and paraphrase a review (1975) that I did of *The Tagmemic Discovery Procedure: an Evaluation of Its Uses in the Teaching of Rhetoric*, by Richard E. Young and Frank M. Koen (1973). (In order to avoid cluttering the text, I will not indicate direct quotes.)

Tagmemic theory postulates that in order to know any "thing" (including abstract concepts), one must understand (1) how it contrasts with everything else in its class, (2) how much it can change and still be itself, and (3) its distribution within the larger system of which it is a part. In other words, one must perceive (1) *contrast*, (2) *variation*, and (3) *distribution*.

Furthermore, any "thing" can be viewed from three perspectives: (1) as an unchanging static entity, (2) as a process, and (3) as a system made up of parts. In other words, borrowing from physics, tagmemicists give us the perspectives of (1) particle, (2) wave, and (3) field.

Finally, a particle, wave, or field can be viewed from the standpoints of contrast, variation, and distribution. Thus, a nine-item set of topics or, in other words, a heuristic emerges. (For its diagrammatic realization, see table 2.)

It seems to me that the tagmemic grid is so complex as to be opaque, and I have found it a hindrance in my composition classes. However, it appears obvious to me that questions implied by the perspectives are valuable and, indeed, I have found them to be so. The tagmemic perspectives give students a way to analyze and move toward an understanding of problematic situations. From the grid, I have drawn the following set of questions:

What are the item's FEATURES?

What are the parts of the SYSTEM?

How does the item OPERATE?

What is the DISTRIBUTION of the item—i.e., how does it fit into the larger system(s) of which it is a part?

How does the item CONTRAST with others in its class?

How can the item be CHANGED?

These questions—and their implications and elaborations, which are demonstrated and discussed in Chapter 9 (pp. 101–3)—encourage students to "walk around" their subject, viewing it from a variety of angles, and this in itself is a useful function of the heuristic.

In the 1973 study, Young and Koen asked of the procedure, "Does it work?" And the answer to that question:

The results of the experiments provide clear support for the proposition that strong personal involvement in an intellectual activity and substantial knowledge of the sub-

Table 2. The Tagmemic Matrix

	Contrast	*Variation*	*Distribution*
PARTICLE	(1) View the unit as an isolated, static entity. What are its contrastive features, i.e., that differentiate it from similar things and serve to identify it?	(4) View the unit as a specific variant form of the concept, i.e., as one among a group of instances that illustrate the concept. What is the range of physical variation of the concept, i.e., how can instances vary without becoming something else?	(7) View the unit as part of a larger context. How is it appropriately or typically classified? What is its typical position in a temporal sequence? In space, i.e., in a scene or geographical array? In a system of classes?
WAVE	(2) View the unit as a dynamic object or event. What physical features distinguish it from similar objects or events?	(5) View the unit as a dynamic process. How is it changing?	(8) View the unit as part of a larger dynamic context. How does it interact and merge into its environment? Are its borders clearcut or indeterminate?
FIELD	(3) View the unit as an abstract multidimensional system. How are the components organized in relation to one another? More specifically, how are they related by class, in class systems, in temporal sequence, and in space?	(6) View the unit as a multidimensional physical system. How do particular instance of the system vary?	(9) View the unit as an abstract system within a larger system. What is its position in the larger system? What systematic features and components make it a part of the larger system?

ject tend to improve the quality of what is written. Even though no formal instruction was provided in conventional/rhetorical and composition skills (such as usage, sentence and paragraph development, logic, methods of persuasion, and arrangement), English teachers regularly rated final essays more acceptable than initial ones. Students also improved in their ability to analyze problematic situations and state problems; and the results of their explorations of problematic data were more complex and varied; they became more sophisticated in testing hypotheses for adequacy; and they wrote essays that were more understandable and more persuasive at the end of the course.

The experiment, however, did not establish that the improved ability to explore problematic data was directly related to the nine-cell discovery procedure. . . . In addition, the tests did not indicate that the theory as presently formulated and the course as it was taught increased students' sensitivity to problematic situations. (Pp. 49–50)

Perkins (1981, pp. 195–96) would agree that there is no hard, fast evidence that heuristics create versatility or originality in thinking.

In rhetorical invention, as in the other departments of our complex art, we have no absolute certainty, but that situation, after all, is not such a disadvantage, for it gives us the freedom to follow our own intuitions and hard-won experiential knowledge, but also the responsibility for knowing what is available, to be sensitively tested in our scene, the composition classroom. Our methods come from our knowledge of the field and its resources and the scholarship and theories behind them, as well as from our own quotidian observant and caring practice with students.

Writing Topics and "Problematization"

I would like to put heuristics into the framework of what Paulo Freire (1982, p. 76) has called "problematization":

Human existence cannot be silent, nor can it be nourished by false words, but only by true words, with which men transform the world. To exist, humanly, is to *name* the world, to change it. Once named, the world in its turn appears to the namers as a problem and requires of them a new *naming*. Men are not built in silence, but in word, in work, in action-reflection.

We hear continually—I heard just yesterday—that students do not read widely enough to gain either background or the ability to think critically. Surely students (and most professors, for that matter) do not read extensively or critically, and surely reading is central to a liberal education—not specialized reading in textbooks or scientific reports, but general reading in books of all kinds, in magazines and newspapers. In our composition classes, we cannot supply the deficit of years, though we can do a great deal to encourage reading and to help students read better. We can help students view their world as a series of problems that invite analysis and discussion, and we can do that with heuristics.

To take a specific example of a problem we all face: We want to judge writing—especially holistically scored finals—on the basis of both form and content. One way to "control" for content is to assign a group of readings—on atomic power, gun control, capital punishment, legislative reapportionment, entitlements, or whatever—and then gear writing prompts to those topics: "In a brief but carefully thought-out essay, analyze the problem of entitlements and propose a solution." But there is another way, provided students have learned to "problematize" their worlds. Assign a topic that all of them have in common, regardless of reading backgrounds. For example, the university itself is a microcosm of the difficulties of any society, with the superaddition of its own particular quirks: inadequate parking, professors who remain isolated from students, dorms, tuition, course requirements, student voice in university governance, adjusting to academic life. . . . None of these is trivial and can result in thoughtful writing if students learn how to recognize and analyze problems.

Obviously, I believe that problematization is the central concern of composition; that being the case, heuristics, properly used, are the most important "methods." After all, Paulo Freire was speaking of peasants just gaining literacy, not of the graduates of Brazil's fancier academies.

5. Style: Syntactic Fluency[1]

Call it what you will—"sentence combining" (SC), "syntactic fluency" (SF), or, my preference, "sentence-manipulation" (S-M)—it is a powerful and wildly popular pedagogical "technology." It begins, actually, with the insightful and graceful work of Francis Christensen (1967), is put on the transformational-generative track by Bateman and Zidonis (1966), is made useful in pedagogy by John Mellon (1969), and is substantially refined by Frank O'Hare (1973).

My purpose, however, is not to outline a history of the sentence combining movement, but to discuss the grammatical, psycholinguistic, and pedagogical principles that help clarify its power—and its limitations.

Transformations in grammar perform four operations:

1. Rearrangement
   1a. Bart sees Betty.
   1b. Betty is seen by Bart.
2. Deletion
   2a. Bart enjoys pornography, and Betty enjoys pornography.
   2b. Bart and Betty enjoy pornography.
3. Substitution
   3a. Bart enjoys pornography, and Betty enjoys pornography.
   3b. That guy enjoys pornography, and that dame does too.
4. Addition
   4a. Bart enjoys pornography. He is a dirty young man.
   4b. Bart, a dirty young man, enjoys pornography.

In principle, a complete syntactic fluency program would deal with all four operations, but, in fact, the programs handle primarily, if not exclusively, rearrangement and addition, so that students can "learn" how to give sentences various possible surface realizations and how to put one sentence within another. For example,

1. Portions of this chapter were adapted from "Prolegomenon to Pedagogical Stylistics," *College Composition and Communication*, 34:1 (Feb. 1983), 80–90. Reprinted with the permission of the National Council of Teachers of English.

Rearrangement
  Extraposition
      5a. To become addicted to ice cream is easy.
      5b. It is easy to become addicted to ice cream.
  Passive
      6a. Barbara slurps pineapple sodas.
      6b. Pineapple sodas are slurped by Barbara.
  Cleft Sentence
      7a. Barbara slurps pineapple sodas.
      7b. What Barbara slurps is pineapple sodas.
Addition
  Noun Phrase Complement
      8a. Jacques disassembles texts. He is the guru of deconstruction.
      8b. Jacques, the guru of deconstruction, disassembles texts.
  Verb Phrase Complement
      9a. I know SOMETHING. My Redeemer liveth.
      9b. I know that my Redeemer liveth.
  Nominative Absolute
      10a. The school year had ended. The students deserted the campus.
      10b. The school year having ended, the students deserted the
            campus.

Behind sentence combining (and *accessibility*, which we will deal with
hereafter) are some relatively simple but highly illuminating linguistic and
psychological concepts, making up a theoretical and explanatory background
that researchers and teachers have largely overlooked or at least failed to account for in the literature.

THE GRAMMAR OF SENTENCE COMBINING

The first principle is the notion of deep and surface structure. (See, for example, Chomsky, 1966.) Until the concept of deep structure was brought into
being, linguists tended to look only at the surfaces of sentences, not at their
complete semantic import. Traditional doctrine classified sentences according
to their clause structure: simple ("The man and the woman spoiled the child"),
compound ("The man and the woman spoiled the child, but the teacher disciplined it"), complex ("The man and the woman spoiled the child because they
were softies"), and compound-complex ("The man and the woman spoiled
the child because they were softies, but the teacher disciplined it")—in other
words, one independent clause *or* two or more independent clauses coordi-
nated *or* one independent clause and one or more subordinate clauses *or* two
or more independent clauses and one or more subordinate clauses.

Transformational generative grammar began to ask about meanings as
well as structures, and a simple sentence, for instance, can, in a strictly defined sense, have the meaning equivalent of two or more sentences, that is, be

semantically equal to a compound or complex sentence, but only in a strictly defined sense.

Which takes us to Charles Fillmore's "case grammar" (1968), a language theory that is crucial for the understanding of both sentence combining and accessibility.

Fillmore points out that a sentence can be viewed as a two-part entity: first a modality (consisting of tense, modal auxiliaries, negative, and other function on the sentence as a whole) and, second, a proposition, consisting of a predicate and the nominals that relate to it. So the sentence *Robinson can beat Hearns* might be analyzed thus:

> *Modality*: present tense, modal aux. "can"
> *Proposition*: beat (predicate), Robinson, Hearns

The nominals *Robinson* and *Hearns*, furthermore, have stable relationships with the predicate, which explains why the analysis above holds also for the passive version of the sentence: *Hearns can be beaten by Robinson*. Now these two versions of the proposition are *not* exactly synonymous in the broader sense, but they are identical in their deep structure—that is, in each it is Robinson who will do the beating and Hearns who will be beaten.

We can assign "roles" to the nominals in a sentence, thus deriving

Predicate	Agent	Patient
beat	Robinson	Hearns

The number of roles is limited to perhaps twenty, for example:

> *Essive*
> *Gertrude* is a historian at Montana State University.
>
> *Instrumental*
> She writes with a *typewriter*.
>
> *Goal*
> Gertrude gave *Klaus* a tie for Christmas.

In less flossy terminology, when we understand a sentence, we know who is doing what with which and to whom, and that is the reason for our taking active and passive versions of the same proposition to be synonymous in an important sense.

It should be obvious that "sentence combining" is actually "proposition combining"; clauses can take nominal, adjectival, and adverbial functions, and deletion rules allow the reduction of propositions when they become parts of speech. Thus, in the following, both the phrase and the clause are nominals filling sentential roles, and each is the semantic equivalent of a one-proposition simple sentence:

11. Peter enjoys *watching his goldfish.*
Predicate	Agent	*Patient*
watch	(Peter)	his goldfish
12. Paul enjoys *whatever Peter likes.*

As the examples on page forty-eight indicate, the grammar of the language affords various ways to combine propositions, perhaps a dozen or so.

The Psychology of Sentence Combining

Syntactic fluency is nothing more than the *unconscious* ability to combine propositions, and reading involves the ability to derive the propositional content from sentences. In fact, we remember the propositions, not the surface structure. (Clark and Clark, 1977, pp. 143–48) Fluent writers are automatic proposition combiners, and fluent readers are automatic proposition decombiners.

For example, when we read the sentence

13. Wanting to be accurate, the scientist who did the calculation was careful.

the information that we gain and store in memory has a propositional form something like this:

14. careful: scientist
    want: (scientist)
    accurate: (scientist)
    do: scientist, calculation

More prosaically, we gain the information that (1) the scientist was careful, (2) it was the scientist who wanted, (3) the scientist was accurate, and (d) the scientist did the calculation—four complete propositions for the price of one sentence, a real cognitive bargain! If readers cannot gain this information, they are not readers of the sentence in question.

From

15. To kill time, Alvin did a crossword puzzle.

we remember something like

16. kill: (Alvin), time
    do: Alvin, crossword puzzle

and after a very short time cannot determine reliably which of the following was the source of meaning:

17. Alvin killed time by doing a crossword puzzle.
18. Doing a crossword puzzle, Alvin killed time.
19. Alvin killed time. He did a crossword puzzle.
20. To kill time, Alvin did a crossword puzzle.

Syntactic fluency is quite another matter. Fluency is nothing more than unconscious mastery of those transformations that one needs to express meaning, but no writer is completely versatile, which is to say that every writer is idiosyncratic, i.e., limited in the range of sentence devices that he or she typically employs. If such were not the case, Hemingway would be a syntactic Faulkner, Faulkner would be a syntactic Joyce, and Joyce would be a syntactic Hemingway. The question of a writer's preference for a given subset of syntactic gambits as opposed to others is at the present completely open, but it is not unreasonable to suggest the influence of cognitive style, reading background, education, and culture. If we take a Burkean view of syntactic fluency as *agency*, then we will investigate it from the standpoints of *agent*, *act*, *scene*, and *purpose*. Such a dialectic would move us beyond the relatively threadbare research now available.

TEACHING SENTENCE COMBINING

Louise Phelps (1981) has nicely delineated important questions regarding syntactic fluency.

First, the matter of *competence*. It is assumed that at some point, quite early in life, people acquire an almost total competence in their native languages. This competence is a reservoir of potential which may or may not be realized in *performance*. Research on sentence combining supports the notion of competence in that brief "treatment" does bring astonishing results. The experimental groups of Mellon (1969) and O'Hare (1973) must have had a substratum of ability, else the brief exposure to sentence combining exercises could not have yielded so gratifyingly. Of course, we cannot measure competence, and in this sense, it is one of those convenient explanatory fictions.

Phelps goes on to say one can assume that, in most instances, sentence combining exercises give students access to tacit knowledge (i.e., competence) and thus give them *technique*; no longer are they bound by their "naive" performance repertory, but are able to switch registers and thus create chords that are, to them, unique.

Phelps concludes with this: technique becomes art when it is used for a purpose; that is, technique for the sake of technique is the goal of practice or drill, but technique for the sake of art is the goal of application.

What is the use and usefulness of sentence combining in a composition program? My answer to that question will be based on experience with ninth- and tenth-graders and with college freshmen, but in addition to Mellon and O'Hare, I would refer the reader to Daiute (1981), Haswell (1981), Morenberg and Kerek (1979), and Ney (1974).

It is enormously important to understand that in some cases sentence combining activates ("triggers") a basic competence, whereas in other cases students seem to acquire/learn a competence or, more accurately, to expand their competence through acquisition/learning. (The difference between acquisition and learning is crucial. See "Developing a Composition Program," pp. 281–97.)

1. *When students have COMPETENCE, brief exposure to sentence building/combining enables them to achieve greater syntactic complexity in performance.*

A deceptively simple technique that I have used with great success works as follows:

(1) On the board write X number of sentences, each with a given structure underlined, thus:

a. *The moon having risen*, the black pines were outlined against the silver snow.
b. The snow, *completely virginal in this remote forest*, was silent and secret.
c. The forest, *a national wilderness area*, was a last retreat from civilization.
d. *On this cold winter night*, the least sound would have broken the spell.
e. The wind, *which had blown during the afternoon*, honored the perfect stillness.
f. Even thought seemed impossible *because ideas are tumultuous*.
g. *Enjoying this moment of eternity*, the skier forgot even the fellowship to be found around a crackling fire.

(2) Without explanation, write a base such as the following on the board:

The man eyed the woman.

(3) Ask a student to add a structure like one of the seven listed on the board, *d*, for example. The result will be something like this: "*On the hot summer day*, the man eyed the woman."

(4) Ask a second student to add another structure, perhaps *a*: "On the hot summer day, the man eyed the women, *the sun glinting in her long blond hair*."

(5) And so on.

On the hot summer day, the man, *totally oblivious*, eyed the woman, the sun glinting in her long blond hair.

On the hot summer day, the man, totally oblivious, eyed the woman, *a willowy creature*, the sun glinting in her long blond hair.

On the hot summer day, *which provided relief from a long spell of rain*, the man, totally oblivious, eyed the woman, a willowy creature, the sun glinting in her long blond hair.

On the hot summer day, which provided relief from a long spell of rain, the man, totally oblivious *because her beauty enraptured him*, eyed the woman, a willowy creature, the sun glinting in her long blond hair.

On the hot summer day, which provided relief from a long spell of rain, the man, totally oblivious because her beauty enraptured him, eyed the woman, a willowy creature, the sun glinting in her long blond hair, *giving it the appearance of spun gold.*

Is the resulting sentence a "good" one? We could answer that question only if we had a total context. Is the ability to produce such sentences—when the occasion demands—valuable to writers? Unquestionably so. Stylistic virtuosity gives the writer options. Exercises such as the one just outlined do provide options for writers.

An interesting note. It seems more effective to identify structures with numbers or letters, as was done above, than with grammatical terminology: (a) nominative absolute, (b) adjective phrase, (c) noun phrase, (d) prepositional phrase, (e) relative clause, (f) adverb clause, (g) verbal phrase. This jargon sidetracks students, causing them to ask for definitions when, in fact, the instructor wants them to imitate.

Two, three, or four periods of such exercises enable many students to increase the complexity of their syntax dramatically. For example:

Before

I was sitting in a bar feeling very low and depressed and down in the dumps. It was one of those days that everything I tried to do went wrong. I felt as though I was carrying the problems of the world on my shoulders. The loneliness and the quietness of the bar made me feel even more depressed. I finished my drink and was ready to leave. As I proceeded to leave, it was then that I saw her sitting there. I then stepped back to the bar and ordered another drink. As I was sipping my drink I thought to myself how lovely she was. She had brown eyes with dark brown hair.

After

On one of those days when everything I tried to do went wrong, I was sitting in a bar feeling very low and depressed and down in the dumps, as though I was carrying the problems of the world on my shoulders. The loneliness and quietness of the bar making me feel even more depressed, I finished my drink and was ready to leave when I saw her sitting there. I then stepped back to the bar and ordered another drink, which I sipped as I thought to myself how lovely she was, with her brown eyes and her dark brown hair.

2. *The lower the competence, the more exercises are necessary.* Students acquire their competence through reading; hence, there is a direct correlation between quantity and quality of reading and the potential for syntactic maturity.

3. *Sentence combining/building is excellent remediation.* With no hard evidence, but a great deal of experience, we have concluded that sentence combining speeds up the acquisition process. Since the technique is largely based on the propositional nature of sentences, and since, as I have said, reading involves proposition decombining, we believe that sentence combining helps with reading as well as with writing.

4. *The American Language Institute at the University of Southern Cali-*

fornia uses sentence combining with non-native speakers. Testimony from my colleagues in the Institute indicates that sentence combining facilitates the acquisition of syntax in English-as-a-second-language instruction.

The now traditional "cued" sentence combining exercises take the following configuration (from O'Hare, 1975):

1. Battaglia glanced at first base.
He went into his windup. (,)
Then he threw a hanging curve that Ryan knocked out of
the stadium. (, *and*)
(Result: Battaglia glanced at first base, went into his windup, and then threw a hanging curve that Ryan knocked out of the stadium.)
2. Ryan was surprised to learn SOMETHING.
No one understood SOMETHING. (*that*)
His paintings represented SOMETHING. (*WHAT*)
(Result: Ryan was surprised to learn that no one understood what his paintings represented.)
3. The people were terrified by SOMETHING.
The people were *in the housing project.*
The project was *near the gas storage tanks.*
Something exploded deafeningly. (a + ly + *explosion*)
The explosion rocked their buildings. (*which/that*)
It smashed dishes. (*ing*)
It cracked ceilings. (*ing*)
It broke windows. (*ing*)
(Result: The people in the housing project near the gas storage tanks were terrified by a deafening explosion that rocked their buildings, smashing dishes, cracking ceilings, breaking windows.)

"Free" combining exercises are very much like those above, but without cues, leaving the student to develop the combinations according to bent and ability. (See Strong, 1973.)

A few words remain to be said about sentence combining, that least interesting but paradoxically now most popular set of methods in our business.

1. On the basis of experience with several thousand ninth-graders, my colleagues and I in the Huntington Beach Project ("Developing a Composition Program," pp. 281–97) have found that cued exercises must precede uncued with severely remedial students. Students working with uncued exercises do not expand their performance repertory as widely as do students who move from the cued to the uncued. Unless they receive the prompting that cued exercises provide, they simply rely on their naive inventory of sentence devices.

2. Sentence combining should always be used selectively, never across the board.

So much, then, for S-M. Our common sense tells us that this technique, in spite of its seductive easiness, must be only a small part of any composition program.

6. Style: Accessibility[1]

The term "accessibility" has to do with ease of reading. For example, fourteen-point type is the most accessible size, and crabbed handwriting is less accessible than typed or printed text. Accessibility, of course, involves much more than *graphic display*. For example, the first sentence in the following pair is less accessible than the second.

1. That Bart thought that Bill believed that Boyd is a thief is odd.
2. It is odd that Bart thought that Bill believed that Boyd is a thief.

It is worthwhile, however, to begin with graphic display, a set of common-sense injunctions that are easily taught, very useful, and universally overlooked in the handbooks and rhetorics.

As all reading teachers know, tables of contents (or outlines), subheads, indentations, italics, and so on can indicate the structure of the text's subject and the most salient points therein. When dealing with a complex referential or conative text, readers learn to use graphic display for guidance; text design can increase or decrease accessibility.

The Psychology of Reading, by Gibson and Levin (1975) paradoxically affords an excellent example of the principle. Here are the subheads from the first chapter:

> A Theory of Perceptual Learning and
> Its Relevance for Understanding Reading
>
> What Is Learned
> Distinctive Features
> Invariants of Events
> Higher-Order Variables
> Processes and Principles
> Differentiation by Abstraction

1. Portions of this chapter were adapted from "Prolegomenon to Pedagogical Stylistics," *College Composition and Communication*, 34:1 (Feb. 1983), 80–90. Reprinted with the permission of the National Council of Teachers of English.

Ignoring Irrelevant Information
Peripheral Mechanisms of Attention
Reinforcement and Motivation in Perceptual Learning
Trends in Perceptual Development
Increasing Specificity
Optimization of Attention
Increasing Economy of Information Pickup
Summary

These subheads, all in the same type size and style, actually obscure structure. Note how the following change in typography reveals the hierarchy of relationships:

A Theory of Perceptual Learning and
Its Relevance for Understanding Reading
WHAT IS LEARNED
Distinctive Features
Invariants of Events
Higher-Order Variables
PROCESSES AND PRINCIPLES
Differentiation by Abstraction
Ignoring Irrelevant Information
Peripheral Mechanisms of Attention
REINFORCEMENT AND MOTIVATION IN PERCEPTUAL LEARNING
TRENDS IN PERCEPTUAL DEVELOPMENT
Increasing Specificity
Organization of Attention
Increasing Economy of Information Pickup
SUMMARY

Now a glance reveals the three principles dealt with in the first section, and so on. Graphic display can reveal the structure of the subject.

LISTING

Listing is also a simple technique that increases accessibility. A study by Frase and Fisher (1977) gives the following examples:

Original
The COU detects the presence of the incoming 28kHz carrier and activates the loop relay to the CO equipment and also activates the compressor and the kHz transmitter.

Revised
The COU detects the presence of the incoming 28 kHz carrier. The COU activates
(1) the loop relay to the COU equipment
(2) the compressor
(3) the 76 kHz transmitter.

TYPOGRAPHIC SEGMENTATION

Frase and Schwartz (1977) suggest that typographic segmentation can increase accessibility. For example,

> The carrier facility may be developed from
>> single or mixed gauge,
>> PIC or pulp (paper) insulated,
>> copper or aluminum
>>> conductor cable with standard sheaths.

PARAGRAPH CUES

A final interesting, though unusual, suggestion regarding the presentation of text. Doctorow, Wittrock, and Marks (1978) increased the accessibility of paragraphs by providing two-word cues. For example,

Letter: Escape
To be assured her brothers would be prepared, she prepared a message in advance. Since specific officials examined all of the slaves' mail, Harriet's message was addressed to a man named Jacob Johnson, who secretly assisted the Underground Railroad, and who was one of the relatively free black men in Maryland. However, even Jacob's mail might be searched, so Harriet had to be cautious. Her message stated: "Inform my brothers to be always devoted to prayer, and when the sturdy aged fleet of vigor glides along to be prepared to unite aboard."

The first cue word ("letter") is a more frequently occurring synonym for the most frequently used word in the passage ("message"). The second word identifies the theme of the passage, though, of course, the word "escape" does not occur.

Cuing paragraphs is so unconventional that it would be unacceptable in most kinds of writing, but, for instance, procedure manuals, contracts, handbooks, and so on could use the technique to great advantage.

INSTANTIATION

In "Brain, Rhetoric, and Style" (pp. 129–57), I have suggested that appositional style, among other features, relies heavily on synecdoche and imagery. I would now go further and claim that the appositionalist typically uses the specific as a conceptual pivot, just as the propositionalist uses the enthymeme. In the essay, I pointed out—commonsensically enough—that successful writers need both appositional and propositional skills; above all, writers must be able to use effective imagery and appropriate examples, a skill that I denote with the term "instantiation." (See "Dramatism in Themes and Poems," pp. 195–203.)

The Art of Readable Writing, by Rudolf Flesch (1949, 1974) is remarkably enlightened and well worth our consideration. On page 9, Flesch tells us, "I am sure you realize by now that this book is not dealing with what usually goes by the names of grammar, usage, composition, or rhetoric. On the contrary, if you want to learn how to write, you need exact information about what kind of language will fit what kind of audience." He then goes on to give a series of useful tips, one of which—in the chapter "How to Be Human though Factual" (pp. 72–83)—interests us particularly.

"Only stories are really readable," he says (p. 72), overgeneralizing, to be sure; then he quotes a *Reader's Digest* editor: "Whenever we want to draw attention to a problem, we wait until somebody does something about it. Then we print the story of how he did it" (p. 72). And that, in fact, is what Flower, Hayes, and Swarts (1980) call the *scenario principle*.

In attempting to understand documents, Flower, Hayes, and Swarts discovered, people explain to themselves by creating anecdotes, dramas. Writers can reverse the process by explaining definitions, principles, and concepts in terms of scenarios, which "represent a more radical kind of transformation than 'readability' revisions, because they actually restructure the information. By creating conditions, agents, and actions, they embed the meaning of a [document] in situations and contexts—they make meaning concrete enough to be *functional* for the reader" (p. 19). Flower, Hayes, and Swarts give examples, a reading of the original document, a rephrasing, and a scenario:

1. Original: No part of such financing shall be used. . . .
Rephrase: Money can't be used. . . .
Scenario: If a borrower has that money on on hand . . . we won't make her a loan so that she can use that money on hand to purchase land or things like that.

2. Original: (Discussion of eligible concerns) Printing: A firm solely engaged in commercial or job printing, if there is no common ownership with a concern ineligible under this paragraph (d)(4) of this section and the printer has no direct interest in the commercial success of the material so produced.
Rephrase: In other words they (this eligible concern) are strictly a job shop printer.
Scenario: You have something that you need printed, you bring it in, they print it up.
(P. 16)

Britt-Louise Gunnarson, a psychologist at Upsala University, found that a change "from the point of view of a law court judging *if a rule was violated*, to the point of view of a person who needed to know *how to act* in order to comply with the law" improved readability of a law regulating negotiations between employees' unions and employers' unions in Sweden, whereas other operations did not: shortening sentences and avoiding nominalizations, embeddings, cross references, unnecessary legalisms ("International Panel on Document Design," 1981).

Swarts, Flower, and Hayes (1980) applied the scenario principle to headings in an insurance policy, substituting "How this policy protects you and your family" for "Protection" and "What you must do for us" for "Eligibility."

Closely allied to the scenario principle is what Frase and Fisher (1977) call "specification," which "consists of making explicit the action taken or the components of a proposition":

Original
Service denial on the physical line requires a disconnect strap at the HMDF to maintain battery and ground on the derived line.

Revised
Service denial on the physical line requires a disconnect strap at the HMDF. The strap maintains battery and ground on the derived line.

Imageability, a variety of instantiation, appears to increase the accessibility of even technical prose. In a study of subjects' memories of texts, de Beaugrande (1979b) found that a passage with low imageability (e.g., "roar and burst of flame") was poorly recalled, but "deafening roar and blinding burst of flame" was well recalled. As I have speculated ("Brain, Rhetoric, and Style," pp. 129–57), imagery is an appositional functor; if this is true, then images embedded in largely propositional texts should create saliency through demanding "whole-brain" activity. And, of course, the readability of a text is a ratio between reading time and memory of contents.

ACCESSIBILITY AND SYNTAX

Case grammar (see pp. 49–50) provides a nice transition to syntax. In fact, the scenarios of some sentences are actually dramatistic, as in table 3.

The coincidence that allows us to correlate grammar, the scenario principle, and the Pentad is worth thinking about, particularly in light of the fact that humans seem "programmed" to seek out agents in both pictures and texts. Segalowitz and Hansson (1979) summarize an extremely significant piece of their work as follows:

Left and right hemisphere processing capabilities for pictorial information about agent (performer of an action) and patient (recipient of an action) relations were assessed in a tachistoscopic study. Subjects were presented pictures in either the right or

Table 3. Sentence Roles

	Grammatical Roles	*Dramatistic Roles*
For revenge	"PURPOSIVE"	PURPOSE
Alvin	AGENT	AGENT
hit	(Predicate)	ACT
Alicia	PATIENT	AGENT
with a noodle	INSTRUMENT	AGENCY
in the kitchen	LOCATIVE	SCENE

For revenge, Alvin hit Alicia with a noodle in the kitchen.

the left visual field depicting an agent-action-patient event. They were asked to locate which side of the drawing contained the agent and, in separate trials, which side contained the patient. Reaction times to locate the agent were significantly faster than to locate the patient, regardless of the field of presentation. The results are discussed in terms of a general nonlinguistic processing constraint that favors agent information. It is suggested that this processing asymmetry may underlie syntactic asymmetries regarding the expression of agents and patients in language. (P. 51)

Currently, the most insightful work in stylistics is that of Joseph Williams. His *Style: Ten Lessons in Clarity and Grace* (1981) is an indispensible treatment of its subject. In the discussion to follow, I will draw freely—and with gratitude—on Williams' work.

Agent-Subject, Patient-Object Correlation

Those sentences that achieve agent-subject and patient-object correlation are, in general, more readable than those which do not.

Williams quotes two paragraphs, in the first of which the order subject-agent-topic-theme and predicate-action-comment-rheme deviates whereas in the second the order is preserved:

A. The nature of black holes in space is the object of investigation by scientists recently. The collapse of a dead star into a point perhaps no larger than a marble results in the creation of a black hole in space. There are profound and little understood changes in the space around it by the compression of so much matter into so little space.
B. Scientists have recently been investigating the nature of black holes in space. A black hole is created when a dead star collapses into a point perhaps no larger than a marble. So much matter compressed into so little space changes the fabric of space around it in profound and little understood ways.

As we shall see, other problems contribute to the relative unreadability of the first passage, but for the moment we are concerned with doers of actions (agents) and recipients of actions (patients) and the grammatical slots that they fill in sentences. For example, a writer can eliminate the unsightly sprawl in 1 by revising as in 2:

1. Determination of foreign policy takes place at the *presidential* level.
2. The *president* determines foreign policy. (Williams, 1981, p. 13)

NOMINALIZATION

I do not intend to survey Williams' book, but would like to pay brief attention to one more principle that he handles: *nominalization*.

When we regularly express an important action not as verb but as a noun, our prose will read like that confused and sluggish writing so common in government, business, and the professions. In chronically indirect and tangled prose, the writer does not express the action of paying by the verb *pay* but by the noun *payment* (or the verbose *compensation*); the action of studying not by the verb *study*, but by the noun *study* (or the more weighty *in-depth investigation*); the action of needing not by the verbs *need* or *must* but as the noun *need* (or the more turgid *urgent requirement*). And then the writer clumps those nouns together into one long compound noun phrase. As a consequence, we have to wade through,

> There is a student loan repayment reliability study need.

or worse,

> There is an urgent requirement for a student loan recompensation in-depth investigation.

instead of skimming through,

> We must find out how reliably students repay their loans. (Pp. 10–11)

As Rulon Wells (1960) pointed out, the verbal style is easier to read than the nominal—but is it a "better" style? Williams (1979a) and Hake and Williams (1981) report that secondary teachers prefer the nominal style in students' writings (as do college teachers under some circumstances). The pessimistic interpretation of that fact: secondary teachers prefer highflown, relatively unreadable pretension to down-to-earth, relatively readable straightforwardness. The optimistic interpretation: secondary teachers naturally look for signs of maturity in student writing, and the ability to nominalize is one of them. The truth is probably both "either" and "or," as well as something in between. Accessibility aside, that style is best which conveys the writer's semantic intention most effectively to the intended audience.

SEMANTIC CLOSURE

One further point concerning syntax, and then we will take a brief look at the readability of units larger than the sentence.

In a useful section of *The Philosophy of Composition* (1977), E. D. Hirsch, Jr. demonstrates that one of the principal factors in the accessibility of sentences is "semantic closure," by which he means deriving the propositional content. As we saw (pp. 48–51), a sentence is either a single proposition or a combination of two or more propositions. If we look at the following awkward sentence, we can begin to understand the operations necessary for a reader to gain semantic closure from it:

> 1. That Vitamin C prevents colds, the scourge of humankind, is known by everyone.

In order to gain closure, the reader must find the superordinate predicate, *is known*, and organize the rest of the sentence around it. "Strategic" *that*, usually called a subordinator, signals that the first predicate, *prevents*, is subordinate; hence the reader withholds closure. The noun phrase "the scourge of humankind" is semantically a complete proposition—(colds are) the scourge of humankind—in an adjectival relationship with "colds." The reader must, then, hold two propositions in short-term memory until he or she reaches the organizational pivot, the predicate "is known."

On the other hand, the active version of the sentence, with the superordinate predicate up front, relieves short-term memory of its burden, for the reader can achieve closure of the propositions *seriatim*:

2. Everyone knows that vitamin C prevents colds, the scourge of humankind.

Schematically,

                                                              is known by
                                                              everyone.

                          (colds are) the
                          scourge of humankind
That vitamin C prevents colds

Everyone knows
                    that vitamin C
                    prevents colds
                                        (colds are) the scourge of
                                        humankind.

Further examples of delayed closure (from Winterowd, 1981):

3. Whatever the family couldn't buy at the country store located at the crossroads five miles from town they did without.
(The family did without whatever they couldn't buy at the country store located at the crossroads five miles from town.)

4. The program was a concert of relatively pleasant newly discovered Appalachian dulcimer music.
(The program was a concert of relatively pleasant dulcimer music that had been newly discovered in Appalachia.)

5. To bake potatoes on an open bonfire, as we did when we were kids, was always a great adventure.
(It was always a great adventure to bake potatoes on an open bonfire, as we did when we were kids.)

BEYOND THE SENTENCE

In the section on form, we will deal at some length with the paragraph, but for the moment, we are concerned with the relationship of paragraphing to the accessibility of texts.

In the first place, many of the old adages about the paragraph are perfectly correct: the maxim of unity ("stick to one subject"), the maxim of coherence ("be sure that transitions are clear"), and the maxim of order ("paragraph organization can be either deductive or inductive"), for instance.

Nearly two decades ago, in "A Tagmemic Approach to Paragraph Analysis," Becker (1966 [1965]) wrote of *equivalence classes* or *equivalence chains* (i.e., sets of coreferential terms) and lexical transition as factors in paragraph coherence. Hirsch (1977), drawing on the work of Kintsch (1974), demonstrates that the more "thematic tags" (i.e., equivalence chains) a paragraph contains, the harder it will be to read.

THEMATIZATION

The theme of a sentence is what the sentence is about, usually, but not necessarily, the grammatical subject; the *rheme* is the information provided about the theme. Schafer (1981) explains the bearing of thematization on accessibility:

Many student paragraphs are comprehensible but difficult to read because themic material is poorly arranged. . . . The problem is not unique to writing. Scinto (1977) studied oral answers to an interviewer's question (Are things on TV real or pretend?) and concluded that the answers of younger interviewees were difficult to understand in part because of faulty pronoun reference but primarily because of poor theme-rheme structuring. In particular Scinto found that the younger interviewees rarely structured their texts by making the rheme of one sentence the theme of the following sentence. Thus, their answers seldom took the form:
John bought the car yesterday.
It was a green Volvo.
Volvo was a wise choice . . . etc.

In "Defining Complexity," Williams (1979) discusses thematization and gives excellent examples.

PARAGRAPH STRUCTURE

In "A Generative Rhetoric of the Paragraph," Christensen (1967) sets forth a series of axioms concerning the paragraph. The most important of the nine are the following five:

1. The paragraph may be defined as a sequence of structurally related sentences. (The relationship, of course, is often semantic rather than structural.)
2. The top sentence of the sequence is the topic sentence. [By "top sentence," Christensen means the most general one.]
3. The topic sentence is nearly always the first sentence of the sequence.
4. Simple sequences are of two sorts—coordinate and subordinate. [An illustration will follow shortly.]
5. The two sorts of sequences combine to produce the commonest kind—the mixed sequence.

In other words, the paragraph is very much like the sentence, with a base to which are added specific details.

Becker (1966) analyzes paragraphs according to their tagmemes (structural units), among which are Topic, Restriction of the topic, and Illustration. While we might doubt that these are universals, the analysis does apply to a great many paragraphs, and certainly it provides a valuable teaching method. (See Winterowd, 1981, pp. 119–27.)

The following paragraph from Christensen (1967) illustrates both Becker's tagmemes and Christensen's axioms:

Topic	Level 1	He [the native speaker] may, of course, speak a form of English that marks him as coming from a rural or an unread group.
Restriction	Level 2	But if he doesn't mind there's no reason why he should change.
Illustrations	Level 3	Samuel Johnson kept a Staffordshire burr in his speech all his life. In Burns's mouth the despised lowland Scots dialect served just as well as the "correct" English spoken by ten million of his southern contemporaries. Lincoln's vocabulary and his way of pronouncing certain words were sneered at by many better educated people at the time, but he seemed to be able to use the English language as effectively as his critics.

—Bergen Evans, *Comfortable Words*, p. 6

De Beaugrande (1979b) has found that inductive order in paragraphs, with specifics first and the most general statement last, seems to facilitate recall. Following Christensen (1967), we can posit that either deductive or inductive order in the paragraph is accessible, but that a bastardization is not.

For example, the following inductive version of the Evans paragraph is accessible and may be more salient than the original:

Samuel Johnson kept a Staffordshire burr in his speech all his life.

In Burns's mouth the despised lowland Scots dialect served just as well as the "correct" English spoken by ten million of his southern contemporaries.

Lincoln's vocabulary and his way of pronouncing certain words were sneered at by many better educated people at the time, but he seemed to be able to use the English language as effectively as his critics.

He [the native speaker] may, of course, speak a form of English that marks him as coming from a rural or an unread group.

But if he doesn't mind being so marked, there's no reason why he should change.

RELATIVE READABILITY

As we have seen, through syntactic maneuvers sentences can be made more or less accessible, and rearrangement of passages can increase or decrease their accessibility also. The variable that can never be completely controlled, however, is the knowledge that a reader brings to the text.

All reading is a tradeoff between what the reader brings to the text by way of background knowledge and the information that the reader gains from the text. The completely informative text would be completely unreadable, for everything in it would be "news." For example—and this is a point missed by strict behaviorists—if I were to have trouble reading a text in advanced mathematics, I would not take a course in reading, but, rather, one in mathematics. Regardless of syntax and paragraph structure, a text presenting complex ideas will be difficult to read—though less so for the expert in the field handled by the text.

Relative accessibility must be judged intrinsically; hence, the question to be asked concerns the writer's semantic intention.

The following sentence from a student paper is relatively inaccessible:

Whatever might annoy our teachers, whom we passionately hated, we thought of.

Two possible reasons for this relatively unreadable syntax are (1) that the student did not have the skill to express the idea any other way and (2) that the student chose a less accessible version rather than one more accessible in order to call attention to the ideas in the sentence.

In the first case, we would be dealing with a matter of writing skills, but in the second, we would address semantic intention: we would judge the syntax to be well or ill motivated in light of what the writer wanted to accomplish. Indeed, as I have said elsewhere in this essay, complexity for the sake of complexity is a common and sometimes justifiable semantic intention. No writer, however, could logically claim that his or her style was *intentionally* more complex than warranted by semantic intention, for that is simply a contradiction.

A Leitmotif in Kenneth Burke's works is that reading involves a tradeoff between information and eloquence: the more we want information, the more annoyed we become by texture, and the less information we demand immediately, the more we enjoy eloquence for its own sake. (See "The Rhetorical Transaction of Reading," pp. 265–72.) At one end of the spectrum, we might say that sets of instructions are, ideally, maximally accessible and hence almost purely information; orations and many essays are eloquently informative; poems, once we have made them part of us, are purely eloquent.

7. Form

On the firm ground of style, among the silver trees in an olive grove on the Cretan hillside, we are mysteriously in repose, for our methodology is clear-cut: we can teach syntactic fluency, editing, accessibility. The "software" is powerful and easily applied. The consolation, however, is a will-of-the-wisp, for we are ever confronted with the inspiriting problem of purpose.

Beyond the eternal grove where style is all—where students could play their sentence games, syntactic Pan songs, lilted to the nymphs of sentence combining—lies the alligator-infested morass of making sense. Making sense.

What you derive from a text as a reader is, in a sense, its form. That is, you usually don't remember the details but retain something of the general tenor and perhaps the structure of the plot or argument. The form of the text for you, the reader, is what you retain in memory.

COHESION

Since cohesion deals largely with intersentential relationships, it serves as an excellent transition between the discussion of style and that of form.

The text is sequaciously cohesive when one gets from T-unit to T-unit without stumbling (not that all readers or all readings go from T-unit to T-unit in a systematic fashion). Halliday and Hasan (1976) explain a good deal of this meaningful sequaciousness.

Cohesion occurs when the interpretation of some element in the discourse is dependent on that of another. The one *presupposes* the other, in the sense that it cannot be effectively decoded except by recourse to it. When this happens, a relation of cohesion is set up, and the two elements, the presupposing and the presupposed, are thereby at least potentially integrated into a text. (P. 4)

According to Halliday and Hasan, the five cohesion devices are

reference (Three blind mice. See how *they* run.)
substitution (The child kicked me in the shins; *the little nipper* is very spirited.)
ellipsis (Would you like to hear another joke? I have a million [more of them]).

conjunction (coordinates, subordinates, transitional adverbs)
lexical cohesion

Robin Bell Markels (1984 pp. 4–22) in particular explores lexical cohesion through (1) item repetition, (2) synonymy, and (3) equivalence, defining cohesion as "unity, as manifested by a recurrence chain" (p. 19).

As Markels' example demonstrates, item repetition is a simple enough concept:

1. The boys climbed the *trees*. The *trees* weren't too tall for them.

Nor is synonymy difficult:

2. The *boy* climbed the fence. The *youth* is a member of a gang. (In this instance, "boy" and "youth" are taken to be coreferential.)

Equivalence is a bit trickier, "an intuitive concept that resists formal definition" (p. 8), according to Markels. For example, in the following "apples" and "they" are not strictly coreferential:

3. I wanted to buy some *apples*. But *they* were sold out.

Markels cites other examples of equivalence from Enkvist (1973):

4. *People* got on and off. At the newstand [*sic*] *Frenchmen*, returning to Paris, bought that day's paper. ("contracting hyponymy")
5. *Tulips* are cheap even in January. But then *flowers* seem to be necessary to Scandinavians during the darkest season. ("expanding hyponymy")
6. The sun *sagged* yellow over the grass plots and bruised itself on the clotted cotton fields. The fertile countryside that grew things in other seasons spread flat from the roads and *lay* prone in ribbed fans of broken discouragement. ("sustained metaphor")
7. *Tulips* are cheap. *Roses* are expensive. ("co-membership of the same world field")

It would seem to be the case that readers will establish some kind of unity for any paragraph that has a definable semantic field. On the other hand, one of Hirsch's main points is that paragraphs with more "thematic tags" (his term for "recurrence chains") are less unified than paragraphs with fewer. (Hirsch, 1977, pp. 126–27.)

Jeanne Fahnestock (1983) has written about what she calls the most basic level, where "an impression of coherence is produced when a reader can go from one clause to the next without losing the meaning." The problem is not so much one of losing meaning as it is of establishing relationships from clause to clause (or T-unit to T-unit), what might properly be called "the grammar of cohesion," dealt with extensively by Halliday and Hasan (1976), Teun A. van Dijk (1977), and Robert de Beaugrande (1980). My own "grammar of cohesion" (which I unfortunately called "The Grammar of Coherence") argues that between T-units in a cohesive paragraph, a finite set of relationships prevails—i.e., on close reading can be supplied by the reader who takes the paragraph to be cohesive. Five of these relationships can always be expressed by a coordinating conjunction and usually with a transitional adverb:

Life is short. [AND/MOREOVER] It is usually tragic. [BUT/HOWEVER] You must make the best of a bad situation. [FOR] The alternative to life is unattractive. [SO/THUS] I advise you to eat, drink, and be merry. [YET/STILL] You must use judgment, [OR] you will abbreviate your already short sojourn.

This essentially inane, cooked-up paragraph can take several forms without disturbing the transitional relationships.

A. Life is short, and it is usually tragic. However, you must make the best of a bad situation, for the alternative to life is unattractive. Thus, I advise you to eat, drink, and be merry. Still, you must use judgment, or you will abbreviate your already short sojourn.

B. Life is short; it is usually tragic; but you must make the best of a bad situation, for the alternative to life is unattractive. So I advise you to eat, drink, and be merry, yet you must use judgment, or you will abbreviate your already short sojourn.

One relationship that cannot be expressed explicitly by a coordinating conjunction is what I call "inclusivity," the marker for which is typically the colon and the grammatical marker of which is the subordinator "that." An example of such a relationship occurs between T-units in a quotation from Kintsch which appears below (p. 69):

A spatial metaphor is useful here. [:/THAT] The memory network is like a universe.

Another sequence that cannot be marked by a coordinating conjunction is question-answer.

However, I leave this argument to the test of experience. "The Grammar of Coherence" (pp. 221–28) explains it sufficiently.

COHERENCE

With a quite wonderful metaphor, Walter Kintsch (1980) characterizes knowledge systems.

We conceive of LTM [long term memory] as a huge propositional network that is organized only in the sense that certain relationships exist among the propositional nodes (e.g., they may have common arguments), and in the sense that related propositions are somehow close to each other. A spatial metaphor is useful here. The memory network is like the universe. In a multi-dimensional space, there are galaxies of knowledge on this or that, with subclusters like star systems. There is a lot of local structure there, as well as some very specific relations within a knowledge cluster, but if observed from enough distance, all we have is a locally uniform space, dense in some regions, full of holes in others. Holes may be filled when new knowledge is acquired through learning, and where someone may have nothing but holes in his knowledge system, others have grown a thicket of nodes. But in some unspecified way these nodes are grown so that related nodes are deposited in neighboring regions of the space. . . . Thus, the knowledge space contains an area where information can be found that has to do with "religion" (including personal, spatio-temporally tagged episodic nodes), and, at some distance from it, a space for "Quantum Theory"—a vast void for most people. (Pp. 7–8)

Like Kintsch, I have no idea how these "galaxies" of knowledge might be precisely specified (since, among other problems, they are personal and idiosyncratic), but the metaphor does explain why a semantic field (whether termed "recurrence chain," "motif," or "theme") has the potential for creating both cohesion and coherence for the reader.

Witte and Faigley (1981) define coherence as "those underlying semantic relations that allow a text to be understood and used." These "coherence conditions are governed by the writer's purpose, the audience's knowledge and expectations, and the information to be conveyed."

A coherent text is one that "adds up" for the reader— that is, the reader feels that he or she has an overall representation of the text's meaning in memory, with no "loose ends," no propositions or concepts that cannot be accounted for in terms of the general representation. But this hazy notion of coherence will become clearer hereafter.

We are seeing that at the semantic level, cohesion and coherence are one and the same, and the notion of "recurrence chains" does not help us a great deal in explaining local sequaciousness, T-unit to T-unit.

Coherence obviously depends on cohesion to some extent—and just as obviously on the world knowledge that a reader brings to the text. For example, the following brief text is coherent only if the reader knows that "Grendel" is the name of a car:

(1) Grendel snorted and staggered. Nonetheless, we reached the park safely.

Context—or scene—is often as important as cohesion in allowing the reader to achieve coherence, my favorite example being a set of instructions found in a phone booth:

(2) Lift receiver.
Deposit coin.
Listen for dial tone.
Dial number.

The enthymeme is unexpressed, but it is supplied by context: The following will enable you to make a phone call.

But give the same text a title, and put it in a book called *Now Poetry*:

AT&T

Lift receiver.
Deposit coin.
Listen for dial tone.
Dial number.

It is no less cohesive, but it is not immediately coherent. Any one of the following enthymemes might create coherence:

Big business is impersonal.
Humans are machines.
If you try hard enough, you can find sexual meanings in anything.

Obviously, the enthymeme specifies intention; therefore, it can be viewed as
the controlling speech act of (not necessarily *in*) a text.

The emerging field of text linguistics restates what rhetoric has been saying for two millennia: "all the levels of language are to be described in terms
of their utilization" (de Beaugrande and Dressler, 1981).

In fact, as I have said, I like to view a text as a set of instructions for
making meaning. Some of those instructions are *exophoric*, "pointing" outward toward the scene, and some are *endophoric*, "pointing" inward, direct-
ing the reader's attention to the text itself. (Northrop Frye, 1963, speaks of
"centrifugality" and "centripetality.") Obviously, the cohesion features outlined by Halliday and Hasan (1976) are endophoric.

MACROSTRUCTURES

Teun A. van Dijk's *Macrostructures* (1980) pursues the distinction between
local and *global* structures, the local being, for example, the syntax of a sentence or the sorts of cohesion relationships dealt with by Halliday and Hasan
(1976), in contrast with such global structures as gist, thesis, theme. Clearly a
text, "the abstract underlying structure of a discourse" (van Dijk, p. 29), has
properties that local analysis cannot account for—primarily a macrostructure or, in fact, a hierarchical series of macrostructures, depending on one's
point of view.

Van Dijk (1980) quotes the following cohesive but uncoherent text:

(1) John was ill, so he called a doctor. But the doctor could not come, because
his wife wanted to go to the theater with him. They were playing Othello, which she
thought they could not miss because Shakespeare is one of the few dramatical authors
who. . . . (P. 40)

The text is *cohesive* for several reasons. In the first place, the inter−T-
unit relationships are perfectly clear (see, "The Grammar of Coherence,"
pp. 221−28), and the cohesion devices (Halliday and Hasan, 1976) are in

place and functioning. Furthermore, the *fact sequence* is acceptable. That is to say, "each fact may be a condition (cause or reason) for the next fact" (van Dijk, 1980, p. 40). ("A fact is an event, action, state, or process in some possible world," van Dijk, 1980, p. 32.) On the other hand, the passage has no topic, no center of gravity. Is it about John, the doctor, Othello, Shakespeare?

The problem with (1) is that it has no controlling *macroproposition*, "a propositional *common denominator* that describes a situation or course of events *as a whole*, such that the constituent sentences denote *normal component actions* of this overall episode" (p. 42). One sort of macrostructure, then, is the macroproposition (which may or not appear in the passage but which must be, in any case, derivable therefrom).

Van Dijk distinguishes between the *semantic* macrostructure and the *formal* superstructure, which can be represented by an outline, for example.

As we should expect, there are also *macrospeech acts*, or, to use van Dijk's own terminology, "local" and "global" speech acts. The example that van Dijk gives (pp. 187–89) is too long for quotation here, but it is easy enough to cook up a brief illustration (using Searle's 1975 categories of speech acts):

(2) A husband at a cocktail party is in conversation with two friends. His wife joins the group and begins to speak.
WIFE: "I apologize for butting in this way." (*expressive*)
HUSBAND: "We were talking about tomorrow's football game." (*representative*)
WIFE: "Don't miss that game under any circumstances." (*directive [ironic?]*)
HUSBAND: "I certainly won't!" (*commissive*)
WIFE: "It is now half past twelve." (*representative*)
HUSBAND: "I hereby pronounce you my timekeeper." (*declaration*)
WIFE: "I repeat: it is now half past twelve." (*representative*)

Though the series of individual speech acts—expressive, representative, directive, commissive, representative, declaration, representative—do not, by some equation, add up to a clearcut macrospeech act, we can assume that the overall intent of the exchange comes to a *directive*: "Let's go home."

As there are macrostructures, there are, of course, macrorules, namely *construction, deletion, evaluation, generalization, interpretation, selection,* and the *zero*-rule. Most of these are self-explanatory, and I choose not to go into them.

The form of a text depends to a great extent on the reader's purpose and strategies. In a study of summarizing abilities, Suzanne Hidi (1984) distinguished *précis* (a shorter version of the original text) from *synthesized summary* ("not only a shortened version, but also one in which ideas are integrated, synthesized and reorganized," p. 2). In summarizing a difficult text,[1]

---

1. The text that Hidi used was M. T. H. Chi, *Knowledge Development and Memory Performance* (Pittsburgh: University of Pittsburgh, Learning Research and Development Center, 1980).

most readers—in the study, eighteen of twenty-five—stick with the précis even though it may not show the dominance of a controlling idea that emerges gradually as the text develops and hence may distort the apparent semantic intention of the original. A linear, paragraph-by-paragraph summary "is based on local integrations rather than on more sophisticated whole-text level reorganizations and syntheses of ideas" (p. 17).

A précis and a summary represent different forms of the same brute data provided by the text. According to Hidi, Levin (1982) has suggested that

> comprehension-directed macro-structure strategies are different from memory-directed macro-structure strategies. The former involves overviewing, skimming the text for main ideas and comprehending them, and paraphrasing larger units. The latter consists of a more thorough analysis and includes the construction of hierarchical representation of text, concretizing main ideas, summarizing and directing higher order questions to those concepts that require inference. (P. 21)

Another—and in my opinion brilliant—slant on macrostructures is Northrop Frye's essay "Myth, Fiction, and Displacement," in *Fables of Identity* (1963).

When we are reading a story, Frye tells us, we are not directly conscious of all local detail, for it would take a "portentous concentration" thus to attend; rather, we tend to make rather large groupings—in the dry language of scientism, as used by van Dijk, we create a series of macrostructures. The result is that we "possess" the story—say the plot of a James novel—not in its sequaciousness, one event following another in memory as they must in time, but rather "there is something oddly discontinuous about our possession of it" (p. 22).

> In the direct experience of fiction, continuity is the center of our attention; our later memory, or what I call the possession of it, tends to become discontinuous. Our attention shifts from the sequence of incidents to another focus: a sense of what the work of fiction was all *about*, or what criticism usually calls its theme. And we notice that as we go on to study and reread the work of fiction, we tend, not to reconstruct the plot, but to become more conscious of the theme, and to see all incidents as manifestations of it. Thus the incidents themselves tend to remain in our critical study of the work, discontinuous, detached from one another and regrouped in a new way. (P. 23)

When we actually digest a story, we have it as *mythos*, or "plot examined as a simultaneous unity, when the entire shape of it is clear in our minds" (p. 24). And as we read, "We are continually, if often unconsciously, attempting to construct a larger pattern of simultaneous significance out of what we have so far read or seen" (p. 25).

At the beginning of his essay, Frye distinguishes between "fictional" and "thematic" literary works, which include most lyrics, essays, didactic poetry, and oratory. In fact, he discusses only fictive literature; yet his argument quite properly implies that fictional and thematic literature, at the top of the hierarchical tree, are identical: they are the theme that the reader derives and that allows him or her to make sense of the details of the work.

The view of structure that van Dijk and Frye share relates to a conception of literacy that is particularly useful. Gavriel Salomon (1983) argues that television, film, and print literacy become more and more isomorphic as one moves from the subskills up the hierarchy toward broad conceptual and managerial skills, or, to put the matter differently, the microrules for decoding print and television are quite different, but the macrorules of interpretation are the same. At the upper levels, the various kinds of literacy come together, a fact that broadens compositionists' view of their field.

A TAXONOMY OF COHERENCE

Phelps (1980) has developed a useful taxonomy of coherence:

underlying coherence: In the reader's judgment, a satisfying macrostructure [enthymeme and "tree"] can be constructed (i.e., is intended and can be inferred from the written text), but it is poorly cued.

partial coherence: The reader can form only an incomplete macrostructure, for lack of an overarching conception of the whole supplied by the writer.

incoherence: Essentially the judgment that a discourse lacks structural features needed to integrate it even partially, probably because the writer has no conception of a satisfying macrostructure.

discoherence: The judgment that structural features cued are in conflict and therefore cannot be integrated. The conflicts are substantive and major and cannot be resolved by cutting out minor bits of meaning.

undercuing: Insufficient cues for successful integration of a macrostructure without reader contribution. Depending on degree, leads to judgment of incoherence, partial coherence, or underlying coherence.

miscuing: Strongly conflicting cues to macrostructural features, making a single consistent integration impossible unless the reader discards some of the meanings expressed by the text. Depending on degree, leads to judgment of discoherence or partial coherence.

THE SEMANTICS OF COHERENCE

Briefly, let's think about the semantics of coherence. A good place to start is at H. P. Grice's well-known cooperative principle (Grice, 1967). The maxims of this principle concern *quantity* (Give the reader all he or she needs to know, and nothing in excess); *quality* (Be reliable and truthful); *relation* (Don't introduce irrelevancies); and *manner* (Be as clear as possible). These principles in a sense define the "face" value of discourse or texts. They are much like the suprasegmental phonemes, tone, pause, and stress: we are aware of them intuitively, and they guide our understanding, but they are never in the foreground of consciousness.

Wolfgang Iser (1978) has made a great deal of the concept of "gaps" in texts, lacunae which must be filled by the reader:

What *is* said only appears to take on significance as a reference to what is not said; it is the implications and not the statements that give shape and weight to the meaning. But as the unsaid comes to life in the reader's imagination, so the said "expands" to take on greater significance than might have been supposed. (P. 168)

Are not these "gaps" *implicatures* which result from violations of the Gricean "contract": *presupposition*, which is knowledge taken as given; and *inference*, knowledge deduced from the text, but not directly stated? Take a simple text as an example:

Tomorrow that man will marry a woman who wears a diamond as big as the Ritz.

The *implication* is (perhaps) that the man is marrying the woman for her money. In attempting to unravel the semantic intention of the text, we assume that the statement is true (quality), that it and its parts are relevant (relation), and that it is as clearly stated as possible (manner). But quantity puzzles us: why the information about the diamond if it is true, relevant, and clear? There is a gap, which we can fill by inference—thus the possibility of the above interpretation, abetted, of course, by our own cynical world knowledge.

But there are other gaps, or other aspects to the gap. The passage begins with a presupposition: that the addressee knows who "the man" is, else the subject of the sentence would need a relative clause or adjective to make identification possible or to define. And the passage is rife with inference: that the man is marrying for money; that the woman is not particularly desirable in and of herself; that the addresser in the passage has made a moral judgment on the man. . . . Thus, it makes very good sense to speak of the constructive act of reading, a point that is made clear by an experiment that is easily replicable. Tell the following story to a group of subjects. Then after ten minutes or so ask them to repeat the story to you.

The company picnic was held on the shores of Lake Crystal. George arrived at the lively, noisy gathering somewhat late, but soon got into the swing of things and was crooning an old song with his comrades, a beer in one hand and a hot dog in the other. After three hours, George was more than ready to leave. He was soaking wet and extremely angry.

Almost surely your subjects will tell you that George either fell or was thrown into the lake, even though the story does not say as much. Furthermore, your subjects will remember the story as if it did directly state its implications. We remember implications as if they were directly stated information. (Clark and Clark, 1977, pp. 154–56)

We cross Iser's "gaps" on the *bridging assumptions* we supply on the basis of our world knowledge, for implications—presuppositions and inferences—are built into the world as we experience it, not into the language.

Some years ago, I was teaching as a visitor at the University of Iowa. From that experience, I have brought several vivid memories, one of which was the execrable food my wife and I were forced to eat day after day at Iowa House, and another of which regards our present subject.

I had been talking about coherence and cohesion with a group of graduate students and in the course of the session cooked up this passage:

My wife and I love abalone. Whenever we go to Salt Lake City, we eat out. Bratten's serves wonderful seafood.

The students, of course, could supply the necessary bridging assumptions to make sense of the text: Bratten's is in Salt Lake City, and the Winterowds eat abalone at Bratten's. Nonetheless, they felt that the text was strange and that it would be unlikely to occur in the real world. At which point I bet them a pound of Amana cheese that, in context, with the proper audience, it could be taken as a real-world instance of language use. Shortly thereafter the class and my wife and I went out to dinner. While waiting in the bar for our table, I casually said, "My wife and I love abalone. Whenever we go to Salt Lake City, we eat out. Bratten's serves marvelous seafood." My wife forthwith responded: "Yes, and and it's strange that, living practically on the seashore, we go to Salt Lake for good seafood." Because of her world knowledge, the utterance was perfectly coherent, with no obvious gaps.

KENNETH BURKE

By this time, it has become obvious that Burke has been a tremendous influence on my thought and, indeed, on my values. That much acknowledged, I will go on to say that I consider his ideas about form to be absolutely seminal (and not widely enough appreciated).

Perhaps the key to his notions is the "psychology of information/psychology of form" tradeoff. The more we pay attention to form, the less information we will gain from the text. As I say in "The Three R's: Reading, Reading, and Rhetoric" (pp. 253–63),

Here, then, is the great irony: the expressive language of poetry is not efficient language. A Coleridgean metaphor comes to mind: the language of poetry is like a pane of glass textured by frost which partially blocks the vision and which calls attention to itself as an object worth contemplating. This irony of texture is precisely—though not completely—explicable in terms of how the cue system works in the psycholinguistic process called reading.

Surprise and suspense depend on the psychology of information—we want to know what happened or will happen. But information is a self-consuming artifact, for once we have it, we lose interest in it. Our interest in form lasts longer. (*Counter-Statement*, pp. 144–46)

Again and again Burke stresses that the appeal of art *as art* lies in form. For example:

So the formal aspects of art appeal in that they exercise formal potentialities of the reader. They enable the mind to follow processes amenable to it. . . . The forms of art, to summarize, are not exclusively "aesthetic." They can be said to have prior existence in the experience of the person hearing or reading the work of art. They parallel processes which characterize his experiences outside of art" (*Counter-Statement*, p. 143).

Form has conative value: when we respond to form we are prepared to respond to opinion. (*A Rhetoric of Motives*, p. 58.) Burke's most widely known statement on the subject is "The Nature of Form," from *Counter-Statement* (pp. 124–52). He defines form in literature as "an arousing and fulfillment of desires. A work has form in so far as one part of it leads a reader to anticipate another part, to be gratified by the sequence" (p. 124).

Syllogistic progression is the form of the perfectly conducted argument, advancing step by step. . . . *Qualitative Progression*, the other aspect of progressive form, is subtler. Instead of one incident in the plot preparing us for some other possible incident of plot . . . the presence of one quality prepares us for the introduction of another. . . . *Repetitive form* is the consistent maintaining of a principle under new guises. . . . *Conventional form* involves to some degree the appeal of form *as form*. . . . *Minor or incidental forms* . . . such as metaphor, paradox, disclosure, reversal, contraction, expansion, bathos, apostrophe . . . which can be discussed as formal events in themselves. (Pp. 124–27)

In a letter to Gorham B. Munson (quoted in Rueckert, 1969, p. 10), Burke says,

Here is why there is so much searching for a definition of form at the present time. Once the plot always centered around a conflict. The scene was set, the conflict began, the big moment was the drawing together of the threads. This was form. It is the form of all drama. In "abstract" writing there is no conflict of this nature. The movement is usually a simple straight line or curving line. There is no plot because *the plot is the hero*; and a plot either does things or does not—it cannot baffle for even baffling itself is a simple plot. Thus, like Joyce, we must turn to the *Odyssey*, or some such, instead of to the tragedy (the psychological novel turned to the tragedy). A challengelike beginning, and a coda end—and in between the main thing is diversity of attack, turning here and then there. With, of course, somewhat of a splurge right before the coda. Then one must devote his time to the minor organisms, trying if possible to make each paragraph a microcosm, with its own formal development. But aside from the beginning, end, and coda, there are, it seems to me just now, no other major functions. The rest are simply *relationships between the parts*, such as ending a conversation or chapter with some speechless act, and so forth. While, of course, the letter or the conversation should have gone through some still smaller curve in themselves.

Since the poem is meant to do something, we look for alignments to see how they work, and when we find out, we have dealt with both form and content. We look at the *equational structure* and see how it functions. Thus, we are looking at purpose, strategy, the symbolic act. (*The Philosophy of Literary Form*, pp. 75–86)

"Correctness" or suitability of form depends on ideology. For an Aristotelian, the *deus ex machina* in *Iphigenia at Aulis* is formally incorrect, but from a thematic point of view, it is completely correct; only God could have rescued her from such a situation. (*Counter-Statement*, pp. 146–47)

FORM FLUENCY

In a remarkable dissertation completed at the University of Southern California, Betty Cain (1981) pursued the following hypothesis:

In producing a discourse, language users exploit a global *form fluency*, which is a tacit competence analogous to syntactic fluency in producing sentences; form fluency comprises four essential processes: *division*, *relationship*, *order*, and *elaboration*.

Cain convincingly demonstrated this hypothesis through analysis of oral impromptu, written impromptu, and multi-draft compositions by freshmen at the University of Southern California.

If we can extrapolate from Cain's study, we can say that (literate) adults have a versatile form competence. In going from task to task, the students changed their global form, but stuck with the same proposition and content. Furthermore, the form fluency is both conceptual and rhetorical. "That is, it functions both intellectually to facilitate thinking, and persuasively, to facilitate the rhetorical identification of readers and writers" (p. 215).

The claim regarding form fluency or competence is, of course, not new with Dr. Cain and can certainly be traced back at least as far as Plato, but among modern rhetoricians, it is Kenneth Burke and Frank D'Angelo who advance the claim most prominently.

Frank D'Angelo's *A Conceptual Theory of Rhetoric* (1975) is a good companion piece to Cain's work. D'Angelo states his premises thus:

The conceptual theory of rhetoric is an explanatory theory of a much deeper sort than that of many rhetorics. The study of conceptual rhetoric is the study of the nature of human intellectual capacities. What are the innate organizing principles, the deeper underlying mental operations, the abstract mental structures that determine discourse? What hypotheses concerning this internalized system will account for the nature of its basic principles? Rhetorical patterns could not be produced in speech or in writing unless they were based on underlying mental processes. Although specific instances of discourse are concrete and individual, they do in fact reflect aspects of underlying, generalized processes. It is probable that innate properties of the human organism must be genetically inherited. In generating discourse, the individual uses this underlying, abstract structure by filling in the details from the universe of discourse around him. (P. 26)

In a sense, D'Angelo is saying that the human mind is the human mind, genetically programmed with certain perceptual, cognitive, and constructive potentials, but he is saying a good deal more: that patterns in rhetoric reflect patterns of mind and "are also to be considered universal patterns of discourse containing structural features which underlie all languages" (p. 57).

Whatever the validity of this claim, we are left with actual discourses and genres in various cultures. In this sense, we are much more interested in scene than gene as we think about form.

RECAPITULATION: A PRACTICAL GUIDE TO FORM

T-Unit

The T-unit is the minimum stretch of discourse that can conventionally be punctuated as a sentence. The practical advantage of using the T-unit rather than the sentence in some kinds of studies is that the T-unit is independent of the idiosyncrasies of punctuation. Here are examples:

One T-unit, one sentence, five propositions: To maintain standards, the university administration urged faculty members who are bibulous to drink temperately while on campus.

Two T-units, one sentence, two propositions: (1) I drink wine every day, (2) but I usually stay sober."

One T-unit, two "sentences," four (perhaps five) propositions: The bibulous professor was trying to maintain his dignity. Trying not to make a fool of himself.

The Grammar of Coherence: Transitions

"The Grammar of Coherence" (pp. 221–28) specifies the relationships that prevail between T-units. I call these relationships "transitions."

The Paragraph

The most important notion about the paragraph is excruciatingly simple, but almost completely overlooked in our textbooks and professional literature. It is simply this: the paragraph as a block of discourse marked by indentation is arbitrary; when I indent, I am setting a patch of text off, just as a period sets a smaller unit apart. However, coherent texts are made up of what Paul C. Rodgers (1966) called *stadia*, and stadia, having psychological reality (Becker, 1966; Young and Becker, 1966), might be called psychological paragraphs.

The indentations that I choose for any one of a variety of rhetorical reasons—or which are mere happenstance—may or may not coincide with stadia. If you reproduce a coherent text without paragraph indentations and ask readers to mark paragraph beginnings, they will mark stadia (Becker, 1966) which may or may not coincide with the paragraphing used by the author. Stadia are psychological; paragraphs are rhetorical. (Sometimes, of course, stadia and paragraphs coincide.)

The following Xerox advertisement[1] is a case in point. Notice that both the "psychological" sentences and the stadia are broken up, presumably for rhetorical purposes:

EVERY DAY THE AVERAGE
BUSINESSMAN COMMUTES TO THE
NINETEENTH CENTURY

(1) It wouldn't take very long for the average twentieth century businessman to feel right at home in the average nineteenth century office.

(2) Because for the most part, the way office workers and executives work and the tools they use are merely refinements of procedures and products invented in the 1800's or before.

(3) The typewriter was patented in 1858. The telephone was invented in 1879 and the ball point pen dates from 1888.

(4) No wonder productivity in the office isn't keeping pace with the times.

(5) At Xerox, helping people work more productively is our business.

(6) Today we produce advanced machines that not only make copies of incredible quality, but automatically reduce, collate, and staple sets together.

(7) Machines that create, store and retrieve documents faster than humanly possible. Machines that print out computer information faster than ordinary computer printers.

(8) And machines that help business professionals, who earn 80% of the salaries paid by American business, create reports with charts, tables, graphics, in hours instead of days.

(9) There's even a special cable—called Xerox Ethernet cable—that can connect these machines into an information network. So that the people in your office and in offices around the country can have the information they need to get their jobs done.

(10) In fact, Xerox people, machines, and services can not only help you stay on top of your job, but even get ahead of it, which can put you a century ahead of where you were yesterday.

In my reading the stadia are made up of rhetorical paragraphs as follows: I = 1, 2, 3, 4; II = 5, 6, 7, 8, 9; III = 10.

Once we differentiate paragraphs from stadia, we can begin to deal productively with the rhetoric of paragraphing. The question with the Xerox ad is not whether the "sentencing" and paragraphing are right or wrong, but whether the company has conveyed its semantic intention through those structures to the intended audience in the given scene.

Lexical Equivalence Chains

These correpond to Halliday and Hasan's (1976) "lexical cohesion." They are readily illustrated, as in the following, where one chain is marked by italics and another by capitals:

MY UNCLE, JOHN A QUARLES, was a FARMER, and HIS *place* was in the country four miles from Florida. HE had eight children and fifteen or twenty negroes and was

1. *The Atlantic Monthly*, 248:6 (Dec. 1981), 21. Reprinted by permission.

also fortunate in other ways, particularly in HIS character. I have not come across a better MAN than HE was. I was HIS guest for two or three months every year, from the fourth year after we removed to Hannibal till I was eleven or twelve years old. I have never consciously used HIM or HIS wife in a book but HIS *farm* has come very handy to me in literature once or twice. In "Huck Finn" and in "Tom Sawyer, Detective" I moved *it* down to Arkansas. It was all of six hundred miles but it was no trouble; *it* was not a very large *farm*—five hundred acres perhaps—but I could have done it if *it* had been twice as large. And as for the morality of it, I cared nothing for that; I would move a state if the exigencies of literature required it.

—*The Autobiography of Mark Twain*

Cohesion

Cohesion comes about when one unit of a text depends on another for its meaning. (Halliday and Hasan, 1976; see pp. 67–68 of the present discussion.) The factors in cohesion are

1. Reference, endophoric and exophoric
2. Substitution
3. Ellipsis
4. Conjunction
5. Lexical cohesion

The Semantics of Coherence

The maxims in Grice's cooperative principle are

Quantity: The addresser will give all information necessary to the subject and no more.
Quality: The addresser will tell the truth.
Manner: The addresser will be as clear as possible.
Relation: Contents of the discourse will be relevant to the subject.

Unintentional violation of the maxims results from inattention or ineptness. Conscious violation of the maxims results in either special rhetorical effect (e.g., irony) or results from mendacity.

Implicatures are meanings not stated directly in the text. *Presupposition* is knowledge taken as given. *Inference* is knowledge deduced from the text, but not stated directly.

"Tomorrow that man will marry a woman who wears a ring with a diamond as big as the Ritz."
Presupposition: The addressee knows who "that man" is.
Inference: The man is marrying the woman for her money.

For an excellent brief discussion of semantics, see Schachter, "Some Semantic Prerequisites for a Model of Language" (1976).

8. Home Base: The English Department

The modern history of composition in colleges and universities is yet to be written,[1] but this needed work must certainly focus on the relationship between literary study and the teaching of writing. Since composition is embedded in English departments, and since English departments are, for all intents and purposes, departments of literature, literary doctrine and practice get translated into the teaching of writing. This much, I think, is obvious.

At least an essay, if not a book, could be written about the influence of the New Criticism on composition,[2] but since that essay is not this one, I will merely say that, in my opinion, New Criticism was largely responsible for the artifactual approach to composition as opposed to the process approach. That is, composition teachers (by default and necessity)[3] had been immersed in the doctrine and methods of New Criticism—text-centered, scrupulously analytic, "objective"—and that critical lore became translated into composition practice: careful analysis of the text; neutrality about opinion as long as the argument was well developed; discussion of literature and essays in class, under the assumption that students would absorb technique from this analysis. And my characterization is, I think, objective.

Compositionists, part of the literary establishment administratively if not philosophically, should be aware of attitudes, modes, values, and practices enfranchised by the currently prevailing literary doctrines, and certainly in this post-structuralist era, reader-response criticism and deconstructionism are the glamorous doctrines.

"Reader-response critics would argue that a poem cannot be understood apart from its results. Its 'effects,' psychological and otherwise, are essential to any accurate description of its meaning, since that meaning has no effective existence outside of its realization in the mind of the reader." (Tompkins,

1. This chapter appeared in *Pre/Text* (Spring 1983) as "Post–Structuralism and Composition" and is reprinted here, in a slightly altered form, by permission of the editors of *Pre/Text*.
In *Writing Instruction in Nineteenth-Century American Colleges* (Carbondale and Edwardsville: Southern Illinois University Press, 1984), James Berlin has done an admirable job of telling the story of our fairly recent history.
2. Colleen Aycock, one of my students, has undertaken such a study for her dissertation.
3. I am aware that this modifier squints.

1980, p. ix.) In Jane P. Tompkins' explanation, reader-response criticism makes perfectly good (common) sense: meaning is not "out there" somewhere in the ether or "down below" on the page, but "up here," in the mind of the reader, yet it took the literary establishment excruciatingly long years to conclude the obvious.

Characteristically, Stanley Fish, perhaps the most accessible of the reader-response critics, puts the case directly on the line:

> Whereas I once agreed with my predecessors on the need to control interpretation lest it overwhelm and obscure texts, facts, authors, and intentions, I now believe that interpretation is the source of texts, facts, authors, and intentions. Or to put it another way, the entities that were once seen as competing for the right to constrain interpretation (text, reader, author) are now all seen to be the *products* of interpretation. (Fish, 1980, pp. 16–17)

These few words, which do not come from the uninitiated fringe of the literary establishment, contain enough implications to occupy a conscientious compositionist for at least a week (a lifetime?). And we will look at these implications hereafter.

DERRIDA, PRESENCE, AND STRUCTURALISM

Fish is small-fry compared with leviathan Jacques Derrida, who has even made *Newsweek* (June 22, 1981) as the secular skeptic *par excellence.* Derrida's deconstructionism is having and will have significant impact on both literature and literacy. In order to understand the scene in which we function as compositionists, we need to get some idea of what deconstructionism is all about. (Might we not, for our own purposes, translate "deconstructionism" as "decomposition" and thus achieve a nice dichotomy: decomposition versus composition? But that gambit draws a battle line where none should exist.)

Derrida's work is largely a reaction against *the doctrine of presence* and *structuralism.*

The metaphysics of presence "locates truth in what is immediately present to the consciousness with as little mediation as possible" (Culler, 1975, p. 32). A useful oversimplification explains that truth is consciousness, exactly in the Platonic sense; we must get behind the words to get at truth. Thus Plato:

SOCRATES. How about the question whether it is a fine thing or a disgraceful thing to be a speaker or writer and under what circumstances the profession might properly be called a disgrace or not? Was that made clear a little while ago when we said—
PHAEDRUS. What?
SOCRATES. That if Lysias or anyone else ever wrote or ever shall write, in private, or in public as lawgiver, a political document, and in writing it believes that it pos-

sesses great certainty and clearness, then it is a disgrace to the writer, whether anyone says so, or not. For whether one be awake or asleep, ignorance of right and wrong and good and bad is in truth inevitably a disgrace, even if the whole mob applaud it.

PHAEDRUS. That is true.

SOCRATES. But the man who thinks that in the written word there is necessarily much that is playful, and that no written discourse, whether in meter or in prose, deserves to be treated very seriously (and this applies also to the recitations of rhapsodes, delivered to sway people's minds, without opportunity for questioning and teaching), but that the best of them really serve only to remind us of what we know; and who thinks that only words about justice and beauty and goodness spoken by teachers for the sake of instruction and really written in a soul is clearness and perfection and serious value, that such words should be considered the speaker's own legitimate offspring, first the word within himself, if it be found there, and secondly its descendents or brothers which may have sprung up in worthy manner in the souls of others, and who pays attention to the other words—that man, Phaedrus, is likely to be such as you and I might pray we ourselves may become.[4]

The equation is obvious: the spoken word is one step removed from the truth, and the written word is a step further. It is the dance of the two veils: strip away the gown of writing to reveal the gossamer of spoken language, behind which lies the naked beauty of the dancer. The metaphor is fruitful: laws of nature, if not decency, prevent the final disrobing, and the unadorned Salome lives only as a chimera in the minds of the beholders. More prosaically, as the structuralists from Saussure onward contended, speech is primary, and writing, which is a representation of speech, is secondary.

The structuralist project in linguistics is built on contrastive analysis. One of the most powerful and useful structuralist doctrines is this: to know any item, you must know how it contrasts with all other items in its class.[5] A homely example will serve here. I know that there is a class called "subcompact cars"; and I also have learned that this class includes Toyotas, Datsuns, Rabbits, Escorts, and so on. However, I have not paid attention to the *features* that differentiate one make from another; thus, on the freeways, I am surrounded by undifferentiated little cars. My unawareness of distinctive features prevents me from classifying them according to make.

The distinctive feature that differentiates the phoneme /d/ from the phoneme /t/ is voicing. Because I am aware of that feature, I know that a "tot" is not a "dot."

Difference. Language is a web of contrasts.

In the Western tradition—from Plato to Walter Ong—writing has been considered the signifier (secondary) of the signifier (primary), which is speech. But Derrida argues that there is no logos behind the words. And suppose

---

4. Trans. Harold North Fowler (Cambridge, Mass.: Harvard University Press, n.d.).

5. This, of course, is one of the prime doctrines of tagmemic theory. See Young Becker, and Pike (1970).

there were. How could you get at it except through language? The problem is that meaning is built of *traces*, and traces are nothing but structures of differences and hence are not "something."

In fact, Derrida tells us in *Writing and Difference* (1978),

It is because writing is *inaugural*, in the fresh sense of the word, that it is dangerous and anguishing. It does not know where it is going, no knowledge can keep it from the essential precipitation toward meaning that it constitutes and that is, primarily, its future. . . . Meaning is neither before nor after the act. (P. 11)

Writing as some action other than mere inscription, that is. And this is precisely why we can speak of "the end of the book," as does Derrida in *Of Grammatology* (1974):

The idea of the book is the idea of totality, finite or infinite, of the signifier; this totality of the signifier cannot be a totality, unless a totality constituted by the signified pre-exists it, supervises its inscriptions and its signs, and is independent of it in its ideality. The idea of the book, which always refers to a natural totality, is profoundly alien to the sense of writing. (P. 18)

Derrida does not mean that there will be no more paperbacks and hardbounds, but that their value will change; they will no longer be the repositories of truths or of definitive statements. The most important moment in a book comes when its own internal logic breaks down and the interpreter can rise to a new synthesis or vision. Which will also be deconstructed.

Derrida's argument is excruciating, but the point he comes to is simply that Saussure both contradicted himself and overlooked the obvious implications of his argument. The contradiction is in the location of meaning in the phoneme, and the lapse is in not seeing that language is *trace* (which is Derrida's term, not Saussure's).

Derrida and the "Science" of Language

To follow the argument that grammatology cannot be a positive science (*Of Grammatology*, pp. 74–93), one must understand the rationalistic movement toward "a real character and philosophic language" (the title of John Wilkins' 1668 treatise), based on the notion that essences could be classified and assigned glyphs or graphemes. In such a language, one could combine the proper signs and *write* in the universal language. (If all humankind had the true concept "soul," and if "+" signified "soul," then we could have a real character.) However, as you can see, this gambit merely evades the notion of speech as the immediate signifier of the signified, and, in fact, ideograms are no more related to essences than are words derived from phonetic alphabets.

Grammatology cannot be one of the sciences of man, for its basic question is "What does 'man' mean?" To answer that question, the *bricoleur* (the exceptionally skilled jack-of-all-trades) must use his or her skill (the *bricoleuse*, that is) at *bricolage*, the handyperson's ability to make do, employing whatever is available to keep things mended and operating. Derrida's translator puts it thus:

> The discourse of anthropology and the other sciences of man must be *bricolage*: the discourses of formal logic, and the pure sciences, one presumes, can be those of engineering. The engineer's "instruments" (according to Lévi-Strauss) are "specially adapted to a specific technical need"; the *bricoleur* makes do with things that were meant perhaps for other ends. (Spivak, 1974, p. xix)

Writing as conceived in the book is not linear and unidimensional, but nonlinear and pluridimensional. The book does not implode; it explodes. In one gesture, Derrida has left man, science, and the line behind. In *Of Grammatology*, he tells us that

> This representation of the anthropos is then granted: a precarious balance linked to manual-visual script. This balance is slowly threatened. It is at least known that 'no major change' giving birth to 'a man of the future' who will no longer be a 'man,' can be easily produced without the loss of the hand, the teeth, and therefore the upright position. A toothless humanity that would exist in a prone position using what limbs it had left to push buttons with, is not completely inconceivable. (P. 85)

So what "science" will be adequate to account for. . . . What? Well, *graphology* won't do the job. First, we don't even have the basic knowledge about substances: wax, clay, paper, quills, ballpoints. Second, we don't have the psychoanalytic knowledge. In fact, "To the extent that the constitution of ideal objectivity must essentially pass through the written signifier, no theory of this constitution has the right to neglect the investments of writing" (*Of Grammatology*, p. 88).

WRITING AND KNOWING

We have seen that "writing" is a form of cognition; its investments are anything that makes it manifest. In studying writing, of course, you are studying cognition, not its content, if there is any. In "Force and Signification," an essay-review of a book by Jean Rousset, Derrida sets forth his most poignant statement concerning writing:

> To write is to know that what has not yet been produced within literality has no other dwelling place, does not await us as some *topos ouranios*, or some divine understanding. Meaning must await being said or written in order to inhabit itself, and in order to become, by differing from itself, what it is: meaning. (*Writing and Difference*, p. 11)

In another place, I have written the following summarizing statement:

> Jacques Derrida . . . argues that we are confined eternally in the dictionary, our knowledge of words deriving only from our knowledge of other words. A concept is

nothing but a structure of meanings, a verbal tapestry hanging—on what? Not a wall, for there is no wall of final Truth behind the arras, only another tapestry of words veiling yet another.

Derrida's work is profoundly interesting, utterly provocative, and, in my own view, often totally wrongheaded. Nonetheless, we should think about consequences.

INDETERMINACY

E. D. Hirsch, Jr., the Lone Ranger of determinate meaning, has finally lost his battle for truth and justice; the bad guys of indeterminacy—led by scragglybearded, bow-legged Jack Derrida, as mean a critter as ever rustled an essay or heisted a book—have won; Hirsch was last seen riding into the sunset some moons ago.

The following contrastive statements are enough to make the point:

Hirsch (1973): Since humane studies, as Dilthey observed, are founded upon the interpretation of texts, valid interpretation is crucial to the validity of all subsequent inferences in those studies. The theoretical aim of a genuine discipline, scientific or humanistic, is the attainment of truth, and its practical aim is agreement that truth has probably been achieved. Thus the practical goal of every genuine discipline is concensus—the winning of firmly grounded agreement that one set of conclusions is more probable than others—and this is precisely the goal of valid interpretation. It must not be dismissed as a futile goal simply because the subject matter of interpretation is often ambiguous and its conclusions uncertain. Certainty is not the same thing as validity, and knowledge of ambiguity is not necessarily ambiguous knowledge. (Pp. viii–ix)

Barbara Johnson (1980): The essays collected in this volume [*The Critical Difference*] have as their common focus . . . "difference" as it structures and undermines the act of reading. But it should already be clear that the meaning of the words *difference* and *reading* cannot be taken for granted. In each essay, they function as two unknowns in a textual equation whose unresolvability is matched only by its ability to engender more textuality. (P. x)

The problem here, as Derrida himself points out, is the rejection of finalism: the text is never finished, by the writer or the reader. This being the case, one must reject *telos* or ultimate purpose, for the text is ever beginning, and yet it is difficult to comprehend how we might understand a text if we have no idea of its purpose. In other words, intention is essential to meaning. That being the case, meaning must be determinate, for it can be nothing else but what the writer intended.

In "Speech Acts and the Reader-Writer Transaction" (pp. 175–93), Dorothy Augustine and I have developed a long and highly technical argument to solve this problem, but for the moment it is enough to realize that Derrida and his followers argue against the determinacy of textual meaning, with the result that the text means, in fact, what it means to me or to you, not what the author intended it to mean. That being the case, the composition teacher is in a bind. One of the key ideas behind teaching composition is this: "I know what you're trying to say in this paper, and I can help you say it better." The strict deconstructionist as a teacher of composition must say, "I think I know what this paper means to me, and I'll explain that to you." In fact, if we give up the idea that meaning is determinate, we pretty much reduce teaching composition to mechanics: syntactic fluency (perhaps), punctuation, verb agreement, and so on.

On the other hand, if we say that no text is completely and finally interpretable, but that some are more so than others, we avoid the red herring of dichotomizing. Everyone can and does argue about the semantic intention of the Bible, but no one performs exegesis on the instructions for assembling a barbecue. In the latter case, we take the text to be determinate if we successfully put the barbecue together. The operation that the text directs is its meaning. In any case, a verbal structure of any length is infinitely complex and just as infinitely vulnerable, but readers do try to make sense, to determine what the writer intended. It is axiomatic in psycholinguistics and reading theory that readers will make every effort to put the text together in a sensible way. In other words, most readers assume that a text will make sense, but a change in attitude can bring about a sudden change in reading strategies.

After all, we can wilfully approach any text as though it were either determinate or indeterminate, though strict "constructionism" is probably a foolhardy stance, as even Hirsch (1973) tacitly admits when he explains the notion of "horizon of meaning":

Most, if not all, meaning experiences or intentions are occasions in which the whole meaning is not explicitly present to consciousness. But how are we to define the manner in which these unconscious meanings are implicitly present? In Husserl's analysis, they are present in the form of a 'horizon,' which may be defined as a system of typical expectations and probabilities. 'Horizon' is thus an essential aspect of what we usually call context. (P. 221)

If the case were binary, yes or no, and either logically or empirically verifiable, we would not *write* about it in any case, though we might well write to convince an audience that the case is really open-and-shut.

A triad of literary and language theorists have synecdochically figured in this discussion: determinist E. D. Hirsch, Jr., the ethical; reader-centered Stanley Fish, most pathetic; and deconstructionist Jacques Derrida, the logical—nicely, that is, allowing us to introduce the classical inventive triad: ethos, pathos, and logos, or attention to writer, to reader, and to content.

CONSEQUENCES

As to consequences, I have argued that determinist Hirsch has been vanquished, and with him, of course, disappears the compositonist's obligation to probe for the student's exact semantic intention: there can be no such entity, and if there were, how might one determine it to be determinate? It is this certainty that our logical and pathetic theorists deprive us of. Being true to the logic of our language theory, we as post-structuralists lose, as I said earlier, our most valuable teaching strategy, summed up as, "I think I know what you're trying to say, and I'll help you say it better."

Insofar as deconstructionist theory has done away with our faith in logos, some ultimate Word, endless dialogue and dialectic will replace conclusiveness: the clearly stated enthymeme, the clincher sentence of the paragraph, the crisp summary conclusion. For better or for worse, a change not only in attitudes and epistemologies, but also in practices.

The virtue of the text is heuristic, its potential for creating more textuality, commentary upon commentary: composition as an open-ended dialogue. And this attitude will have at least two diverse practical consequences.

First, "accepted" texts—rather than those produced by students—will become even more firmly entrenched as the basis for composition instruction. In the "pathetic" class, students will respond to literature in the ways suggested by Norman Holland (1975a, 1975b, 1975c), David Bleich (1975a, 1975b), and even Louise Rosenblatt (1976, 1978). In the "logical" class, under the aegis of the Derridean hermeneutics, cultural documents—such as *Civilization and Its Discontents*, already the basis for a comp class taught by a respected colleague of mine—will be the afflatus for further textuality: freshman writing as deconstructionist interpretation.

Second, the "banking" concept of education, so excoriated by Freire (1982; see "Black Holes, Indeterminacy, and Paulo Freire," pp. 307–13), will receive the *coup de grace*. Under the banking concept, a teacher communicates skills and knowledge to students, but when education becomes "problematized"—to call on Freirean terminology once more—students view learning as a process with no final goal, a plunge into the abyss of textuality, the end of the book, the end of certainty.

In the post-structuralist era, gobbledygook and obscurity are enfranchised. Though some moderns remain as brilliantly clear as Stanley Fish, others take the new climate as a license to obfuscate—for example, this from Derrida (or his translator, or both):

The system of writing in general is not exterior to the system of language in general, unless it is granted that the division between exterior and interior passes through the interior of the interior or the exterior of the exterior, to the point where the immanence of language is essentially exposed to the intervention of forces that are apparently alien to its system. (*Of Grammatology*, p. 43)

And it would be easy to compile a whole chrestomathy from the greater and lesser lights of modern criticism, especially the deconstructionists.

I am not arguing that reading should be easy (simple-minded?). I am only saying that writers whose motive is to *inform* me should make my task easier, not more difficult. There are ways to make complex ideas *more* accessible rather than less so, and there are authors who help me gain their meanings. The epigones of deconstructionism want me to put forth total effort, utter commitment, to gain their meanings; they eschew writing strategies that would make their texts more accessible.

Well, different strokes for different folks. Considering both the brevity of life and its richness, I normally choose not to labor through obscure texts that could be more accessible without losing their intellectual complexity. If your purpose is to inform, then you should do everything possible to make your text more accessible. However, in the current literary climate, accessibility is devalued, regardless of purpose. And such will be the case in composition. The more student writing can approximate the opacity of the going literary theory, the more it will be valued—provided punctuation and spelling are regular. The compositionist—a true believer in clear writing—will be a heretic in an establishment that values complexity for its own sake, arhetorically, regardless of purpose, audience, or scene.

Post-structuralism debunks, first, the long tradition of talk-write pedagogy in composition; second, the whole idea of a "science" of composition as well as "scientific" research in the field; third, the authority of handbooks and rhetorics, the whole textbook tradition.

In popular lore and in the scholarly literature, an ideal of natural language has run deep—namely, that students can speak effectively, even eloquently, and that, therefore, they should simply write like they talk, hence, the talk-write pedagogy. (For example, Zoellner, 1969.) Post-structualism may well accomplish what recent linguistic studies (e.g., Keenan and Bennett, 1977; Kroll and Vann, 1981) probably could not, convincing teachers that there are radical differences between "talking" and "writing" and that commonsense advice about writing like you talk is nonsense. In the first place, as Derrida argues convincingly in *Of Grammatology*, speech is no more primary than writing since writing is a way of thinking and is associated with inscription only accidentally. Furthermore, as the post-structuralists do not to my knowledge point out, writing is an array in space whereas speech is an array in time, and the spatial-temporal distinction makes a very great deal of difference: we can thumb through a book to find information, or scan the tome, strategies that are not possible with, for instance, tape recordings.

Two scholarly traditions take composition to be one of their fields: the humanities and the social sciences. The humanities, of course, are largely rationalistic and traditional: one does humanistic research in the library; the social sciences are largely empirical: one does research in the laboratory or in the field.

If one allows Derrida's argument, there can be no science of composition, just as there can be no science of grammatology, and attempts to posit such a science are mere "scientism," subscribing to the easiest scientific shibboleths without pondering their ramifications. Nonetheless, the prevalent attitude is scientismic:

Cognitive science is a recently emerging field at the crossroads of psychology, linguistics, philosophy, computer science, anthropology, sociology, and education. Its goal is to create a unified science of cognition and communication, with the specific concerns of the several subdisciplines forming an integrated whole. The undertaking might appear utterly utopian, were it not for the growing realization that the individual questions for each discipline may well be unanswerable without the framework of the whole theory. For example, the attempts to derive both semantics and pragmatics from syntax have been a notorious weakness of linguistics; what is needed is rather a theory of how knowledge is utilized (psychology) and how humans interact in society (sociology). (de Beaugrande, 1982, p. 229)

Insofar as this author terms his endeavor "scientific," he is a victim of both hubris and delusion—or so the deconstructionists would tell us; he is clearly talking about *bricolage*, not science.

And textbooks? Because composition has been within the humanities, textbooks have influenced both theory and teaching in strange ways. Consider, for example, school grammars: in 1762, Bishop Robert Lowth published his extraordinarily influential *Short Introduction to English Grammar*, which, as Edward Finegan (1980, pp. 23–26) argues, served as the model for much that appears even in current handbooks and standardized tests. But anyone who has taught composition knows that handbooks and rhetorics most often stem from tradition and that tradition gives them their authority—which is, after all, the source of authority in the humanities.

It is Derrida who most unequivocally pronounces the end of the book, and publishers should beware: the reaction against the authority of accepted texts will be doubled and quadrupled in regard to those peripherals, the handbooks and rhetorics. Composition will increasingly become a textbookless class.

While "definitive" texts will be devalued, exploratory writing will gain stature, and that, of course, is a mixed blessing. Students need to use writing to work ideas and attitudes out, writing that is inconclusive, open-ended—exploratory writing. On the other hand, definitive, "determinate" explanatory writing is both rewarding and very useful. But those sorts of texts will be devalued in favor of others that fit the value systems of the post-structuralists.

Finally, both reader-centered theorists and deconstructionists are profound skeptics, and that skepticism will spill over into composition. The incisive debate of the New Criticism will be replaced by a long, drawn-out, enigmatic shrug of the shoulders.

9. On Teaching Composition

THE DOMESTICATION OF THE SAVAGE FRESHMAN

We can take as our text this passage from *The Domestication of the Savage Mind*, that marvelous book by Jack Goody (1977):

> Perhaps I may put the central difficulty I find in terms of personal experience. In the course of several years of living among people of "other cultures," I have never experienced the kinds of hiatus in communication that would be the case if I and they were approaching the physical world from opposite ends. That this experience is not unique seems apparent from the contemporary changes occurring in developing countries where the shift from the Neolithic to modern science is encapsulated into the space of a man's lifetime. The boy brought up as a bricoleur becomes an engineer. He has his difficulties, but they do not lie at the level of an overall opposition between wild and domesticated minds, thoughts, or approaches, but on a much more particularistic level. (Pp. 8–9)

Since 1962—the date of *The Gutenberg Galaxy*, by Marshall McLuhan—a new period in humanistic scholarship has developed: "the era of literacy." In 1963, Goody and Watt published their now classic essay "The Consequences of Literacy," and Havelock's *Preface to Plato* appeared the same year. For whatever reason, literary theory became literacy oriented, focusing on the act of reading—literature in the reader—rather than on the autonomous text. At the same time, composition was being rehabilitated as a not-quite-respectable discipline, whereas before about 1962, composition was most emphatically not respectable within the humanities.

The politics of literature and literacy are a major aspect of the history of both ideas and education, of intellectual currents and teaching, but this discussion is not that one. (However, see "The Politics of Meaning," pp. 337–53.) I merely want briefly to explore the implications of literacy theory.

As I have said, speech is an array in time, whereas writing is an array in space. This simple fact is basic to the explanation of the consequences of literacy and is made salient, easily enough, by the reminder that you can leaf through a book, but not a tape recording. And, of course, writing, as opposed to speech, always involves the mediation of technology.

"The spoken word, however abstract its signification or however static the object it may represent, is of its very nature a sound tied to the movement of life itself in the flow of time" (Ong, 1977, p. 20). Spoken language, Walter Ong goes on to say, encourages a sense of participation with life, an unmediated experience of the stream of thought. For this reason, print alienates us from the most basic human condition: one person talking face-to-face with another, the living ideas shaped in the give-and-take of dialectic.

Literacy alienates in another sense, however—one that Paulo Freire deals with brilliantly. When we ask a Brazilian peasant to acquire literacy (or a savage freshman to acquire that sort of literacy sanctioned by us as academics), we are asking that the person alienate him- or herself from the native culture, for literacy is not merely technique; rather, it is a cultural and personal value. (The story of this sort of alienation is marvelously told by Richard Rodriguez in *Hunger of Memory* [1982].)

In *Education for Critical Consciousness* (1981 [1973]), Paulo Freire tells the story of Maria, who fortuitously triggered a breakthrough in his theory of literacy. Freire had conceived a simple "technology" of literacy, based on the concept of "generative words." For example, the Portuguese word *favela* ("slum") breaks into three syllables which illiterates can readily learn: *fa-ve-la*. On the basis of this insight, they can quickly learn phonemic families:

    fa-fe-fi-fo-fu
    va-ve-vi-vo-vu
    la-le-li-lo-lu

After a number of these exercises, the students can go on to create words with the various combinations. (*Education for Critical Consciousness*, pp. 82–83) When he first began his work, Freire wanted to test his ideas and asked Maria ("an old woman, a very good woman—a peasant, illiterate—she worked with us in our home—she was a cook" [quoted in Mackie, ed., 1981, p. 60]) to be his subject. Maria quickly grasped the principle, but after fifteen minutes grew tired; the essentially meaningless routine bored her, and she was unwilling to go on. Freire concluded that "the way really would be to challenge from the beginning the intentionality of consciousness and not the other way in which I was thinking. . . . *I would have to challenge the critical consciousness from the beginning*" (Mackie, ed., p. 61).

If Maria—an old woman, a very good woman, a peasant, illiterate— were to develop her critical consciousness in the process of becoming literate, she would not docilely ask, "Do you think I was able to help you?" After which "She left my library and in five minutes more she came back with a cup of coffee for me" (p. 60). Revolutionaries—whether Freire, Castro, or Lenin—know that literacy sets the stage for revolution, and revolution, from the standpoint of the *status quo*, is the ultimate alienation.

Think of the savage freshman, certainly not illiterate, but ignorant of the culture that values, for instance, Addison, Lamb, and Eiseley. Surely *The*

Norton Reader is as strange to this youngster as the printed text is to a member of a preliterate society. And to enter the new culture of English 101, the student must accept new values and in so doing repudiate, to a certain extent, his or her native culture. As Goody says, "The boy brought up as a bricoleur becomes an engineer," and certainly the girl brought up in a central city broken home containing no books and few magazines becomes a best-selling author and the doyenne and darling of the editors of *The Norton Reader*. But in either case, not without enormous sacrifice.

George Dillon (1981) characterizes the sort of culture we ask our students to join when they migrate from their villages in Beverly Hills or Watts to the university—as Olson (1977) terms them, the World of Text as opposed to the World of Utterance:

Text embodies many of the traditional values of the liberal arts education, offering as it does the means of emancipation from the confines of received opinion and the limiting (though often sustaining) solidarity with family and peer groups. If we think of education as inducing or enabling students to move from Utterance to Text, we can see why composition teachers have traditionally viewed their work not merely as imparting a prerequisite for a liberal education but as the very heart of a liberal education itself. (Dillon, 1981, p. 23)

And one of the prime instruments of that education is the expository essay, which

has a rhetorical purpose beyond "conveying information": it attempts to convince the reader that its model of experience or the world is valid. It does not seek to engage the reader in a course of action, however, but rather in a process of reflection, and its means of convincing are accordingly limited to the use of evidence and logical proof and the posture of open-mindedness.

In "Dramatism in Themes and Poems" (pp. 195–203), I deal extensively with Dillon's characterization of the expository essay, agreeing with him in the main, but modifying his viewpoint to a certain extent. For the moment, this genre, as defined above, can stand as the symbol for the liberal education, the discourse of the university, the language and thought model that we ask freshmen to acquire as the first and most important step in their domestication. And I should go on record as being profoundly in favor of this cultural goal.

The naturalization rites of English 101 raise thorny problems, not the least of which is that many students must develop both arhetorical skills and rhetorical abilities.

SKILLS

Shaughnessy's justly admired study of basic writers, *Errors and Expectations* (1971), documents what every composition teacher has learned from experience: some students need massive help with such fundamentals as capitalization, not to mention punctuation and verb agreement. Yet both Lester Perelman (in a study not yet published, 1983) and George Hillocks (1982) find that "marking" papers for mechanical errors is unproductive; indeed, Perelman reports that such response is counterproductive.

The arithmetic here is fairly simple. We are endowed with only so much ability to attend. The beam of our attention need not be a laser in its sharp narrowness: it has been clinically demonstrated that there is both broadened and narrowed attention, broadened implying that "the subject can scan or perceive a relatively large number of stimuli (or stimulus aspects) simultaneously" (Mirsky, 1978; see also Pirozzolo and Rayner, 1977). Nonetheless, we cannot attend profoundly to semantic intention and at the same time invest a great deal of concentration in mechanical niceties. The fact that fluent writers can revise as they go demonstrates both the versatility of attention and the small psychic investment they find necessary for editing.

For basic writers who have consciously and painstakingly learned editing skills, however, the psychic investment of regularizing the text is virtually overwhelming. For these beginners, much of the writing process is not automatic; they must ponder each mark of punctuation, each verb and its subject, each pronoun and its antecedent. A good analogy is the first few days of transition from a familiar typewriter to a word processing computer. The writer making the transition must invest attention heavily in manipulating the machine, at the expense of semantic intention. In the process of gaining fluency, it is well not to attempt serious composing, but to copy manuscripts or merely play around.

At some point, the student who has not acquired editing skills must consciously learn them. (See Krashen 1976, 1978; and "Developing a Composition Program," pp. 281–97.) For numerous reasons, I argue that direct teaching and learning should be delayed until ninth grade. Piaget and Vygotsky would seem to agree that at about fourteen the youngster is cognitively mature, and Walter Loban's fine study, *Language Development: Kindergarten through Grade Twelve* (1967), contains tangential evidence that fascinates me and that has not, to my knowledge, been discussed.

In 1953, Loban started a longitudinal study of 338 children who entered kindergarten in Oakland. The subjects were carefully selected to represent a cross section of the total kindergarten population. When the study terminated (with high school graduation or the subjects' reaching age eighteen), Loban had an amazing 211 left in his sample.

On the basis of the *Minnesota Scale for Paternal Occupations*, Loban created three socioeconomic groups of thirty-five each: High, Low, and Random. Now the point I want to make is this. On verbal skills in general, oral and written, all three groups made jumps at ninth grade, a development that I like to call "the Piaget leap." However, in writing skills at grade eleven, the High group makes another jump, and the Low group either plateaus out or declines, depending on the skill being measured. I like to call this phenomenon "the aspiration paradox." I hypothesize on the basis of the evidence that the High socioeconomic group is preparing for college, getting ready for admission to premed or engineering, aspiring to the state that represents their value systems. But, then, into UCLA and CCNY—and into virtually every other college and university between these two geographic extremes—do wander members of the Low group, encouraged by the American dream, their own intelligence and intellectual curiosity, scholarships, missionary efforts on the part of recruiters: for whatever reason, they opt, unwittingly in most cases, for the cultural ideal embodied in English 101. And part of that ideal is "the doctrine of correctness," the adamantine historical fact that verbs must agree and pronouns must refer and periods must end units called "sentences."

It is now that they are caught as never before in the contradiction between learning language skills and acquiring rhetorical abilities. Since the ground here is a bit tricky, we must take care not to lose our footing.

The language features that constitute proofreading are perfectly obvious and perfectly systematic; that is to say, with almost complete certainty you or I could regularize any text: capitalizing, punctuating, making verbs and pronouns agree and pronouns refer unambiguously, for we have unconsciously acquired—or even perhaps consciously learned—these systems. The freshman who has not acquired or learned them must do so. That much seems to be a fact about American higher education, and this "fact" raises two issues: 1) Is it ethical to demand that everyone master written standard English? 2) Ethical or not, how is this mastery best accomplished? (A matter that is discussed fully in "Developing a Composition Program."

As to ethics, my argument is short and direct: we should do everything possible to make all language skills available to all students, but we should not demand that every student reach some X level of proficiency in any writing skill. After all, it is undoubtedly the case that some bright, even extremely gifted, students will not be able to master the skills of academic literacy, for some are certainly "miswired" for this kind of learning, and others surely have erected such "affective filters" that only extensive psychotherapy would prepare them to learn. As a case in point regarding the complexity of the problems we face with students who cannot or will not learn what some call "grammar," ponder the varieties of aphasia and realize that aphasia is only one of many possible causes for disability in learning language skills.

However, we make all sorts of accommodations for other disabled students. In fact, any red-blooded director of admissions would leap at the chance to recruit a gifted quadriplegic, blind, deaf-mute woman for medical school, and any right-thinking medical school dean would rearrange his whole enterprise to make her into a neurosurgeon. Think of the headlines:

FIRST BLIND DEAF-MUTE QUADRIPLEGIC
GRADUATES FROM MED SCHOOL
Plans residency in
neurosurgery at Memorial Hospital

But pity the literacy-disabled men and women who opt for State. If English A doesn't wash them out, English B will.

We are asking these young men and women to attend not only to a new genre—or a variety of new genres—but also to attend scrupulously to the surface form of their texts, and in doing this, we dichotomize objectives, teaching skills which are related to algorithms and expecting students to acquire rhetorical abilities and cultural values.

A Composition Class Is a Writing Class

Don't shoot! I surrender!

But maybe the proposition that "a composition class is a writing class" is not so obvious as it sounds. Of course, we all know of comp classes that are exclusively lecture, in format and spirit very much like Psychology 101 or Astronomy 103; however, I am not talking about those obvious deformities. We all agree that writing should take place in a composition class and might even concur, I think, with the suggestion that we substitute the term "workshop" for "class" so that colleagues and administrators will know that we are not so much interested in disseminating knowledge as in conferring the skills and art of composition. Analogically, we are in some ways nearer to the violin and art teacher, to the instructor in a poetry workshop, or even to the football and basketball coaches than we are to our colleagues who disseminate knowledge through lectures and discussions. We are, in fact, extremely Freirean. We don't "deposit" knowledge in the heads of our students, but rather teach them (coach them) in writing.

For the moment, let's think of writing as a performing art. The students should see the teacher as a writer, and among the countless ways there are to convince our apprentices that we are at least competent, if not masters, are three that I have found useful.

The first and simplest is this: give the students copies of your writings, published or unpublished articles, personal essays, technical writings such as proposals and reports, memos, poems, stories—whatever you feel will evidence your capability and versatility. I think it extremely useful for teachers to demonstrate that they are skilled writers of not only the loftier texts such as personal essays or scholarly articles, but also of lowlier forms, such as letters of complaint or even personal letters; after all, one needs a good deal of skill to produce an effective memo. And needless to say, skilled performance in any art is its own reward.

Second, complete at least some of the writing assignments that the class undertakes—especially when the assignment is an impromptu essay—and submit the results to the class for their reactions.

Third, you might try what I call "give-a-topic." I explain to students that frequently I will give them a topic and ask them to write on it for fifteen minutes in class, but I also ask them to have a "bank" of topics from which they can draw to give me an assignment that I will write on the blackboard as they are composing at their seats. The virtue of this method is its immediacy; students see me as a writer who is at times successful, but often unsuccessful. With my text on the board, students can begin to discuss the breakdowns and patchwork of this text or the serendipitous strategy which made another successful. After the students have discussed my writing, I ask them to exchange papers with a neighbor and briefly discuss the triumphs and tragedies that they find in these short impromptus.

I shall take my own freshman composition class as what Kenneth Burke calls a "representative anecdote," the kind of synecdoche that allows one to characterize a whole genus through one of its members.

The Students

Believing staunchly in the democracy of the composition class, we do not track students at the University of Southern California; hence, our class members are likely to represent the whole spectrum of the student body: the privileged, those kids who drive Jaguars, BMWs, and even Rolls Royces, and who glitter with the appurtenances and aura of wealth; Chicanos and blacks from the area around USC, admitted on scholarships because they show exceptional academic promise; the gifted, the not-so-gifted, and a few, a very few, who must have been admitted to the university for reasons other than past achievement or any sort of academic promise.

There was Kim, with her understatedly expensive wardrobe and ever impeccably manicured nails. (She was majoring in international marketing—and I assume there is such a major—because she likes people and wants to travel.) Roger, a faculty brat, was very bright, extremely witty, and a perfect delight. Tom, a self-made young man of eighteen, had made killings in real estate and was so preoccupied with the field that his ten essays for the course all dealt with real estate. I had no jocks, and to that extent, my class was atypical. And then there was Mary Ann, the lovely but extremely shy Chicana.

Let's focus on Kim, Roger, and Mary Ann, taking them to represent the whole range of students that I encountered.

I suspect that Kim was bright, but her intelligence didn't show through the brick wall of conventional decorum she had inherited. She was prompt with her work, courteous, alert in class—and completely dull. She needed shaking out of her five-paragraph-essay value system and modus operandi. Here is a sample of her work early in the semester:

If Change Were Possible, How
Would You Change Your Life?

After giving serious thought about what I would like to change in my life, I have come to the conclusion that I am very fortunate. I can not think of a major aspect I would like to have different about myself, yet I am not near to saying that I do not want to change at all. There is an intermediate stage that I would call improvement, and I believe that there is room for improvement in everyone.

One part of my personality, which I feel insecure about, does need enhancement: expressing my opinions publicly. Personal expression, I think, is the most important factor in communication and the interchange of thought or opinions is the key to success in marketing and international affairs, both of which I am interested in. In these fields it is necessary to persuade another person to be interested in what you are offering which can only be done by showing confidence and relaying your message well. . . .

In some ways, Roger was as much of a problem student as Kim: he wanted more and more challenges, and he kept me busy keeping him productively busy. For him, reading, thinking, discussing, and writing were already a way of life. Here is a sample of Roger's work at the beginning of the semester:

What you are reading right now on the few pages in front of you is the end product of an idiosyncratic writing process. Not long ago, the author began writing the words in front of you, hoping that through a descriptive, unorthodox essay he could bring you, perhaps, to a revelation of the method in his composing.

Notice first that the author has written this short essay in the third person. It is important that an author be conscious of himself and be able to envision himself as someone else would, noticing his little peculiarities, as it is for him to survey the world and its people. The writer, in order to relate his own experience to an audience, must understand himself so that he may compare and contrast himself with the readers, identifying himself with them while at the same time enlightening them as to his individuality and unique knowledge. The author in this essay is, in short, attempting in front of an audience to critically analyze an aspect of his life. He is, for a change, observing himself.

Mary Ann, the lovely Mary Ann, was the perfect case study of the bright, willing student who enters higher education with massive language problems. Her writing for my class was totally engaging, but in mechanics would have been completely unacceptable to the educated community. (In my opinion, the community is wrong, but my opinion does not rescue the hundreds of thousands of young people whose language keeps them out of the system.) Here is a sample of Mary Ann's unedited writing:

If change were possible, how would you change your life? If change were possible, I would save my other half. In December of 1957 a young man and a very lady were to be wed. This young man was determined in his character. He was 23 years old and fresh out of the army. This young man was named Ramon _____. This lady was kind-hearted in her character. She had just turned 16 years by 3 months. This young was named Mary _____, and soon to be our mom.

Ramon and Mary were married the 28 to december of 1957. Two years were to pass and they would start thier family. Mary was to give birth in the beginning of the year 1959. It was February 4, 1959, 4 o'clock in the morning and Mary would give birth to a pair of bouncing baby girls, only to know that one was to die.

The first girl was healthy as can be. Her name was Jessie. the second girl had a hole in her heart, and doomed. Her named was Mary Ann. Mary Ann was to die in four months because of her heart. Four months passed and both girls were living.

At the sixth month, Jessie's Heart would stop. This is the life I want to save. My other half.

THE PROFESSOR

I viewed myself as a coach, a facilitator, a resource person, and sometimes chairman of the discussion sessions. But most of all, *I wanted the students to view me as a writer and to see me in the act of writing.* For this reason, I gave the class members offprints of pieces that I had published here and there in the past; I showed them copies of drafts-in-progress; I also engaged in give-a-topic.

CLASS ACTIVITIES

Three sorts of activities occupied us during our class sessions: (1) developing writing topics; (2) responding to writing done by class members; (3) working with miscellaneous activities, the nature of which I will explain hereafter.

Developing Writing Topics

The first principle is this: if any student wanted to complete some kind of writing for any reason, other than to fulfill the requirements of my class, I encouraged him or her to grab the ball and run. I have no hesitation about giving credit in a writing class for essays that will be submitted in another class. Sometimes, indeed, the students found their own interests and purposes and hence their own topics, having nothing to do with their class requirements at the university.

The writing that I accepted for the class fell into three categories: (1) self-sponsored, (2) required, but not by my class, and (3) assigned in my class. In the best of all possible worlds, the purposes of all writing in a composition class would come from outside that class, but in the postlapsarian university, it is simply necessary to have assigned topics, for students must write if they are to learn to write, and self-sponsorship is fairly rare—and, unfortunately, assigned writing is infrequent outside the English department, especially in freshman classes. The need to develop topics in a writing class, as opposed to merely assigning them, has, in fact, great advantages, for in developing topics, class members learn heuristic and problem-solving skills.

A Representative Assignment. Early in the semester, I ask students to write about some problematic aspect of the university: the physical plant (parking is a popular topic), the administration, the curriculum, whatever. In explaining how to go about this assignment, I use the cafeteria as my case in point, for it is a truth universally acknowledged that all cafeterias in higher education are problematic. (One of my students last year suggested that the problem is not at all with the cafeteria, which, according to him, serves tasty, wholesome food at a reasonable price, but students' attitudes toward the cafeteria. In order to solve the cafeteria problem, then, this young man suggested changing the patrons, not the establishment.) In any case, when I ask the class if the cafeteria is a problem, I get virtually total agreement that it is: the food isn't good, the prices are too high, the place smells, and so on.

Well, then, we have an opportunity to investigate in detail, do a report which we can submit to the proper authorities, and perhaps bring about change. But how does one go about investigating the cafeteria? Here are some suggestions that I give the class and that we discuss in some detail.

1. First, we want to record as many *features* of the cafeteria as possible, preferably on a sheet of paper or index cards. "What sort of data would you want to obtain?" I ask, and I get answers such as the following:

Dimensions. Brightness of lighting. Seating capacity. Noise level. Patronage during various hours. Odors. Costs. Decor. Utensils. Number of employees. . . .

2. Now I suggest that the investigator has a mountain of more or less unrelated data, which is a good entry to the subject, but which must somehow be systematized. So I ask students to think about the cafeteria as a *system* with interrelated parts.

They begin to analyze the relationship of the kitchens to the serving lines, the location of the cash registers, the layout of the serving area, and so on. What had been a montage of features becomes a blueprint or diagram, with the emphasis on relationships.

3. A blueprint is, after all, static, and a cafeteria is a *dynamic operating unit*, so I now suggest that we set the place in motion and begin to think about traffic flows (and the amount of time it takes to get through the lines, which is easily determined with a stopwatch), the movement of food from kitchen to serving line to trays, the movement of trays from the clean stack to their final destination in the washer. . . . In short, we now have a third perspective on our subject, and, as usual, we record our data and impressions in detailed notes.

4. A fourth perspective is based on *contrast*, i.e., how does the subject— in this case, the cafeteria—contrast with other items in its class, namely, eating establishments? The students now can compare cafeteria prices and quantities with those of McDonald's; they can compare the cafeteria with fine restaurants and greasy spoons. The basic question is simply this: How does the item differ from other members of its class? And the implication is that the variation will be either favorable or unfavorable.

5. The fifth perspective asks students to look at what might, for lack of a better term, be called *distribution*. The cafeteria, a system in itself, is part of multiple larger systems. Since it is part of the physical plant and layout of the university, location may be an important consideration. It is also part of the financial structure of the university, and one would like to determine its economics, whether it breaks even, makes money, or loses money. It is also

part of the administrative structure of the university: someone is head person at the cafeteria, and he or she reports to someone else, and so on. Perhaps administrative structure is one of the problems.

For convenience, we can term these five perspectives *features, system, operation, contrast,* and *distribution.*

Once the students have considered all five of these angles for a week or so—gathering information, letting ideas germinate, rethinking tentative conclusions—they can begin to ask themselves the question that will lead ultimately to a piece of writing: "On the basis of my current knowledge, what changes would I recommend?" After having gathered ideas and data for several days, the student is ready to present the background that will make his or her recommendations telling.

This heuristic is, of course, adapted from Young, Becker, and Pike, *Rhetoric: Discovery and Change* (1970).

I have received analyses of the parking problem at the university, of the problems of the handicapped at the university, of registration procedures, of various curricula, of admissions policies, and so on. I could, of course, have simply assigned students to analyze a problem at the university and to make recommendations concerning it. However, it is one of my ironclad rules that I will not give an assignment (or a suggestion) without providing some guidance for completing the job. In fact, the results of the heuristics that I just outlined are quite amazing, constituting a revolution for many students who have never systematically analyzed anything.

Varieties of Writing. During the semester, I encourage students to do a wide spectrum of kinds of writing; in fact, I suggest topics that will elicit such variety. Kinneavy (1971) provides what I have found to be the most useful and defensible schema for classifying discourse types.

Explanatory writing—the "how" of complex problems and the "why" of opinions—creates an ethos (writer)-pathos (reader) relationship of expert to novice. I cannot really give an explanation, as a felicitous speech act, of something that I do not believe I know, and equally I cannot give an explanation to someone who knows as much about the subject as I do. (Since the ethos-pathos relationship of explanatory writing is that of master to novice, think about the strange logic of having freshmen write explanatory essays about literature for English professors.)

Exploratory writing—the tentative outlining of problems, ambivalence—creates an ethos-pathos relationship of equal to equal. The concerned writer is laying out the territory for one concerned reader or group of readers.

Argument—the setting forth of "conclusive" research, scientific evidence, irrefutable logic (library papers, scientific reports, *Summa theologica*)—creates an interesting rhetorical situation, in which the writer (ethos) almost disappears, and the substance (logos) appeals not to a reader (pathos), but to a universal audience. (Perelman, 1969.)

The simple point about explanation, exploration, and argumentation (the divisions of exposition) is that they create different writer-reader ratios and hence provide excellent practice for novices who need means and motives to develop control of tone, style, and form.

Persuasion differs from exposition or referential discourse in this respect: persuasion attempts to create the basis for action. In the referential modes, the writer informs; in perusasion, the writer "woos" through "courtship" (Burke, 1969, pp. 208–12), and though persuasion most often involves an indirect threat—the consequences—its basis is reader-orientation (pathos): the benefits of acquiescence. In referential discourse, the writer assumes a more or less take-it-or-leave-it tone, disinterestedness. In persuasive discourse, the ethos and pathos are equally prominent, for I would persuade you only of that which I believed good for me and that I believed you would believe was good for you.

Regardless of these intricacies, the real point about encouraging students to write in a variety of modes is simple enough: other modes and other problems create the opportunity for versatility to develop. So many of our compositionists are *mono*-tonous!

The Journal. The journal is the *continuo* of my comp classes. Almost all writing is a public performance, intended for an audience, and performances, no matter how familiar the hearers, are tinged with anxiety and threat. That's what makes them exciting, both for Placido Domingo and those who have paid to hear him: risk and fulfillment, tragedy and triumph. Imagine the utter boredom of an art form consisting only of masterpieces. That's why, upon occasion, I am assured by my infallible intuition, Domingo sings in the bathtub, for the sheer joy of singing, even as you or I. The journal is singing in the bathtub: always a complete success, never threatening.

Think of the logic. The primary, if not the only, audience for the journal is the writer him- or herself, an ethos-ethos ratio, if you will. The journal, then, is a success if it engages the writer.

Of course, I review journals two or three times a semester, checking for *quantity*, and indicating to students that I'm interested in all of their writing, but I assure class members that their own evaluations are the only important ones. And then, perversely, I always give the journals a grade, A to F, telling the students that I will not record the grade, but that it reflects my reaction to, my interest in, the journal. Invariably the students who receive less than A for their journal work ask me how to improve the grade, and I answer thus: "What do you care about *my* opinion? If you're satisfied with the journal, that's all that counts. I have assigned a grade merely to give you my reaction, but it's your reaction that's important."

Following Rohman and Wlecke (1964), I suggest outrageous analogies, existential sentences, and meditations as profitable journal exercises. (Winterowd, 1981, pp. 29–54)

Response to Writing

Developing writing assignments through class discussion takes about one-third of the class time during the semester, one day in three. We spend another one-third of our time responding to the writing produced by the class. This response takes several forms: small group discussion, conferences, and whole-class discussion. I reproduce four or five of each group of papers I receive and use these for class discussion.

In my essay "From Classroom Practice to Psycholinguistic Theory" (pp. 299–306), I make the point that "feedback," response, is the single most important help that writing students can receive. Both Hillocks (1982) and Perelman (1982) presented strong evidence that the conference, whatever its form, is the most effective method of instruction. What these researchers imply is simply that writers need rich feedback, which is best provided dialectically, in the give-and-take of discussion. One-on-one is not the only form of conference. Whole-class discussion of a piece of student writing is a kind of conference.

However, before students feel right about submitting their work to the scrutiny of the whole class in open discussion, an air of trust and confidence must be established. The witty, cynical instructor will poison the atmosphere to such an extent that discussion can never be a comfortable, effective learning experience. The atmosphere in the composition class must be loving, not brittle.

Writers acquire competence through the dual process of reading and of receiving response to their own writing. The varieties of response sessions in my class provide this necessary feedback, through which students learn without really knowing that they are learning.

However, most students are not ready to give the most useful, or even pertinent, response to the writing of their peers. It takes training to become an effective critic-teacher, and I use a heuristic to give my students help in generating constructive comments, questions, and suggestions regarding their own writing and that of others. Once again, to repeat a point I made earlier, I rely on the Jakobson framework and propose the following list of questions as starting points for response to writing:

Concerning *audience*: For whom is the writing apparently intended? Laypersons? Experts? Readers with strongly held views regarding the subject? Other questions?

Concerning *writer*: What is the purpose of the piece? What is the writer's attitude toward the subject? Toward the audience? How can/does the writer establish his/her authority? Other questions?

Concerning *content*: Is the thesis clear? Is the evidence adequate? Is the logic compelling? What needs to be added? Deleted? Substituted? More examples? More specific detail? Other questions?

Concerning *medium*: Is the format adequate? (Does it meet the demands of genre?) What about graphics? Are subheads and lists used effectively? What about formal demands such as footnotes? Other questions?

Concerning *style*: Appropriateness? Readability? Tone? Proofreading? Other questions?

These sets of questions are no panacea, but they do provide useful points of departure for instruction, and they do make students aware of the manifold problems involved in producing a successful text.

Students need constructive response to their writing—the more, the better.

Other Activities

In the writing workshop, we do spend a bit of time analyzing models: essays by such writers as Isaac Asimov and Loren Eiseley for the marvelous use of metaphor; Tom Wolfe for the idiosyncrasy of his prose style; Mark Twain, because I think his prose is superb in its ease. We consider the organization of this essay, the beginning of that one, and the argumentative techniques in another. In short, we use a limited amount of professional writing in quite traditional ways, usually as models. We tend to discuss the ideas of the essays produced by the class more intensely than we do the ideas in the readings. My class is a *writing* workshop, not a remedial or developmental reading class—and certainly not a class in sociology, literature, the history of ideas, women's liberation, Chicano studies. . . . If reading is a problem—and to some extent it is for most students—then the institution must supply the resources needed to teach reading; however, I am convinced that it is a disastrous though common error to turn a writing workshop into a reading class.

Another important activity: exercises in style. Most freshmen have a great reserve of stylistic *competence* which they have never drawn upon; that is, most of their ability is latent, having never been activated in *performance*. It is fairly easy to activate this competence, to help students expand their repertory of stylistic options.

Other students, such as Mary Ann, have limited competence (not limited potential) and need quickly to internalize the syntactic resources of the language. Systematic work with sentence combining is, I am convinced, an effective pedagogical technique with students who need to build a reservoir of competence. I send these students to the writing lab, where they regularly work with a sentence combining program under the supervision of a tutor.

But students with competence need only be made aware of the potential that they have already internalized through reading, and I use style games and parodies to create this awareness. (For an example of such a game, see pp. 52–53.)

When she entered my class, Eleanor's style was prim and proper and about as palatable as cold, unseasoned grits. After two or three class sessions of style games, she began to realize her considerable powers as a prose stylist:

A tall skinny guy, being towed by his mother, who was towing his father, with an old bent grandma shuffling along at the rear, passed by us, and we both laughed out loud at the same time. Then it was just us on a hot summer day in July. We stood in front of a building which claimed to be the oldest one on campus, two about-to-be college girls, freshly graduated from high school and smiling our completed orthodontia smiles because we were happy. We looked around carefully in every direction, absorbing all the sights, and I remember we were feeling very independent without having Mom, Dad, and Grandma tagging along with us for any reason.

It was only the two of us standing there together, each one blocking for the other as she stole furtive glances at the tell-tale map she held in her hand. People passed by and looked at us—we were always mistaken for sisters. Friends since the sixth grade, standing there in anticipation, anxious to begin our new adventure. Keeping that beastly but necessary little map well out of sight, we walked around through that whirling mid-summer Los Angeles hot air.

Under "miscellaneous activities" I could list such mundane matters as brief lectures on lapses in grammar and usage that seem endemic to the class. And I never pack the schedule so full that the spontaneous is impossible, those happy moments when a class member or a professor gets an idea and wants to try it on the group. (In the right kind of class atmosphere, such moments are fairly frequent. One of the most delightful in my career was a marvelous parody of myself, staged by one of my students on a day when I was particularly cantankerous. The performance was inspired, and I deserved the good-natured rebuke.)

THE CONVENTIONS OF EDITED STANDARD ENGLISH

Of course, we want students to master the conventions of edited standard English: spelling, punctuation, verb agreement, reference, parallelism, and so on. The writing workshop, however, is not the place to handle such matters; for this sort of remediation, every writing program needs a carefully designed and well administered laboratory. (See "Developing a Composition Program," pp. 281–97.)

SOME REMARKS ABOUT THE STUDENTS

What you can achieve with your students in one semester—or two or three or more—depends on various factors, not the least of which are the reading the student has done and motivation.

Classified according to their reading backgrounds and their experiences with composition in high school, students fall into these categories:

1. *Avid readers who have taken three or four years of composition in high school*: These students have acquired competence through reading and have performed in composition classes. (Composition instruction *does* make

a difference. See Bamberg [1978].) Many of these students should be exempted from normal freshman writing courses, but should be encouraged to take creative writing or advanced composition.

2. *Avid readers who have not taken composition in high school*: These are the students we cherish. Since they have acquired competence through reading, they gain the ability to perform in a very short time, and we can credit ourselves with superb teaching skill and success.

3. *Minimally able readers*: These students are able to function in higher education. They can get through their psychology and history texts. But they have never read avidly for pleasure. They have the potential to learn to write serviceable, if not inspired or graceful, prose. If they are motivated, their work will be adequate, but it won't glitter. To achieve miracles with these students, we would need to make them into avid readers and give them the time to acquire competence through reading.

4. *Disabled readers*: They are also the disabled writers, the basic writers who were the subjects of Shaughnessy's (1977) study.

5. *Students with second language problems*: Like Mary Ann, these students need special help.

MOTIVATION

There are many easy and superficial ways to discuss motivation. For instance, as we saw earlier, it is axiomatic that people learn second languages and second dialects for one of two general reasons, or for both: (1) integrative, to be accepted by a language or dialect group, and (2) instrumental, to use language for some purpose, as my son learned New Testament Greek as a scholarly tool.

However, among the lessons that Paulo Freire (1981, 1982) has taught us is this: illiterate people learn to read and write only after they see themselves as participants in and shapers of their cultures. As long as they are instruments, they see no compelling need for reading and writing, but when they conceive of themselves as agents, they quickly become literate.

Consider a typical freshman composition student. She (or he) is from a middle class home in which books and writing are not prime values; neither her mother nor her father, both college graduates, is particularly "bookish." She has not been nurtured by the values of "high" literacy in the tradition of the liberal arts. Now try to motivate that student by telling her—as I have told countless students in the past—that she is now on the threshold of the world of culture and intellect and that she needs finely tuned writing ability to integrate herself. Tell her further that her writing skill will serve as an instrument whereby she may well be able to gain prestige, power, and wealth in the great world out there. That student, typically, will go blank. In the first place, she knows perfectly well that she can achieve at least middle class affluence and respectability without becoming superbly or even, perhaps, reasonably literate.

Our sermons—which we believe sincerely—don't wash with many of our students, which is *not* to say that integrative and instrumental motives don't fuel the efforts of many others.

The classroom is in many respects a self-contained universe, a space lab with its own life-support system, in tenuous contact with the teeming and troubled planet earth. If students begin to see themselves as shapers of the culture of their composition classes, they will, I believe, become engaged, and that is one reason for making the writing workshops a cooperative, democratic venture.

Which suggests that (1) The teacher must not be magisterial and pontifical. In fact, I define the teacher's role in the coda to this essay and will say no more at this point. (2) Classes must be heterogeneous, not homogeneous. I could never understand the rationale for segregating the super deluxe and the rejects from the great masses of students. "Tracking" demoralizes the students who are excluded from advanced (i.e., elite) sections and equally demoralizes instructors who must deal with the less-than-the-best. (The impulse to teach only those who need the least teaching is somehow like the doctor who wants to deal only with healthy patients. After all, the rejects among our students present the greatest challenges and hence the greatest rewards.) Moreoever, tracking creates inefficient teaching in composition workshops. Writers need to develop the ability to address varied audiences, and in the dialect of the workshop, the more able learn from the less able just as surely as the reverse.

In years of practical experience and diligent scholarship, I have never encountered a compelling argument for tracking.

To end this discussion on the downbeat, there is the interesting study of motivation by Williams and Alden (1983). These researchers found that most students of composition are extrinsically motivated (i.e., grade hungry):

Results indicate that extrinsically motivated students tend to view writing as unimportant in our society, that they would not take a composition course if it were not required, and that they do not enjoy writing. Furthermore, they tend not to revise papers before turning in a final draft, not to value teacher comments, and not to believe that writing can be taught.

Such is the challenge.

GRADING

The composition teacher—coach, cohort, mentor—must finally deliver an evaluation on students' work, and this necessity creates a problem: students know that, after all, their coach is also their stern judge, delivering grades that will further their careers or exclude them from med school, that will put them on the honor role or in bad graces with parents who sacrifice to pay for their educations.

In the best of all possible worlds, composition workshops would be ungraded, but this earth is not, I think, that Utopia we long for. Hence, we composition teachers must be graders.

I have developed a system that, I believe, is a valid teaching experience and that removes a large part of the onus we must feel when, at the end of the semester, we record a less-than-glittering final grade for the student's accomplishments during the term.

First, I believe that no one should be graded on his or her total output of writing. Certainly I am not judged by everything I write. Much of my stuff never peregrinates beyond my study, some of it ending in the wastebasket and some of it winding up in files on the assumption that, like wine, it will improve with careful aging. Hence, I tell my students that they will be graded on one-half (usually five) of the total papers they complete during the semester.

I do not grade individual papers as they come in, but discuss them with students in conference, use them for class discussion, make them the subject of small-group readings and critique sessions.

Toward the end of the term, students have a sense of their best and their less-than-best, and they choose the best for thoroughgoing revision. (I leave the final two weeks of the term for revisions and am available for conferences. I will give endless advice, but I will not undertake revisions myself.) The five papers that the students choose as their best work are then submitted for independent grading by two of my colleagues.

At the the beginning of the term, I enter an agreement with two other composition teachers: I will grade their students' packets, and they will grade those submitted by my students. The graders assign a grade to each paper in the group and an overall grade. In other words, each student of the three instructors in the "grading group" receives two independent evaluations of his or her work. If the two grades coincide (for instance, B and B), that is the grade the student receives. If the grades differ by one point (say, B and C), the student receives the benefit of the doubt. If the two grades differ by more than one point (say, A and C), I act as the arbiter.

Here is the grading policy that I include in my statement (not syllabus) for my composition course:

In order to qualify for a grade, you must complete *all* of the assigned work. You will receive various kinds of responses to each piece of writing that you submit, but I will not assign grades to the individual papers. (I'll give you plenty of "feedback" in written comments and conferences.) From the ten papers, you will choose the four [now revised to five] that you think are most promising and will revise and polish those, to submit as the primary basis for your grade in the course. A panel of readers will determine the grade to be assigned for the papers you submit.

Perhaps most important, students must prepare a cover sheet for each essay, explaining their purpose, their audience, and the problems they encountered in doing the paper.

Here is a sample cover sheet:

Plea Bargaining: Justice Behind Closed Doors

Assignment: The essay was to present an analysis of a problematic situation, and in effect, stimulate the interest of the reader regarding this problem.

Audience: The paper is intended for the educated person who has limited knowledge of the process of plea bargaining in the courts.

Abstract: Plea bargaining is an extremely serious and complex process in the administration of justice. I have attempted, therefore, to analyze the process and provide the reader with some of the points of view regarding plea bargaining. First, I explain what plea bargaining is and why it is considered a problematic situation. Second, I explain what the courts, judges, attorneys, defendants, and society think about the plea bargaining in our courts.

Special problem: There exists enough material on this situation to write a few books, so it was difficult to condense the subject material and still provide an adequate analysis.

Because my files were lost in a move, I cannot attest to the statistical validity of this system, but I can give an old-timer's impression. Most of the time, the evaluators agree. All of the time, the students feel that they've gotten a better deal than they would with the idiosyncratic and personal reactions of the instructor.

The system, of course, recommends itself philosophically, if not statistically. It does away, to a large extent, with the teacher-as-evaluator syndrome, a problem that Britton et al. (1975) argue is one of the most destructive in our business.

Coda: On Teaching Composition[1]

I have never known a composition teacher without a theory of his or her complex art. Often those theories, hard won through the demanding and exhilarating quotidian effort to meet the diverse needs of the far too many students that are part of our lot, remain tacit, unenunciated and hence unexamined. But probe a bit in the coffee room or during the inevitable Friday evening cocktail party, and the committed compositionist who fights and struggles against enunciated theory and against enunciating one will begin to take a stand, forced by dialogue to piece together a rationale, which often turns out to be a *raison d'être*, so totally engaging is the business to which we devote our time and energy. We tend, I think, to be a serious bunch, though not grimly or humorlessly so, and our motives are fairly clean since our vocation offers neither glory nor riches. I shall not go on to extoll us for the purity of our motives, but will say that as academics go, we are not more bibulous or mendacious than our colleagues, and we must, by the nature of our calling, be somewhat more tolerant and giving than most others.

All of us work on the basis of theories, else we teach by chance, mind-

---

1. This "coda" was originally published in *Freshman English News* and is reprinted here, in a slightly altered version, by permission of the editors of *FEN*.

lessly. But our business is to teach a complex art, not theories about it, and in this respect, tacit theories, developed by sensitive, intelligent teachers are less seductive than those "up front."

In one of my essays (pp. 159–74), I argue that three values fuel language, give it saliency: Authority, Beneficence, and Commitment, the ABC's of language transactions. For example, the force of a claim

I claim that most composition teachers are guided by theories.

depends largely on the epistemic authority of the speaker or writer, and the force of a pronouncement of sentence

I sentence you to ten days in County Jail.

depends on the civil authority of the judge.

Since a promise implies beneficence on the part of the promiser toward the promisee, the following does *not* count as a promise:

I promise to punch you in the nose if you interrupt me again.

And I cannot make a vow without commitment.

These are only examples of the dance of values that makes language work; the ABC's are the critical mass in semantic intention. And I think that the ABC's, abstracted from language and applied to human actions in general, illuminate some of our most important concerns—such as teaching composition.

The teacher must have Authority, not conferred by a board of trustees, a dean, or a superintendent, but assumed through knowing what one is about, gained from the sense that classroom practices and course goals are well motivated, i.e., that they are part of a theory of composition. Vatic authority is, of course, spurious; the inspired teacher who is ignorant of other theories and research in the field is a dogmatist, not an authority.

And yet, the true authority is not magisterial, for Beneficence tempers the self-confidence that knowledge and experience create. The magisterial authority in a lecture class such as history or chemistry can be (awe) inspiring—one thinks of the John Houseman character in *Paper Chase*. But composition is a "hands on" subject, a performing art, and to be effective, the master must demonstrate a genuinely Beneficent *attitude*, by word, deed, and manner—which is only a fancy way of saying that the composition teacher must care deeply about his or her students.

And be genuinely Committed to students, the art of composition, and the art of teaching it. Composition teachers who really want to be doing literature exclusively, part-timers who will do anything to pick up a buck (a minority group, I think), those who work in composition because it is a "hot" field offering the chance for a quick reputation—these colleagues of ours lack Commitment.

Teaching with Authority, but without Beneficence and Commitment, is bullying.

Teaching with Beneficence, but without Authority or Commitment, turns out most frequently to be maudlinism.

Teaching with Commitment, but without Authority and Beneficence, constitutes fanaticism.

The best composition classes always crackle with intense human relationships; when the teacher is a bully, a maudlin sentimentalist, or a fanatic, these relationships are diseased and destructive. As I have argued in "Syntax, Readability, Intention, and the Real World" (1980c), attitude is the ground of intention, and intention is the direct precursor to action. In this sense, the ABC's of value are the all in teaching composition: Authority, Beneficence, Commitment.

References to Part I

Abbreviations: *B&L, Brain and Language*; CCC, *College Composition and Communication*; CE, *College English*; RITE, *Research in the Teaching of English*.

ADAMS, JAMES L. (1979). *Conceptual Blockbusting: A Guide to Better Ideas*. New York: W. W. Norton.

ATLAS, MARSHALL A. (1979). *Addressing an Audience: A Study of Expert-Novice Differences in Writing*. "Document Design Project Technical Report No. 3." Pittsburgh: Carnegie-Mellon University.

AUGUSTINE, DOROTHY (1981). "Geometries and Words: Linguistics and Philosophy: A Model of the Composing Process." *CE.* 43:3 (March), 221−31.

―――, and W. ROSS WINTEROWD (forthcoming). "Speech Acts and the Reader-Writer Transaction."

AUSTIN, J. L. (1962). *How to Do Things with Words*. Oxford: Oxford University Press.

BAILEY, RICHARD W. and ROBIN MELANIE FOSHEIM, Eds. (1983). *Literacy for Life: The Demand for Reading and Writing*. New York: MLA.

BAMBERG, BETTY (1978). "Composition Instruction Does Make a Difference: A Comparison of College Freshmen in Regular and Remedial English Courses." *RITE.* 12: 47−59.

BARRITT, LOREN (1981). "Writing/Speaking: A Descriptive Phenomenological View." Kroll and Vann, Eds. *Exploring Speaking/Writing Relationships*.

―――, and BARRY M. KROLL (1978). "Some Implications of Cognitive-Developmental Psychology for Research in Composing." Charles M. Cooper and Lee Odell, Eds. *Research on Composing*.

BATEMAN, DONALD and FRANK ZIDONIS (1966). *The Effect of a Study of Transformational Grammar on the Writing of Ninth and Tenth Graders*. Urbana, Il.: NCTE.

BEACH, RICHARD (1976). "Self-Evaluation of Extensive Revisers and Nonrevisers." *CCC.* 27 (May), 160−64.

BECKER, A. L. (1966). "A Tagmemic Approach to Paragraph Analysis." *The Sentence and the Paragraph*. Urbana: NCTE.

BENDERLY, BERYL LIEFF (1981). "The Multilingual Mind." *Psychology Today*. (March), 9–12.

BENNETT, TINA L. (1977). "An Extended View of Verb Voice in Written and Spoken Personal Narrative." Keenan and Bennett, Eds. *Discourse Across Time and Space*.

BERLIN, JAMES A. (1984). *Writing Instruction in Nineteenth-Century American Colleges*. Urbana, Il.: NCTE.

BERTHOFF, ANN E. (1978). *Forming, Thinking, Writing: The Composing Imagination*. Rochelle Park, N.J.: Hayden.

BISSEX, GLENDA L. (1980). *GNYS at WRK: A Child Learns to Write and Read*. Cambridge, Mass. Harvard University Press.

BLEICH, DAVID (1975a). *Readings and Feelings: An Introduction to Subject Criticism*. Urbana, Il.: NCTE.

—— (1975b). "The Subjective Character of Critical Interpretation." *CE*. 36:7 (March), 739–55.

BOND, SANDRA J., JOHN R. HAYES, and LINDA S. FLOWER (1980). *Translating the Law into Common Language: A Protocol Study*. Pittsburgh: Carnegie-Mellon University Press.

BRIDWELL, LILLIAN S. (1980). "Revising Strategies of Twelfth Grade Students' Transactional Writing." *RITE*. 14:3 (Oct.), 197–222.

BRITTON, JAMES (1978). "The Composing Processes and the Functions of Writing." Cooper and Odell, Eds. *Research on Composing*.

——, TONY BURGESS, NANCY MARTIN, ALEX McLEOD, and HAROLD ROSEN (1975). *The Development of Writing Abilities (11–18)*. London: Macmillan Education.

BURKE, KENNETH (1968). "The Anaesthetic Revelation of Heron Liddell." *The Complete White Oxen*.

—— (1968). *The Complete White Oxen*. Berkeley: University of California Press.

—— (1968). *Counter-Statement*. Berkeley: University of California Press.

—— (1969). *A Grammar of Motives*. Berkeley: University of California Press.

—— (1957). *The Philosophy of Literary Form*. Revised Edition. New York: Vintage.

—— (1969). *A Rhetoric of Motives*. Berkeley: University of California Press.

—— (1961). *The Rhetoric of Religion*. Boston: Beacon Press.

CAIN, BETTY (1981). *Form Fluency in Transactional Discourse of College Freshmen: An Exploration Toward a Grounded Theory*. Dissertation. University of Southern California.

CAMBOURNE, BRIAN (1981). "Oral and Written Relationships: A Reading Perspective." Kroll and Vann, Eds. *Exploring Speaking/Writing Relationships*.

CAPLAN, BRUCE and MARCEL KINSBOURNE (1981). "Cerebral Lateralization, Preferred Cognitive Mode, and Reading Ability in Normal Children." *B&L*. 14:2 (Nov.), 349–70.

CARAMAZZA, ALFONSO, JOEL GORDON, EDGAR B. ZURIF, and DAVID De Luca (1976). "Right-Hemispheric Damage and Verbal Problem Solving Behavior." *B&L*. 3:1 (Jan.), 41–46.

CAYER, ROGER L. and RENEE K. SACKS (1979). "Oral and Written Discourse of Basic Writers: Similarities and Differences." *RITE*. 13:2 (May), 121–28.

CHALL, JEANNE S. and ALLAN F. MIRSKY, Eds. (1978). *Education and the Brain*. The Seventy-seventh Yearbook of the National Society for the Study of Education. Part II. Chicago: The National Society for the Study of Education.

CHARROW, VEDA (1979a). *Let the Rewriter Beware*. Washington, D. C.: Document Design Center, American Institutes for Research.

―――― (1979b). *What Is Plain English Anyway?*. Washington, D. C.: Document Design Center, American Institutes for Research.

CHOMSKY, NOAM (1966). *Deep Structure, Surface Structure, and Semantic Interpretation*. Cambridge, Mass.: MIT Press.

CHRISTENSEN, FRANCIS (1967). *Notes Toward a New Rhetoric*. New York: Harper & Row.

CLARK, HERBERT H. and EVE V. CLARK (1977). *Psychology and Language: An Introduction to Psycholinguistics*. New York: Harcourt Brace Jovanovich.

COHEN, MORRIS R. and ERNEST NAGEL (1962). *An Introduction to Logic*. New York: Harcourt Brace Jovanovich.

COLLINS, JAMES L. and MICHAEL M. WILLIAMSON (1981). "Spoken Language and Semantic Abbreviation in Writing." *RITE*. 15:1 (Feb.), 23–35.

COOPER, CHARLES R. and LEE ODELL (1976). "Considerations of Sound in the Composing Process of Published Writers." *RITE*. 10 (Fall), 103–15.

――――, Eds. (1978). *Research on Composing: Points of Departure*. Urbana, Il.: NCTE.

CORBETT, E. P. J. (1965). *Classical Rhetoric for the Modern Student*. New York: Oxford University Press.

CULLER, JONATHAN (1975). *Structuralist Poetics: Structuralism, Linguistics, and the Study of Literature*. Ithaca: Cornell.

DAIUTE, COLETTE A. (1981). "Psycholinguistic Foundations of the Writing Process." *RITE*. 15:1 (Feb.), 5–22.

D'ANGELO, FRANK (1975). *A Conceptual Theory of Rhetoric*. Cambridge, Mass.: Winthrop.

DAY, PATRICIA SPENCER and HANNA K. ULATOWSKA (1979). "Perceptual, Cognitive, and Linguistic Development after Early Hemispherectomy: Two Case Studies." *B&L*. 7:1 (Jan.), 17–33.

DE BEAUGRANDE, ROBERT (1979a). "The Processes of Invention: Assocation and Recombination." *CCC*. 30:3 (Oct.), 260–67.

―――― (1979b). "Psychology and Composition." *CCC*. 30:1 (Feb.), 50–57.

―――― (1980). *Text, Discourse, and Process*. Norwood, N.J.: Ablex.

―――― (1982). "Psychology and Composition." Martin Nystrand, Ed. *What Writers Know*.

―――― and WOLFGANG DRESSLER (1981). *Introduction to Text Linguistics*. London and New York: Longman.

DELLA-PIANA, GABRIEL (1978). "Research Strategies for the Study of Revision Processes in Writing Poetry." Cooper and Odell, Eds. *Research on Composing*.

DENNIS, MAUREEN and HARRY A. WHITAKER (1976). "Language Acquisition Following Hemidecortication: Linguistic Superiority of the Left over the Right Hemisphere." *B&L*. 3:3 (July), 404–33.

DERRIDA, JACQUES (1974). *Of Grammatology*. Trans. Gayatri Chakravorty Spivak. Baltimore: Johns Hopkins University Press.

―――― (1978). *Writing and Difference*. Trans. Alan Bass. Chicago: University of Chicago Press.

DILLON, GEORGE F. (1981). *Constructing Texts: Elements of a Theory of Composition and Style*. Bloomington: Indiana University Press.

DIMOND, STUART J. and J. GRAHAM BEAUMONT, Eds. (1974). *Hemisphere Function in the Human Brain.* New York: John Wiley and Sons.

DOCTOROW, MARLEEN, M. C. WITTROCK, and CAROLYN MARKS (1978). "Generative Processes in Reading Comprehension." *Journal of Educational Psychology.* 70:2 (April), 109–18.

EMIG, JANET (1971). *The Composing Processes of Twelfth Graders.* Urbana, Il.: NCTE.

——— (1978). "Hand, Eye, Brain: Some 'Basics' in the Writing Process." Cooper and Odell, Eds. *Research on Composing.*

ENKVIST, NILS ERIK (1973). *Linguistic Stylistics.* The Hague: Mouton.

FAHNESTOCK, JEANNE (1983). "Semantic and Lexical Coherence." *CCC.* 34:4 (Dec.), 400–416.

FELKER, DANIEL B., Ed. (1980). *Document Design: A Review of the Relevant Research.* Washington, D. C.: Document Design Project, American Institutes for Research.

———, FRANCES PICKERING, VEDA R. CHARROW, V. MELISSA HOLLAND, and JANICE C. REDISH (1981). *Guidelines for Document Designers.* Washington, D. C.: Document Design Project, American Institutes for Research.

——— and ANDREW M. ROSE (1981). *The Evaluation of a Public Document: The Case of FCC's Marine Radio Rules for Recreational Boaters.* Washington, D.C.: Document Design Project, American Institutes for Research.

FILLMORE, CHARLES J. (1968). "The Case for Case." Emmon Bach and Robert T. Harms, Eds. *Universals in Linguistic Theory.* New York: Holt, Rinehart and Winston.

FINEGAN, EDWARD (1980). *Attitudes Toward English Usage: The History of a War of Words.* New York: Teachers College Press, Columbia University.

FISH, STANLEY (1980). *Is There a Text in This Class?* Cambridge, Mass.: Harvard University Press.

FLESCH, RUDOLF (1974 [1949]), *The Art of Readable Writing.* New York: Harper & Row.

FLOWER, LINDA S. and JOHN R. HAYES (1979). *A Process Model of Composition.* Pittsburgh: Carnegie-Mellon University.

——— (1980). "The Cognition of Discovery: Defining a Rhetorical Problem." *CCC.* 31 (Feb.) 21–32.

——— (1981). "A Cognitive Process Theory of Writing." *CCC.* 32 (Dec.), 365–87.

———, ———, and HEIDI SWARTS (1980). *Revising Functional Documents: The Scenario Principle.* Pittsburgh: Carnegie-Mellon University Press.

FRASE, LAWRENCE T., and DONALD L. FISHER (1977). "The Comprehensibility of Technical Writing." Unpublished MS. NIE Writing Conference. Los Alamitos, Calif.

———, and BARRY J. SCHWARTZ (1977). "Typographical Cues That Facilitate Comprehension." Unpublished MS. NIE Writing Conference. Los Alamitos, Cal.

FREED, RICHARD (1981). "Using the Right Brain." *WLA Newsletter.* No. 17 (Spring), 3–4.

FREIRE, PAULO (1981 [1973]). *Education for Critical Consciousness.* Trans. various. New York: Continuum.

——— (1982 [1970]). *Pedagogy of the Oppressed.* Trans. Myra Bergman Ramos. New York: Continuum.

FRIEDERICI, ANGELA D., PAUL W. SCHOENLE, and HAROLD GOODGLASS (1981). "Mechanisms Underlying Writing and Speech in Aphasia." *B&L.* 13:2 (July), 212–22.

FRIES, CHARLES CARPENTER (1952). *The Structure of English.* New York: Harcourt Brace.

FRYE, NORTHROP (1963). *Fables of Identity.* New York: Harcourt Brace Jovanovich.

FULTZ, VIRGINIA (1978). "A Study in the Correlation between CLEM Tests and Problem-Solving Tasks: A Consideration of Their Possible Application to Rhetoric." Unpublished MS. University of Southern California.

GARDNER, HOWARD and ELLEN WINNER (1979). "The Development of Metaphoric Competence: Implications for Humanistic Disciplines." Sheldon Sacks, Ed. *On Metaphor.* Chicago: University of Chicago Press.

GAZZANIGA, MICHAEL S. (1975). "Review of the Split Brain." *UCLA Educator.* 17:2 (Spring), 9–12.

GEERTZ, CLIFFORD (1973). *The Interpretation of Cultures.* New York: Basic Books.

GIBSON, ELEANOR J. and HARRY LEVIN (1975). *The Psychology of Reading.* Cambridge, Mass.: MIT Press.

GLASSNER, BENJAMIN (1980). "Preliminary Report: Hemispheric Relationships in Composing." *Journal of Education.* 162: 74–95.

——— (1981). "Writing as an Integrator of Hemispheric Function." Kroll and Vann, Eds. *Exploring Speaking/Writing Relationships.*

GLOBUS, GORDON G., GROVER MAXWELL, and IRWIN SAVODNIK, Eds. (1976). *Consciousness and the Brain: A Scientific and Philosophical Inquiry.* New York and London: Plenum Press.

GOODY, J. (1977). *The Domestication of the Savage Mind.* Cambridge: Cambridge University Press.

———, and I. P. WATT (1963). "The Consequences of Literacy." *Comparative Studies in History and Society.* 5: 304–45.

GORDON, ROBERT M. (1980). "The Readability of an Unreadable Text." *The English Journal.* 69 (March), 60–61.

GRAVES, DONALD H. (1975). "An Examination of the Writing Processes of Seven Year Old Children." *RITE.* 9:3 (Winter), 227–41.

——— (1982). *Writing: Teachers & Children at Work.* Exeter, N.H.: Heinemann.

GRICE, H. P. (1975). William James Lectures, Harvard University. Published in part as "Logic in Conversation." P. Cole and J. L. Morgan, Eds. *Syntax and Semantics.* Vol. 3: *Speech Acts.* New York: Seminar Press.

HAKE, ROSEMARY L. and JOSEPH M. WILLIAMS (1981). "Style and Its Consequences: Do as I Do, Not as I Say." *CE.* 43:5 (Sept.), 433–51.

HALLIDAY, M. A. K. and RUQAIYA HASAN (1976). *Cohesion in English.* Bath, G.B.: Longman.

HARTLEY, JAMES, Ed. (1980). *The Psychology of Written Communication.* New York: Nichols.

HASWELL, RICHARD H. (1981). "Within-Group Distribution of Syntactic Gain Through Practice in Sentence-Combining." *RITE.* 15:1 (Feb.), 87–96.

HAVELOCK, ERIC A. (1963). *Preface to Plato.* Cambridge, Mass.: Harvard University Press.

HIDI, SUZANNE (1984). *Summarization of Complex Texts.* Toronto: The Ontario Institute for Studies in Education, Centre for Applied Cognitive Science.

HIGGINS, E. T. (1973). *A Social and Developmental Comparison of Oral and Written Communication Skills.* Unpublished doctoral dissertation. Columbia University.

HILL, ADAMS SHERMAN (1897). *The Foundations of Rhetoric.* New York: Harper & Brothers.

HILLOCKS, GEORGE, JR. (1982). "The Interaction of Instruction, Teacher Comment, and Revision in the Composing Process." *RITE.* 16:3 (Oct.), 261−78.

HIRSCH, E. D., JR. (1973). *Validity in Interpretation.* New Haven, Conn.: Yale University Press.

―――― (1977). *The Philosophy of Composition.* Chicago: University of Chicago Press.

――――, and DAVID P. HARRINGTON (1981). "Measuring the Communicative Effectiveness of Prose." *Writing: The Nature, Development, and Teaching of Written Communication.* Vol. 2: *Writing: Process, Development and Communication.* CARL H. FREDERICKSEN and JOSEPH F. DOMINIC, Eds. Hillsdale, N.J.: Lawrence Erlbaum.

HITCHCOCK, ALFRED M. (1923). *Composition and Rhetoric.* New York: Henry Holt.

HOLDAWAY, DON (1979). *The Foundations of Literacy.* Exeter, N.H.: Heinemann.

HOLLAND, NORMAN N. (1975a). *The Dynamics of Literary Response.* New York: W. W. Norton.

―――― (1975b). *5 Readers Reading.* New Haven, Conn.: Yale University Press.

―――― (1975c). *Poems in Persons: An Introduction to the Psychoanalysis of Literature.* New York: W. W. Norton.

HOLLAND, V. MELISSA and ANDREW M. ROSE (1980). *Understanding Instructions with Complex Conditions.* Washington, D.C.: Document Design Project, American Institutes for Research and Pittsburgh: Carnegie-Mellon University.

HUMES, ANN (n.d.). "An Instructional Model of the Composing Situation." Southwest Regional Laboratory Technical Note. Los Alamitos, Calif.: SWRL. *Information Design Journal* (Fall 1981).

"International Panel on Document Design" (1981). *Simply Stated.* No. 20 (Sept.), 1; 4.

IRMSCHER, WILLIAM (1972). *Holt Guide to English.* New York: Holt, Rinehart and Winston.

ISER, WOLFGANG (1974). *The Implied Reader: Patterns of Communication in Prose Fiction from Bunyan to Beckett.* Baltimore: Johns Hopkins University Press.

JAKOBSON, ROMAN (1960). "Linguistics and Poetics." Thomas A. Sebeok, Ed. *Style in Language.* Cambridge, Mass.: MIT Press.

JOHNSON, BARBARA (1980). *The Critical Difference: Essays in the Contemporary Rhetoric of Reading.* Baltimore: Johns Hopkins.

JONASSEN, DAVID H. (1982). *The Technology of Text: Principles for Structuring, Designing, and Displaying Text.* Englewood Cliffs, N.J.: Educational Technology Publications.

The Journal of Business Communication (1981). 18:4 (Fall).

KASDEN, LAWRENCE N. and DANIEL R. HOEBER, Eds. (1980). *Basic Writing: Essays for Teachers, Researchers, and Administrators.* Urbana, Il.: NCTE.

KEENAN, ELINOR O. (1977). "Why Look at Unplanned and Planned Discourse." Keenan and Bennett, Eds. *Discourse across Time and Space.*

―――― and TINA L. BENNETT, Eds. (1977). *Discourse across Time and Space.* Southern California Occasional Papers in Linguistics No. 5. Los Angeles: University of Southern California.

KERN, R. P., T. G. STICHT, D. WELTY, and R. N. HAUKE (1976). *A Guidebook for the Development of Army Training Literature*. Washington, D. C.: U. S. Army Institute for the Behavioral and Social Sciences, Human Resources Organization.

KINNEAVY, JAMES L. (1971). *A Theory of Discourse*. Englewood Cliffs: Prentice-Hall.

KINTSCH, WALTER (1974). *The Representation of Meaning in Memory*. Hillsdale, N.J.: Lawrence Erlbaum.

―――― (1980). "Psychological Processes in Discourse Production." Technical Report No. 99. Institute of Cognitive Science. Boulder: University of Colorado.

KLEIN, RAYMOND and ROSEANNE ARMITAGE (1979). "Rhythm in Human Performance: 1½ Hour Oscillations in Cognitive Style." *Science*. 204 (June 22), 1326–28.

KOESTLER, ARTHUR (1967). *The Act of Creation*. New York: Dell.

KRASHEN, STEPHEN D. (1976). "Second Language Acquisition." M. Burt and others, Eds. *Personal Viewpoints on Aspects of ESL*. New York: Regents.

―――― (1978). "On the Acquisition of Planned Discourse: Written English as a Second Dialect." *Proceedings of the Claremont Reading Conference*. Claremont, Calif.

KROLL, BARBARA (1977). "Combining Ideas in Written and Spoken English: A Look at Subordination and Coordination." Keenan and Bennett, Eds. *Discourse across Time and Space*.

KROLL, BARRY M. and ROBERTA J. VANN, Eds. (1981). *Exploring Speaking/Writing Relationships: Connections and Contrasts*. Urbana, Il.: NCTE.

LABOV, WILLIAM (1969). *The Study of Nonstandard English*. Urbana, Il.: NCTE.

LAKE, DEBORAH A and M. P. BRYDEN (1976). "Handedness and Sex Differences in Hemispheric Asymmetry." *B&L*. 3 : 2 (April), 266–82.

LEVIN, F. (1982). "Pictures as Prose-Learning Devices." A. Flammer and W. Kintsch, Eds. *Discourse Processing*. Amsterdam: North-Holland.

LEVY, JERRE (1980). "Cerebral Asymmetry and the Psychology of Man." M. C. Wittrock, Ed. *The Brain and Psychology*.

――――, and MARYLOU REID (1976). "Variations in Writing Posture and Cerebral Organization." *Science*. 194 (Oct. 15), 337–39.

LEY, ROBERT G. and M. P. BRYDEN (1979). "Hemispheric Differences in Processing Emotions and Faces." *B&L*. 7 : 1 (Jan.), 127–38.

LOBAN, WALTER (1976). *Language Development: Kindergarten Through Grade Twelve*. Urbana, Il.: NCTE.

LORD, ALBERT B. (1960). *The Singer of Tales*. Cambridge, Mass.: Harvard University Press.

LURIA, A. R. (1973). *The Working Brain: An Introduction to Neuropsychology*. Trans. Basil Haigh. New York: Basic Books.

MACKIE, ROBERT, Ed. (1981). *Literacy and Revolution: The Pedagogy of Paulo Freire*. New York: Continuum.

MACLEAN, PAUL D. (1978). "A Mind of Three Minds: Educating the Triune Brain." Chall and Mirsky, Eds. *Education and the Brain*.

MARKELS, ROBIN BELL (1984). *A New Perspective on Cohesion in Expository Paragraphs*. Carbondale and Edwardsville: Southern Illinois University Press.

McKEEVER, WALTER F. and MICHAEL S. DIXON (1981). "Right-Hemisphere Superiority for Discriminating Memorized from Nonmemorized Faces: Affective Imagery, Sex, and Perceived Emotional Effects." *B&L*. 12 (March), 246–60.

McLUHAN, MARSHALL (1969 [1962]). *The Gutenberg Galaxy: The Making of Typographic Man*. New York: New American Library.

McQUADE, DONALD, Ed. (1979). *Linguistics, Stylistics, and the Teaching of Composition*. Akron: University of Akron.

MELAS, D. D. (1974). *Difference of Themes in Assigned and Unassigned Creative Writing of Elementary School Children*. Unpublished Doctoral Dissertation. Buffalo: SUNY.

MELLON, JOHN C. (1969). *Transformational Sentence-Combining*. Urbana, Il.: NCTE.

MINER, EARL (1976). "That Literature Is a Kind of Knowledge." *Critical Inquiry*. 2 (Spring), 487–518.

MIRSKY, ALLAN F. (1978). "Attention: A Neurological Perspective." Chall and Mirsky, Eds. *Education and the Brain*.

MORENBERG, MAX and ANDREW KEREK (1979). "Bibliography on Sentence Combining: Theory and Teaching, 1964–1979." *Rhetoric Society Quarterly*. 9:2 (Spring), 97–111.

MOSCOVITCH, MORRIS (1976). "On the Representation of Language in the Right Hemisphere of Right-Handed People." *B&L*. 3:1 (Jan.), 47–71.

MURRAY, DONALD M. (1980). "Writing as Process: How Writing Finds Its Own Meaning." Timothy R. Donovan and Ben McClelland, Eds. *Eight Approaches to Teaching Composition*. Urbana, Il.: NCTE.

NEWMAN, J. B. and M. W. HOROWITZ (1965). "Writing and Speaking." *CCC*. 16: 160–64.

NEY, JAMES W. (1974). "Notes Toward a Psycholinguistic Model of the Writing Process." *RITE*. 8:2 (Fall), 157–59.

NYSTRAND, MARTIN (1979). "Using Readability Research to Investigate Writing." *RITE*. 13:3 (Oct.), 231–42.

———, Ed. (1982). *What Writers Know: The Language, Process, and Structure of Written Discourse*. New York: Academic Press.

OBLER, LORAINE K., ROBERT J. ZATORRE, LINDA GALLOWAY, and JYOTSNA VAID (1982). "Cerebral Lateralization in Bilinguals: Methodological Issues." *B&L*. 15:1 (Jan.), 40–54.

ODELL, LEE and CHARLES R. COOPER (1980). "Procedures for Evaluating Writing: Assumptions and Needed Research." *CE*. 42:1 (Sept.), 35–43.

O'HARE, FRANK (1973). *Sentence Combining: Improving Student Writing without Formal Grammar Instruction*. Urbana, Il.: NCTE.

ONG, WALTER (1977). *Interfaces of the Word: Studies in the Evolution of Consciousness and Culture*. Ithaca: Cornell University Press.

ORNSTEIN, ROBERT E. (1975). *The Psychology of Consciousness*. New York: Penguin.

OXENHAM, JOHN (1980). *Literacy: Writing, Reading, and Social Organisation*. London: Routledge & Kegan Paul.

PERELMAN, CH[AIM] and L. OLBRECHTS-TYTECA (1969). *The New Rhetoric: A Treatise on Argumentation*. Trans. John Wilkinson and Purcell Weaver. Notre Dame: University of Notre Dame.

PERELMAN, LESTER (1980). "The Revisions of Freshman Writers." Discussion of work in progress. University of Southern California.

——— (1982). ["Factors Affecting Student Performance in Composition"]. Unpublished Ms. University of Southern California.

PERKINS, D. N. (1981). *The Mind's Best Work*. Cambridge, Mass.: Harvard University Press.

PERL, SONDRA (1979). "Composing Processes of Unskilled College Writers." *RITE*. 13:4 (Dec.), 317–36.

———— (1980a). "A Look at Basic Writers in the Process of Composing." Kasden and Hoeber, Eds. *Basic Writing*.

———— (1980b). "Understanding Composing." *CCC*. 31:4 (Dec.), 363–69.

PETTIGREW, JOAN (1981). "Studies of the Composing Process: A Selective Review." *Research in Composition Newsletter*. 3:1 (Fall).

PETTY, WALTER (1978). "The Writing of Young Children." Cooper and Odell, Eds. *Research on Composing*.

PHELPS, LOUISE WETHERBEE (1980). *Acts, Texts, and the Teaching Context: Their Relations within a Dramatistic Philosophy of Composition*. Dissertation. Case Western Reserve University.

———— (1981). Lecture. University of Southern California.

———— (1984). "Dialectics of Coherence: Toward an Integrative Theory." *College English*. 46:6 (Oct.), 58–75.

PIANKO, SHARON (1979a). "A Description of the Composing Processes of College Freshman Writers." *RITE*. 13:1 (Feb.), 5–22.

———— (1979b). "Reflection: A Critical Component of the Composing Process." *CCC*. 30:3 (Oct.), 275–78.

PIROZZOLO, FRANCIS J. and KEITH RAYNER (1977). "Hemispheric Specialization in Reading and Word Recognition." *B&L*. 4 (April), 248–61.

PRESSMAN, REBECCA (1979). *Legislative and Regulatory Progress on the Readability of Insurance Policies*. Washington, D. C.: Document Design Center, American Institutes for Research.

"The Process of Document Design" (1981). *Simply Stated*. No. 18 (July), 1–4.

RADCLIFFE, TERRY (1972). "Talk-Write Composition: A Theoretical Model Proposing the Use of Speech to Improve Writing." *RITE*. 6:2 (fall), 187–99.

"Readability Formulas as Guides to Rewriting" (1982). *Simply Stated*. No. 29 (Sept.), 1–2, 4.

REDISH, JANICE (1979a). *How to Draft More Understandable Legal Documents*. Washington, D.C.: Document Design Center, American Institutes for Research.

———— (1979b). *Readability*. Washington, D.C.: Document Design Center, American Institutes for Research.

RODGERS, PAUL C. (1966). "A Discourse-Centered Rhetoric of the Paragraph." *The Sentence and the Paragraph*.

RODRIGUEZ, RICHARD (1982). *Hunger of Memory: The Education of Richard Rodriguez*. Boston: David R. Godine.

ROHMAN, D. GORDON and ALBERT O. WLECKE (1964). *Pre-Writing: The Construction and Application of Models for Concept Formation in Writing*. East Lansing: Michigan State University.

ROSE, ANDREW M. and LOUIS A. COX (1980). *Following Instructions*. Washington, D.C.: Document Design Project, American Institutes for Research.

ROSE, MIKE (1980). "Rigid Rules, Inflexible Plans, and the Stifling of Language: A Cognitivist Analysis of Writer's Block." *CCC*. 31:4 (Dec.), 389–401.

———— (1984). *Writer's Block: The Cognitive Dimension*. Carbondale and Edwardsville: Southern Illinois University Press.

ROSE, STEVEN (1976). *The Conscious Brain*. New York: Vintage.

ROSENBLATT, LOUISE M. (1976 [1938]). *Literature as Exploration*. Third Edition. New York: Noble and Noble.

—— (1978). *The Reader, the Text, the Poem*. Carbondale and Edwardsville: Southern Illinois University Press.

RUECKERT, WILLIAM H. (1969). *Critical Responses to Kenneth Burke: 1924–1966*. Minneapolis: University of Minnesota Press.

SALOMON, GAVRIEL (1983). "Television Literacy and Television vs. Literacy." Fosheim and Bailey, Eds. *Literacy for Life*.

SAWKINS, M. W. (1970). *The Oral Responses of Selected Fifth Grade Children to Questions Concerning Their Written Expression*. Dissertation. Buffalo: SUNY.

SCHACHTER, JACQUELYN (1976). "Some Semantic Prerequisites for a Model of Language." *B&L*. 3:2 (April), 292–304.

SCHAFER, JOHN C. (1981). "The Linguistic Analysis of Spoken and Written Texts." Kroll and Vann, Eds. *Exploring Speaking/Writing Relationships*.

SCHMULLER, JOSEPH and ROBERTA GOODMAN (1979). "Bilateral Tachistoscopic Perception, Handedness, and Laterality." *B&L*. 8:1 (July), 81–91.

SCHNITZER, MARC L. (1978). "Toward a Neurolinguistic Theory of Language." *B&L*. 6:3 (Nov.), 342–61.

SCINTO, L. F. (1977). "Textual Competence: A Preliminary Analysis of Orally Generated Texts." *Linguistics*. 194: 5–34.

SEARLE, JOHN R. (1975). "A Taxonomy of Illocutionary Acts." P. Cole and J. L. Mason, Eds. *Minnesota Studies in the Philosophy of Language*. Minneapolis: University of Minnesota Press.

—— (1978). *Speech Acts: An Essay in the Philosophy of Language*. Cambridge: Cambridge University Press.

SEGALOWITZ, NORMAN and PETER HANSSON (1979). "Hemispheric Functions in the Processing of Agent-Patient Information." *B&L*. 8:1 (July), 51–56.

The Sentence and the Paragraph (1966). Urbana, Il.: NCTE.

SHAUGHNESSY, MINA P. (1977). *Errors and Expectations: A Guide for the Teacher of Basic Writing*. New York: Oxford University Press.

SHUY, ROGER W. (1981). "Four Misconceptions about Clarity and Simplicity." *Language Arts*. 58:3 (May), 557–61.

Simply Stated. The monthly newsletter of the Document Design Center, American Institutes for Research.

SOKOLOV, A. H. (1969). "Studies of the Speech Mechanisms of Thinking." M. Cole and I. Waltzman, Eds. *A Handbook of Contemporary Soviet Psychology*. New York: Basic Books.

SOMMERS, NANCY (1980). "Revision Strategies of Student Writers and Experienced Adult Writers." *CCC*. 31:4 (Dec.), 378–88.

SPERRY, R. W. (1976). "Mental Phenomena as Causal Determinants in Brain Function." Globus, Maxwell, and Savodnik, Eds. *Consciousness and the Brain: A Scientific and Philosophical Inquiry*.

SPIVAK, GAYATRI CHAKRAVORTY (1974). "Introduction." Derrida. *Of Grammatology*.

STALLARD, C. K. (1974). "An Analysis of the Writing Behavior of Good Student Writers." *RITE*. 8:206–18.

STALTER, WILLIAM (1978). "A Sense of Structure." *CCC*. 29 (Dec. 1978), 341–45.

STERNGLASS, MARILYN (1980). "Creating the Memory of Unheard Sentences." Freedman and Pringle, Eds. *Reinventing the Rhetorical Tradition.* Conway, Ark.: L&S Books for the Canadian Council of Teachers of English.

STRONG, WILLIAM (1973). *Sentence Combining: A Composing Book.* New York: Random House.

SWANEY, JOYCE HANNAH, CAROL J. JANIK, SANDRA J. BOND, and JOHN R. HAYES (1981). *Editing for Comprehension: Improving the Process Through Reading Protocols.* Pittsburgh: Carnegie-Mellon University.

SWARTS, HEIDI, LINDA S. FLOWER, and JOHN R. HAYES (1980). *How Headings in Documents Can Mislead Readers.* Pittsburgh: Carnegie-Mellon University.

TAYLOR, DENNY (1983) *Family Literacy: Young Children Learning to Read and Write.* Exeter, N.H.: Heinemann.

TEN HOUTEN, WARREN D. and CHARLES D. KAPLAN (1973). *Science and Its Mirror Image.* New York: Harper & Row.

TOMPKINS, JANE P., Ed. (1980). *Reader-Response Criticism: From Formalism to Post-Structuralism.* Baltimore and London: Johns Hopkins University Press.

TULVING, ENDEL (1972). "Episodic and Semantic Memory." Endel Tulving and Wayne Donaldson, Eds. *Organization of Memory.* New York: Academic Press

UCLA Educator (Spring 1975).

VAID, JYOTSNA and WALLACE E. LAMBERT (1979). "Differential Cerebral Involvement in Cognitive Functioning of Bilinguals." *B&L.* 8:1 (July), 92–110.

VANDE KOPPLE, WILLIAM J. (1982). "Functional Sentence Perspective, Composition, and Reading." *CCC.* 30:1 (Feb.), 50–63.

VAN DIJK, TEUN A. (1977). *Text and Context.* London: Longman.

——— (1980). *Macrostructures: An Interdisciplinary Study of Global Structure in Discourse, Interaction, and Cognition.* Hillsdale, N.J.: Lawrence Erlbaum.

VISIBLE LANGUAGE (1980). 14:4.

VONNEGUT, KURT (1976). *Slapstick, or Lonesome No More.* New York: Dell.

VYGOTSKY, L. S. (1962). *Thought and Language.* Trans. E. Hanfmann and G. Vakar. Cambridge, Mass.: MIT.

WAPNER, WENDY and HOWARD GARDNER (1981). "Profiles of Symbol-Reading Skills in Organic Patients." *B&L.* 12:2 (March), 303–12.

———, SUZANNE HAMBY, and HOWARD GARDNER (1981). "The Role of the Right Hemisphere in the Apprehension of Complex Linguistic Materials." *B&L.* 14:1 (Sept.), 15–33.

WASON, PETER C. (1980). "Conformity and Commitment in Writing." *Visible Language.* 14:4, 351–63.

WELLS, RULON (1960). "Nominal and Verbal Style." Thomas A. Sebeok, Ed. *Style in Language.* Cambridge, Mass.: MIT Press.

WILLIAMS, J. D. (1983). "Covert Language Behavior during Writing." *RITE.* 17:4 (Dec.), 301–12.

——— and SCOTT D. ALDEN (1983). "Motivation in the Composition Class." *RITE.* 17:2 (May), 101–12.

——— and MICKY RIGGS (1981). "Subvocalization during Writing." Unpublished MS. University of Southern California.

WILLIAMS, JOSEPH M. (1979a). "Defining Complexity." *CE.* 40:6 (Feb.), 595–609.

——— (1979b). "Non-Linguistic Linguistics and the Teaching of Style." D. McQuade, Ed. *Linguistics, Stylistics, and the Teaching of Composition.*

——— (1981a). "The Phenomenology of Error." *CCC.* 32:2 (May), 152–68.

———— (1981b). *Style: Ten Lessons in Clarity and Grace*. Glenview, Ill.: Scott, Foresman.

WINTEROWD, W. ROSS (1970). "The Grammar of Coherence." *CE*. 31:8 (May), 828–35.

———— (1971). "*Dispositio*: The Concept of Form in Discourse." *CCC*. 22:1 (Feb.), 39–45.

———— (1972a). "Beyond Style." *Philosophy and Rhetoric*. 5:2 (Spring), 88–110.

———— (1972b). "The Realms of Meaning: Text-Centered Criticism." *CCC*. 23:5 (Dec.), 399–405.

———— (1973). "'Topics' and Levels in the Composing Process." *CE*. 34:5 (Feb.), 701–09.

———— (1975). Review of *The Tagmemic Discovery Procedure: An Evaluation of Its Uses in the Teaching of Rhetoric*, by Richard Young and Frank M. Koen. *Philosophy and Rhetoric*. 8:3 (Summer), 183–87.

———— (1976a). "The Rhetorical Transaction of Reading." *CCC*. 27:2 (May), 185–91.

———— (1976b). "The Rhetoric of Beneficence, Authority, Ethical Commitment, and the Negative." *Philosophy and Rhetoric*. 9:2 (Spring), 65–83.

———— (1977). "Getting It Together in the English Department." *ADE Bulletin*. No. 55 (Nov.), 28–31.

———— (1978). "Creativity and the Comp Class." *Freshman English News*. 7:2 (Fall), 1–4; 12–16.

———— (1979). "Brain, Rhetoric, and Style." D. McQuade, Ed. *Linguistics, Stylistics, and the Teaching of Composition*.

———— (1980a). "Developing a Composition Program." A. Freedman and I. Pringle, Eds. *Reinventing the Rhetorical Tradition*.

———— (1980b). "The Paradox of the Humanities." *ADE Bulletin*. No. 64 (May), 1–3.

———— (1980c). "Syntax, Readability, Intention, and the Real World." *Journal of English Teaching Techniques*. 10:1 (Summer), 21–33.

———— (1981). *The Contemporary Writer*. Second Edition. New York: Harcourt Brace Jovanovich.

———— (1982a). "Teaching Composition Across the Curriculum." *The Writing Instructor*. 1:2 & 3 (Winter/Spring), 55–65.

———— (1982b). "The Three R's: Reading, Reading, and Rhetoric." William E. Tanner and J. Dean Bishop, Eds. *Rhetoric and Change*. Mesquite, Tex.: Ide House.

———— (1983a). "Black Holes, Indeterminacy, and Paulo Freire." *Rhetoric Review*. 2:1 (1983), 28–36.

———— (1983b). "Dramatism in Themes and Poems." *CE*. 45:6 (Oct.), 581–88.

———— (1983c). "From Classroom Practice into Psycholinguistic Theory." A. Freedman and I Pringle, Eds. *Learning to Write: First Language/Second Language*. New York and London: Longman.

———— (1985). "The Politics of Meaning." *Written Communication*. 2:3 (July 1985), 269–92.

WITTE, STEPHEN P. and LESTER FAIGLEY (1981). "Coherence, Cohesion, and Writing Quality." *CCC*. 32:2 (May), 189–204.

WITTROCK, M. C., Ed. (1977). *The Human Brain*. Englewood Cliffs, N.J.: Prentice-Hall.

————, Ed. (1980a). *The Brain and Psychology*. New York: Academic Press.

———— (1980b). "The Generative Process of Reading." Address. 8th Annual Conference on Rhetoric, Linguistics, and Literature. University of Southern California. *The Writing Instructor* (1983). 2:4 (Summer).

YOUNG, RICHARD (1976). "Invention: A Topographical Survey." Gary Tate, Ed. *Teaching Composition: Ten Bibliographical Essays*. Fort Worth: Texas Christian University.

———— and ALTON L. BECKER (1966). "Toward a Modern Theory of Rhetoric: A Tagmemic Contribution." Janet A. Emig, James T. Fleming, and Helen M. Popp, Eds. *Language and Learning*. New York: Harcourt Brace Jovanovich.

————, ALTON L. BECKER and KENNETH L. PIKE (1970). *Rhetoric: Discovery and Change*. New York: Harcourt Brace Jovanovich.

————, and FRANK M. KOEN (1973). *The Tagmemic Discovery Procedure: An Evaluation of Its Uses in the Teaching of Rhetoric*. Ann Arbor: University of Michigan.

ZOELLNER, ROBERT (1969). "Talk-Write: A Behavioral Pedagogy for Composition." *CE*. 30:4 (Jan.) 267–320.

Part II

Essays on Composition/Rhetoric

Invention

Brain, Rhetoric, and Style

In 1975, one of my students—now Dr. Ronald Shook of Utah State University—called the latest issue of the *UCLA Educator* to my attention. The journal contained the collection of essays, edited by Merlin Wittrock, that was reissued by Prentice-Hall as *The Human Brain* (1977). At about the same time, Stephen Krashen joined the linguistics faculty at the university, and he and I began a close association from which I have learned and continue to learn a great deal, not only about such arcana as conjugate lateral eye movement and Korsakov amnesia, but also about the practicalities of giving remedial students and foreign speakers the skills of literacy in English.

If my introduction to brain theory was casual, my subsequent work has been systematic and fairly broad ranging, stopping short of following histological and biochemical studies.

"Brain, Rhetoric, and Style" was a pioneer effort, the first attempt to apply the new discoveries concerning hemisphericity to the problems of literacy, though Earl Miner had published "That Literature Is a Kind of Knowledge" in 1976.

If the essay had done nothing more than begin the definition of propositional and appositional texts (and writing styles), it would, I think, have justified itself. But the concept of metaphor developed in the essay seems valuable, as does the exploration of LH, RH, and reading.

When the essay was first published, it pointed, I think, toward the future of composition/rhetoric studies. It still does.

It may be well to start our speculations with the obvious before we begin to probe the not-so-obvious and

This essay appeared originally in *Linguistics, Stylistics, and the Teaching of Composition*, ed. Donald A. McQuade (Akron: University of Akron, 1979).

even the esoteric. Obviously, then, the skilled writer of exposition must be able to generalize (state or adumbrate a thesis) and then to organize the exposition of that thesis in some meaningful way. This idea can be stated in a variety of terms; the writer of exposition must be able to think deductively, must be coherent in the development of ideas, must be "logical." And just as obviously, the skilled writer must be able to supply appropriate local detail, to texture the exposition so that it is something more than an elegant structure in which all of the major segments fit.

In this essay, I will argue that the writer needs those skills which are characteristic of both the left and the right hemispheres of the brain; I will further suggest that some unsuccessful writers are extremely left-hemispheric while some are extremely right-hemispheric; finally, I will suggest that the skills of both hemispheres can be taught (though a great deal of empirical work must be done before we will be on solid ground in this regard).

So this essay will concern composition, but our interest does (and must) spill over from that homely subject into the headier realms of poetry. In fact, I believe that there can be no sharp division between composition theory and literary theory without the impoverishment of each. I intend *not* to keep a sharp focus in these pages, but to maintain a lambency of interest.

As composition is the construction of texts, so reading is their reconstruction, and composition theory must take account of reading theory. In fact, it is virtually impossible to consider the construction of texts without also dealing with their reconstruction.

All of which is to say, really, that the following essay will deal with reading and writing in the light of brain theory—the reading of *anything* and the writing of *anything*.

This discussion calls upon the most reliable theories of brain func-

tion and uses the consensus of brain researchers for its conclusions and speculations. The reader must determine for him- or herself where conclusiveness ends and speculation begins, for I do not hesitate to use brain theory and research metaphorically, heuristically. The facts about the brain are accurate; in this paper, I often use them as speculative instruments.

And yet I think that alert readers will know perfectly well when the paper becomes highly speculative, for I have made every attempt to keep not only my audience but myself oriented. No small task, when one considers the drama and glamour of brain theory, the seductive possibilities of using one finding about cognition or brain mechanism for much more than it is worth.

All in all, however, I have approached my materials with caution. I hope that my readers agree on two points: where I am relatively assured in my conclusions, I have good warrant for my certainty; when I am less assured, I have nonetheless pointed the way for future inquiry and research.

By "rhetoric" in the following discussion, I mean the generation, reception, and pragmatics of natural language and even more narrowly, reading and writing.

The story of brain and language began in the mid-nineteenth century when, performing an autopsy on an aphasic, the French neurologist Paul Broca found massive damage to an area of the left cerebral cortex and concluded that this area—now identified with his name—was the speech center. It is indeed known to be *one* of the areas controlling speech.

Since Broca's discovery—and especially since the end of World War II—brain research has been pursued with increasingly dramatic results.[1] An ecumenical endeavor involving neurologists, neurosurgeons, biochemists, linguists, and psychologists (among others), brain science has, as the following pages will demonstrate, much to contribute to rhetoric and stylistics, and, conversely, both of these fields have much to contribute to brain science. For example, in discussing the brain as mechanism of language, A. R. Luria tells us that expression begins with a *motive* or general idea, while perception (decoding, understanding) ends with the interpretation of the motive lying behind the utterance.[2] That is to say, rhetoric is the alpha and omega of the brain's handling of speech, for rhetoric is, in large part, the study of motives.

However, I do not want to give the impression that brain research is meaningful to rhetoric and stylistics only in the large philosophical sense; its details help clarify many of the premises of these fields and suggest pedagogical strategies.

LEFT-BRAIN, RIGHT-BRAIN

Our interest in the brain centers on hemisphericity, the different ways in which the left hemisphere (LH) and the right hemisphere (RH) function.

The LH controls the right hand, and the RH controls the left hand. By and large, in right-handed people language is a function of the LH, often called the "dominant hemisphere." Localization studies by such researchers as Wilder Penfield have resulted in "maps" [of brain function.]

The two hemispheres of the brain are joined by the *corpus callosum*, a white sheet of axons or nerve fibers that provides the communicative link between the two halves of the brain. If the corpus callosum is severed (through a surgical procedure known as *commissurotomy*), the left hand quite literally does not know what the right hand is doing if there are no visual or verbal clues. Obviously, commissurotomized patients are a major source of knowledge about the functioning of the hemispheres.

Information from the left side of the visual field is transmitted to the RH, and information from the right side of the visual field is transmitted to the LH. Since language is, by and large, a function of the LH, if the right portion of the visual field is covered in a split-brain (commissurotomized) patient, only the RH receives information, and as a result, the patient cannot name items shown to him or her even though there is evidence that this patient knows what the items are. For instance, in the situation just described, a patient will be able to use a spoon properly, but will not be able to name it.

While it is generally agreed that the LH is the side of the brain with language, the role of the RH in regard to language is disputed. One study suggests that the RH *does* have language, which is released when the control of the LH is weakened or removed, as in the case of massive injury to or removal of the LH.[3]

An even more dramatic view of the RH and language is provided by the study of three subjects, nine and ten years old, who had either the RH or the LH removed before five months of age. The study concludes the following: (1) both the LH and the RH are efficient in phonemic discrimination; (2) both the LH and the RH provide "an adequate substrate for semantic skills"; (3) the LH is far better at syntax than is the RH.

"What is the characteristic of the left hemispheric defect? It appears to be an organizational, analytical, syntactic, and hierarchic problem rather than a difficulty with the conceptual or semantic aspects of language."[4] In regard to the LH, those adjectives have resonance: organizational, analytical, syntactic, hierarchic.

Perhaps the best-known terms for characterizing the hemispheres are J. E. Bogen's *propositional* (LH) and *appositional* (RH), in regard to which he hazards the generalization that "simultaneous patterns rather than sequential order distinguish appositionality from propositionality."[5] As we shall see, the terms "propositional" and "appositional" have great meaning for the present discussion, implying as they do that the LH is sequential, logical and that the RH, on the other hand, works with an all-at-onceness, atemporally and nonsequentially.

In this discussion, I will suggest that language use can be rated on a scale according to its degree of propositionality or appositionality. On the one hand, some language use approaches the pure propositionality of mathematics or symbolic logic; that is, it is structure almost without specific content. Other language use is almost purely appositional in the sense that idea after idea or image after image occurs in a string of appositions, with no apparent propositional connection. At these extremes, language is, I think, pathological, and indeed the best illustrations of what I mean come from the language of schizophrenics.

In a later section of this paper, we will return to my notions of propositional and appositional language, particularly in relation to the teaching of written composition.

To characterize the RH, then. It is often called the "dark," "intuitive" side of the brain. In the normal right-handed person, either it has very little language or its language function is suppressed by the "dominant" LH. The RH is superior at establishing part-whole relationships, that is, at gestalt formation or closure.[6] (As will be seen, this idea is extremely important.) For instance, with the left hand (controlled by the RH), the split-brain patient is proficient at determining what a whole object will be on the basis of feeling one part of that object; from the part, the patient can infer or construct a gestalt. With the right hand, this is impossible. The RH emotes, learns, remembers, and initiates responses. It is superior in "managing spatial tasks."[7]

Robert D. Nebes provides a succinct description of the activity of the RH:

It is evident that the right cerebral hemisphere makes an important contribution to human performance having functions complementary to those of the left hemisphere. The right side of the brain probably processes information differently from the left, relying more on imagery than on language, and being more synthetic and holistic than analytic and sequential in handling data. It is certainly important in perceiving spatial relationships. It is also probably the neural basis for our ability to take the fragmentary sensory information we receive, and construct from it a coherent concept of the spatial organization of the outside world—a sort of cognitive spatial map within which we plan our actions.[8]

If we think about the process of speech—which characterizes the LH—we begin to get a notion of how the LH must operate: "what is essentially involved in language production is the programming of an idea, itself containing no intrinsic temporal order, into a sequence of linguistic units, which are also intrinsically unordered."[9] As Luria characterizes the process, first "the motive or general idea of the expression . . . is coded into a speech scheme and put into operation with the aid of internal speech; finally, these schemes are converted into narrative speech, based on a 'generative' grammar."[10] The temporal nature of these operations is illustrated by the fact that, in some cases at least, the speaker must choose or project a structure before selecting a lexical item, as in the following: *"That she didn't recognize Jim surprised Mary."*

In sum,

The left (dominant) hemisphere (in right-handers) begins to play an essential role not only in the cerebral organization of speech, but also in the cerebral organization of all higher forms of cognitive activity connected with speech—perception organized into logical schemes, active verbal memory, logical thought—whereas the right (non-dominant) hemisphere either begins to play a subordinate role in cerebral organization of these processes or plays no part whatsoever in their course.[11]

I cannot resist ending this characterization of the hemispheres with a paradox—which will seem a good deal less paradoxical as our discussion progresses. I have implied that the LH is the logical half of the brain and that the RH works in images, alogically. Now ponder Einstein's description of his own cognition:

The words of the language, as they are written or spoken, do not seem to play any role in my mechanism of thought.

The psychical entities which seem to serve as elements in thought are certain signs and more or less clear images which can be "voluntarily" reproduced and combined.[12]

As Nebes hints, perhaps the apparent inverse relationship between creativity and verbal skills could be due to the overtraining of verbal skills at the expense of nonverbal abilities.[13]

BRAIN, CREATIVITY, AND THE COMP CLASS

It is a common experience in composition classes to find two diametrically opposed styles, the one which is highly general, the student writer never seeming able to get down to cases, and the other which is extremely specific and concrete, but chaotic, as if the writer is unable to order ideas and impressions, unable to establish the logical connections and hierarchies among them. In the one style, we have the skeleton of coherence without the substance of tangible content; in the other, there is substance without form.

We can characterize the highly abstract but "coherent" style as propositional and the concrete style as appositional. We will further discuss the characteristics of propositionality and appositionality, but for the moment, we must relate these styles to brain function.

As we have seen, the LH is the propositional side of the brain; it works well with deductive structures, handling the ghostliness of symbolic logic and the bare-bonedness of the syllogism and the sorities with a proficiency of which the RH is incapable. The RH is the appositional side of the brain, "seeing" with an all-at-onceness, taking a gestaltist view of sensory input, perceiving patterns in the gouache which the LH would process as merely a jumble of disconnected fragments. (It is the RH that enables us to recognize faces.)

That much said, we can look at some specific examples of propositional and appositional styles.

Some years ago, quite by chance, I found an article on schizophrenic language.[14] When I read the piece it occurred to me that the author, Brendan Maher, could well have been speaking of the more extreme cases of propositionality and appositionality that I had discovered in my composition classes. Here are two examples of schizophrenic language:

PROPOSITIONAL

The subterfuge and the mistaken planned substitutions for that demanded American action can produce nothing but the general results of negative contention and the impractical results of misplacement, of mistaken purpose and unrighteous position, the impractical serviceabilities of unnecessary contradictions. For answers to this dilemma, consult Webster.

APPOSITIONAL

I hope to be home soon, very soon. I fancy chocolate eclairs, Doenuts. I want some doenuts, I do want some golden syrup, a tin of golden syrup or treacle, jam. . . . See the Committee about me coming home for Easter my twenty-fourth birthday. I hope all is well at home, how is Father getting on. Never mind there is hope, heaven will come, time heals all wounds, Rise again Glorious Greece and come to Hindoo Heavens, the Indian Heavens. The Dear old times will come back. We shall see Heaven and Glory yet, come everlasting life. I want a new writing pad of note paper.

"Normal" students write themes that are only a shade less schizoid than the passages quoted above. The following two themes are reproduced exactly as I received them, with all errors intact.

PROPOSITIONAL

Before a person can say whether the best things in life are free, he must first deturmine what in his opinion the best things are. Naturally every person has his own ideas concerning the objects or things that are important.

I believe that friendship, health, and beauty are three of the most important things a person can enjoy. When I say "beauty" I mean having things around you that you like or being places that make you feel good.

When I say that friendship is not fun, I don't mean that you can go out and buy five dollars worth of it when you need a friend. Instead of using money you use yourself. Your ideals and attitudes to buy friends. To fit into a group you must drop some and maybe most of your attitudes before you will be considered normal in the group. If you don't, you will be considered rebellious or off-beat and become an outcast from that group. Therefore, to have friends is to pay by changing yourself for their benefit.

Good health is very important to me because without it I can not enjoy myself. To maintain a healthy physical condition one must get the proper amounts of exercise, food, and sleep. Exercise and sleep are free but food is by no means free. Every time one turns around he is paying for food by working at some type of job to get money for food.

Beauty is the only thing that comes close to being free. Aside from having to buy most of the articles that a person likes to have—such as a car, skiis or any other material object—beauty is mostly free. I love to go into the forest and enjoy nature's beauty. The trees, forest creatures, brooks and streams all mean a lot to me. I enjoy hunting and camping in the forest and just walking there alone, thinking to myself. But to keep these forests we must pay to see that some careless hunter or camper doesn't burn them down. We have to set aside parks and wilderness areas so they aren't cut into lumber by the mills. These parks all cost money. Everywhere you go, you have to pay some way or another.

APPOSITIONAL

Are Motion Pictures Too Real?
"Film" Scene Is 'Too Real'"
Sao Paulo, Brazil (Reuters)—An assistant movie director shooting a Brazilian style western, fell dying with a rifle bullet in his back during a gunfight scene, Meridional News Agency reported here Wednesday.

Police halted film-making while they tried to find out who fired the fatal shot at Martino Martini as film extras blazed off blank ammunition.

So far there has been no explanation of how there came to be a live bullet among the blanks.

Martini was a talented young member of the "new wave" of Brazil's film industry. The film, "Obliged to Kill," was to be completed in 10 days' time."
Senta of Vienna

"Brunette Senta Berger of Vienna has lone been a glowing face in nondescript German movies. Last year fame took a leap across Europe and the world after she played the lusciously blonde German girl friend of a Russian soldier in the American-produced "The Victors." "I (Senta) was the aggressive girl in the film scenes. I stood out because when you're aggressive, audiences watch you." Senta also stood out, as mail from men everywhere proclaimed, because she is full-faced, full-bosomed, full-hipped—a frankly full female."
"The 'Love Goddess' who never found love."—Marilyn Monroe

"Here (Miss Monroe) fans saw her pictures as reflections of her beauty, fame, fortune, and sex. They show the evolution of the Love Goddess in all her sexuality—the role that Marilyn knew and enjoyed and most feared to lose. First—and most famous—was the 1949

nude calendar pose, which brought her a worldwide flood of welcome publicity while she was just a long-haired model who had had a few walk-on parts in the movies."

Elizabeth Taylor and Sophia Loren among the few, are too explicit in their acting on and off the scene. Producers seem to put realism in front of morals and dignity.
The public wants more sex from female actresses, more realistic looking and sounding killings, etc.
The Walt Disney type program is fast becoming absolete. Programs on the educational line seem to have died. I want to go to a movie to be intertained by good acting, but moral conduct.
Now days, I walk away from a movie with a sick feeling in my stomach.
My feelings are caused by simpley vulgar intertainment. Of course, there are a few good movies, such as Lorance of Arabia and others, but to the handfull that are acceptable in my terms, there are hundredes that are poor. The producers' ought to put this realistic tought into good and moral acting.
Not this garbage that is turned out in mass production.
"Of Human Bondage"
"Some women can't help what they are
. . ."
"There would always be men in her life . . . all kinds of men . . . and always Phillip to come back to . . . to degrade and despise."
As the billboard, a half naked woman!

The propositional and the appositional styles can be contrasted on the basis of these factors, among others:

PROPOSITIONAL	APPOSITIONAL
Stated topic (enthymeme)	Implied topic
Organizational rigidity	Organizational flexibility
General examples, if any	Specific examples

Backgrounded style [15]	Foregrounded style
Little presence [16]	Great Presence

In the propositional essay, the topic is clearly stated; at the end of the second paragraph, we know that the writer considers health, friendship, and beauty to be three of the best things in life, and we can predict with virtual certainty that the essay will explore these three values to determine whether or not they are free. The progression will be, in Kenneth Burke's term, syllogistic.

It follows, then, that organization is predictable. The first two paragraphs enunciate the topic (which might, indeed, have been stated in one complex sentence), and the following three paragraphs each explore one aspect of the topic. Our expectations concerning organization are thwarted only by the writer's failure to supply cloture in the form of a summative paragraph.

There are no real examples in the piece, no narrative concerning a friendly relation, no anecdote concerning ebullient good health, no specific image of a beautiful place. The prose floats at least thirteen feet above the rich earth of specificity.

This lack of examples creates the backgrounded style and deprives the writing of presence, which is the sort of palpability that evokes attention from the reader.

Comments on the appositional essay would be the obverse of those on the propositional: the topic is unstated, there is no real organization, and the examples (which are the substance of the essay) create foregrounding and presence.

Although the ability to carry on propositional thinking is undoubtedly a sign of maturity, maturity in writing involves the ability to unite the appositional with the propositional in appropriate contexts. Such is the implication of Aristotle's mention of inductive thinking and of the whole concept of presence. (Such also, of course, is the implication of the poetic theory that this discussion will elaborate.) Of course, writing teachers have intuitively understood this point all along. The master comment on the propositional theme above would be, I suppose, "Get down to cases. Give me some concrete examples. Help me to see what you're talking about, to experience." The "master" comment on the appositional theme would be, "Get a thesis, state it or imply it clearly, and then organize and explore your ideas."

When we give such advice, we are quite literally asking students to change the ratios between their cerebral hemispheres. In this regard, Luria tells us that

it must be remembered that the absolute dominance of one (the left) hemisphere is not by any means always found, and the law of lateralization is only relative in character. According to recent investigations (Zangwill, 1960; Subirana, 1969), one-quarter of all persons are completely right-handed, and slightly more than one-third show marked dominance of the left hemisphere, whereas the rest are distinguished by relatively slight dominance of the left hemisphere, and in one-tenth of all cases the dominance of the left hemisphere is totally absent.[17]

Clearly, in the classroom we must take account of the fact that we will encounter instances of extreme LH or RH dominance, and I would postulate that in the example themes above, we have seen probable instances of such dominance. The situation becomes even more complicated when we realize that *literacy may create or facilitate lateralization.*[18] Learning to read and write may well increase the dominance of the LH.

Can we conclude, then, that the appositional writer may increase proportional skills through intensive practice in reading and writing? Such would seem to be the case. Are appositional writers in general less literate than propositional writers are? At present, there is no answer to that question. In the absence of such evidence, I would suggest that carefully structured reading and writing exercises may well increase the versatility of the appositionalist.

Drawing on work that I have done in the past[19] and on my experience with secondary students in the Huntington Beach Union High School District, I am at present constructing materials intended to give the appositionalist propositional skills. The materials are yet to be tested, but, in general, they are based on a progression from algorithmic to heuristic to aleatory exercises. In the materials, this progression will be applied to instruction in all of the "stadia" of discourse: sentence, paragraph, essay.

The paragraph is the handiest example of what I am getting at. Drawing on both tagmemic theories and the theories of Francis Christensen, I ask students to construct paragraphs according to algorithms— for instance:

(1) Make a general statement about your English class.	My English class is boring.
(2) Qualify, restrict, or explain that statement.	We never do interesting things in the class.
(3) Illustrate the restricted statement three times.	We spend a lot of time diagramming sentences. The teacher makes us read a lot of old-fashioned poetry. Every day we do grammar drills in our workbooks.

The result is a recognizable paragraph, with levels of generality and local details.

The next step is heuristic: to recombine the "tagmemes" in the algorithmic paragraph in as many ways as possible:

(1) In my English class, we spend a lot of time diagramming sentences. The teacher makes us read a lot of old-fashioned poetry, and every day we do grammar drills in our workbooks. My English class is boring. We never do interesting things in the class.

(2) Because we never do interesting things in my English class, it is boring. We spend a lot of time diagramming sentences, and the teacher makes us read a lot of old-fashioned poetry. Not only that, we do grammar drills in our workbooks every day.

(3) We spend our time doing uninteresting things in my English class: diagramming sentences, reading old-fashioned poetry, and doing grammar drills in our workbooks. My English class is boring.

The aleatory phase of instruction relies on creative devices such as metaphor and analogy to suggest relationships that can be expressed in paragraphs, the forms for which students have presumably "internalized" through their algorithmic and heuristic work. For example,

> Compare a recent journey—to another country, another city, another part of your own city—with each of the following:
> threading a needle
> a nightmare
> attending a play or a film
> eating a tart apple
> smelling a freshly painted room
> touching suede
> solving a math problem
> Use the ideas that your comparisons generated to write a paragraph—or several paragraphs—about the journey.

One other possibility concerning the appositionalist is intriguing and deserves careful investigation. If the general skills of propositional thought are both learnable and transferable, then it might well be possible to increase the appositionalist's versatility by providing him or her with extensive exercises in propositional reasoning, e.g., syllogisms, enthymemes, sorites, and problems in symbolic logic.

As to the propositionalist, I can only suggest that intensive exposure to the most appositional of all written discourse may well bring about greater versatility. I am speaking, of course, of the reading and writing of lyric poetry. However, the common method of "explaining" the lyric poem by propositionalizing all of its images (a subject which is explored fully in a later section of this paper) should, according to my logic, tend to increase the propositional nature of the writing. It would seem, then, that "reader response" criticism and free writing would be in order.

Finally, of course, the ultimate goal is to increase the creativity of all writers—the ability to generate writings (whether poetic or non-poetic, temporal or atemporal) that satisfy the writer's need for expression, the reader's need for understanding and empathy, and the world's need for meaningful communication. This creativity consists of the ability to use both propositional and appositional modes appropriately, and it comes about only in the proper environment.

Insofar as the composition classroom is an environment, it must be characterized by an atmosphere of freedom and by writing tasks that are liberating. (Drills and exercises can be liberating at certain times for certain purposes with certain students.)

Carl Rogers defines creativity as "the emergence in action of a novel relational product, growing out of the uniqueness of the individual on the one hand, and the materials, events, people, or circumstances of his life on the other."[21] The conditions that foster creativity are *psychological safety* ("Accepting the individual as of unconditional worth. . . . Providing a climate in which external evaluation is absent. . . . Understanding empathically")and *psychological freedom.*[22]

In his magnificent book *The Act of Creation*[23] Arthur Koestler has developed a model of the creative act. The creative person has been able to *bisociate* by leaping from one *matrix* to another. An excellent example of both matrix and leap is provided by James L. Adams in *Conceptual Blockbusting.*[24]

At sunrise on the first morning, a monk laboriously climbs to the summit of a mountain, where he spends the rest of the day and all of the night meditating. At sunrise on the second day, he comes down the mountain on the same trail by which he ascended. Is there any time in his journey downward at which he would be in exactly the same spot as he was on the journey upward?

If one stays in the verbal matrix, this is a difficult problem to solve, but if one leaps to the visual matrix, the solution becomes obvious. Picture the monk going upward and downward simultaneously. Obviously he would meet himself at some point on the trail.

Koestler sets up three categories of creativity: comedy, in which there is a collision of matrices; science, in which there is an integration of matrices; and art, in which matrices are juxtaposed. The comic effect comes about, for example, through the juxtaposition of the ridiculous with the sublime; Kepler analogized the role of the Father in the Trinity with that of the sun in the solar system, thus integrating two matrices; in tragedy the matrix of the play is juxtaposed with the audience's knowledge that the play is just a play.

As there is matrix-hopping, so there is hemisphere-hopping: in fact, the two are apparently the same at times. Fluency in thought, like fluency in writing, is the ability to use both the appositional and the propositional, an ability that is very much like John Crowe Ramsom's description of metaphysical poetry (as opposed to physical and Platonic poetry):

Platonic poetry is too idealistic, but physical poetry is too realistic, and realism is tedious and does not maintain interest. The poets therefore introduce the psychological device of the miracle. The predication which it permits is clean and quick but it is not a scientific predication. For scientific predication concludes an act of attention but miraculism [in the form of the metaphysical conceit] initiates one. It leaves us looking, marveling, and reveling in the thick *dinglich* substance that has just received its strange representation.[25]

The RH is the master of appositional, *dinglich*, all-at-onceness of images; the LH is the master of metaphor, analogy, and proposition.

The fluent writer is a hemisphere-hopper.

RIGHT-HANDED METAPHOR AND LEFT-HANDED SYNECDOCHE

In a paper that I coauthored with Timothy Crusius, one of my students,[26] we analyzed the nature of metaphor. As Christine Brooke-Rose[27] and Laurence Perrine,[28] among others, have pointed out, metaphor can have any of a great variety of grammatical forms. For example:

predicate nominal sentence
   All the world's a stage . . .
genitive construction
   the bird of time
appositive
   the black bat, night
vocative
   O wild West Wind, thou breath of Autumn's being . . .
deixis
   Be watchful of your beauty, Lady dear!
   How much hangs on *that* lamp, you cannot tell.

Indeed, metaphor may depend on context alone:

Eat, drink, and be merry, for tomorrow you die.

This would not be metaphorical if uttered by a guard delivering the last meal to a condemned prisoner.

The metaphor, then, with its variety of grammatical forms, emerges through our knowledge of the world (and in this discussion, I ignore the difference between metaphor and simile). If I say "From Los Angeles, I sailed to New York in a great silver ship," your metaphorical interpretation of that statement will depend upon your knowledge of United States geography and modern transportation systems, though, of course, it is quite possible that I took a sailing ship through the Panama Canal or around the Horn.

Whatever its form, the metaphor is meaningless as metaphor unless, to use Richards' terms, we can identify its tenor and vehicle, which is to say, in fact, that all metaphors are somehow a vehicle predicated of a tenor, or, if you will, that all metaphors *can be* expressed as a predicate nominal sentence.

	Tenor	(is/are)	*Vehicle*
All the world's a stage	world		stage
the bird of Time	Time		bird
the black bat, night	night		black bat
O wild West Wind, thou breath of Autumn's being	wild West Wind		breath of Autumn's being
Be watchful of your beauty . . . that lamp. . . .	beauty		lamp
Eat, drink, and be merry. . . .	life		a day
Sheathe thy impatience	impatience		sword
the tawny-hided desert crouches	desert		lion

I am not arguing, of course, that when we process language we go through the kind of transformation that I have illustrated, and specifically I am avoiding the argument over the nature of deep structure or whether it has any psychological reality. Quite obviously, however, metaphors are, to use Bogen's term, *propositional* in nature.

Not only are they propositional—they are verbal in a specific way. Suppose I say to you, "Eat, drink, and be merry, for tomorrow you die." And suppose you ask me what I mean. I can propositionalize: "Well, I was only trying to tell you that 'life is but a day.'" Suppose further that you are still unsatisfied and ask me to clarify my meaning; I will tell you bluntly that I mean "life is short." With "*short*," I will have arrived at an *intermediate term*, beyond which I can still go to make my meaning more explicit: Life is only a few hours in the sum of eternity; birth is like waking in the morn, and death is like going to sleep at night; in one day, there is time for few pleasures. . . .

Another example. A particularly obstreperous child says to me, "Oink, oink!"

"What do you mean by that?"

"I mean that *you are a pig.*" (propositionalization)

"Why am I a pig?"

"Because you're *unpleasant*." (intermediate term)

"Why am I unpleasant?"

"Because you're greedy, rude, fat, smelly. . . ."

In both of these examples, we have seen that there are *intermediate* levels beyond which we can go in explanation of the metaphors and also that there are *rockbottom* levels beyond which we cannot go. The rockbottom level is the most specific level of explanation.

It is now perhaps apparent why I say that metaphor is a particularly verbal kind of figure. We explain metaphor by resorting to sets of terms, *not to counter-images*. (Shortly, we will be considering imagery, and we will see that explanations of images take place through the construction of counter-images; this difference in explanatory strategies clarifies the difference in function and effect between metaphor and image.) I believe that we always explain metaphor with *rockbottom terms* or with further metaphors, which in turn can be explained with rockbottom terms:

Eat, drink, and be merry, for tomorrow you die.

Birth is (like) waking in the morn, and death is (like) going to sleep at night.

Life is a day.

Life is short.

Enjoy yourself while you can.

The particularly verbal nature of metaphor becomes clearer when we compare metaphor with image. One of the most famous of all imagist poems is this, by William Carlos Williams:

The Red Wheelbarrow

so much depends
upon

a red wheel
barrow

glazed with rain
water

beside the white
chickens.

How do we begin to "explain" this image? To be sure, we can metaphorize it: red wheelbarrow (tenor) is purity, childhood, life, machine, etc. (vehicle). However, such a reading of the poem is simply unwarranted, as our complete uncertainty

about vehicle indicates. In the case of imagery, it seems that the poem should not mean, but be. And yet the poem *does* mean, but *not* in any metaphorical sense. Whereas metaphor in poetry is relatively easy to explain or "explicate," the image is elusive and difficult.

Take the first few lines of "The Love Song of Alfred Prufrock," for example. Ignoring certain "embedded" metaphors, we can see that these lines present an alternation of metaphors and images:

Let us go then, you and I,

When the evening is spread out against
    the sky
Like a patient
    etherized upon a table;   *metaphor*

Let us go, through certain half-deserted
    streets,
The muttering retreats
Of restless nights in one-night cheap
    hotels
And sawdust restaurants with oyster-
    shells: *image*

Streets that follow like a tedious
    argument
of insidious intent   *metaphor*
To lead you to an overwhelming
    question . . .

Oh, do not ask, 'What is it?'
Let us go and make our visit.

In the room the women
    come and go
Talking of Michelangelo [30]   *image*

Note how relatively easy it is to explain the meaning of the metaphors. Since the evening is spread out against the sky like a patient etherized upon a table, the evening is passive, inert, in someone else's hands, sick, hovering between life and death, stifling. But note also how difficult it is to explain the "meaning" of the images. "In the room the women come and go/Talking of Michelangelo"—but what does that *mean*?

In fact, I think, the only way for me to explain what that image means is to present counter-images and thus to construct a set of images, of which the original would be a part. The original image, then, would be a *synecdoche*, a part standing for the whole category that constituted the meaning of the one image for me.

My purpose here is to discuss the nature of poetry, not literary criticism, and yet I cannot resist an instructive and essentially relevant digression to illustrate my point about metaphorical versus synecdochic explication. Years ago, I read Yeats' account of the composition of "Leda and the Swan." As I recall, Yeats talked about getting so caught up with the *image* of the poem that nothing else mattered, and I think that the *experience* of the poem gives the reader something of the inexpressible—or at least inchoate—intensity of a painting of the same subject. Insofar as the poem "works," it does so as an image, not as a statement. But what can one *say about* an image? As we have seen, it is relatively easy to talk about metaphor, to explicate the metaphor in essentially metalinguistic terms. No metalanguage serves to clarify the image as image, however. (How would one give a metalinguistic explication of "The Red Wheelbarrow"?)

It turns out, I think, that the need to explicate—whatever the source of that need—forces us to metaphorize the image, a result that in itself is neither good nor bad. For instance, here is Richard Ellmann on "Leda and the Swan":

Could power and knowledge ever exist together in this world, or were they, as he

(Yeats) had reason to suspect, contraries ever at war? Was wisdom the ripe fruit obtainable only when the sense of taste was gone?[31]

In this ingenious (and to me, at least, particularly rich) interpretation of the poem, Ellmann uses the gambit of metaphorization:

Zeus is power.

Leda is knowledge.

Rape is war.

I am hinting strongly, of course, that metaphor relates closely to what we know about the LH, that it is naturally easier to explain "meanings" in LH than in RH terms, and, finally, that explications which we might characterize as RH will sound naive, typically beginning with that sure clue to the affective "fallacy," "This remainds me of . . ."

Let's think about images in poetry. One of the powers of metaphor, certainly, is that it propositionalizes *imagistically* (or usually does so): "night is a black bat," "the stars are the candles of the night," "life is but a walking shadow," "we devour our time like am'rous birds of prey," and so on. "Eat, drink, and be merry" is more powerful than its reduced propositionalized version ("life is a day") precisely because it is more imagistic in quality. But as we have seen, one of the important characteristics of metaphor is its amenability to metalinguistic explanation.

The image has a "purity" which is quite arbitrary and depends wholly on the reader in that any reader can metaphorize any image, as we have seen to be the case with both "The Red Wheelbarrow" and "Leda and the Swan." When the image is "pure," explication becomes difficult, if not impossible, for, as we shall see, it is difficult to talk about the meanings of images.

I want to use "Prufrock" as my example, for it is the first modern poem that I took seriously. In 1948 on the banks of the Truckee River in Reno, Nevada, I decided to make the first step toward overcoming my all-too-obvious philistinism: I would get to know Eliot. (Joyce was second on my agenda. Twenty-nine years later, I realize that I have not reached my cultural goal and never will. Nonetheless.)

I began to read "Prufrock," resolving that I would understand its every word and then memorize the whole. The details of this experience—even the setting—still live vividly for me. With the first few lines, I gained a tremendous sense of power, for I could well understand the evening's being an etherized patient stretched out against the sky. I had words to express my understanding and sensed that I could argue cogently in favor of my interpretation.

Immediately, though, I was frustrated. How could I explain the full sense that I got from the images? (I did not yet have that term.) What did sawdust restaurants with oyster-shells "mean"? Even more puzzling: women in a room talking of Michelangelo? Of course, I resorted to a strategy that embarrassed me even then: "These passages remind me . . ." The only way I could begin to express what had happened to me in my reading was to give examples of similar scenes and events from my own experience. Even at the age of eighteen, I realized that such naive understanding was unacceptable—though I was not awfully precocious, and though I was a student at

one of the most humble and practical state universities. I was stymied—in just the same way that most readers of poetry are stymied when they want to or are forced to discuss their experience of imagistic poetry.

We have not, I assure you, wandered from our purposes: to discuss LH and RH in the experience of reading poetry. We have seen that there is good reason to characterize metaphoric interpretation as LH, and there is equally good reason to characterize the interpretation of images as RH.

You will recall our characterization of RH thought as *appositional, holistic, imagistic*. There is good reason to believe that the RH power of imaging is necessary even for some kinds of propositional thought. For example, in solving problems involving certain kinds of disjunction, the RH seems to be essential. In answering the following, the LH seems adequate: "Jim is taller than Bill. Who is taller?" But in the following, experiments have shown that imaging seems necessary: "Jim is taller than Bill. Who is shorter?"[32] And, of course, if our logic follows, the metaphor (which propositionalizes images) must be bihemispheric while the image can be associated largely with the functions of the RH. (Does bi-hemisphericity explain the power of metaphor, which, Longinus tells us, simply sweeps us away and thus is the most rhetorically cogent of the figures?)

Particularly skilled at establishing part-whole relationships, the RH is quite literally synecdochic in operation, synecdoche being the figure in which part stands for the whole: *All hands on deck! A fleet of twenty sails. I give my heart to you.* (Metonymy is the figure in which something closely associated with the object term is substituted for the term: *The crown commands, The pen is mightier than the sword.* For our purposes, the distinction between synecdoche and metonymy, like that between metaphor and simile, is ignored.)

To understand the argument regarding images in poetry, one must understand the psychological concept of the *cognitive category*,[33] itself a metaphor that explains a perfectly obvious property of thought: the tendency of the mind to categorize, the necessity to do so. When a child first learns to recognize four-footed creatures, all quadrupeds are quite likely to be "doggies." Experience enables the child to make differentiations and thus establish new, refined categories: "moo-cows," "kitties," "horsies." The child—or adult—makes differentiations very rapidly, on the basis of one or two examples. When the child sees one "horsie" and differentiates it from "doggie," the new category is established, the one horse being a synecdoche, a part representing the whole category. For many freshmen in college, a poem is a poem is a poem, but after a brief time in a literature class, the "poetry" becomes lyrics, narratives, sonnets, odes, etc. Thus, cognitive categories are hierarchical in arrangement and are created by and large through the observer's purpose.

In the experience of reading, an image is a synecdoche in just this sense: it is meaningful to the reader insofar as he or she can relate it to a set of like images, i.e., place it in a cognitive category. For this reason, in its effect the image is likely to be highly personal, even idiosyncratic.

An eminent brain researcher, Sir John Eccles, states the idea this way:

Our speculation has been extended to cover in principle the simplest aspects of imagination, imagery or the re-experiencing of images. In passing beyond this stage we may firstly consider a peculiar tendency to association of imagery, so that the experience of one image is evocative of other images, and these of still more and so on. When these images are of beauty and subtlety, blending in harmony and capable of being expressed in some language, verbal, musical or pictorial, so that transcendent experiences can be evoked in others, we have artistic creation of a simple or lyrical kind.[34]

While we might argue with the adjective "simple" in the above, certainly Eccles describes the lyrical experience.

All of this means, then, that a perfectly forthright explanation of the "meaning" of a poetic image is likely to be unacceptable in the academy, where the tradition demands "logical," impersonal explications.

In a brief essay, Roman Jakobson makes suggestions that relate to my argument here.[35] He points out that aphasia suppresses either the ability to express similarity (metaphor) or the ability to express contiguity (metonym). It would seem, then, that metaphor and metonym (or synecdoche) are polar functions of language, even if they cannot be associated directly with LH and RH.

Another intriguing hint comes from a theory about the genesis of language. Harry J. Jerison postulates that language evolved as a marking system, not as a system of communication.[36] Wolves and other predators mark their territory with urine, their highly developed olfactory sense making this possible, whereas man, who has never had a highly developed olfactory system, signaled with sounds. In other words, language was first used to produce (evoke) images, and it still is so used. Whether or not Jerison is right—and we will never know—certainly the power of the image is mysterious and basic, felt in our right-handed, logical culture, but largely inexpressible because of our hemispheric bias.

According to the logic of this argument so far, the bilateral symmetry of the organ within our skulls—anatomical symmetry with complementarity of function—destines us for the poetic experience, both productive and receptive. If it turns out in fact that most people take no joy in poetry, find no real meaningfulness in it, we must look for a social influence of enormous power—enough to overcome "basic human nature," and we realize that even jails have not been successful at that.

I would suggest that we look at our right-handed schools, which both reflect and influence the development of our culture. In most literature classes—from the public schools through graduate seminars—it is impossible to respond to the synecdochic quality of poetry in the way that I have argued is necessary, using the LH-RH distinction at least as the analogical basis for my argument. The emphasis on *explication de texte* and the critical essay warps the total poetic experience and serves, I think, to alienate people from poetry.[37]

LH, RH, AND READING

What we know about brain function helps us understand the process of reading. In the following, I will not cover territory already explored in standard sources, but will attempt to suggest new directions for inquiry and explain some of my own recent insights.[38]

First, I would like to point out some obvious, but generally unnoticed, characteristics of texts and the reading process.

Texts can be roughly categorized on the basis of their *temporal organization* and their poetic or *nonpoetic character*. (For "temporal organization" we could substitute "appositional or propositional organization" or "lyric or nonlyric form.") Most novels and dramas, narrative poems, and other works take chronological sequence as their principle of organization. Lyric poems and some modern works of prose fiction and drama do not take chronological sequence as their organizing principle. Nonpoetic works such as sets of instructions, journals, logs, and so on are chronologically organized. Nonpoetic works such as collections of sayings, the larger structure of the present discussion, and other writings do not take chronological sequence as their organizing principle.

Recently, I encountered a perfect description of an atemporal, nonpoetic text: specifically, a study of William Faulkner, written by John T. Irwin. Irwin's description is well worth repeating:

As I look back on the writing [of the book], I suppose that, stylistically, I was trying to weave a kind of seamless garment, and that that was necessary because the structure of what I was trying to reveal exists only as a whole, exists not as the sum of its elements, not by the simple addition of those elements, but rather through the simultaneous multiplication of every element by every other element. What I tried to evoke was a kind of synergism in which the structure in its irreducible wholeness is infinitely more than simply the sum of its parts, for, strictly speaking, *considered as structure, a continuous system of differences*, it has no parts, no independently meaningful, logically separable units. . . .

At one point I simply had to ask myself if I thought that it was possible to present a holistic, simultaneous structure in the temporal, successive medium of written discourse. My answer was, "Of course not"—not if by "present" one meant "explain." But it seemed to me that I could come as close as possible to presenting that structure by trying to embody it in the structure of my own text. The model I used as a starting point for that attempt was the musical, motival structure of Lévi-Strauss's *The Raw and the Cooked*. In order to achieve the multiple counterpointing effect that is the great strength of that method, I had to try to create within my text a kind of multidimensional imaginative space in which there existed the possibility of simultaneously placing every element side by side with every other element.[39]

In this connection one might also— with great trepidation—evoke Marshall McLuhan.

Diagrammatically, what I am saying works out like this:

	TEMPORAL		A-TEMPORAL
POETIC	novels dramas etc.	. . .	lyric poems some novels some dramas
		.	etc.
NON-POETIC	sets of instructions journals logs, etc.	. . . .	collections of sayings essays etc.

The distinction between poetic and non-poetic writings is determined by the reader, a bald statement that could well be (and indeed has been) the subject of a long essay in itself. What I mean is simply that the poetic/nonpoetic distinction is determined by the purpose of the reader. I can read *Heart of Darkness* as a fiction (poetic), as a treatise on colonialism (nonpoetic), as a document in the autobiography of Conrad (poetic *or* nonpoetic).

Related to, but distinct from, the contrast between poetic and nonpoetic writings is the nature of the reading experience itself. In *informational reading*, the purpose is to learn something, to gain information, the reader always aware of context, the text relating to or having the potential of relating to something "out there" in the real world of concepts and ideas. It is the kind of reading that most reading theorists talk about: the efficient processing of a text for *meaning*, which is commonly defined as "the reduction of uncertainty."[40] I am suggesting that most reading theorists deal with the multiple experiences of reading as if they were intended solely for the purpose of gaining information about the world "out there."

But there is another world, the world of the possible, which is the root of the distinction that Northrop Frye makes between poetic and nonpoetic texts. The poetic text delineates a possible world. The text that delineates an actual world is not poetic.[41]

I am not suggesting, of course, that the distinctions I outline are clearcut. Is a work such as *In Cold Blood* or even *The Grapes of Wrath* a delineation of an actual world? The answer, as I have said, lies in the purpose of the reader, but it is obvious that some texts, like *The Grapes of Wrath*, have more potential for being taken as nonpoetic than do others, such as *Vathek*.

When the work is (taken as) poetic, the delineating of a possible world, the reading experience is quite different from that of the non-poetic work in that the reading becomes solipsistic, the purpose being to *immerse* oneself, not to test the text against reality or to gain information. If there is such a phenomenon as *informational reading* on the one hand, there is also such an experience as *esthetic immersion*.

At the moment, I am reflecting on my own writing problem here. It seems to me that I need some way to "verify" the distinction I am making between informational reading and esthetic immersion. I need support—preferably in the form of unimpeachable authority—but I think there is no such "outside support" to be found in the scholarship of reading or of literary theory. The best authority is oneself, one's own experience of reading. In the experience of esthetic immersion, the ties with reality (with the "context," in Roman Jakobson's term) are either cut or suppressed. One lives more or less exclusively in the world of the work, and there are no "practical" consequences to the reading. Everyone who passionately reads poetry or fiction has had this experience.

But there is a paradox. Since we read with our minds, *not* our eyes, the text is meaningful only insofar as we can relate it to our experience, and as we make this relation, we change the nature of our experience by expanding it, so that, through reading, we gain knowledge. Consider (with Kenneth Burke) *Madame Bovary*, a prime example from the naturalistic school. Flaubert has "displaced" the mythic underpinning of his tale to give it its lifelike quality. But, as Frye says,

The realistic writer soon finds that the requirements of literary form and plau-

sible content always fight against each other. Just as the poetic metaphor is always a logical absurdity, so every inherited convention of plot in literature is more or less mad.[42]

As Burke points out, the novel is nothing more than a definition of the god-term of its title, Madame Bovary. Just as the poet displaces myth to give it credibility, verisimilitude, life-likeness, so the reader who is esthetically immersed displaces. The esthetic purpose of reading *Madame Bovary* is to define "*Madame Bovary*." Once that definition is made, the reader has a powerful tool for understanding reality; he or she is in command of the complex concept "*Madame Bovary*," which can be used to illuminate and deal with experience. In the reading, the naturalistic content is "displaced" to make way for the experience of the novel. For this reason, the most improbable possible world *can be* as real in the act of reading as the most probable. In esthetic immersion, *Madame Bovary* is no more real than one of Philip José Farmer's outrageous fictions. The more "real" the novel is to the reader, the less of a poem it becomes. The poem has a reality of its own. This reality is, of course, in the mind of the reader, a mythic reality.

Frye's outline of the process whereby we grasp the mythic reality of the fiction—the plotted poetic work—squares nicely with brain theory. When we read a fictional work,

continuity is the center of our attention; our later memory, or what I call the possession of it, tends to become discontinuous [appositional]. Our attention shifts from the sequence of incidents to another focus: a sense of what the work of fiction was all *about*, or what criticism usually calls its theme. And we notice that as we go on to study and reread the work of fiction, we tend not to reconstruct the plot, but to become conscious of the theme, and to see all incidents as manifestations of it. Thus the incidents themselves tend to remain, in our critical study of the work, discontinuous [a-temporal], detached from one another and regrouped in a new way.[43]

The fiction becomes mythos and thus takes on the character of lyric.

Put into "brain" terms, Frye is describing the reading of fictions in this way. The images (RH) are perceived in their temporal sequence (LH). In retrospect, the sequentiality of the images disappears, and the work becomes a gestalt (RH). Any one of the images becomes a synecdoche (RH) for the whole. In discussing *Moby-Dick*, for instance, any one of the synecdochic images, frequently the substance of one chapter, can become "the point of entry"—"The Candles," "The Try-Works," "The Doubloon." In this sense, the mythos of the fiction is analogous to the cognitive category.

The experience of reading should convince us that the most closely reasoned essays have the same organizational principle as fiction: the temporal, in that A must come before B in order for B to make sense, and B must come before C—though it is the case that few essays in my experience have this kind of tight logic, most not being of the nature of St. Thomas Aquinas. Once we have finished reading, we have the "meaning" or the equivalent of mythos, but seldom can we put the details of the argument together in a satisfactory fashion.

Other dynamics are working here, however. In writings based on temporal sequence, it should be the case that readers would attempt to "re-duce" them to mythos or "meaning." One of my students has suggested, though, that there may well be—and probably are—readers who tend always to be reductive and others who tend always to be constructive. In her experiment, Judith Walcutt presented a variety of kinds of prose to readers: poems, recipes, sets of instructions, and so on. She revealed these texts to her subject readers in small increments, in effect uncovering them virtually line by line. What she found is that some readers always tend to "reduce," to seek out the central mythos or meaning, while other construct their own possible worlds—poems, fictions, fantasies, speculations—on the basis of the individual segments of the text as they are revealed.

Reductive readers seem determined to make *the* sense out of the text; constructive readers seem to be triggered into their own creative processes by the synecdochic nature of the individual segments of the text. In our terms, reductive readers seem to be LH, while constructive readers seem to be RH.

So far we have been dealing primarily with those texts which are organized on the basis of what Kenneth Burke terms syllogistic progression.[44] Lyrics and other writings do not have such a structure. The sections of "The Waste Land," for example, could well be rearranged without affecting the integrity of the work as a whole.[45] Or compare *Moby-Dick* with *The Moonstone*. To be sure, *Moby-Dick* has a chronological organization based on the sequence of the voyage, but its organization is primarily lyric, the individual chapters being synecdochic for the whole.

We will return to the a-temporal (lyric, appositional) mode hereafter, but for the moment, I would like to relate our key terms—esthetic immersion and informational reading, temporal and a-temporal organization—more clearly to what we know about brain function.

Ordinary consciousness, Robert E. Ornstein says, "involves analysis, a separation of oneself from other objects and organisms."[46] The experience of esthetic immersion in reading is, then, not ordinary consciousness, but extraordinary. One does not analyze, does not "stand back" and achieve separation from the text. The informational reader must maintain contact with context, with the world "out there" which the text deals with; the text at every moment relates to context and, conversely, gives one access to context. Esthetic immersion, resulting from a willing suspension of disbelief, breaks that contact.

Esthetic immersion is a matter of *attention*. If I am reading a set of instructions for operating a new electric razor, the razor itself—"out there"—will be literally or figuratively before me; there will be an attention ratio between the set of instructions and their referent. But, as Frye point out, in poetic discourse there is no such ratio, poetic discourse constructing, by definition, only possible worlds, worlds, that is, of the imagination.

Attention is, to be sure, neurologically determined. "It is well known to psychologists that those features of the most elementary, involuntary attention of the type which is attracted by the most powerful or biologically significant stimuli can be observed very early on, during the first few months of the child's development."[47] Voluntary attention, however, "is not biological in its origins, but a social

act. . . . It can be interpreted as the introduction of factors which are the product, not of the biological maturing of the organism, but of forms of activity created in the child during his relations with adults, into the organization of this complex regulation of selective mental activity."[48]

In Piaget's characterization of cognitive growth, one finds two parameters. First, the child discovers "otherness," that he or she is separated from the world "out there," a process that begins almost at birth and is completed at about eight years. Second, the child develops the ability for operational and abstract thinking, "the possibility of utilizing formal operations, which are completely abstract, conceptual tools."[49] The child begins to understand reality, gains the ability to use abstract thinking to deal with that reality, growing from the world of story to the world of science, developing the possibility of using reading as a tool for manipulating the world, i.e., the possibility of informational reading.

For the child, "Little Red Riding Hood" is an experience; for the adult, this myth can be regarded as an allegory concerning puberty and the onset of menstruation.[50] When the tale is used in an attempt to understand some facet of reality (of context), the reading is informational, not esthetic immersion.

Now, it is obvious that the development of cognition creates the possibility for *using* stories, particularly in Western societies, which are characterized as LH.[51] Crimes based upon fictions—cinematic, video, or prose—are only the most blatant examples. Nonetheless, the ability to experience stories—with wonder, intense curiosity about "what happens next," with terror, with absorption—remains always a possibility, though Western cognitive styles and, in particular, Western pedagogy tend to suppress and devalue this ability. *After* the experiences of reading, the adult also has the possibility of using the story as a cognitive instrument, a definition of a situation, the title or the name of a character becoming a tool of communication or a pivot for rational thought. During the experience of esthetic immersion, the story is *never* an instrument; I would like, almost, to say that it is prerational.

Note well: I am not dichotomizing; I take account of *both-and* as well as *either-or*. Almost simultaneously, the story can be *both* myth *and* instrument for the reader, so infinitely complex is the experience of reading.

The story is temporal (LH), *in medias res* being the most apparent example. "Processing" a story must be very much like processing a sentence or other verbal sequence, which in surface form must be a spatial-temporal sequence, the events in the story, like the phonemes or graphemes in the sentence, coming one after another, both conveying meanings, which by definition are atemporal. An analogy is the "deep structure" of a sentence, which has no linear or temporal dimension, so that both *I smoke cigars* and *Cigars are smoked by me* convey the same meaning in the sense that (a) predication and reference are the same and (b) roles are the same, i.e., in both versions we know that the same person is performing the same action with regard to the same thing. Any sensory array can be dealt with in two ways: serially (one at a time) or holistically. In reading, it appears that the RH processes data visuo-spatially, while the LH

processes it verbally. "Thus, while the left hemisphere goes through and sequentially transforms each letter into an internal acoustic code (i.e., names them), the right hemisphere examines all the letters simultaneously looking for a variation in shape."[52] If the terms "event" or "scene" are substituted for "letter," this must pretty well describe the process of reading temporally organized works.

However, we must distinguish between process and experience, since reading *anything* must involve somewhat the same process at one level. Even though reading a mystery by Dorothy Sayers (syllogistic progression) and a collection of poems by Adrienne Rich is based on the same "decoding" procedures, these procedures can be and usually are radically different in the larger sense—that is, we read the Sayers mystery from first page to last sequentially to get the meaning, but we can and probably do read the collection of poems in an almost random way. The experience of reading each may be immersion in the world of the possible, but there are differences, of course, for reading a murder mystery is not reading a series of poems. The similarity of the two experiences is in the connections that one does or does not make between the texts and the world "out there"—the immediate *uses* that one makes or does not make of the reading.

The best example of the atemporal text is the lyric. (Not all lyrics are appositional in form since the completely appositional lyric can be rearranged significantly with no loss of "coherence.") Many lyrics—perhaps the best ones—simply evaporate when one attempts to explicate them, for they are experience, transmitted from poet to reader, near the subjective pole of the subjective-objective dichotomy. Eccles gives a spectrum of experience that illuminates the nature of the "pure" lyric.

(a) The vision of an object. (The object can be touched, photographed, etc.)
(b) A pin prick. (Can be seen by an observer; can be duplicated in an observer; observer can see the wince of pain and hear the cry.)
(c) Ache or pain in a visceral organ. (Cannot be seen or duplicated, but can be generally described, even in a clinical sense.)
(d) Mental pain or anguish. (Not a consequence of physical stimulation, but can achieve public status through descriptions and clinical reports.)
(e) Dreams, memories (fantasies, etc.). Gain public status through "the wealth of communication that there is between observers."[53]

The subject matter of the lyric—dreams, memories, reveries, fantasies—is RH. The imagistic quality of lyrics if RH.

We can perform an experiment that will demonstrate the reading experience offered by the lyric—and again, I differentiate experience and process, for in process, the reading of a lyric might well be as sequential as reading a set of instructions (or, might be "attacked" as if the steps in their sequence were arranged appositionally, the holistic processing of serial displays being always a possibility). The *inner* process of reading a lyric, regardless of attack strategies, is quite different from the *inner* process of reading instructions.

Reprinted below is Lowell's "Colloquy in Black Rock." Read this poem in the following way: jump about from stanza to stanza, image to image, even word to word in a quite random way, until you feel that

you "know" the poem. Then ask yourself the sense in which you know it. Ask yourself, further, how you might go about transmitting that knowledge to another; ask yourself, indeed, whether you have knowledge of the poem in any traditional sense, i.e., in any sense that would allow you to provide a conventional, logical *explication de texte*.

Colloquy in Black Rock

Here the jack hammer jabs into the
    ocean:
My heart, you race and stagger and
    demand
More blood-gangs for your nigger-brass
    percussions,
Till I, the stunned machine of your
    devotion,
Clanging upon this symbol of a hand,
Am rattled screw and footloose. All
    discussions

End in the mud-flat detritus of death.
My heart, beat faster, faster. In Black
    Mud
Hungarian workmen give their blood
For the martyr Stephen, who was stoned
    to death.

Black Mud, a name to conjure with: O
    mud
For watermelons gutted to the crust,
Mud for the mole-tide harbor, mud for
    mouse,
Mud for the armored Diesel fishing tubs
    that thud
A year and a day to wind and tide; the
    dust
Is on this skipping heart that shakes my
    house,

House of our Savior who was hanged till
    death.
My heart, beat faster, faster. In Black
    Mud
Stephen the martyr was broken down to
    blood:
Our ransom is the rubble of his death.

Christ walks on the black water. In Black
    Mud

Darts the kingfisher. On Corpus Christi,
 heart,
Over the drum-beat of St. Stephen's choir
I hear him, *Stupor Mundi*, and the mud
Flies from his hunching wings and beak
 —my heart,
The blue kingfisher dives on you in fire.[54]

I posit that your experience of the poem can now be characterized something as follows: your "knowledge" consists of a series of images in apposition and a mood or emotion. I think, indeed, that the following equation is valid: *images in apposition + mood or emotion that they engender = knowledge of the lyric.* Our knowledge of the lyric is RH and thus difficult to express, unless we propositionalize, so that perhaps the only true "explication" of a lyric is another lyric.

A more superficial point can be made about "Colloquy in Black Rock": it offers many possibilities for rearrangement—but that, of course, is precisely the nature of apposition.

The power of the lyric is the experience that our right-handed civilization is organized to deprive us of. Which leads me to conclude with this from Eccles:

Entrancing displays of imagery that are reputed to be of great beauty and clarity can be experienced by ordinary people under the influence of hallucinogenic drugs such as mescaline or LSD. In parenthesis it should be noted that there are very few transmutations into literature or art of the transcendent esthetic experiences alleged to be enjoyed by drug addicts. One would suspect that in these conditions there would be an especial tendency for the formation of ever more complex and effectively interlocked patterns of neuronal activity involving large fractions of the cortical population of neurones. This would ac-

count for the withdrawal of the subject from ordinary activities during these absorbing experiences. Not unrelated to these states are the various psychoses where the inner experiences of the patients also cause them to be withdrawn.[55]

LH, RH, AND PRESENCE

One of the most important documents in "the new rhetoric" is *The New Rhetoric: A Treatise on Argument*, by Chaim Perelman and L. Olbrechts-Tyteca.[56] Among several key notions in the work is that of *presence*, the means whereby style gives arguments status, vividness, and extralogical power.

Presence seems to have these characteristics. First, that object or concept to which one directs attention assumes thereby more presence than other objects or concepts. In other words, the act of attention endows presence. Second, the image creates presence. Third, presence is conferred by holism. Perelman says,

Presence acts directly on our sensibility. As Piaget shows, it is a psychological datum operative already at the level of perception: when two things are set side by side, say a fixed standard and things of variable dimensions with which it is compared, the things on which the eye dwells, that which is best or most often seen, is, by that very circumstance, over-estimated. . . . Certain masters of rhetoric, with a liking for quick results, advocate the use of concrete objects in order to move an audience. . . . It should also be observed that the effort to make something present to the consciousness can relate not only to real objects, but also to a judgment or an entire argumentative development. As far as possible, such an effort is directed to filling the whole field of consciousness with this presence so as to isolate it, as it were, from the hearer's overall mentality.[57]

And Perelman quotes Bacon:

The affection beholdeth merely the present: reason beholdeth the future and sum of time. And therefore the present filling the imagination more, reason is commonly vanquished; but after that force of eloquence and persuasion hath made things future and remote appear as present, then upon the revolt of the imagination reason prevaileth.

After reading Perelman, we have a fairly good sense of what presence consists in, and yet an exact specification eludes us.

Aristotle, of course, had the same intuitions about presence that Bacon, Perelman, and many others have had. Logical proofs, he tells us in the *Rhetoric*, are developed through deduction on the basis of the enthymeme or through induction on the basis of example. In rhetoric, of course, the example does not have the power of statistical validity—and yet, Aristotle and our experience tell us, it does have great power: the power of creating presence.

As you can well foresee, I am about to argue that presence in argument comes about largely through RH functions. I am referring to the synecdochic power of the example-image, with its ability to evoke a cognitive category and to change that category by becoming a part of it. In this sense, the image not only creates presence by "triggering" the imaging power of the RH, but is also strictly dialectic, in that it adds to the available cognitive data of the perceiver.

We can postulate that the image affects cognition in at least two ways: first, by adding to and thus changing the cateory through enlarge-

ment, and, second, by triggering the creation of a new category. Paradoxically, the enlargement of a category always involves the creation of a new category due to hierarchical structure.

We can further postulate that some examples are *confirmative*, or *disconfirmative*, evoking in the reader (or hearer) that set of images, memories, and associations that represent an already existing category and thus creating presence, which results in adherence to or rejection of an idea through tacit demonstration that the subject under consideration is familiar. In this sense, they serve as the grounds for argument, and, as Perelman explains, argument can begin only on the basis of shared assumptions.[58]

Some examples are *constructive*, creating presence by triggering the construction of whole new cognitive categories in the reader or hearer and thus making whole new avenues of thought possible.

Some examples, of course, are *misfires*, neither confirming nor constructing either because they have not received attention or because they are so far outside the audience's experience that they cannot evoke or trigger the formation of a new set.

One function of style, assuredly, is to serve as an attention-getting device: inflection and emphasis in spoken discourse and figures of grammar in written.

I would argue that, to a large extent, presence is the lyric component of argument. The purest deduction is an abstract set of statements which are relationally valid; the purest induction is a set of examples in apposition. Deduction is typically LH; induction is typically RH. Rhetoric—as Aristotle posited—must use both deduction and induction, for rhetorical situations and subject matter are both right-handed and left-handed.

This discussion of presence leaves me dissatisfied, uneasy, realizing as I do that it consists largely of hints and generalities when the topic assuredly deserves a more thorough handling. Yet I have decided not to omit this section, for I would hope my stumbles, misfires, and occasional insights will generate interest and further thought and research.

CONCLUSION

Earl Miner has addressed himself to brain theory as it relates to the old speculation about literature as knowledge. Miner tells us that

The poet has not the Eureka discovery but the constant assistance of the right-hemispheric Muse. The artist must draw continually on typical right hemispheric activity. When that proves infeasible, "inspiration" is gone, "invention" is dried up. And while sustaining creativity with the right, the artist must also continually draw on left-hemispheric activity for elaboration and consistency of detail. Much more must the poet among artists rely on the linguistic performance of the left, to give his sustained creativity an intelligibility and word-brightness. It is such distinctions that give aesthetic knowledge its appositional character, its virtual or provisional status.[59]

From the standpoint of the aesthetic reader, bihemispheric activity seems equally crucial. For example, I have assembled some evidence (tentative though it may be) that extremely LH readers have no sense of the kind of episodic knowledge that poetry conveys. A typical comment, from one of my friends, is that poems and stories are "meaningless" to him: he is unable to imagine or visualize the synecdochic content.

If my speculations are correct, poetry is the paradoxical attempt to convey episodic knowledge verbally, which, of course, can never be totally successful.

My friend Jay Martin has posited that Henry Miller confronted himself with a dual problem, to speak the unspeakable and to say the unsayable. As both Miller and D. H. Lawrence demonstrated, the unspeakable can be spoken, though often at enormous personal risk and sacrifice; however, each also demonstrated the ultimate futility of attempting to say the unsayable, and both artists, late in their careers, turned to painting.

In an inspired, fascinating, and outrageous book, *The Origin of Consciousness in the Breakdown of the Bicameral Mind,* Julian Jaynes has posited that consciousness as we know it developed very late in the evolution of humanity.[60] Lawrence and Miller struggled in their work to reunite consciousness, to bring about a harmonious balance between the propositional knowledge of the LH and the appositional knowledge of the RH, and in this, I think, they were typical of all poets.

But, of course, our concern is not with brain physiology and most assuredly not with cell structure and function. In fact, the rhetorician is not so much interested in brain as in mind.

Modern brain studies—as this discussion has tried to show—give us a new and unique understanding of mind, which must result in productive new directions for theorizing, scholarship, and experimentation in rhetoric and stylistics. If the paper stimulates that activity, it will have served its purpose.

NOTES

1. A brief and lucid account of this history is Steven Rose, "The Development of the Brain Sciences," in *The Conscious Brain* (New York: Vintage, 1976), pp. 21–48.

2. A. R. Luria, *The Working Brain: An Introduction to Neuropsychology*, trans. Basil Haigh (New York: Basic Books, 1973), pp. 306–7.

3. Morris Moscovitch, "On the Representation of Language in the Right Hemisphere of Right-Handed People," *Brain and Language*, 3 (Jan., 1976), 47–71.

4. Maureen Dennis and Harry A. Whitaker, "Language Acquisition Following Hemidecortication: Linguistic Superiority of the Left over the Right Hemisphere of Right-Handed People," *Brain and Language*, 3 (July, 1976), 404–33.

5. J. E. Bogen, "Some Educational Aspects of Hemispheric Specialization," *UCLA Educator*, 17 (Spring, 1975), 27. An expanded version of this issue of the *UCLA Educator* is now available: M. C. Wittrock and others, *The Human Brain* (Englewood Cliffs, N.J.: Prentice-Hall, 1977).

6. Bogen, 27.

7. Michael S. Gazzaniga, "Review of the Split Brain," *UCLA Educator*, 17 (Spring 1975), 9–12.

8. Robert D. Nebes, "Man's So-Called 'Minor' Hemisphere," *UCLA Educator*, 17 (Spring 1975), 13–16.

9. Stephen D. Krashen, "The Left Hemisphere," *UCLA Educator*, 17 (Spring 1975), 17–23.

10. Luria, p. 306.

11. Luria, p. 78.

12. "Letter to Jacques Hadamard," *The Creative Process*, ed. Brewster Ghiselin (New York: New American Library, n.d.), p. 43.

13. Nebes, p. 16.

14. Brendan A. Maher, "The Shattered Language of Schizophrenia," *Psychology Today*, 2 (Nov., 1968), pp. 30–33. See also S. R. Rochester, J. R. Martin, and S. Thurson, "Thought-Process Disorder in Schizophrenia: The Listener's Task," *Brain and Language*, 4 (Jan., 1977), 95–114.

15. To use the foregrounded style is "to present phenomena in a fully externalized form, visible and palpable in all their parts, and completely fixed in spatial and temporal relations." "On the other hand [in the backgrounded style], the externalization of only so much of the phenomena as is necessary for the purposes of the narrative, all else left in obscurity; the decisive points of the narrative alone are emphasized, what lies between in nonexistent; time and place are undefined and call for interpretation; thoughts and feelings remain unexpressed, are only suggested by the silence and the fragmentary speakers; the whole, permeated with the most unrelieved suspense and directed toward a single goal (and to that extent far more of a unity) remains mysterious and 'fraught with background.'" Erich Auerbach, *Mimesis: The Representation of Reality in Western Literature*, trans. Willard R. Trask (Princeton: Princeton Univ. Pr., 1968), pp. 6, 11–12.

16. See the section on presence in this essay.

17. Luria, pp. 78–79.

18. Adam F. Wechsler, "Crossed Aphasia in an Illiterate Dextral," *Brain and Language*, 3 (April, 1976), 164–72.

19. Much of that work is assembled in *Contemporary Rhetoric: A Conceptual Background with Readings*, ed. W. Ross Winterowd (New York: Harcourt Brace Jovanovich, 1975).

20. Richard E. Young and Alton L. Becker, "Toward a Modern Theory of Rhetoric: A Tagmemic Contribution," and Francis Christensen, "A Generative Rhetoric of the Paragraph," in *Contemporary Rhetoric*, pp. 123–43.

21. Carl R. Rogers, "Toward a Theory of Creativity," *Creativity and Its Cultivation*, ed. Harold H. Anderson (New York: Harper and Row, 1959), p. 71.

22. Rogers, pp. 78–80.

23. Arthur Koestler, *The Act of Creation* (New York: Dell, 1967).

24. James L. Adams, *Conceptual Blockbusting: A Guide to Better Ideas* (San Francisco: W. H. Freeman, 1974).

25. John Crowe Ransom, "Poetry: A Note in Ontology," in *Critical Theory since Plato*, ed. Hazard Adams (New York: Harcourt Brace Jovanovich, 1971), p. 880.

26. "The Apprehension of Metaphor," *Language and Style*, 14 (Winter 1981), 20–33.

27. Christine Brooke-Rose, *A Grammar of Metaphor* (Atlantic Highlands, N.J.: Hillary House, 1958).

28. Laurence Perrine, "Four Forms of Metaphor," in *Contemporary Rhetoric*, pp. 19–37.

29. In *Collected Earlier Poems*. Copyright 1938 by William Carlos Williams. Reprinted by permission of New Directions Publishing Corporation.

30. In *Collected Poems 1909–1962*. Copyright 1936 by Harcourt Brace Jovanovich, Inc. Reprinted by permission of the publisher.

31. I found this quotation written in the margin of my copy of Yeats, probably dating from about 1959. Apparently as long as twenty-five years ago, I had begun to have intuitions about metaphor and image.

32. Alfonso Caramazza, Joel Gordon, Edgar B. Ziff, and David de Luca, "Right Hemispheric Damage and Verbal Problem Solving Behavior," *Brain and Language*, 3 (Jan., 1976), 41–46.

33. Frank Smith, "On Making Sense," in *Comprehension and Learning* (New York: Holt, Rinehart and Winston, 1975), pp. 9–48.

34. John C. Eccles, *Facing Reality* (Heidelberg and Berlin: Springer-Verlag, 1970), p. 57.

35. Roman Jakobson, "The Metaphoric and Metonymic Poles," in *Critical Theory since Plato*, pp. 113–16.

36. Harry J. Jerison, "Evolution of the Brain," *UCLA Educator*, 17 (Spring 1975), 1–8.

37. This is much the same point that Keith Fort makes in his excellent essay, "Form, Authority, and the Critical Essay," *College English*, 32 (March, 1971), 629–39.

38. For an overview of reading theory, I suggest Frank Smith, *Understanding Reading*, Third Ed. (New York: Holt, Rinehart and Winston, 1982).

39. John T. Irwin, *Doubling and Incest/Repetition and Revenge: A Speculative Reading of Faulkner* (Baltimore: Johns Hopkins, 1975), pp. 6–7.

40. Smith, *Understanding Reading*, pp. 35–38.

41. This idea occurs again and again in Frye. See, for instance, "Nature and Homer," in *Fables of Identity* (New York: Harcourt Brace Jovanovich, 1963).

42. Northrop Frye, "Myth, Fiction, and Displacement," *Fables of Identity*, p. 36.

43. Frye, p. 23.

44. Kenneth Burke, *Counter-Statement* (Los Altos, Cal.: Hermes Press, 1953), p. 124.

45. See W. Ross Winterowd, "Beyond Style," *Philosophy and Rhetoric*, 5 (Spring, 1972), 88–110.

46. Robert E. Ornstein, *The Psychology of Consciousness* (New York: Penguin, 1975), p. 61.

47. Luria, p. 258.

48. Luria, p. 262.

49. Rose, p. 200.

50. I have encountered such an interpretation, though I cannot cite the source. The point is not so much that such an interpretation *was* made, but that it *might well be* made.

51. Ornstein discusses the problem of hemispherical dominance in whole societies as do Warren D. Ten Houten and Charles D. Kaplan, *Science and Its Mirror Image* (New York: Harper and Row, 1973).

52. Nebes, p. 15.

53. Eccles, pp. 52–53.

54. Robert Lowell, *Lord Weary's Castle and the Mills of the Kavanaughs* (New York: Harcourt Brace Jovanovich, 1951), p. 11. Reprinted by permission of the publisher.

55. Eccles, pp. 57–58.

56. Trans. John Wilkinson and Purcell Weaver (Notre Dame: Notre Dame University, 1969).

57. Perelman and Olbrechts-Tyteca, pp. 116–18.

58. Perelman and Olbrechts-Tyteca, pp. 65–114.

59. Earl Miner, "That Literature Is a Kind of Knowledge," *Critical Inquiry*, 2 (Spring, 1976), 505.

60. Julian Jaynes, *The Origin of Consciousness in the Breakdown of the Bicameral Mind* (Boston: Houghton Mifflin, 1976).

The Rhetoric of Beneficence, Authority, Ethical Commitment, and the Negative

In one sense, this essay results from my reading of four quite extraordinary works: Charles Fillmore's "The Case for Case," John Robert Ross's "On Declarative Sentences," J. L. Austin's *How to Do Things with Words*, and John Searle's *Speech Acts*. To a certain extent "The Rhetoric of Beneficence" is an essay in grammar and speech act theory. It is also, however, an essay in the philosophy of good reasons. It pleases me to realize that a set of values is the fuel that makes language go and that those values are the ones named in my title. (Note that they show up in the last section of the first part of this book, the "Coda: On Teaching Composition.")

There are two aspects of the essay that I wish I had been wise enough to avoid. In the first place, I regret the attempt to explain language values in terms of a binary chart; my interest in linguistics trapped me in the same cul-de-sac that linguists had built for themselves. Furthermore, I wish that I had stated the obvious: that the values I identify—beneficence, commitment, and authority—are scenic, as is the whole of semantic intention. The implication of my essay is that the values are built into language, much as the genetic code is built into humans, when, in fact, we know that meaning is "out there," in what Jakobson calls "context" and Burke calls "scene," and "up there" in the minds of the audience, not "down there" on the printed page, for that page is only a set of instructions for the derivation of meaning.

In the following discussion, I would like to explore rhetorical force in sentences. Arguments in the rhetorical sense can, of course, never be mere sentences (or at least I cannot imagine a sentence which is also a rhetorical argument), even though they can be such in the logical sense. However, as I will suggest toward the end of this paper, what we find out concerning the rhetorical force of sentences can be extended to true rhetorical arguments and to literature. In fact, starting with analysis of

This essay is reprinted from *Philosophy and Rhetoric* (Spring 1976), by permission of The Pennsylvania State University Press, University Park, PA.

the sentence has the virtue of concision and neatness, advantages to be prized in an area so large and essentially messy as rhetoric.

The first point I want to make concerning *intention* has been stated again and again. Simply, we cannot fully interpret a sentence until we can supply an intention for it. If I say to you, "I'll be here tomorrow," you cannot really take the sentence as anything but a mere utterance (which it undeniably is) until you can determine what I'm getting at. The ambiguity of the sentence (which, undoubtedly, a context would eliminate) concerns precisely what I am calling intention. Namely, you must know whether I am *promising* or *stating*. I can clarify this point—if it needs clarification—through an anecdote. Suppose that Dorothy comes into my office and I say to her, "You're looking lovely today." And suppose that she answers, "What do you mean by that?" The fact that she must ask my meaning indicates that meaning has not been *consummated*, indicates, in fact, she she is suspicious of my intention, though it would never occur to me

or to you that she wanted a definition of the sentence in the conventional sense. Her question has indicated her uncertainty about my intention.

It turns out that there is a class of verbs which can be used to specify intention whenever and wherever it is in doubt. These are the *performatives*, verbs with which the saying is the doing. When an ordained minister in the proper setting (etc.) says, "I hereby *pronounce* you man and wife," he is not only saying something; he is doing it. To state the point another way: the saying is the doing.

Among the performative verbs are the following: advise, answer, appoint, ask, authorize, beg, bequeath, beseech, caution, cede, claim, close, command, condemn, counsel, dare, declare, demand, empower, enquire, entreat, excommunicate, grant, implore, inform, instruct, offer, order, pledge, pronounce, propose, request, require, say, sentence, vow, warn, write.[1]

If you put any of these verbs into declarative, positive, first person sentences in the present tense, you have performative sentences. Thus:

Performative	Nonperformative
I (hereby) *advise* you to stop smoking.	Advise me to stop smoking.
I (hereby) *answer* your question.	I don't answer your question.
I (hereby) *appoint* you chairman.	They appoint you chairman.
I (hereby) *ask* you the time.	I asked you the time.

Notice that we gain some clarification of the nature of performatives by the fact that they easily take the modification of the adverb *hereby*.

That much is interesting, and has been extremely useful to ordinary

language philosophers such as Austin and Searle. But it turns out that performatives are extremely interesting to rhetoricians also. A minor interest has already been stated. When a declarative sentence is nonperformative, its intention can be made explicit by stating the sentence in question as the object of a performative verb.

Let me give just a couple of brief examples to clarify this point. The sentence *You should stop smoking* might well be ambiguous as to intention, even in context, but the following sentence is unambiguous: *I (hereby) advise you that you should stop smoking.* Such also is the case with the following two sentences: *I'll never take another drink. I (hereby) vow that I'll never take another drink.*

Performative verbs *state* intentions, and thus I like to call them "verbs of intention." Each of the verbs, like all verbs, can, of course, be nominalized, and thus they give us names for intentions:

I'll pick the strawberries. I (hereby) *state* that I'll pick the strawberries. (The sentence is a statement.)
You might like sherry. I (hereby) *suggest* that you might like sherry. (The sentence is a suggestion.)

It seems self-evident (to me, at least) that intention is a part of meaning in sentences, and ordinary language philosophy lends me support, for the total speech act consists, roughly, of *utterance acts* (the mere uttering of morphemes, words, etc.), *propositional acts* (predicating and referring), *illocutionary acts* (stating, questioning, promising, threatening, etc.), and *perlocutionary acts* (achieving effects, such as frightening, convincing, informing).[2] And I am arguing that performatives are verbs of intention.

But, indeed, the discussion so far has been pretty much old hat, covering a hoary noggin. The rhetorician will become interested in the concept of performatives just at the point where the grammarian will be roused from his lethargy by the possibility of structural analysis. And it is to the structure of the performative proposition that I would now like to turn.

I draw my first premises (which, I think, will finally be pretty much self-evident) from the concepts advanced by Charles Fillmore in his now classic essay "The Case for Case."[3] Fillmore argues that, from one point of view, a sentence is a two-part structure, consisting of modality and proposition. The modality consists of such functions-on-the-sentence-as-a-whole as tense, modal auxiliaries, and so on. Thus, in *I smoke cigars*, the modality is simply present tense, and in *Norma can make pancakes*, the modality is present tense plus the modal *can*. The modality, however, need not concern us; it is the proposition that we must explore. The proposition in a sentence is made up of a predicate plus the grammatical "roles" or "cases" that function with the predicate and in relation to one another. Thus, for instance, we can analyze the proposition of *Jeff changes the oil* as

Predicate	Agent	Neutral
change:	Jeff	the oil

The proposition of *George gives Mary a whack with a bat* is something like this:

Predicate	Agent	Goal	Neutral	Instrumental
give:	George	Mary	a whack	with a bat

The names that I have chosen to give the roles in the example sentences are not significant. Fortunately, in our analysis of the propositions of performative sentences we need not concern ourselves with identifying and naming the various roles that can enter into nonperformative sentences, for performatives are relatively simply in their propositional structure.

pare this with *I hereby ask you to give me a dollar*. Clearly, the intent is that the speaker (Agent) will benefit. On the basis of this evidence alone, we can posit that the proposition of the performative sentence contains either Agent or Agent-Beneficiary (as the subject); either Oblique or Oblique-Beneficiary (in some sentences, as the indirect object usually); and Neutral. It is also the case that with some verbs, the benefit

Predicate	*Agent*	*Oblique*	*Neutral*
advise:	I	you	to be cautious
(I advise you to be cautious.)			
close:	I		this session
(I close this session.)			
pledge:	I	(to you)	that I'll be there
(I pledge [to you] that I'll be there.)			

Arbitrarily, we will choose the terms *agent, oblique,* and *neutral.* As we have seen, the Agent will always be expressed by a first person pronoun (I or we), and as we have already seen, there will frequently be an Oblique role, normally expressed by *you.*[4] Finally, there is a third role, the one which we have chosen to call Neutral. This is easily demonstrated, and is more easily explained through demonstration than otherwise: Clearly, however, this analysis, in its simplicity, leaves out virtually all of the information that is of interest to rhetoricians in their analysis of propositions. What it omits, in fact, is what I call the principle of *benefaction.*[5] Take the following sentence as an example: *I hereby bequeath you my watch.* It is a fact of the meaning of the sentence that the referent of the Oblique case will be the beneficiary of the consequence of my statement, and that person must believe that I intend him or her to be the beneficiary or the meaning of the sentence is not consummated. Com-

that Oblique receives will be *negative,* as in *I hereby condemn you to death.* (Later we will give full discussion to the principle of the negative. For the moment, I only want to argue that we can begin to understand the nature of the performative proposition by positing a feature—Beneficiary.) A survey of the performatives that we are dealing with will illustrate how the principle of beneficence works in the proposition. The following chart (fig. 1) will be incomplete, in that it will deal with only one use of each performative when, in fact, more than one use or "sense" might be possible.

Undoubtedly, the chart raises a great many questions, and it is admittedly sketchy. It is merely intended to suggest how benefaction is a grammatical-rhetorical principle just a bit further, stopping short, I hope, of running it into the ground. If I say, "I inform you that you've won the lottery," clearly the Oblique role is beneficiary, but if I say, "I inform you that you are guilty," the

Figure 1. Role Structure

Sentence (Pred. italicized)	Agent	Agent Benef	Oblique	Oblique Benef	Neutral
I *advise* you to save your money.	+			+	×
I *answer* your question.	+			+	×
I *appoint* you chairman.	+			+	×
I *ask* you the time.		+	+		×
I *authorize* you to act for me.	+			+	×
I *beg* your indulgence.		+	+		×
I *bequeath* you my watch.	+			+	×
I *beseech* you to stop.		+	+		×
I *caution* you to be careful.	+			+	×
I *cede* my claim to you.	+			+	×
I *claim* my rights from you.		+	+		×
I *close* this session.	+				×
I *command* you to stop.	+		+		×
I *condemn* you to death.	+			−	×
I *counsel* you to study.	+			+	×
I *dare* you to jump.	+		+		×
I *declare* a moratorium.	+				×
I *demand* satisfaction from you.		+		−	×
I *empower* you to vote.	+			+	×
I *enquire* after the answer (from you).		+	+		×
I *entreat* you to stop.		+	+		×
I *excommunicate* you.	+			−	
I *grant* (you) your claim.	+			+	×

(Fig. 1., continued)

I *implore* your forgiveness.		+	+		×
I *inform* you of my intention.	+			+	×
I *instruct* you to turn right.	+		+		×
I *offer* you a cigar.	+			+	×
I *order* you to study.	+		+		×
I *pledge* my support to you.	+			+	×
I *pronounce* you man and wife.	+			+	×
I *propose* marriage to you.		+		+	×
I *request* your presence.		+	+		×
I *require* your reply.		+		+	×
I *say* X to you.	+		+		×
I *sentence* you to jail.	+			−	×
I *vow* revenge on you.	+			−	×
I *warn* you of X.	+			+	×
I *write* my opinion.	+				×

Oblique role is hardly beneficiary in any ordinary sense of that word. Thus, I posit the feature +/− Beneficiary.

In any case, I think that "playing around" with the semantics of benefaction will tell anyone a good deal about the rhetorical force of performative sentences. As I will point out later, we need other principles to account for the force of such sentences as *I command you to stop*, for we feel, I think, that accounting for the force of this and others in terms of benefaction is highly tenuous and makes us uneasy. For the moment, I am content if I have demonstrated that benefaction is a rhetorical principle in performatives. (Regardless of whether or not anyone agrees with my individual analyses.)

According to our definition, the following sentence is not a performative: *I'll give you my watch*. Is this to say that the principle of benefaction is not operative in its force? Or that we cannot specify its intention? For I would claim that performatives are verbs of intention and that all intentions can be *stated* by performatives. This is to say that *all* sentences have performative force, nothing more and nothing less.

From this point on, I must adopt a convention. I will assume (with a great many modern linguists) that sentences have both deep and surface structures, but I want to avoid the argument over whether or not this claim has any psychological validity. When I speak of deep structure of sentences, I am only saying something like the following: some implicit elements of sentence meaning can be made explicit through paraphrase or metalinguistic analysis. I will not try to capture my notions of deep structure—if there is any such thing—with a metalanguage. Rather, I will use natural language. What I intend is easily enough illustrated. The sentence *The log is ashes* puzzles no one. *Ashes* is predicated of *log*, and we all know what logs and ashes are. Yet the sentence is paradoxical in that, if the log is ashes, it is no longer a log. I would capture this idea by *capitalizing* what I take to be the deep structure content. In other words, what the sentence *means* to me is something like the following: SOMETHING THAT WAS the log is ashes.[6]

In an extremely intricate article, J. R. Ross argues that underlying all declarative sentences there is a performative sentence.[7] In other words, surface declarative sentences which are nonperformative are Neutral roles in a performative proposition which does not appear on the surface. Let's go back to *The log is ashes*. What Ross is saying, essentially, is that the deep structure of the sentence looks something like this: I HEREBY STATE/SAY TO YOU THAT the log is ashes. Predicate (state/say): Agent (I), Oblique (you), Neutral (the log is ashes). In effect, Ross's argument and the one that I have been advancing meet at this point, for I have been claiming that all sentences must have intentive force and that performatives are the verbs of intention.

Unfortunately, Ross's argument is so intricate that it defies easy sum-

mary. In general, he sets out to argue for his analysis on the basis of surface features that are explicable if one posits deep structure performative verbs. An example will perhaps suffice to give some indication of his method.

The noun phrase which follows *as for* must have some connection with the clause that follows it. Thus:

As for the students, they enjoy basketball.
* As for the students, hydrogen is a gas.

It is also the case that if a pronoun follows *as for*, it generally cannot be a reflexive-intensive:

As for her, she liked chocolate.
* As for herself, she liked chocolate.

How, then, do we explain the following?

As for myself, I like chocolate.

We can do so by positing that I HEREBY STATE THAT as for myself, I like chocolate. Granted: in and of itself, this is a weak argument; however, Ross assembles a whole variety of surface manifestations which can be explained by the performative analysis, and in their totality, they are impressive.

Ross's work makes us more comfortable with the present argument as it moves along, for Ross demonstrates that there is empirical evidence to support what we are advancing.

We have come to the point, then, that we can state directly: all *declarative* sentences gain their intentive force in some way from performatives. We are not positing deep structure in the conventional sense of that term, but are arguing only that all declarative sentences must have a performative interpretation for meaning to be consummated. In other words, to understand my declarative sentence S fully, you must know whether I am *promising, stating, threatening*. . . . But with a brief argument, I would like to progress beyond this point and say that *all sentences* gain their intentive force through performatives. The sentence *Will you buy me a beer?* is an interrogative in form, a question by type, and a request in force. I HEREBY REQUEST OF YOU *will you buy me a beer?* The sentence *Stop making noise!* is an imperative in form and a command in force: I HEREBY COMMAND/ORDER YOU (to) *stop making noise!* And so on.[8]

Now then, consider a sentence such as *I order you to appear*. It is hard for me to conceive that the principle of benefaction is important here. We can tell a story, thus supplying a context, and thereby demonstrate that benefaction is operative, but taken at "face value," the sentence seems to be beneficiary-free. Where does its "face value" come from? The answer, I think, is that *order* is a verb of *authority*. I can give you an order only if somehow I have the authority to do so. You will take the statement as an order only if you believe that I have the authority. It would make no sense for a private to order a general to retreat—unless the private felt that he had the authority, perhaps moral.

Or take a sentence such as *I promise to be good*. If my child says this to me, I will not take it to be a promise unless I believe that he has made an *ethical commitment*.

What I am suggesting, of course, is that we expand our notion of rhetorical force from the principle of

beneficence to include *authority* and *ethical commitment*.

Perhaps a brief summary is in order here. We have said that performatives are verbs of intention and that they, in some sense, are either in the structure of or underlie the structure of all sentences. We have argued that the propositional structure of performative sentences demands that we take account of a principle that we have termed *beneficence*. (This principle apparently does not operate in all performative sentences.) And we are further arguing that at least some performatives (in fact, a great many) gain part or all of their rhetorical force from the principles of *authority* and/or *ethical commitment*.

Insofar as the argument holds water, have we not constructed a triad of values?

Note that we have been talking about rhetorical (perlocutionary) force. Therefore, we have been largely looking back on sentences from the standpoint of the hearer. That is to say, if *I* don't really believe that *you* intend me good, I will not interpret your sentence as *advice*. If *I* do not believe that *you* believe you have authority, I will not take your sentence as a *command*. If *I* do not believe that *you* have ethical commitment, I will not take your sentence as a *promise*.

I would like to propose, then, that the three *values* which give sentences their force are *beneficence*, *authority*, and *ethical commitment*.

The proposal immediately becomes shaky, however, when we begin to think of Wayne Booth's *A Rhetoric of Irony*.[9]

Suppose that I am an eighteenth-century cleric and that I am in a conversation regarding the deplorable state of the Irish peasantry. Suppose, further, that I *say*, "Use the children for food. That's a modest enough proposal." I am ostensibly saying something like this: I HEREBY *PROPOSE* TO YOU THAT YOU *use the children for food.* Or am I saying something like that? If that is indeed what I'm saying, the reaction of my hearer will probably be analogous to that of the legendary college freshman who horrifiedly takes Swift "seriously." Am I not really suggesting, in my intention, that all-important logical predicate: *negative?* In other words,

[NOT (SUGGEST (eat children))].

Here, it seems to me, we have stumbled onto a terribly interesting point. As was said earlier, the definition of performative sentences precludes negatives. A negative sentence is simply not a performative. Thus, its potential force is cancelled. Is that not precisely the case with irony? The "face value" force of the ironic sentence is simply cancelled. The reader, perceiving irony, is left in a momentary quandary, in puzzlement. But since a negative implies its opposite, only one choice is available. In fact, notice what happens in the case of "A Modest Proposal." The negative cancels the performative value of the statement "I propose that . . . ." for "I do *not* propose that . . ." is not a performative. The statement is automatically transformed into the utterance "Don't eat children," which, of course, is not a performative. For it to have force, it must gain its performative interpretation and becomes, by our logic, an exhortation: I HEREBY EXHORT YOU *don't eat children.*

But, you will say, the eating of children is not what "A Modest Pro-

posal" is all about, and, of course, you're perfectly right. Once the reader has arrived at the true performative value of the piece, he or she can begin to get at the real meaning.[10]

If we are ambitiously claiming the construction of a grammar of rhetorical force in sentences, we can now add the fourth term to our triad, and we arrive at *beneficence, authority, ethical commitment,* and the *negative.* Since we have added the negative, Kenneth Burke should be happy with our argument, in part at least. As he says,

There are many notable aspects of language, such as classification, specification, abstraction, which have their analogues in purely nonverbal behavior. But the negative is a peculiarly linguistic resource. And because it is so peculiarly linguistic, the study of man as the specifically word-using animal requires special attention to this distinctive marvel, the negative.[11]

Three tasks now remain to us: (1) to see how our "grammar" works out in performative sentences, (2) to explore the uses of the grammar in understanding rhetoric, and (3) to do the same as regards "pure" poetry.

The "proof" of our four-value grammar is in its applications. Do the principles of benefaction, authority, ethical commitment, and the negative activate the intentive force of sentences and larger stretches of discourse?

We can begin with an apparently easy case: *I hereby answer your question.* Notice that this sentence, in its deep structure, contains a role that is deleted in the surface structure: *I hereby answer your question* FOR YOU. This deleted role is clearly the Oblique + Beneficiary, and the principle of benefaction is seen to be part of the force of the sentence. Do authority and ethical commitment operate? If the question is something like *What time is it?* and I glance at my watch before replying, authority and ethical commitment are such minor factors in the force of the sentence (if indeed they are present at all) that we can ignore them. If I am Milton Friedman and the question to me is *How soon will stagflation end?* then authority is indeed a force in the performative answer.

In *I hereby authorize you to act for me*, both authority and benefaction are apparent, for the sentence confers authority upon you. On the other hand, *I hereby beg your indulgence* is activated by the Agent + Beneficiary role and, I think, ethical commitment. One clearly needs no authority to beg, but the verb *beg* itself implies commitment (which I think is always ethical, so that our term "ethical commitment" may be tautological). Such also is the case with *I beseech you to stop*.

With *I hereby close this session*, no benefaction is readily apparent (even though all of the participants, including the chairman, might sigh with relief that the session has finally ended), but authority is clearly necessary for the act of closing.

I would argue that with true commands, there is no benefaction, but, of course, "pure" authority. When a drill sergeant issues a command and troops obey it, neither the sergeant nor the troops benefit in the direct sense that the beseecher who is successful or the questioner who is answered does.

With *I hereby condemn you to death*, the principle of authority is apparent, and, of course, we have the Oblique role with the feature − Beneficiary.

When we come to *I hereby dare you to jump*, we obviously encounter problems. In the first place, a dare is usually characterized as "just for the hell of it." One needs no authority to dare, and certainly no ethical commitment (in fact, just the opposite). The very word "dare" implies amorality, so perhaps our clue here is to be found in the parenthetical conclusion of the last sentence, leading us to construct the roles for "dare" as Agent with the feature − Beneficiary and Oblique with the same feature. It seems to me undeniable that "dare" is in some sense a "valueless" verb, unless we take the value to be a mere solipsistic ego.

Finally, I would like to discuss *say*. Compare *I hereby say X to you* with *I hereby state X to you*. In most senses, *to say X* is to be less forceful in intent than *to state X*. We feel a good deal easier substituting *utter* for *say* than to substitute it for *state*. In fact, it seems to me that *state* is more value-laden than *say*. We can equate *utter* with Searle's notions of utterance acts and propositional acts, diminishing the importance of illocution and perlocution.[12]

As regards the illocutionary and the perlocutionary act, there seems to be a spectrum of force, of intention and effect. The utterance of *I hereby say X* can be taken as very nearly a pure *locutionary act*,[13] as opposed to *i*llocutionary and *per*locutionary, strangely devoid of intention and effect.

I would claim, tentatively at least, that there is a whole class of performative verbs which are like *say* in their lack of forcefulness.

I hereby *write* my will.
I hereby *signal* my presence with flags or smoke signals.

I hereby *utter* my displeasure.
I hereby *wire* the time of my arrival.[14]

Thus, in a sentence such as *I hereby say X to you*, we seem to have the roles Agent and Oblique, without the feature Beneficiary, and the principles of authority and ethical commitment seem to be absent or at least subdued.

An argument, however, is never just the *saying* or *uttering* of X; it is *stating, claiming, affirming*. For some hundreds of words now, I have been carrying on an argument, and if that argument has been effective, it has been so not just because you, the reader, have agreed with its "content," but also because you have tacitly accepted my authority and my ethical commitment. To be sure, part of my authority may come from the source of publication, and you may indeed be compelled to accept my ethical commitment "at face value." It is, however, obvious that you would not read seriously if you did not believe that I have the authority to argue as well as commitment to my argument.

In regard to this paper, the principle of beneficence is extremely interesting, and that interest hinges on two senses of the verb *argue*. Notice the difference between *I argue with John* and *I argue that X*. The first implies conflict; the values implied by the first use of *argue* are strangely similar to those of *dare*. In fact, if I am in a heated argument, I would be uneasy with the performative *I hereby argue with John*. The argument itself transcends the speech acts that compose it and becomes a symbolic conflict, logomachy. In that kind of argument, the principle of authority is suspended, for the hearer will not grant my authority, nor is there an element of beneficence in

such a situation. It is a truism that no one wins an argument. And I would like to point out the reason for this: it is because the principle of the negative becomes overriding. No one finally gets anything out of it. Its structure is

	Agent	Oblique	
Predicate	− Bene	− Bene	*Neutral*
argue	I	with you	about X

Arguments *concerning*, as opposed to arguments *about*, proceed on the basis of authority and ethical commitment, precisely because my argument is forceful if you believe that I know what I'm taking about and can be trusted. (We have here, then, the "ethical argument" in its classical sense.)

Obviously, authority is not enough for an argument to proceed. We have all experienced situations in which The World's Greatest Authority on X used his authority as a weapon for browbeating an audience, and, of course, the result is always hostility rather than conviction. But perhaps at this point the discussion is verging on truism.

Finally, I would like to speculate about "pure" rhetoric and "pure" poetry.

For our paradigm of "pure" rhetoric, we can turn to advertising—any ad, though I will construct one that is archetypal. The advertisement, in the first place, activates itself by stressing the principle of beneficence; the product being sold will do something *for you*. But again, this point is merely truistic; advertisers assuredly do not stress negative features of their products. The very fact that there are no "if's," "and's" or "but's" in the advertisement indicates its authority, as do testimonials, selective data, and so on. And, of course, there is no question about the ethical commitment of the ad if one takes it at its face value. What we see here is that "pure" rhetoric relies heavily on authority and ethical commitment and that its "proposition" includes the role Oblique + Beneficiary. Rhetoric differs from coercion in its stress on benefits to the audience; it is the pathetic argument *par excellence.*

"Pure" rhetoric always strongly implies an audience. The "argument concerning" that we have just discussed does not imply an audience in this strong sense. While I am reluctant to start a new chain of ideas that would carry us far afield, I would like to suggest that Perelman's notion of the "universal audience" will help us understand the nature of "arguments concerning." [15]

Perhaps the best known statement concerning "pure" poetry is Archibald MacLeish's "A poem should not mean, but be," and, of course, the notion of "pure" poetry has preoccupied critics since the inception of the New Criticism decades ago. As Allen Tate explains the objectivist dogma:

We must return to, we must never leave, the poem itself. Its "interest" value is a cognitive one; it is sufficient that here, in the poem, we get knowledge of a whole object. If rational inquiry is the only mode of criticism, we must yet remember that the way we employ that mode must always affect our experience of the poem. I have been concerned in this commentary with the compulsive, almost obsessed, application of an all-engrossing principle of pragmatic reduction to a formed realm of our experience, the distinction of which is its complete knowledge, the full body of the experience that it offers us. However we may see the completeness of poetry, it is a problem

less to be solved than, in its full import, to be preserved. [16]

In general, I think that the New Critics would like to reduce poetry to mere saying or uttering. Tate brings me to suppose that what *I* get from *your* poem is the experience of the poem itself. In fact, I believe it perfectly possible for me to take the poem as an utterance. Indeed, a whole string of critics describe an experience of reading which seems to be hermetically sealed from the motives that make an argument an argument or that can make rhetoric "pure." To investigate the notion would require a second, and very long, essay, but the experience is epitomized by Sartre in his statement that "reading is a free dream." [17] What I would like to suggest, however, is that a "pure" poem has no performative force. The poem itself is "pure" expression, and the reading act itself is what I like to call "esthetic immersion." The poet needs no authority, for he is making no claims, giving no orders, advancing no premises. [18]

We have said that our analysis is from the viewpoint of the perlocutionary act, the element of the total speech act in which "things happen." But, as Northrop Frye points out again and again, in poetry nothing happens. [19] And if poetry makes something happen in the real world, it is no longer "pure" poetry.

In fact, as I have demonstrated, the "pure" poem is easy to conceptualize, but it is impossible to find. Like the concept of a point in geometry, it is a convenient fiction. A geometrician can certainly "define" a point, even though he or she could not show you one. The whole problem with much literary criticism in the twentieth century has been its tendency to imply that the abstract concept "pure poem" has physical reality. No one can point to a "pure" poem.

This, I think, is precisely because poets perform speech acts, and readers assume that speech acts have been performed—cannot, indeed, avoid assuming otherwise.

As my example of a "poem" that cannot be "pure," I will use a tale that everyone is familiar with and that, indeed, so easily supports my argument that I might be accused of loading the evidence in my own favor. I refer to *Heart of Darkness*— and I will be extremely brief in my discussion of it.

A perfect reader might indeed take it as a pure poem, having no evidence of the author's authority or ethical commitment, but that would be to miss the whole *esthetic* point of the tale, for it is, among other things, an allegory concerning the darkness of the human heart, a propagandistic attack on colonialism, a fictionalized history of the Belgian Congo, a segment of Conrad's biography, and so on. I *know* all these things, for I have studied Conrad's journals, the historical background of the tale, and so on. Thus, it is literally impossible for me to read the story as "pure" since I am unable to lobotomize myself at will. And if I were not the informed reader, but came to *Heart of Darkness* in pristine ignorance of its background? It is simply demonstrable and a commonsense assumption that: the more "ignorant" the reader, the more likely he or she is to be confused and frustrated in the reading. It is a fact that a hypothetical "pure" reader will be no reader at all. As reading theory currently points out, reading is a transaction involving raw information from a page (in the form of black squiggles), a visual system, an extremely limited short-term memory, and a mind that brings with it a total background of experience, emotions, cultural and ethical sets, and so forth. In that transaction, the mind is by all odds the most important factor.[20]

What constitutes the difference in the reading experience that one has with an argument in favor of birth control and with a poem about the brevity of life? The difference lies, I think, in what Philip Wheelwright calls the weight of the "assertorial tone":

Statements—for we here consider the molecular order of meanings—vary with respect to the manner in which they are susceptible to affirmation and denial, ranging all the way from "heavy" assertorial tone—which characterizes the literal statement, the proposition—to "light" association or semiaffirmed tension between two or more symbols. A poetic statement differs from a literal statement not, as Dr. Richards used to maintain, in that one has a merely subjective, the other an objective reference—at least this is an unnecessary and generally irrelevant difference; but in their manner of asserting. There are differences of what might be called *assertorial weight*. A literal statement asserts heavily. It can do so because its terms are solid. It must do so because we are practical busy creatures who want to know just where we stand. A poetic statement, on the other hand, consisting as it does in a conjunction or association of plurisigns, has no such solid foundation, and affirms with varying degrees of lightness.[21]

I would suggest that we can look to the principles of *beneficence, authority, ethical commitment,* and the *negative* as terms that can be

used (must be used?) to discuss assertorial tone and thus differentiate
a text that we take to be rhetoric
from one that we take to be poetry.

An example that I cannot resist is
the following. Suppose that we open
a volume titled *Now Poetry*, and
suppose that we find this as the first
poem in the volume.

AT&T

Lift receiver.
Deposit coin.
Listen for dial tone.
Dial number.

In the volume, *Now Poetry* this sequence has little assertorial tone; in
a phone booth, it has a great deal.

If we read *A Modest Proposal*
from the "purely" objective point of
view, which we have argued is impossible in practice, we will look at
its structure, its style, its verbal wit,
and so on. If we take it as irony, the
principle of the negative suddenly
appears, and, as we have demonstrated, when the negative appears,
the piece must become an "argument." With argument comes beneficence: Swift is arguing in favor of
something to someone. And need we
point out that the poet's authority
and ethical commitment are necessary components of our uptake on
the piece?

We have come a long way now,
perhaps too far. I see another essay
looming over the horizon, one that
will explain in detail how I have
made the leap from the sentence to
the poem or whole argument. At this
point, I only want to hint at what my
answer might be. As Northrop Frye
points out, the text lives in our minds
not as a series of events in a plot, but
as a gestalt, as a meaning.[22] I think
we can say that that meaning is activated by the performative that we

apply to it: I hereby *lament* that. . . .
I hereby *argue* that. . . . I hereby
urge you to. . . . But as we read,
moving from sentence to sentence,
we are involved in the intricate
dance of values that make us take
sentences as intentive. We are caught
up in the rhetoric of beneficence, authority, ethical commitment, and the
negative.

NOTES

1. John Robert Ross, "On Declarative
Sentences." *Readings in English Transformational Grammar*, ed. Roderick A.
Jacobs and Peter S. Rosenbaum (Waltham, Mass.: Ginn, 1970), pp. 222–23.
2. John Searle, *Speech Acts: An Essay
in the Philosophy of Language* (Cambridge: Cambridge University, 1969),
pp. 22–26.
3. *Universals in Linguistic Theory*,
ed. Emmon Bach and Robert T. Harms
(New York: Holt, Rinehart and Winston, 1968).
4. Analysis of this oblique role would
reveal that it is complicated. For example, look at the structural properties
of the oblique as it appears in sentences
which are quoted a bit later in this essay.
I advise *you* to save your money.
I answer your question (*for you*).
I beg (*of you*) your indulgence.
I bequeath (to) *you* my watch.
I beseech (of) *you* to stop.
It would clearly be possible for us to sub-
categorize a variety of functions of
the oblique. However, this operation is
unnecessary to the argument being
advanced.
5. I am not completely happy with the
terms "benefaction," "beneficence," and
"beneficiary." As Professor Henry Johnstone pointed out to me in a letter, "I
don't see how you can appeal to beneficence without falling into the quicksand
of utilitarianism. Beneficent in the long
run or in the immediate present? Beneficent in the opinion of the recipient or in
that of experts? One man's beneficence is

another man's maleficence. The possibility of these questions strongly suggests to me that beneficence belongs to a wholly different category than, say, intention. It also seems to me to belong to a quite different category from what you call the negative." Perhaps these objections can be obviated (though my uneasiness will remain) by referring to Searle's "rules" for the performance of illocutionary acts. One of these is the "Sincerity Rule." In a *request*, for instance, it can be stated this way: "S[peaker] wants H[earer] to do A[ct]" (*Speech Acts*, p. 66). In other words, if I *request* that you stop beating my dog, you will not really take my statement as a request unless you believe that I really want you to do A—that I am sincere. And you cannot believe that I want you to do A unless you believe that the result of A will be in some sense desirable for me. Thus, I will tentatively cling to my terms "beneficence," "beneficiary," and "beneficent." I am talking, really, about conditions that seem to activate language, not about the philosophical question of what is fully good or beneficial.

6. Emmon Bach, "Nouns and Noun Phrases," *Universals in Linguistic Theory.*

7. "On Declarative Sentences."

8. As Professor Henry Johnstone pointed out to me in a letter, it is not the case that the performative versions of sentences must have the same meaning as the nonperformative versions, only the same intention—as *stating, vowing, ordering,* etc. As Johnstone points out, "I walk into a room with a green chair. I say, 'That chair is red.' My statement is false. Someone else walks into the room and says, 'I hereby state, "That chair is red."'" His statement is true. A true statement cannot have the same meaning as a false statement. Therefore, you cannot have in mind that a performative could literally have the same meaning as a nonperformative." Precisely.

9. (Chicago: University of Chicago, 1974.)

10. I am diffident at this point. I really don't know just how far I would push my idea about the negative in regard to irony, and if I did pursue the idea, I don't know exactly where the chase would lead me. However, the whole notion is intriguing enough that I am reluctant to strike it from my essay.

11. "A Dramatistic View of the Origins of Language," *Language as Symbolic Action* (Berkeley and Los Angeles: University of California, 1966), p. 419.

12. *Speech Acts*, pp. 22–26.

13. For a discussion of the concept "locutionary act," see J. L. Austin, *How to Do Things with Words* (New York: Oxford University Press, 1962), pp. 94–107.

14. Ross ("On Declarative Sentences," p. 243) lists members of a class which he calls "verbs of linguistic communication." A look at his list indicates that some of these verbs are more forceful than others; in some cases, we feel uneasy in substituting them for *utter*. His list includes *said, stated, asserted, declared, claimed, screamed, whispered, told, wigwagged, snorted.*

15. Concerning the "universal audience," see Ch. Perelman and L. Olbrechts-Tyteca, *The New Rhetoric: A Treatise on Argument*, trans. John Wilkinson and Purcell Weaver (Notre Dame: Notre Dame University, 1969), pp. 30–35.

16. "Literature as Knowledge," *Critical Theory Since Plato*, ed. Hazard Adams (New York: Harcourt Brace Jovanovich, 1971), p. 491.

17. "Why Write?" *Critical Theory Since Plato*, p. 1063.

18. In regard to this point, see Richard Ohmann, "Speech, Action, and Style," *Literary Style: A Symposium*, ed. Seymour Chatman (London and New York: Oxford University, 1971). Ohmann says, "Frye speaks of literature as a 'body of hypothetical verbal structures,' with the polemical emphasis on the word 'hypothetical.' For present purposes, I would shift the focus slightly, and say that a work of literature is also a series of hypothetical *acts*, grounded in the convention for verbal action that we have all thoroughly learned. In fact I would go farther, and say that literature can be accurately *defined* as discourse in

which the seeming acts are hypothetical. Around them, the reader, using his elaborate knowledge of the rules for illocutionary acts, constructs the hypothetical circumstances—the fictional world—that will make sense of the given acts. This performance is what we know as mimesis" (pp. 253–54).

19. For example: "So we begin to see where the imagination belongs in the scheme of human affairs. It's the power of constructing possible models of human experience. In the world of the imagination, anything goes that's imaginatively possible, but nothing really happens. If it did happen, it would move out of the world of imagination into the world of action." "The Motive for Metaphor," *The Educated Imagination* (Bloomington: Indiana University, 1984), p. 22.

20. The best summary of current reading theory is Frank Smith, *Understanding Reading* (New York: Holt, Rinehart and Winston, 1971).

21. "The Logical and the Translogical," *Critical Theory Since Plato*, p. 1109.

22. See, for instance, "Myth, Fiction, and Displacement," *Fables of Identity* (New York: Harcourt Brace Jovanovich, 1963).

Speech Acts and the Reader-Writer Transaction
(with Dorothy Augustine)

This essay is a "sequel" to "The Rhetoric of Beneficence, Authority, Ethical Commitment, and the Negative." As we discussed the implications of that earlier essay, Augustine and I began to see that we could begin to explain some of the problems of intentionality in discourse and, at the same time, relate speech act theory to the larger, traditional body of knowledge, rhetoric.

On and off again, Dorothy Augustine and I worked on this essay for two years—including one long session in the steaming oppressiveness of a Gulf summer while she was teaching at the University of Houston. We were enthusiastic when our somewhat raucous, always invigorating dialect generated the concept of rhetorical performatives—those controlling verbs that invite an addressee to disagree and hence to enter into dialectic with the addresser. As we say in the paper, "we hope to show how the sources of composition depend on a special kind of language game explicitly realized by a special class of performative verbs."

I

In the first chapter in *Speech Acts: An Essay in the Philosophy of Language*, John Searle marks the distinctions and relationships between (1) talking, (2) characterizing talk, and (3) explaining talk.[1] We are *talking* (or writing prepared talk) now, for instance, and our ability to do this underlies the possibility of writers and readers to *characterize*

This essay appeared originally in *Convergences*, ed. B. Petersen (NCTE forthcoming). Reprinted with the permission of the National Council of Teachers of English.

this kind of talk as rhetoric or written discourse or composition. Furthermore, our characterizing statement may be *explained* by rules that experienced writers and readers know or can invent, in this case, rules which govern sentences, introductory paragraphs, contextual frames, cohesion, and the like.

Needless to say, rhetoricians do a lot of talking in order to explain what they characterize as discourse. Only recently, however, has this talk focused on the characterizing statements themselves. We have started to examine conventional characterizations of rhetoric or composition, such as those found in textbooks from Aristotle to Peter Elbow, in terms of questions like "What happens when writers write?" or "Do paragraphs produced in the real world resemble those prescribed by textbook rules?"[2] Sooner or later, these analyses of writing will generate evidence sufficient to counter the convention and to offer characterizing propositions about the nature of composing that can be explained with rules or models that are simple, general, and testable.

That rhetoric, specifically composition, involves an implicit dialogue is one proposition of this kind, for it characterizes written discourse as a transaction between writer and reader, a transaction relying on the writer's and reader's tacit knowledge of the regularities of conversation. All of us whose native language is English, for example, conform to certain "rules" of turn-taking in conversation, and we adhere to what the philosopher H. P. Grice describes as "the cooperative principle."[3] These tacit rules or regularities have only recently been discovered as underlying the surface forms and even the content of conversation. Unlike Moliere's Monsieur Jourdain, however, none of us is surprised that we have been speaking according to these rules or regularities all our lives. We recognize them as "intuitively valid," as linguists like to say. Furthermore, such linguistic or philosophic discoveries help explain why researchers in rhetoric have shifted from attempts to characterize the written word (the "facts") to attempts to characterize the generating of texts (the underlying rules which regulate the "facts").[4]

Of course, composition is unlike conversation in obvious ways. It is

prepared or rehearsed, unlike most conversation; it is more formal in its vocabulary and syntax; and, perhaps most obvious, it appears one-sided, a monologue. Nevertheless, successful composition may be described as *implicit* dialogue if for no other reason than that the concept of "reader" requires writers to pay attention to regularities of behavior which involve a partner in the discourse, a "silent" partner, to be sure, but one who is equal and, ideally, equally competent in the linguistic business at hand.

Sophisticated writers, for example, are hardly surprised by the statement that they have invented a reader. Everyone understands that writers' workshops are valuable and good editors are sought after precisely because writers need to test the possible and probable "responses" they have projected (consciously or unconsciously) to their theses, proofs, points of view, etc. One may, therefore, consider the hypothetical responses projected by writers as a correlate to the conversational "cues"—silent and spoken—that speakers constantly receive from listeners in live dialogic situations: Speakers "know" whether they should continue to speak, stop to explain a point, back up or skip ahead because of the listeners' verbal and non-verbal signals. These signals can be as blunt as a listener's interrupting a speaker with a request for information or clarification, or they can be as subtle as a listener's dilated pupils, interpreted by the speaker as silent affirmation of what is being said.[5] There are no immediate cues of that kind, however, in the writer-reader transaction, and this may be the most fundamental reason for the writer to invent the reader, to project the hypothetical responses which will indicate whether the reader is "going along" with the claim, argument, proposal, or other *illocutionary act* initiating the discourse or any of its parts.[6] If the writer projects a *perlocutionary* response that challenges or questions an initiating illocution, then that response must be addressed in the compositional forms and content of proof, qualification, concession, background, refutation, etc., and the resulting discourse will assume the features of the language game which we call rhetoric. A simple illustration in speech act format can clarify this notion:

Illocution	(I *assert* to you that) The Equal Rights Amendment is misunderstood by a majority of voters.
Perlocution	(I *challenge* you to) Prove it!

Rhetorical discourse, in Chaim Perelman's words, will manifest the writer's facility for generating the reader's "adherence to the theses" offered for his assent.[7] Implicit in Perelman's description of rhetoric's function is the presupposition that someone "out there" will object to "the thesis." As far back as Aristotle (rhetoric is "the faculty for observing . . . the available means of persuasion," *Rhetoric*, 1355b), theoreticians have described the function of rhetoric and the work of the rhetor without paying too much attention to the *causes* of either—the hypothetical responses of an idealized audience, responses on the order of "Prove it!" or "Says who?" or "So what?".

At this point, a bridge from one aspect of the tradition, invention, may be helpful in order to relate the above to a more familiar concept.

Invention, most of us feel, is the first of the rhetorical arts because when a writer provides form without the substance of a topic, we find it abhorrent to our ideal of a rhetoric's function. But topics—the methods and procedures for discovering issues, lines of agreement, problems, for assessing values or beliefs, etc.—should be understood as more than prescriptive inducements to substantive "thought." By employing the topic of definition, for example, writers would presuppose or project readers to ask, "What do you mean by *that*?" when a "that" has just been introduced into the discourse. Likewise, we would rely on cause and effect when we hypothesize that a reader will question the relationship between what we claim to be antecedent and consequent. Whatever topic we use, consciously or unconsciously, felicitously or not, we attempt to address and satisfy what we project as the probable response to our overall or localized illocution in the discourse, our *advice, argument, assertion, claim, proposal, request, warning,* or other speech act underlying the surface structure of what we are communicating to the reader. We do that, for the most part, because of our competence as speakers and listeners in everyday "language games" with their intrinsic rules for generating form, style, and even content. The "logic" of invention, seen in this light, is hardly a set of rules imposed from without. It is already there, in the structure of human dialogue as a coherent series of inter-influences.

This short illustration is not meant to reappropriate the tradition by redefining its parts, but to demonstrate how the "how" of classical thought may be distinguished from the "why" of current research in composition.[8] What has come to be known as the current-traditionalist school refers more or less to the posivitist philosophy that reality is external and fixed, and that language functions as a container for and carrier of meaning. The epistemic philosophy of the new rhetoric, on the other hand, understands meaning to emerge from rhetorical situations, each with its own rules of evidence, etc.[9] In this view of reality, language acts as a kind of chemical reagent, a device for detecting and identifying each situation and the particular set of rules attending it, as you that. . . ."[10] For example, the first sentence of this paragraph must be considered as the subordinate clause of an underlying or deep structure sentence represented roughly as "We *state* to you that 'The implications of research in philosophy and linguistics for rhetorical theory are rich.'" The main clause, identified by a performative verb and therefore indicative of a speech act, together with the subordinate clause, form what we will call the "super-intention." We can illustrate the relationships by means of the familiar tree diagram.

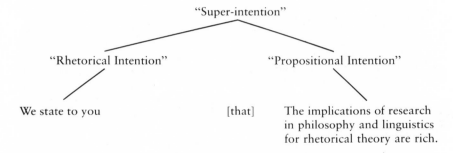

well as the agency of our definitions and evaluations of the world.

II

The implications of research in philosophy and linguistics for rhetorical theory are rich. But chief among them, we believe, is this: every declarative sentence that we read or hear, write or speak, may be represented as the subordinate clause (what we will call the "propositional intention") of an underlying main clause. The dominant or main clause of the sentence (what we will call the "rhetorical intention") is identified by illocutions on the order of "I *advise* (*assert, claim, joke, warn*) [to]

Propositional intentions, then, account for most of the surface structures of what we read or hear in discourse. "Rhetorical intentions," indicative of and accounting for the *purpose* of introducing the proposition(s) of the subordinate clause are, for the most part, "understood" in composition (as well as in conversation), much like the deep-structure "you" of the imperative. The problem is, rhetorical intentions are more highly subject to misinterpretation by readers than by listeners, for there are no "live" cues to rely on in facing a page of print. This is one of the reasons why composition is a much more complicated language game than the spoken word and its (usually immediate) response.

A less apparent handicap for writers is the fact that rhetorical intentions are represented by the performative values of the underlying dominant clause, and there are many performative verbs with their own accompanying semantic environments. Referring to our first sentence again, for example, a reader may have interpreted the rhetorical intention to be governed by an underlying performative like *claim* rather than *state*. That would be a perfectly reasonable "reading" of the rhetorical intention. For in the first sentence of the first paragraph of a major division of an essay, rhetorical intentions are more properly realized in performative values tending toward "proofs," which a performative verb like *claim* would warrant, and with the accompanying semantic "up-take" of readers *expecting* clarification of terms and points of view which *claim* would require (and which *state* would not require, or at least not as strongly as *claim* would). One would not expect as full a discussion to follow a statement as a claim; the meaning of the two illocutions realized as intentions justify different perlocutions or responses on the part of the reader. Other possible rhetorical intentions for the same proposition as it appears above in the surface structure may be explicitly realized in performatives like *propose, offer, argue, maintain, inform, instruct, pronounce, declare,* or even *advise*. All of these performatives could represent the intention governing that particular proposition (though we expect a majority of readers will vote for *claim*). Indeed, the competent reader may have held all the possible verbs in suspension—in a rhetorical juggling act—until in reading further, one "meaning" was confirmed (and the others disconfirmed) by the content, style, and form of what followed. No competent reader, however, would have interpreted the same proposition to be governed by a rhetorical intention informed by a performative like *deny, warn,* or *enquire*.

To illustrate this point of the reader-writer transaction further, we can factor out what we take to be the dominant clauses or the performative values or the rhetorical intentions or the purposes of any stretch of discourse as follows:

Super-intention

Rhetorical Intention	*Propositional Intention*
I *declare* to you that	. . . government of the people, by the people, for the people, shall not perish from the earth.
I *insist* to you that	My Mistress' eyes are nothing like the sun.
I *instruct* you that	(You) Lift receiver, deposit coin, listen for dial tone.
I *question* that	It is a truth universally acknowledged, that a single man in possession of a good fortune, must be in want of a wife.
I *vow* to you that	I am not a crook.
I *tell* you that	(You should) Call me Ishmael.

Though we do not expect a perfect match between the rhetorical intentions we have assigned and those that the reader might, the point is that we could all agree that the above is a *possible* and reasonable list of rhetorical intentions which make purposeful sense of the list of corresponding propositions. Naturally, one could interpret a "vow" as a "lie," but that fact only serves to reinforce our point: underlying performative values will govern the purpose of discourse, whether those values are intended by the writer-speaker or responded to by the reader-listener. Where gross discrepancies occur between writers' underlying intentions and readers' responses, we have the "misunderstanding" that I. A. Richards valiantly tried to account for in his analyses of the surface meanings of discourse.

Such a deep-structure analysis is easily tested and validated in terms of the real-world responses we hear every day to declarative sentences. A possible response to

(1) Prices slumped,

for example, might be rendered in ordinary conversation as "Are you serious?" The deep structure of that response may be represented as

(2) Do you ((claim) (joke)) to me that "Prices slumped"?

And we mark such responses as the surface structure of sentence 2 as coherent precisely because we understand the listener is searching not only for the semantic or propositional intention of the speaker, but also, and more important, for the speaker's rhetorical intention or purpose in relating the proposition. The listener, in fact, is making an at-tempt to reconstruct the performative verb of the underlying dominant clause. She must understand the super-intention, the whole of the discourse, before she can make sense of any of its parts.

What we are saying is simply this: writers can make their intentions explicit by supplying the deep-structure performative verbs which account for their rhetorical purposes; if readers have understood the writer's intentions, then they can reconstruct and make explicit the deep-structure performative(s) of the main clause(s).

Notice the ambiguities in the following speech acts and how they might be resolved:

(3) S: Two dollars on Sea Biscuit!
    H: Are you *betting* or *bidding* on Sea Biscuit?
(4) S: I shall return.
    H: Are you *promising* or *threatening* me that you'll come back?
(5) S: You should learn Greek.
    H: Are you *suggesting* that I learn Greek or *ordering* me to?

And for anyone who has taught freshman English, a classic example of a misunderstanding will come to mind:

(6) Swift: We should breed, fatten, and slaughter the poor of Ireland.
    Freshman: Are you *advocating* the proposal that we should breed, fatten, and slaughter the poor of Ireland?

The fact that we do not normally pose such responses as those in 2–6, proves that as readers and listeners we are superbly efficient, most of the time, in constructing and reconstructing rhetorical intentions.

Of course, in the semantic environment of satire, as in 6, the competence allowing for a deep-structure "analysis" is essential, because understanding the *propositional* intention alone, that is, what appears in the surface structures of the essay, is insufficient for comprehending Swift's *purpose* in his proposal.[11] The naive reader may understand perfectly the semantic import of the surface structures of the entire essay or their reduction to a "thesis," but he will misconstrue Swift's *rhetorical intention* in communicating that proposition if his competence in language games does not allow the necessary "deep-structure analysis" of possible performative verbs in the main, underlying clause. Such a reading demonstrates the difference between what Searle calls "brute facts" and "institutional facts." His famous football analogy bears repeating here:

Imagine a group of highly trained observers describing an American football game in statements only of brute facts. . . . [W]ithin certain areas a good deal could be said, and using statistical techniques certain "laws" could even be formulated. For example, we can imagine that after a time our observer would discover the law of periodical clustering: at statistically regular intervals organisms in like colored shirts cluster together in a roughly circular fashion (the huddle). Furthermore, at equally regular intervals, circular clustering is followed by linear clustering . . . and linear clustering is followed by . . . linear interpenetration . . . But no matter how much data of this sort we imagine our observers to collect and no matter how many inductive generalizations we imagine them to make from the data, they still have not described American football. What is missing from their description? What is missing are all those concepts which are backed by constitutive rules, concepts such as touchdown, offside, game, points, first down, time out,

etc., and consequently what is missing are all the true statements one can make about a football game. The missing statements are precisely what describes the phenomenon on the field *as a game of football*. . . . No one, I guess, would try to offer a description of football in terms of brute facts, and yet, curiously enough, people have tried to offer semantic analyses of languages armed with only a conceptual structure of brute facts and ignoring the semantic rules that underlie the brute regularities.[12]

Satire, like the underlying rules of football, may be understood as an institutional (semantic) fact, and Swift's essay, like men in colored jerseys running about on a striped field, may be understood as a collection of brute facts or regularities. Competence in understanding football and satire is the ability of the players and observers to rely on constitutive rules which explain why the participants behave in such and such a way. In understanding "A Modest Proposal," readers rely on the regularities of linguistic behavior not available for observation, an unconscious repertoire of skills, if you like, one of which is the ability to refer to *possible* performatives and probable rhetorical intentions which will make sense of Swift's surface structures. The naive graduates into sophistication not because he finally reads "A Modest Proposal" more closely (the familiar pedagogical admonition to reconcile, in effect, more brute facts), but because he reconstructs Swift's underlying, tacit, illocutionary *denial* of what is on the page, a rhetorical reading. The transaction between reader and writer, to be sure, depends upon their sharing the same institutional fact, governed and explained by constitutive rules. Even more profound, however, is their ability to agree on the performative value(s) or rhetorical intention(s) communicating and interpreting the institutional fact(s) they share. "A Modest Proposal" affords the extreme example in demonstrating how the "constitutive rules" of speech act transaction between writer and reader accounts for the "institutional fact" of ridicule by wit, satire.

Though this essay is not meant to treat in a practical way models of instruction or the English curriculum, we cannot resist touching on an object lesson here. A naive interpretation of Swift's essay can be traced to a thin repertoire of rhetorical skills, to the reader's paltry store of experienced rhetorical intentions. Young adults in the twentieth century have been primarily educated, perhaps as no other previous generations, in the "scientific" style and to writing, themselves, in the expository mode. Neither does more than attempt "to inform," only one of the three aims of discourse, "to persuade" and "to please" being considered irrelevant to the "plain, dispassionate style" of certitude in reporting and describing objective phenomena. If rhetoric is reduced to explanation, rhetorical intentions can only be realized and interpreted as statements of clarification made bearable by brevity and sincerity.[13] The linguistic, psychological, and cultural effects of such education can only be guessed at, but one likely result fits neatly into our case for constructing and reconstructing rhetorical intentions in written discourse. If student writers-readers are educated to exercise and expect only those rhetorical intentions on the order of "I *inform*," "I *instruct*," or, at the most, "I *advise*," then of course they do exactly that. Underlying rhetorical intentions on

the order or "I *deny*," "I *joke*," or "I *criticize*," all possible, underlying indicators of Swift's propositions in "A Modest Proposal," lie outside the student's culturally acquired constitutive rules of composition. Notice that the naive reader will participate in the speech act initiated by Swift. The misunderstanding, however, occurs because the performatives appropriate to satire, or even to persuasion or argument, are missing from the reader's experiential inventory of those that govern writers' purposes and readers' expectations in discourse.

To summarize this section: In any speech act which is consummated by the reader's appropriate perlocution, where the exchange of intention and response is coherent or felicitous, an underlying explicit performative clause is understood by the participants to carry the rhetorical intention or purpose of the discourse. (Needless to say, the performative clause may appear in the surface structure: "I promise that I'll return" versus "I'll return.") As the rhetorical constituent of the super-intention, the main, performative clause will govern both the writer's and the reader's attitudes toward the subject matter of the discourse, represented by the propositional content (predication and reference) in the subordinate clause. The preceding sentence, for example, is subordinate in the deep structure to the main clause "We claim that:" *We claim that* "As the rhetorical component of the super-intention. . . ." We do not *question, deny, criticize, suggest,* or *admit* the proposition. We do not, in fact, allow for any other performative value to govern the purpose of our communicating the propositional intention, though up to this point we have not stated any claims in the literal or surface features of this essay. And yet the reader will have understood or reconstructed our *purpose* by having responded to the *claim* which is implicit in the previous paragraphs. Perhaps that response or perlocution is on the order of "So what?" or "Prove it!" The next section is meant to continue the implicit dialogue here by our addressing what we project to be potential responses to our implicit claim.

III

Consider the following two two-sentence speech acts (for the time being, we will substitute the more general terms, intention and response, for the more specialized terminology of speech act theory):

explained in the philosophers' taxonomies of performative values, it has not been discussed by theorists interested in the "constitutive rules" of rhetorical discourse. In exploring the anomaly, we hope to show how the sources of composition and the reader-writer transaction depend on a special kind of speech act explicitly realized by a special class of performative verbs in the initiating illocution and a challenge or denial (or what is projected as a challenge or denial) in the perlocution.

The philosopher's analysis of 7a and 8a clarifies and defines the conditions which must be in force in order that admissions and assertions be valid or true or taken to be valid or true of a state of affairs. Searle's taxonomy classifies a speech act informed by verbs like *admit* as "declaratives," and those informed by verbs like *assert* as "representa-

(7)   (a)   Intention:
I *admit* (*christen, condemn, confess, congratulate, declare, pronounce, sentence, will,* . . .) ([to] you) that "x."
      (b)   Response:
I *affirm* (*agree, assent, concede, grant, regret,* . . .) ([to] you) that "x."
(8)   (a)   Intention:
I *assert* (*claim, insist, propose, request, suggest,* . . .) ([to] you) that "x."
      (b)   Response:
I *challenge* (*deny, doubt, object, question, refute,* . . .) ([to] you) that "x."

Both responses are coherent with their respective initiating intentions. But 7b is coherent with 7a only, whereas both 7b and 8b are coherent with 8a. In the real world, in other words, with necessary conditions of felicity [14] and cooperativeness having been met, one kind of illocution may elicit a perlocutionary challenge, denial, doubt, etc., while another may not. This is an interesting anomaly, and while the phenomenon has been characterized and

tives." [15] We could, for instance, distill from any real-world utterance on the order of 7a the abstraction, *I declare to you that a certain state of affairs exists*; from 8a, the abstraction, *I declare to you that a certain state of affairs exists "as such."* And as Searle's analysis has already shown, the semantic environments of each class of performatives invest the "I" and the "you" of the main clause with certain social and epistemic privileges and constraints; conditions of felicity and cooperativeness are givens in 8 as well as in 7 in order that the speech acts be consummated by appropriate and coherent perlocutions or perlocutionary effects. One performative like *admit* is *promise*, for example, and to make a promise involves a complex understanding of underlying rules that must be adhered to by the participants in the speech act in order that the promise be consummated. Clark and Clark outline these underlying rules or felicity conditions:

Imagine that Alan says to Ben "I promise you that I will go home tomorrow." The rules Alan must adhere to are these:
  (1) *Propositional content rule.* The propositional content "I will go home tomorrow" must predicate a future act of Alan (which it does.)
  (2) *Preparatory rule.* Alan must believe that Ben would prefer Alan's

The same conditions would hold true for *admit* and all the other performatives in 7a, with adjustments, of course, for the semantic restrictions of the verb. For example, *admit* would predicate a past action by the speaker, not a future one, as with *promise*, and so on.

But felicity conditions having been met, an audience does not have the option to challenge an illocution or intention informed by a verb like *promise* or *admit*. Verbs like *admit* must belong to a sub-class of performatives which are explicitly *arhetorical*, that is, a speech act initiated by a performative like *admit* is composed of one illocution and one perlocution, of one "conversational turn" each by the participants. The evidence for this rule is illustrated in 9, with unacceptable perlocutions marked "*":

(9) (a) (I admit that) I was smoking behind the barn.
    (b) Well, I hope you'll never do that kind of thing again.
        I'm glad you had the courage to say so.
        Welcome to the club!
        In that case, you're forgiven.
    (c) * You can't prove that.
        * Are you certain of what you're saying?
        * Who cares?
        * I don't believe you.

going home tomorrow; and Alan must also believe that it is not obvious to Alan or Ben that Alan would go home tomorrow in the normal course of events.
  (3) *Sincerity rule.* Alan intends to go home tomorrow.
  (4) *Essential rule.* By uttering this sentence, Alan undertakes an obligation to go home tomorrow.
If any one of these rules is not fulfilled, Alan could be said to be making an "infelicitous" promise. Hence these rules are often called the *felicity conditions* of a promise.

Rhetoric begins, as Kenneth Burke has shown us, with the human option to say NO, and one cannot respond to an *admission* with a perlocutionary *denial* or *challenge*. In arhetorical language games, all of the constituents of the illocution will be recognized as valid by the audience: the authority of the speaker to make such an utterance (ethos); the real-world truth of the proposition (logos); and the influence of both on the audience (pathos), all obtaining in the responses in 9b. Such an illocutionary act will not be challenged by any perlocutionary effect on the order of "Prove it" (logos); or "So what" (pathos), or "Says who" (ethos), all indicative of the responses in 10c. As J. L. Austin remarks on a smaller category of illocutions, informed by what we think of now as the "classical" performatives such as those in 7a, the saying is the doing. One may as well challenge a lunar eclipse as to respond to 7a or 9a, respectively, with any of the alternatives in 8b or 9c.

Suppose, though, that felicity conditions are violated, resulting in a defective speech act. The "scenes" may be described briefly by positing some perlocutionary effects in which the negative *may* obtain. We can use a well-worn illocution in the example.

(that is, challenges to ethos, pathos, and logos) in which defective, arhetorical speech acts may be seen to "violate reality." But notice also that, the sincerity of the exchanges notwithstanding, the speech acts represented in 10 describe a burlesque of reality principles, the foundation of a farcical scene by Shakespeare or Woody Allen perhaps, a violation of expectations built upon a violation of the constitutive rules of arhetorical speech acts.

When an illocution carries the rhetorical value of a performative like *assert*, however, the constitutive rules describe a different kind of language game, for any or all three of the constituents may be denied, questioned, challenged, objected to, refuted, etc., without violating the preparatory rules of felicity or coop-

(10) (a) Illocution: I pronounce you man and wife.
        Perlocution: But you can't marry us. You're not a priest.
   (b) Illocution: I pronounce you man and wife.
        Perlocution: Nice try, but you've got the wrong couple. We're the parents of the groom.
   (c) Illocution: I pronounce you man and wife.
        Perlocution: But we want to be confirmed.

In 10a, the response is to ethos, in that the audience believes the speaker not to have the authority invoked by the pronouncement. In 10b, the response is to pathos, in that the audience understands itself to be outside the act of the utterance; it is inappropriate or irrelevant to their real-world concerns or situation. In 10c, the response is to logos, in that the proposition of performing a marriage is inappropriate, inconsistent, or incoherent in the "scenic" state of affairs. Notice the traditionally rhetorical contexts

erativeness. Suppose, for example, that the proposition in 9a, "I was smoking behind the barn," is preceded by the rhetorical intention indicated by a performative like *suggest*, a clearly rhetorical performative:

(11) (a) (I suggest that) I ((was) (may have been)) smoking behind the barn.

All of the possible perlocutions in 9b are also possible as responses to 11a. But the following perlocutions, unacceptable challenges to authority, truth, or relevance in 9, are permitted as responses to a suggestion:

(11) (b) You can't prove that.
Are you certain of what you're saying?
Who cares?
I don't believe you.

If the response to an intention informed by an arhetorical performative verb is one of negation or challenge, then, either some principle of reality or some condition for felicity was violated, as in 9c or 10. If a "negative" perlocution obtains (or is projected) to an intention informed by a rhetorical performative, as in 8b or 11b, the initiating intention-response pair will extend to what we characterize as dialogue, discourse, or composition. The person initiating the speech act will attempt to address the challenges to her authority to offer such a proposition, the truth of the proposition, or the real-world relevance of the proposition to the audience. Performatives like *assert*, therefore, may be thought of as belonging to the subclass, *rhetorical*, with the semantic power of initiating a potential series of turn-takings. We can take a well-publicized illocution this time to illustrate the point:

(12) (a) Linus Pauling: ((I *assert* (*claim*, . . .) that)) Megadoses of Vitamin C will help to prevent disease.
(b) Audience: I *deny* (*question*, . . .) that you have the authority to make any claim about nutrition and health.

In 12b, the audience directs the response to the credentials of the writer, the ethical constituent of the illocution. In 12c, the response is directed at the truth or validity of

the state of affairs as represented by Pauling, the logical constituent of his claim:

(c) Audience: I *deny* (*question*, . . .) that megadoses of C can prevent disease.

In 13d, the response is directed toward the relevancy of the claim to the real-world concerns or situation (pathos) of the audience:

(d) Audience: I *deny* that your claim is meaningful for me (because I am allergic to Ascorbic Acid . . .).

Of course, the audience may affirm as well as deny, accept as well as question any or all of the constituents of the illocution. In that case, however, rhetoric does not follow; the exchange begins and ends in a two-sentence language game of one turn each for the participants. There is no ensuing "art of the probable," no attempt to "remedy misunderstandings," no need to depend upon the constitutive rules of argument or persuasion in order to present evidence for one's case.

But, quite simply, a significant condition attached to rhetorical intention(s) realized as underlying performative clauses on the order of 8a is the writer's presupposition that a challenge or a negative *may* direct the reader's response. It is this potential response that teases the concept of rhetoric from the universe of discourse.

One "rule" governing rhetoric is this: the writer must hedge his rhetorical bet by addressing and resolving the denials or challenges to any or all of the constituents of his super-intention informed by a verb such as *assert*. In doing so, the writer will compose more than subject matter; he will at least attempt to bring together or reconcile the differing views or presuppositions toward the materials of the discourse—his authority to speak on the subject, the relevance of the subject to the reader, and the real-world "truth" of his proposition(s). If the writer is successful, he will have established a new meaning for any proposition, any "x"; he will have communicated "news." The following represents the underlying model of the reader-writer transaction in successful discourse.

style or arrangement are beside the point. A speaker or writer whose intention is to make an admission, confession, pronouncement, promise, etc., need only learn or have available for imitation a certain linguistic "ritual." The performative values of verbs like *admit* carry with them proscribed forms and styles signified by the writer's (or speaker's) reliance on ritualized language (the priest reading from a prepared text in performing a ceremony; legislators employing legal consultants to check on the wording of a newly written bill; etc.) This attention to the ritual

> Writer: I *assert* to you that "x."
> Reader: I *deny* that ("x" is a true representation of reality).
> (I have any stake in "x").
> (you have the authority to assert "x").
> Writer: I *offer* (n "proofs" that "x" is true).
> (n "proofs" that "x" is relevant to you).
> (n "proofs" that I am a credible source).
> Reader: I *require* (q "proofs" for the truth of "x").
> (. . . .)

And so on. Not so surprisingly, one could reduce any finished piece of rhetoric to the abstract turn-taking described above. The evidence which is generated to address potential negative responses to the writer's intention(s) will mark the form of discourse as representative of the ego-sharing that is involved in all language games. If subject matter transforms to subject in the process of composing, that is exactly what is involved.

One way of looking at the topics of invention or prescriptions for style and arrangement is that they are implicit codifications of probable, negative responses by audiences to writers' intentions. Indeed, in arhetorical situations, represented in 7 or 9, considerations such as

of the speech act marks the behavior of the participants as outside the probable. It is either "correct" or it isn't. As a matter of fact, in some arhetorical situations, any deviation from the "text" nullifies the speech act. A verdict of guilty may be overthrown on a "linguistic" technicality as well as an evidential one: the defendant was not "formally" charged; a witness was not properly interrogated. Formal or stylistic latitude, at any rate, is very narrow in the speech acts which identify civil, religious, or social speech acts realized as contracts.

One may even entertain the notion here that some academic "styles," especially in the sciences, tacitly militate against the reader's option to say NO; rigidly proscribed form in an essay is, in a sense, indicative of a contract, an arhetorical speech act initiated by performatives like *declare*, *inform*, or *pronounce*, in which, preparatory conditions having been satisfied, a negative response is ruled out. Scientific papers do not "argue"; for the most part, their authors "declare" that such-and-such is the case because a certain process was overlaid on a certain set of givens, a theoretical or practical ritual that the investigators report on. That writers in the humanities should allow that model of research and communication to influence their own practice is understandable in a "scientific age," but it has taken a terrible toll. The inordinate amount of time and attention given to form and style in composition courses based on current-traditionalist notions of rhetoric would seem to bring about the arhetorical situation in which students "expect" no response, except perhaps that of assent, in their reading and their own writing. Is it any wonder that despite the recent renaissance in emphasizing invention, heuristics, problem-solving and other aids for investing students' writing with substance, point of view, purpose, *meaning*, their essays may still lack the fullness of their "real-life" talent for dialogue and debate.

In the next section, then, we intend to show how and why the theory laid out above can significantly affect the teaching and learning of writing.

IV

Rhetorical situations are marked by debate over propositions, exchange of views and evidence, influence over decision-making, with persuading the audience toward a particular action or idea as the final cause. This is so whether or not an audience apart from the writer is addressed or conceived. The phenomenon of the writer's "changing his mind," or his thesis, in the process of composing is, after all, a familiar one to accomplished writers, and this first-hand knowledge, if nothing more, strongly suggests that underlying the surface structures of written discourse we may "discover" the rules for rhetorical competence.

We have posited that these rules may be made explicit by referring to the concepts describing spoken dialogue and specifically to speech act theory and the intention-response model of philosophy and linguistics. A preliminary analysis of rhetorical intentions made tenable the idea that the successful reader-writer transaction depends upon both participants constructing and reconstructing the same (or a semantically equivalent) performative verb in the main, deep-structure clause of the declarative sentence serving as a statement of thesis or topic. Furthermore, we demonstrated that rhetorical intentions are marked by a special subclass of performative verbs. This subclass of rhetorical performatives has the semantic potential to elicit responses which are coherent with the rhetorical or the propositional intentions, but which, nevertheless, may deny or challenge any or all of the constituents of the super-intention. If a challenge to the authority of the writer, the truth of the proposition, or the relevance of either to the reader does ensue (and the writer must suppose that any or all may), then an underlying, extended, and implicit series of speech acts describes the form and content of the resulting discourse.

Given that summary, we would like to make two practical observations.

First, if our case is valid, it represents in abstract what every competent writer and reader knows intuitively. (To misquote a truism of linguistic research, none of us knows consciously the "rules" of composition, but we all read and write as though we do.) That is, our attempt to raise the rules of composition to formal representation should not be interpreted as a vague prescription for classroom practice, but as a descriptive model of rhetorical competence in writers and readers. Teaching speech act theory to naive writers in the hope that they will translate its maxims and terminology into their practical struggles with the written word would seem to be as vain an endeavor as teaching them grammar in the hope that their editing problems will disappear. The point is that, just as competent speakers know the rules for putting the parts of speech together, though they may not be able to define "noun" or to give an example of one, competent writers and readers know the rules for successful transaction in discourse, though they may not be able to define "rhetorical intention" or be consciously aware of responding to them. Humans "acquire" linguistic competence through exposure to models—mostly imperfect. We do not subsequently "imitate" the models so much as creatively adapt them to own purposes in, as Chomsky puts it, manipulating the world.

The proper "use" of our theory, it seems to us, is as an aid to the teacher's formal understanding of the discipline more than as an immediate editing tool for the student. Until very recently in composition research, we have been more or less concerned with the interaction of underlying systems of linguistic behavior—the teacher's and the student's—with little attention to the systems themselves.[17] This essay, as we stated at the start, is one more attempt in a growing body of research in rhetoric to realign our thinking about composition and its processes. Like some others who have looked at received "characterizing statements" of rhetoric and found them to misrepresent our realities, we implicitly questioned some tenets of the tradition by explicitly offering a novel characterization of the system itself.

Second. At the same time, we have to admit that many if not most of our students cannot yet claim rhetorical competency. And so we have to address a potential response of the reader: Who cares about theoretical adjustments to the tradition when I have students who consistently compose two-sentence paragraphs and cannot formulate a recognizable thesis? We admit that our answer must disappoint any immediate expectations of practical payoffs. For in order to rely on the constitutive rules for rhetoric, writers and readers need the time to "acquire" rule-governed behavior rather than just "learn" formulae.[18] A history of reading "just for fun" is the necessary condition for reconstructing, say, Swift's rhetorical intention in "A Modest Proposal." Experience in writing "just for the hell of it" is prerequisite to formulating and constructing super-intentions. Competent writers and readers have long, and wide, apprenticeships. Paradoxically, they come as students to our classes with little need for "instructions." Since they have already internalized the rules, they learn only to perfect their game.

For those students lacking such an apprenticeship, we can only point to the wrong-headedness of much of the English curriculum in perpetuating incompetency, delivered of attitudes toward reading and writing that, according to Clinton S. Burhans,[19] depend on myth and unexamined assumptions about language and literacy. In previous sections, we touched on the counter-productiveness of college-level courses in writing taught solely in terms of exposition and their emphasis on form and style. We would argue that if a "learned" form makes the meaning in a piece of writing rather than the writer making the meaning in the process of rhetorical give-and-take, she must always be judged as "naive." As for reading, it is safe to say that naive writers at any level of instruction need exposure to all the modes of discourse, all the divisions of rhetoric's implicit dialogue, critical essays as well as fiction, argumentation as well as biography, so that form and style can be understood to develop in any piece of writing as a function of underlying speech acts, not as ends in themselves. As teachers of composition, we can rephrase T. S. Eliot's profound quip about the difference between mature and immature poets to read "Competent writers steal; naive writers copy." Competent writers will rely on the whole range of possible intention-response environments for meaning they have been exposed to in their reading, and they will do a mental cut-and-paste job in adapting those possible "models" of implicit dialogue to their own writ-

ing.[20] Our prescription, then, must be stated as a goal: adjustment of the curriculum to present characterizations of literacy—what it is that writers-and-readers do.

The major division of speech acts between rhetorical and arhetorical describes a novel concept, and a valid one we believe, of the transaction between writer and reader. It has allowed us to characterize rhetoric as a corollary to recent, valid descriptions of language. Understood as such, rhetoric is rich in possibilities for research which may qualify either the characterizing statement or the explanation we gave for it in the preceding pages. Our concept, moreover, marks much of the tradition as intuitively sound. But it also indicts much of the practice which refers to convention as pedagogically short-sighted and even counter-productive to the means and ends of a society in which dialogue rather than dicta is preferred.

NOTES

1. London and New York: Cambridge University Press, 1969.

2. Linda Flowers and John R. Hayes provide protocol analyses of writers thinking aloud in the process of composing, showing that writers are guided by creative goal-setting rather than by "learned" rules ("A Cognitive Process Theory of Writing," *College Composition and Communication*, 32 [December 1981], 365–87). "Studies That Challenge Traditional Paragraph Prescriptions" is the heading for seven entries in a recently published annotated bibliography, Marian Price, "Recent Work in Paragraph Analysis: A Bibliography," *Rhetoric Society Quarterly*, 12 (Spring 1982), 127–31.

3. Simply put, in adhering to the cooperative principle, speakers are informative, truthful, relevant, and clear, "and

listeners interpret what [speakers] say on the assumption that they are trying to live up to these ideals." Herbert H. Clark and Eve V. Clark, *Psychology and Language* (New York: Harcourt, Brace, Jovanovich, 1977), 122.

4. "Rhetoric," in other words, "can be viewed as an inherent system which is 'discoverable,' rather than as a set of rules imposed from without." Dorothy Augustine, "Geometries and Words: Linguistics and Philosophy: A Model of the Composing Process," *College English*, 43 (March 1981), 221–31.

5. The anthropologist Edward Hall has reported on an extended experiment meant to explore why any two conversants were seen to move in close physical synchrony when they were studied on slow motion film:

[Finally] two people in conversation were wired to electroencephalographs to see if there was any comparability in brain waves. Two cameras were set up so that one focused on the speakers, the other on the EEG recording pens. When two people talked, the recording pens moved as though driven by a single brain. When one of the individuals was called out of the conversation by a third person, the pens no longer moved together. . . . The only thing that destroyed synchrony was if one of the people was called out of the conversation by a third party. Synchrony stopped, and a new chain was set up with the new interlocutor.

Beyond Culture, (Garden City, N.Y.: Anchor Books, 1977), p. 73.

6. Any speech act is composed of illocution and perlocution, or intention and response; for example, *Illocution*: I advise you to stop smoking; *Perlocution*: I answer that your advice is unrealistic. The examples are abstractions, for normally we speak to each other "indirectly": "Why don't you stop smoking, for heaven's sake?" "It isn't that easy."

In speech act theory, an illocution initiates a purposive exchange of inten-

tion(s) and response(s). An illocution is always a "performative sentence," indicated by the main verb being one of the class of true, linguistic verbs which includes *advise, answer, appoint, ask, assert, authorize, beg, bequeath, beseech, caution, cede, claim, close (a meeting), command, condemn, counsel, dare, declare, demand, deny, empower, enquire, entreat, excommunicate, grant, implore, inform, instruct, order, pledge, pronounce, propose, request, require, say, sentence, vow, warn, write.* Perlocutions may also be thought of as performative sentences, though, of course, the semantic environment requires that the main verbs include those performatives in the subclass of "response performatives," such as *answer, cede, challenge, enquire, deny, require,* etc.

7. The naive writer has no such facility for inventing readers or for projecting their probable or potential responses to what is being said in the composition. Mina Shaughnessy reports, for example, that the basic writers with whom she worked had trouble locating their own intentions, let alone projecting responses—their own as well as others'. "Without [the] conviction that he has 'something to mean,' the writer cannot *carry on the kind of conversation with himself that leads to writing*" (italics added). And the point is not simply that student-writers like Shaughnessy's lack rhetorical purposes, for the problems of basic writers, she reminds us, are the problems of all writers, writ large: "Without these dialogues [with oneself], thoughts run dry and judgment falters." (*Errors and Expectations* [New York: Oxford Univ. Press, 1977], 81–82.)

8. A recent collection of essays treating the subject is James J. Murphy, ed., *The Rhetorical Tradition and Modern Writing* (New York: The Modern Language Association, 1982).

9. Patricia Bizzell maintains that successful writing-across-the-curriculum programs are informed by epistemic notions of rhetoric. ("Cognition, Convention, and Certainty," *PRE/TEXT*, 3 [1982].) The paradox appears that were writing-across-the-curriculum in-

troduced before the new rhetoric's emergence, there might not have been a common mechanism to account for success or failure; everyone would have had access to the causes only through his or her discipline's "objective" definition of rhetoric and its function.

10. This analysis of deep-structure intentions is adapted from John Robert Ross, "On Declarative Sentences," in *Readings in Transformational Grammar*, R. A. Jacobs and P. S. Rosenbaum, eds. (Waltham, Mass.: Ginn, 1970), 222–72.

11. A full discussion of the underlying intention in Swift's "A Modest Proposal" is given in W. Ross Winterowd, "The Rhetoric of Beneficence, Authority, Ethical Commitment, and the Negative," *Philosophy and Rhetoric*, 9 (Spring 1976), 65–83.

12. *Speech Acts*, 52–53.

13. In *Literacy and the Survival of Humanism*, Richard Lanham attacks the C-B-S (clarity, brevity, sincerity) "model" of writing on the same grounds, though with a different aim. (New Haven, Conn.: Yale University Press, 1983.)

14. Felicity conditions, discussed below, are those presuppositions about the speaker, the listener, and the proposition "which an illocutionary act must fulfill if it is to be successful and non-defective." John Lyons, *Semantics*, II (London and New York: Cambridge University Press, 1977), 733.

15. John R. Searle, "A Taxonomy of Illocutionary Acts," in *Minnesota Studies in the Philosophy of Language*, K. Gunderson, ed. (Minneapolis: University of Minnesota Press, 1975), 344–69.

16. *Psychology and Language*, 242.

17. This situation has been given much attention in sociolinguistic studies of standard vs. nonstandard dialects in the schools. See, for example, William Labov, *The Study of Nonstandard English* (Champaign, Ill.: The National Council of Teachers of English, 1970), 39–42.

18. Stephen Krashen advises that we should think of literacy as a "second dialect," and that the teaching of writing can profit from the pedagogy of second language learning. More specific to our concern here, Krashen distinguishes between "acquiring" or internalizing the rules of a second language through social interaction—and therefore achieving full competency—and "learning" a second language—consciously recalling and intellectually applying the rules of its grammar so that one is "understood" by competent speakers, but is also identified by them as "speaking with an accent" or "making mistakes." The critical age for acquiring a second language or dialect is, depending on the researcher, as early as six but no later than adolescence.

19. "The Teaching of Writing and the Knowledge Gap," *College English*, 45 (November 1983), 639–56.

20. Finally, one more note on the theory. Below is a tentative classification of performatives distinguishing between those that are rhetorically weighted (entailing a potential negative response in the perlocution) and those that are arhetorical (entailing only an affirmative in the perlocution). Again, some discrepancies may occur between our designations and the reader's; we stress that our classification is a possible and reasonable ordering of the more familiar performatives.

Arhetorical Performatives	*Rhetorical Performatives*
answer	advise
appoint	assert
ask	beg
authorize	beseech
bequeath	caution
cede	claim
close (a meeting)	counsel
command	entreat
condemn	implore
confess	offer
dare	propose
declare	request
demand	require
grant	?tell
inform	warn
instruct	write
order	. . .
pledge	

promise
pronounce
?say
sentence
vow
. . .

Further subclassifications are possible. For instance, all arhetorical verbs warrant the authority of the "I" in the main clause (as judge, priest, teacher, etc.) to perform the speech act, but so do some in the rhetorical class. *Advise, counsel,* and *warn* are ethically charged, and evidence of the writer's authority to perform those services for the reader will make those speech acts rhetorically felicitous. This observation may lead us to expect a disproportionate reliance by the writer on the "ethical proofs" in essays of advice, counsel, or warning. Our educated suspicion would point toward that expectation being borne out through analysis. Also, the assumption taken from cognitive psychology that personal narrative is the first stage in those that lead to rhetorical competency is given a theoretical boost by the appearance of verbs like *confess, declare, inform, instruct, pledge, pronounce,* or *vow* in the arhetorical column, none of them admitting a complexity of underlying rules by the writer's needing to project a response. Intentions, after all, must be practiced before possible and potential responses can be projected. These observations, indicative of future studies, may make coherent rigorous analysis and our best intuitions.

Dramatism in Themes and Poems

Several of my essays explore "other knowledge," that realm of meaning that is not "logical" and sequential, but imagistic, "dramatistic"—or, to use the jargon of modern psychology, "episodic" as opposed to "verbal" knowledge: "Brain, Rhetoric, and Style," "Black Holes, Indeterminacy, and Paulo Freire," and "The Politics of Meaning" as well as this one. In fact, a bit of tampering could make all of those essays into one: they add up to a coherent whole.

In the essay, I say, "[Kenneth] Burke's dramatistic view of meaning would have preempted post–structuralists such as Derrida if they had been aware of [his work through the years]." I want, then, to give Burke the centrality that he deserves.

In "Brain, Rhetoric, and Style," I used the term "appositional prose"; this essay is an elaboration on my definition of the term.

The following discussion will concern the radical dramatism of language and the implications of that view for composition classroom practice. If literary theory comes in by the way, so much the better.

The Art of Readable Writing, by Rudolf Flesch, was a popular success when it was published in 1949, and it still remains in print (25th anniversary ed., rev. and enlarged: New York: Harper & Row, 1974). Though seriously flawed by the readability formula with which it concludes, the book is remarkably enlightened. For example, early on Flesch says, "I am sure you realize that this book is not dealing with what usually goes by the names of grammar, usage, composition, or rhetoric. On the contrary, if you want to learn how to write, you need exact information about what kind of language will fit what kind of audience." (p. 9). He goes on to give a series of tips:

1. "Find out what people know, and what they don't know, and write accordingly." (P. 19)
2. Find an angle or slant, *which is likely to result from illustrations.* (Pp. 26–35)

This essay appeared originally in *College English* (Oct. 1983). Reprinted with the permission of the National Council of Teachers of English.

3. Think about your ideas; give them a chance to gel. "There has to be one idea that is sharply in focus, and a clear grouping of everything else around it." (P. 37)

4. "Ordinarily—not always, but more often than not—writing proceeds like this: collecting material—trying to find a good approach—spending some time on something else—getting a sudden bright idea—planning and organizing—writing—revising. The most mysterious—and most fascinating—part of the whole process is the one you don't read about in the handbooks: the search for a good approach, the period when you abandon the search, and the moment when, out of nowhere, an idea pops into your mind." (P. 49)

In the chapter "How to Be Human Though Factual" (pp. 72–83), Flesch becomes most dramatistic. "Only stories are really readable," he says (p. 72). Then he quotes a *Reader's Digest* editor: "Whenever we want to draw attention to a problem, we wait until somebody does something about it. Then we print the story of how he did it" (p. 72). In effect, Flesch stated the *scenario principle* of Linda Flower and John Hayes: functional prose should be structured around a human agent performing actions in an understandable context.[1] One might sum up in a few words: present ideas dramatistically. And the injunction—from whatever source—has great intuitive appeal.[2]

One of the most important of dramatistic theoreticians, Kenneth Burke, offers this clearcut formulation of dramatism in *A Grammar of Motives* (1945; rpt. Berkeley: University of California Press, 1968):

In a rounded statement about motives, you must have some word that names the *act* (names what took place, in thought or deed), and another that names the *scene* (the background of the act, the situation in which it occurred); also, you must indicate what person or kind of person (*agent*) performed the act, which means or instruments he used (*agency*), and the *purpose*. (P. xv)

Burke now ruefully wishes he had included Attitude in his "grammar of motives."[3] We shall happily do so, putting the Hex- on the Pentad.

From the cursed center formed by the pivotal six, we can move northward into the realm of malice and the lie or southward into the system of the text: the drama of human relations at one pole and drama at the other. Our discussion can be so ambiguous as to leave our reader undecided as to whether we are talking about politics or poems—and, in fact, we are undoubtedly dealing with both.

Burke's technical term for "drama" in *A Grammar of Motives* is "representative anecdote" (pp. 50–124), which in one sense was defined by Flower and Hayes. The compositionist's adage "Give appropriate examples" covers the case adequately. In another sense, however, "representative anecdote" means "conceptual pivot" and is equated with a family of terms: "enthymeme," "thesis," "topic sentence," "theme." The representative anecdote, in other words, can be either support or conceptual pivot, and in the case of drama (such as *Samson Agonistes*, *Madame Bovary*, or "The Rime of the Ancient Mariner") is both support and conceptual pivot—the all. A woman as a rat in a Skinner box is quite different from a man whose great-great-great . . . grandpa was a monkey is quite different from a child whose destiny is angel's wings and a harp: the story of humankind as *Beyond Freedom and Dignity*, *The Origin of the Species*, or the Bible.

Let me use the ferrule (or slapstick) to make my point: we are here dealing with revolution. Burke is telling us that we progress not only via enthymemes (logical propositions), but also, importantly, via *synecdoches* (representative anecdotes), which explains why *Samson Agonistes*, *Madame Bovary*, and "The Rime of the Ancient Mariner" provide an essential kind of knowledge. Humans live not by enthymemes (theses, topic sentences) alone.

tative" rather than "syllogistic" progression.

Burke's dramatistic view of meaning would have preempted post–structuralists such as Derrida if they had been aware of *Counter-Statement* (1931), *Permanence and Change* (1935), *Attitudes Toward History* (1937), *The Philosophy of Literary Form* (1941), *A Grammar of Motives* (1945), and *A Rhetoric of Motives* (1950).

The following quotations, in apposition, get us at the crux of Burke's ideas. First, from *The Philosophy of Literary Form* (rev. ed.; New York, Vintage, 1957).

FRÈRE JACQUES, DORMEZ VOUS?

Burke is so nonchalant about his epistemology that one can easily react with "So what?" Of course, Burke's theories of knowing are subjective, drawn from his own experience, naively one suspects, as if he were reflecting on the way his own mind works and presenting the results as a theory. The Boikwoiks not only attempt to explain knowing, but demonstrate repeatedly how their author knows. The terms that apply most aptly are "synecdoche," "terministic screen," "logologic," and "apposition." Synecdoche (representative anecdote) is often the pivot; the synecdoche implies (makes inevitable) a set of terms (terministic screen); logologic enables one to trace, tease, Joyce, wring the possible meanings from the set of terms and hence arrive at the meaningfulness of the synecdoche. Order is virtually always appositional rather than logically sequential; or, to use Burke's own terminology, the arguments most often represent "quali-

Where does the drama get its materials? From the "unending conversation" that is going on at the point in history where we are born. Imagine that you enter a parlor. You come late. When you arrive, others have long preceded you, and they are engaged in a heated discussion, a discussion too heated for them to pause and tell you exactly what it is about. In fact, the discussion had already begun long before any of them got there, so that no one present is qualified to retrace for you all of the steps that had gone before. You listen for a while, until you decide that you have caught the tenor of the argument; then you put in your oar. Someone answers; you answer him; another comes to your defense; another aligns himself against you, to either the embarrassment or gratification of your opponent, depending upon the quality of your ally's assistance. However, the discussion is interminable. The hour grows late, you must depart. And you do depart, with the discussion still vigorously in progress.

It is from this "unending conversation" . . . that the materials of your drama arise. Nor is this verbal action all there is to it. For all these words are grounded in what Malinowski would call "contexts of situation." (Pp. 94–96)

And then this:

Men seek for vocabularies that will be faithful *reflections* of reality. To this end, they must develop vocabularies that are *selections* of reality. And any selection of reality must, in certain circumstances, function as a *deflection* of reality. Insofar as the vocabulary meets the needs of reflection, we can say that it has the necessary scope. In its selectivity, it is a reduction. Its scope and reduction become a deflection when the given terminology, or calculus, is not suited to the subject matter which it is designed to calculate. (*A Grammar of Motives*, p. 59)

And finally, from *A Rhetoric of Motives* (1950; rpt. Berkeley: University of California Press, 1969):

So we must keep trying anything and everything, improvising, borrowing from others, developing from others, dialectically using one text as comment upon another, schematizing; using the incentive to new wanderings, returning from these excursions to schematize again, being oversubtle where the straining seems to promise some further glimpse, and making amends by reduction to very simple anecdotes. (P. 265)

Language not only conveys meaning, it makes it; and it does so not only *in* a context, but *because of* or *through* a context. To many, all of this might sound particularly Fishy,[4] but snide allusions, though gratifying to churls, are *non sequiturs*, leading us away from the constructive dialectic of conversation to the destructiveness of logomachy.

CONSTRUCTING TEXTS: CONCEPTUAL PIVOTS AND ACCEPTABLE ARGUMENTS

In the fourth century B.C., Aristotle placed the enthymeme at the very heart of rhetoric: "Rhetorical proof . . . takes the form of an enthymeme, this being, in general, the most effective among various forms of persuasion."[5] Compositionist synonyms for enthymeme are, among others, "thesis" and "topic sentence." The point is this: throughout Western history, logic—formal and informal—has been the accepted method in expository and persuasive writing. Among others, Walter Kintsch and Teun A. van Dijk present evidence that readers attempt to organize their knowledge of a text around the highest level generality that they can derive (that is, around the enthymeme).[6] If the writer is an enthymeme monger, then the reader is an enthymeme seeker, and the coherence of a text depends on the reader's ability to find the highest level generality and then "tree" the rest of the ideational content.

Note, for instance, the design of an article in the February 1982 issue of *The Atlantic*. Above the title is this teaser: "An unruly market may undo the work of a giant cartel and of an inspired, decades-long ad campaign." Then the title: "Have You Ever Tried to Sell a Diamond?" With extraordinary efficiency the editors have strongly implied the enthymeme even before the article begins—something like this: in spite of the diamond cartel's campaign to convince us that diamonds are forever, the value of the stones will drop if people start trading them like other commodities.

Burke is, of course, famous for having substituted *identification* for *persuasion* as the goal of rhetoric (see *A Rhetoric of Motives*, pp. 19–20), but his most revolutionary departure from the classical and accepted tradition has gone unnoticed. Burke enfranchises and consistently uses what might be called a non-Aristotelian conceptual pivot, the "representative anecdote." In *Counter-Statement* (1931; rpt. Berkeley: University of California Press, 1968) Burke had talked about the "individuation" of "patterns of experience" (pp. 29–62). In *A Grammar of Motives* he brings the idea to fruition, for a representative anecdote is precisely an individuation (in other words, a synecdoche).

Dramatism suggests a procedure to be followed in the development of a given calculus, or terminology. It involves the search for a "representative anecdote," to be used as a form in conformity with which the vocabulary is constructed. For instance, the behaviorist uses his experiments with conditioned reflex as the anecdote about which to form his vocabulary for the discussion of human motives; but this anecdote, though notably *informative*, is not *representative*, since one cannot find a representative case of human motivation in animals, if only because animals lack that property of linguistic rationalization which is so typical of human motives. A representative case of human motivation must have a strongly linguistic bias, whereas animal experimentation necessarily neglects this. (P. 59)

Propositional
enthymeme as conceptual
    pivot
organizational rigidity
general examples, if any
backgrounded style
little presence

It goes without saying that some of the most useful representative anecdotes are works of literature.

Put into the admonitory terms of the composition handbook, Burke's ideas might read something like this: Find a representative anecdote (instead of a thesis or enthymeme), and

follow its implications as far as you can, dramatistically. Make certain that the anecdote has the proper "circumference," i.e., that it has enough "scope" to serve your purpose.

In an earlier essay I characterized two general prose styles, which I called "propositional" and "appositional."[7] A slightly modified version of that characterization applies here:

Appositional
representative anecdote as
    pivot, or no apparent pivot
organizational flexibility
specific examples
foregrounded style[8]
great presence[9]

The propositional style is best represented by the typical essay in *Atlantic* or *Critical Inquiry*; any reader of Burke has found countless examples of the appositional.

I have not chosen the terms "propositional" and "appositional" promiscuously, but have lifted them directly from Joseph Bogen's characterization of two different kinds of thought processes.[10] I don't want, at this point, to summarize either my work or current knowledge of hemispheric specialization. Suffice it to say that Burke has outlined a non-traditional (though that word is far too weak) method of argumentation and uses that method consistently in his own work. We have the dramatistic way of knowing, explaining, and arguing: a method that is based on synecdoche, not enthymeme. The handbook admonition "Support your argument with appropriate examples" is turned on its head and becomes "Follow the leads of your example to their limits."

One suspects that Burke's tacit advice and its concommitant method have kept him outside the traditional mainstream. Certainly Derrida and Fish, both of whom unwittingly recapitulate much of Burke's thought, do not mention him as far as I know.

DECONSTRUCTING TEXTS: DRAMATISTIC INTERPRETATION

If we are to speak of interpretation, we must return briefly to meaning, and we shall do so via this stunningly modern statement which appeared in *Counter-Statement* (1931):

In some cases the matter to be recovered is so remote, is in a channel of thinking or feeling so alien to our own, that even a savant's "restoration" of the environmental context is not adequate. This is always true in some degree—though historical relativists have tended to make too much of it. For in the last analysis, any reader surrounds each word and each act in a work of art with a *unique* set of his own previous experiences (and therefore a unique set of imponderable emotional reactions), communication existing in the "margin of overlap" between the writer's experience and the reader's. And while it is dialectically true that two people of totally different experiences must totally fail to communicate, it is also true that there are no two such people, the "margin of overlap" always being considerable (due, if nothing else, to the fact that man's biologic functions are uniform). Absolute communication between ages is impossible in the same way that absolute communication between contemporaries is impossible. And conversely, as we communicate approximately though "imprisoned within the walls of our personality," so we communicate approximately though imprisoned within the walls of our age. (Pp. 78–79)

We shall resist the temptation at this point to enter the fray concerning determinacy of meaning, except to

say that Burke got there before many of our unwitting epigones rediscovered the continent.

Both Aristotle and the handbooks, of course, discuss deductive argument, based on the enthymeme, and inductive argument, based on the example—but it is a mistake to assume that the Aristotelian example and the Burkean representative anecdote are identical, as one of my students, James Comas, pointed out to me in a paper, from which I quote with his permission:

In the *Rhetoric*, Aristotle first mentions example as the rhetorical counterpart to induction in dialectic. (I.2.8) The Greek word for "example" is *paradigma* from the verb *paradiknú-nā*, meaning to exhibit beside, to show side by side. The word is a compound, from *para-* beside + *digma* sample, pattern, plan; the verb form of *digma* can also mean to furnish a sample and to make a proof. The *paradigma*, then, is not the simple furnishing of a sample, but furnishing a sample beside, or next to, something else. But what is this *something else*? Aristotle gives us an answer, I think, when he defines *paradigma* as having the structural relation of part to part:

It is neither the relation of part to whole, nor of whole to part, nor of one whole to another whole, but of part to part, of like to like, when both come under the same genus, but one of them is better known than the other. (I.2.19)

The *something else* is another sample, another "part"; the *paradigma* then is the relationship of two (or more) samples to each other and to the genus under which they are classified. Thus, even though Aristotle speaks of example in the singular (*paradigma* instead of the plural *paradigmata*), the concept implies more than one sample.

The example, then, is always a tripartite structure (or minimally tripartite structure); there are the two samples and the genus under which they are classified. The representative anecdote, on the other hand, is a binary structure, the synecdochic structure of part to whole; and Aristotle tells us explicitly that the example is not the "relation of part to whole, nor of whole to part." Thus, the representative anecdote has little in common with Aristotle's concept of the example.[11]

Both deduction and induction lead the reader to *a* central idea. By and large, I think, readers demand enthymemes and are impatient with texts from which no fairly clearcut general idea is to be derived—as if knowledge itself could always be summed up in a neat proposition.

In following the representative anecdote, what does one derive, if not an enthymeme? Burke's answer is "the terminological structure that is evolved in conformity with it" (*A Grammar of Motives*, p. 60). And "Once we have set seriously to work developing a systematic terminology out of our anecdote, another kind of summation looms up. We might call it the 'paradigm' or 'prototype'"— the perfect example implied by Burke's terminology, as the Act of Creation is the perfect instance of dramatistic action (p. 61).

We learn to single out certain relationships in accordance with the particular linguistic texture into which we are born, though we may privately manipulate this linguistic texture to formulate still other relationships. When we do so, we invent new terms, or apply our old vocabulary in new ways, attempting to socialize our position by so manipulating the linguistic equipment of our group that our particular additions or alterations can be shown to fit into the old texture. We try to point out new relationships as meaningful—we interpret situations differently; in the subjective sphere, we invent new accounts of motive.[12]

And that passage, though it antedates the first mention of representative anecdote by ten years, is a fair description of how the writer uses the device and of how the reader will interpret (*if* he or she consents to the terms of such a text).

The great disadvantage of the representative anecdote is that it does not lead readily to the closure of an enthymeme. Its great advantage is that it does not force such closure.

CAVEAT EMPTOR

Burke did not invent the representative anecdote. He discovered it in his own work and thought. According to my description (based originally on the work of ninth-graders and college freshmen), Burke writes appositionally. (And I suspect that apposition and representative anecdote imply one another.)

It goes without saying that Burke has always been outside the mainstream of language theory and literary criticism.[13] It is not too much, I think, to claim that Burke's method has been a major reason for his exclusion from the most select clubs; in any case, the appositionalist following the leads of his representative anecdote has not been much in evidence in the "schools" of criticism, the faculties of English departments, or the pages of the standard journals.

I have wondered how many appositionalists triumph in our college writing classes, and how many fail—for I am certain that Burke is uniquely brilliant, but that he is not unique in his conceptual strategies. I wonder, further, how many frustrated, baffled appositionalists fail to reach college, having been soundly defeated in high school. And I wonder yet further if perhaps expectations are changing, if post–structuralism is not preparing a generation of readers who will be satisfied with the open rather than the closed text.

Finally, we ask: "What practical value does all of this stuff about appositional writing and representative anecdotes have?"

First, we should be sensitive to the "styles" of our appositionalist students, giving their writing the kind of respectful attention that so many critics have failed to give Burke.

Second, we should teach students to use all there is to use in the effort to build an understanding of the world, and certainly the representative anecdote is marvelously heuristic.

Third, we should be realistic: the appositionalist is at a disadvantage in almost every writing situation, whether within the academy or without.

Fourth, we should realize that the situation is changing. Post–structuralism is enfranchising the kind of writing that Burke has been doing since the 1930s.

But that's the subject for another paper, isn't it?

NOTES

1. *Revising Functional Documents: The Scenario Principle* (Document Design Project Technical Report No. 10; Pittsburgh: Carnegie-Mellon University, 1980).

2. One can bring evidence from a great variety of sources to bear on the issue. For example, it may well be that the brain is simply programmed to seek out *agents*. (See Norman Segalowitz and Peter Hansson, "Hemispheric Functions in the Processing of Agent-Patient Information," *Brain and Language*, 8 [1979],

51–56.) Case grammar gives a dramatistic slant to the study of deep structure and syntax. Unlike structural and transformational grammar, the question of case grammar is, in a strategic oversimplification, "Who did what and with which and to whom?" And, of course, a principle of readability is that in sentences with agents, the agent should be in the subject slot. (See Joseph Williams, *Style: Ten Lessons in Clarity and Grace* [Glenview, Ill.: Scott, Foresman, 1981], p. 13.)

3. Burke has made this avowal numerous times: in 1978 at a conference at the University of Southern California and in 1980 at the MLA convention, among others.

4. See Stanley Fish, *Is There a Text in This Class?* (Cambridge, Mass.: Harvard University Press, 1980), pp. 1–17.

5. *The Rhetoric of Aristotle*, trans. Lane Cooper (New York: Appleton-Century-Crofts, 1932), p. 5.

6. "Toward a Model of Text Comprehension and Production," *Psychological Review*, 85 (1978), 363–94.

7. "Brain, Rhetoric, and Style," *Linguistics, Stylistics, and the Teaching of Composition*, ed. Donald McQuade (Akron, Ohio: University of Akron Press, 1979).

8. To use the foregrounded style is "to present phenomena in a fully externalized form, visible and palpable in all their parts, and completely fixed in spatial and temporal relations." "On the other hand [in the backgrounded style], the externalization of only so much of the phenomena as is necessary for the purposes of the narrative; all else left in obscurity; the decisive points of the narrative alone are emphasized, what lies between is nonexistent; time and place are undefined and call for interpretation; thoughts and feelings remain unexpressed, are only suggested by the silence and the fragmentary speakers; the whole, permeated with the most unrelieved suspense and directed toward a single goal (and to that extent far more of a unity), remains mysterious and 'fraught with background.'" Erich Auerbach, *Mime-*

sis: The Representation of Reality in Western Literature, trans. Willard R. Trask (Princeton, N.J.: Princeton University Press, 1968), pp. 6; 11–12.

9. Presence is "the means whereby style gives arguments status, vividness, and extralogical power. Presence seems to have these characteristics. First, that object or concept to which one directs attention assumes thereby more presence than other objects or concepts. In other words, the act of attention endows presence. Second, the image creates presence. Third, presence is conferred by holism." ("Brain, Rhetoric, and Style," p. 176.)

10. "Some Educational Aspects of Hemispheric Specialization," *The Human Brain,* ed. M. C. Wittrock, et al. (Englewood Cliffs, N.J.: Prentice-Hall, 1977), pp. 133–52.

11. "'Secret Agents,' 'Representative Anecdotes,' and Aristotle's 'Example,'" unpublished paper.

12. Kenneth Burke, *Permanence and Change* (1935; rpt. Los Altos, Cal.: Hermes, 1954), p. 36.

13. For a perspective on Burke's reputation and reception, see William H. Rueckert, ed., *Critical Responses to Kenneth Burke: 1924–1966* (Minneapolis: University of Minnesota Press, 1969).

Creativity and the Comp Class

It was in 1976 at Janice Lauer's annual summer rhetoric seminar that I first realized the power and usefulness of creativity theory. In a wonderfully informative and entertaining slide show and lecture, D. Gordon Rohman of Michigan State University gave a substantial outline of the field and demonstrated its applicability to the concerns of composition teachers. Rohman having gotten me under way, I began to read systematically and extensively. Much of the work on creativity theory, I found, is nugatory or downright silly, but a good deal is enlightening and challenging; I also found many of the same themes repeated again and again in the literature.

It seemed to me, then, that a "factor analysis" might be a way to get at the essence of creativity theory, so I began to catalogue themes as they appeared, under various guises, in the works that I went through. The result of that catalogue is "Creativity and the Comp Class"—and I still believe that it is an excellent introduction to its field and that its field is important to composition.

On March 14, 1977, I sat down to begin preparing the original version of the strange "paper" that follows. I had spent a year reading in and thinking about creativity theory, convinced that this field would be a fruitful source of ideas for composition and that the concepts embodied in it might well be crucial.

Early on in my reading, I began to perceive that certain issues and ideas were recurrent, running through many of the discussions and informing a great deal of the empirical research. Thus, I began to do a "factor analysis" of creativity theory. The result was a large brown box stuffed with 4 × 6 cards. (Prufrock may well have measured out his life with coffee spoons. I measure mine with brown and grey boxes.)

The original version of the paper was prepared for students in my seminar "Problems in the Theory of Discourse." In this revision, I have tried to maintain my sense of audience: a group of interested, respected colleagues who take their

This essay appeared originally in *Freshman English News* (Fall 1978). Reprinted with the permission of the editors.

subject matter, but not themselves, seriously. The revisions themselves consist in certain expansions and in the deletion of remarks that would be meaningless out of the context of the seminar that was going on during the spring semester of 1976.

I would like to think that this "factor analysis" is a reasonable survey of creativity theory and, furthermore, that it will be a heuristic for teachers of composition.

Items cited in the text are listed fully in the bibliography at the end of the paper.

Analogy

We shouldn't be afraid of analogy, and probably ought to use it as a rough-and-ready heuristic in teaching. (For example, see Rohman and Wlecke). Koestler (pp. 199–211) tells how Kepler used an absolutely screwy analogy: the role of the Father in the Trinity with that of the sun in the solar system.

I have been accused by my students of making outlandish analogic leaps, but I will keep on doing so, for they are productive. Recently I was quite willing to leap from speech act theory into a theory of master values (Winterowd, "The Rhetoric of Beneficence, Commitment, Authority, and the Negative"), and I fully intend to do a study of literature from the standpoint of these values.

Archetypes

The concept is basic to Northrop Frye. I'm not sure how to play around with this notion in regard to creativity—except to say that archetypes are not artifacts and must emerge from the language transaction. Notice that Koestler discusses the archetype (pp. 358–65).

Attitude

The best work on this (that I have found, anyway) comes from the self-actualization fellows. In *The Farther Reaches of Human Nature* (pp. 57–71), Maslow distinguishes between primary and secondary creativeness, roughly the initial inspiration and the subsequent work of creating the final product. (More about this later in another connection.) He lists some characteristics of the *peak experience* as primary creativeness: giving up the past, giving up the future, innocence, narrowing of consciousness, loss of ego, loss of self-consciousness, disappearance of fears, lessening of defenses and inhibitions, strength and courage, acceptance, trust (vs. trying, controlling, striving), Taoistic receptivity, integration of the being-cognizer, permission to dip into primary processes (poetic, metaphoric, primitive, mystic, etc.), esthetic perceiving rather than abstracting (which I call concretization), fullest spontaneity, fullest expressiveness, fusion of the person with the world.

In other words, primary creativity involves hanging loose, giving up inhibitions, relying on intuition, etc. It is perfectly clear that in the composition class, we are dealing with both primary and secondary creativity. At the primary stage, the more we let students be themselves, the more successful we're likely to be as teachers. Paradoxically, primary creativity demands concentration, but not "discipline." We should never confuse the mechanical aspects of writing with the more spontaneous, less controlled aspects. Outlining, editing, ordering—all of these belong to secondary creativity. If we don't keep the two separate, we are bound to create havoc.

I can think of my own process of composition. It begins in chaos and ends in a kind of order. For example, I could show you the genesis of some of my papers (not that I'm claiming they're highly creative); what you'd find is a movement from outlandish chaos toward more and more control and form. In fact, when I began this "factor analysis," I was trying to work myself up to a point that would result in some kind of coherent and relatively unique insight concerning creativity in language. In fact, the process was successful, for I completed a long paper, "Brain, Rhetoric, and Style," which is now in the process of publication.

And this makes me think of an interesting point. I *wanted* to come up with something! And if nothing had resulted from the work, the experience would have been bitter for me. I wanted to arrive at the point where I could say (to myself) "Eureka!" For it is a fact that the main purpose of this sort of moiling is the exhilaration of that Eureka. In a way, it doesn't matter if, subsequently, criticisms and contradictions let the air out of the balloon.

Bisociation

This notion permeates Koestler, of course. It's a fruitful one for me. For example, I can look at the graduate students in our rhetoric-linguistics-literature program and see how extremely gifted people have been set off by the forced bisociation of the program.

In general, I think that bisociation is a good educational principle—and, of course, it's an old one. However, you can't bisociate thin gruel with Irish stew and come up with anything but either a thickened version of gruel or a watered-down version of stew. In other words, the bisociated fields both need some depth.

On *Nova* a couple of weeks ago I was listening to Watson and Crick talk about their discovery of the double helix. Interestingly enough, Watson the biologist did the crystallographic thinking, and Crick the physicist made his greatest input in the biological component of the theory.

I also think that bisociation is an interesting principle in language. Can't we see it as the function of metaphor? Irony? Paradox?

It is reasonable to assume that creative uses of language rely on a particular kind of bisociation. For example, from the standpoint of reading theory—the efficient processing of information—anything that gets in the way of efficiency is "noise." The text itself is transparent. However, in poetry the text is *not* transparent; as I have pointed out ("The Three R's: Reading, Reading, and Rhetoric"), the textual irony of poetry comes about precisely because the text reifies itself, dissociates itself from message. In short, the dissociation of the what and the how is one of the features of poetry.

Could we go on to say that style is bisociation? Roughly, a good news article has no style in the sense that it can be processed with maximum efficiency, but a work of art has style. Of course, we are talking here about a spectrum—and also about reading as a rhetorical transaction. It is possible for me to read *anything* either as information or as art. Do you see what I'm getting at?

A good heuristic forces bisociation. Think of Burke's ratios. Or think of the tagmemic grid.

Blocks

In *Conceptual Blockbusting,* Adams lists three kinds of blocks to creativity, and I find these both commonsensical and tremendously useful when applied to the classroom. If every writing teacher would go through an awareness session based on these blocks, comp classes would be more productive places. For your convenience, I will give you Adams' list.

(1) Cultural and Environmental —e.g., taboos and lack of cooperation and trust among colleagues

(2) Emotional
    (a) fear of taking a risk
    (b) no appetite for chaos
    (c) judging rather than generating
    (d) inability to incubate [My interpretation: the urge always to be going, rather than sometimes meditating.]
    (e) reality and fantasy—the inability to separate the two

(3) Intellectual and Expressive
    (a) flexibility in use of strategies [I can't help commenting on the current tendency in "good" schools to emphasize the three-point topic sentence, the five-paragraph theme, and so on—not to mention the mindless dichotomizing of "creative" and "expository" writing. I cite Keith Fort's essay, as well as Winston Weathers' piece in *FEN.*]
    (b) importance of correct information
    (c) expressive blocks in general [Create your own lists.]

Character of the Creator

Right now, without batting an eye, I could do a 500-page essay on this subject. For instance, Eyring says one characteristic is "inability to understand the obvious." I'll give you some citations: Fromm in Anderson, pp. 48–53; Rogers in Anderson, pp. 73, 75–78; Guilford in Anderson; Hilgard in Anderson; Adams, pp. 49–73; Bruner, *On Knowing,* pp. 24–28. What I'm going to do is read through my notes and then give you my idea of the creative person.

The creative person has the ability to become completely absorbed, eliminating the Cartesian duality between self and world. Along with this absorption come a variety of paradoxical traits: self-confidence coupled with an accepting attitude toward others; a feeling of omnipotence with the ability to be surprised in a childlike way; the ability to make the end-goal the activity of the here-and-now, giving each step in the process teleological value, the process itself becoming the end. Of course, flexibility in thinking is an obvious characteristic, but less obvious is the ability to think in what Maslow calls esthetic terms, seeing "things" in their concrete particularity, not as abstract schemata. The creative person, needless to say, is quite likely to be "different," not one of the crowd. And on and on and on.

A few thoughts. The person who is creative in language obviously becomes involved with the language at least to the partial exclusion of "context" or "content." One characteristic that all of our authorities note is the playfulness of the creative person, and I think that the creative user of language plays language games, as did Joyce. The notion of creativity as play squares with the concentration on process as an end in itself, for a true game is an end in itself, the playing is what matters.

I seem to keep coming back to the

composition classroom. Playfulness relates to primary creativity—with words, with sentences, with ideas. Secondary creativity has to do with skills, sociolinguistic facts of life, to the problems of effectively communicating with some reader in some time, at some place, for some purpose.

Needless to say, primary and secondary creativity do an intricate dance during the process of composition.

Coherence

Poincaré (as quoted in Ghiselin) says that the ordering of elements is more important than the elements themselves, and it seems that one can have an intuitive sense, at a glance, of this coherence, this *elegance*.

In language, we must differentiate between coherence that can be traced in features of the text and coherence that arises only in the mind of the beholder (is constructed by the mind of the beholder). This is an old idea with me. To carry it just one step further, might we not say that there are three kinds of coherence: that of the semantic field, that of features of the text, and that of—what shall I call it?—the beholding mind? Weathers, for instance, talks about the list as an alternate grammar for writing, and the list gains coherence because of the semantic field that it establishes.

More about coherence when we get to "form."

Concretization and Symbolization

Here's an idea that is really productive. See Koestler, 182–86; Guilford, 153–54; Maslow, *Toward*, 89; Maslow, *The Farther*, 69. Koestler says that the subconscious allows us

to concretize and symbolize abstract problems—for example, Kekulé's snakes.

Maslow says that the creative person has the ability to perceive esthetically. "The end product of abstracting is the mathematical equation, the chemical formula, the map, the diagram, the blueprint, the cartoon . . . the theoretical system, all of which move farther and farther from raw reality . . . The end product of esthetic, of nonabstracting is the total inventory of the percept, in which everything in it is apt to be equally savored, and in which evaluations of more important and less important tend to be given up. Here greater richness of the percept is sought for rather than greater simplifying and skeletonizing."

Now let me speculate. The ability to concretize doesn't necessarily depend on analytic intelligence. (In fact, the relationship between creativity and intelligence is questionable.) It is, I think, a fact that in literary theory and in the comp class, much of our thrust and our evaluation is based on concretization. "Give me details." "We like the poem because it gives us experiences, not concepts." And so on.

Suppose that we were able to make students more creative. (I think that we are able to do so.) Then they would become more concrete in their writing (would become creative as they became more concrete?). They would simply become better writers from most of the standards that we apply—editing aside.

One way to make students more concrete-creative is to give them some touchy-feely-smelly. But I doubt the efficacy of this method. All of the evidence seems to indicate that creativity arises from (1) self-image and (2) the right environment. Obviously, we can't change the student's image of him/herself overnight, but we can immediately create the right environment. (More about environment later.)

It's almost truistic to point out that there's creative reading as well as creative writing. Readers who can't enjoy the poem in its concrete particularity don't enjoy poetry. I think that from both ends of the spectrum this inability to produce or perceive the concrete results from constipation. In order to enjoy particularity or to produce it, you've got to let yourself go, to let the mind rove freely and uncritically, to be almost unpurposive and certainly to be unanalytical to a certain extent.

All of this suggests both reading and writing exercises. It also suggests a classroom ambience that I find exceptionally attractive.

No, I'm not saying that only the highly creative should go on in the comp class. Remember the concepts of primary and secondary creativity. If you'll think about it, every heuristic encourages a letting-go. I'd make this bet: get students onto and into a powerful heuristic, and then work seriously with it: the result, somewhere along the path, will be zaniness, laughter, "irresponsibility." Such, in any case, has been my experience.

For more concerning "concretization" and "symbolization," see "hemisphericity."

Conditions for Creativity

Rogers (in Anderson) lists inner conditions: (1) openness to experience and extensionality, (2) an internal locus of evaluation, (3) the ability to toy with elements and concepts, (4) selectivity, an evidence of discipline, an attempt to bring out the essence, (5) the eureka feeling, (6) the anxiety of separateness and aloneness, (7) desire to communicate and share. *Conditions fostering constructive creativity:* psychological safety, psychological freedom.

From almost all of the sources, we get a sense of what a classroom would be like if it were designed to foster creativity—and I mean "classroom" with the features +/− concrete. In the first place, the teacher must gain the trust of the students, and this is not done through criticism and evaluation, which is not to say that both of these factors are not at some point inevitable. However, the martinet will not be successful, nor will the cynic. The creative classroom will inevitably be characterized by a degree of chaos, but also by warmth and trustingness.

All of this sounds so perfectly sensible to me—and yet I am in a continual fight with my neighbors, who see the classroom as a place in which kids, sitting neatly in rows, are bent over their books or exercises silently for fifty-minute stretches or are decorously raising their hands to answer questions that are posed. In fact, the kinds of classrooms that my neighbors want are almost bound to be unproductive. One of the problems is that my neighbors confuse skills with education, believing that skills are education, not just a part of it. And they feel that decorum is necessary for the learning of skills.

skills	learning strategies
decorum	original thought
information	spontaneity

Much of what I'm saying sounds truistic, but I'll say it nonetheless.

De-energization

I picked this notion up from May's *The Courage to Create*. Statements like "human possibilities are unlimited" are de-energizing, for they terrify us. Creativity demands limits. In this same sense, the general theme topic is de-energizing. Remember Pirsig's story about having a student write on one brick in a certain building? I've been working on some exercises that fascinate me—the old narrowing-the-topic bit. What I noticed is that as I narrowed, I began to get whole floods of ideas. You might think about the possibility that narrowing is energizing.

Definition

Here are a few:

"creativity is the ability to see (or to be aware) and to respond."—Fromm, in Anderson

"the emergence in action of a novel relational product, growing out of the uniqueness of the individual on the one hand, and the materials, events, people, or circumstances of his life on the other."—Rogers, in Anderson

"the occurrence of a composition which is both new and valuable." Murray, in Anderson [Note that both Rogers and Murray stress synthesis.]

"an act that produces effective surprise." Bruner, *On Knowing*

"the process of bringing something into being."—May, *The Courage to Create*

Desire to Communicate

It is worth noting that both Rogers and Anthony Storr stress the desire of the creator to communicate the creation.

Destructiveness

Koestler, May, and others point out that creating something new involves destroying something old. At least, it must disrupt the old, rigid patterns of mental organization. This is why May says that creativity takes courage.

I guess students need courage to break the matrices of their neat five-paragraph essays and the strictures that their uptight teachers put on them.

Displacement

In *Fables of Identity*, Northrop Frye says that as we are reading fiction, we are directly concerned with continuity, but after we have read, we lose sight of and interest in sequaciousness. Our knowledge is of what is generally called *theme*, and theme consists of subject, allegory (Hamlet personifies indecision, for example), and *mythos*, which is the work "as a simultaneous unity, when the entire shape of it is clear in our minds." It is *dianoia*, and Frye does argue that the same *mythos* can have various "surface" realizations. Frye says, "because myths are stories, what they 'mean' is inside them, in the implications of their incidents. No rendering of any myth into conceptual language can serve as a full equivalent to its meaning . . . Its life is always the poetic life of a story, not the homiletic life of some illustrated truism." Naturalism and realism are just indirect mythologies, to which Frye applies the term *displacement*. "Literary shape cannot come from life; it comes from literary tradition, and so ultimately from myth."

Koestler also talks about displacement (189—91). For example, realizing that a pendulum *weight* can also serve as a *hammer* to drive a nail to hang the pendulum on. An extreme example of displacement is the total shift from one frame of reference to another, accompanied by a "reversal of logic." For example, electric motors resulted from the accidental reversal of function of the dynamo.

Ecstasy

Among others, May talks about it.

Ego

It is worth noting that Fromm includes in the creative attitude not the loss of ego, but its heightening: experiencing oneself as the true center of the world.

Elegance

Here is one of the great principles, stated best by Poincaré in Ghiselin.

Now, what are the mathematic entities to which we attribute this character of beauty and elegance, and which are capable of developing in us a sort of esthetic emotion? They are those whose elements are harmoniously disposed so that the mind without effort can embrace their totality while realizing the details. This harmony is at once a satisfaction of our esthetic needs and an aid to the mind, sustaining and guiding. And at the same time, in putting under our eyes a well-ordered whole, it makes us foresee a mathematical law. Now, as we have said above, the only mathematical facts worthy of fixing our attention and capable of being useful are those which can teach us a mathematical law. So that we reach the following conclusions: The useful combinations are precisely the most beautiful, I mean those best able to charm this special sensibility that all mathematicians know, but of which the profane are so ignorant as often to be tempted to smile at it.

I could probably get myself into hot water here—for I'd argue that the most creative use of language is the most elegant, which would mean the most economical possible to achieve the desired effect, just exactly the point that Hirsch makes in *The Philosophy of Composition*. But clearly that puts us into just the kind of argument that literary scholars adore, and since I'm not a literary scholar, I'll retreat before I advance.

Yet the principle of elegance makes good sense, and it relates to the principle of coherence that we have already discussed. *Please note this:* it also relates to Northrop Frye's ideas about reading literature in "Myth, Fiction, and Displacement" (*Fables of Identity*). Namely, we remember not the sequence of events in the plot, but the *mythos* or *dianoia*. In other words, after we read a plotted work it becomes, if you will, lyric. *And those works that we do remember are precisely the most elegant*— not the most intricately plotted or elaborate, but the most elegant in Poincaré's terms.

Encounter

This is a fertile idea, one of the two or three that I gained from May. Encounter amounts to absorption, intensity, engagement. Therefore, escapist creativity is that which lacks encounter. Encounter is the intense interrelation with the world, and the "World is the pattern of meaningful relations in which a person exists and in the design of which he or she participates." In regard to what I said above, note this: "We cannot *will* to have insights. We cannot *will* creativity. But we can *will* to give ourselves to the encounter with intensity of dedication and commitment." And that is an important statement!

What May is saying is this: creativity results from encounter, but we cannot will creativity; what we can will is encounter. In a sense, that's what I'm doing right now; I'm willing encounter. And it's amazing how mundane encounter can be. In my case right now, it involves a bunch of 4 × 6 cards, a typewriter, a pleasant study—and me. I guess it also involves what I've called commitment, or perhaps it's commitment that creates encounter. Would you think that possibly commitment is the spring of action for creativity?

Environment and Conditions

Congenial surroundings and stimulating company, according to Eyring. You've already heard from Rogers. Look at Lasswell and Mean in Anderson and also at Adams.

Eureka

A commonly noted phenomenon—one that all of us have experienced. (Rogers in Anderson, p. 77; Poincaré and Mozart in Ghiselin, p. 38, p. 45; Bruner, *On Knowing*, pp. 19–20.) The most thoroughgoing discussion is throughout Koestler.

In my own writing, the Eureka concept is fairly interesting. In much of what I do, there is certainly no Eureka, but most of what I do is only secondarily creative, not primarily. In a couple of instances—imaginative writing aside—I think that I've been genuinely creative, that is, have come up with something new. One of these creations resulted from a decided Eureka moment, the insight coming in a flash and needing only a couple of hours to be written down. In the other instance, the Eureka phenomenon was incremental, accruing over a period of days and over a space of pages. Needless to say, there have been no Eurekas in these pages so far.

Evaluation

We must put the concept of evaluation into a rhetorical framework. What seems original and valuable to me, the producer, may be stale and useless to you, the beholder—in just the way that the corniest poem may tickle the freshman who wrote it and make you yawn or regurgitate. So I can evaluate my own creative elation, but you evaluate a product.

Specifically in regard to verbal creations (and other artistic creations) Koestler (pp. 333–44) talks about *infolding*, by which he means implication: *im − plie = fold in*. It is through implication that the artist captures the audience. Infolding creates economy and forces the reader to intrapolate, extrapolate, and transform. Related to implication also are originality and emphasis. Do we have a rubric for evaluation? *Originality, emphasis, economy.* That's a start, at least.

Hilgard (in Anderson) makes an interesting point: to be creative, one must be able to break out of sets. For example, if you have just used a hammer as a hammer, your ability to use it in novel ways will be decreased (p. 168). From the standpoint of evaluation, if a hammer can be only a hammer, it is not a creative product. The creative product must rearrange our "frames." So along with originality as a criterion, I think I'd put *unexpectedness*. (Of course, in language creativity this quality is obviously a must.)

In "Creativity in Perspective," Anderson makes the point that evaluation can be *external, internal,* or *dyadic*: (1) you evaluate my product, or (2) I evaluate my product, or (3) we discuss the product and arrive at a mutual evaluation.

Poincaré on *elegance* is worth quoting: Which conceptions are elegant? "They are those whose elements are harmoniously disposed so that the mind without effort can embrace their totality while realizing the details. . . . The useful combinations are precisely the most beautiful. . . ." Here's what interests me: compare Poincaré's statement with Frye's notion of *mythos*.

You'll recall that Frye talks about two kinds of literature—in my terms, not necessarily his, lyric and narrative. In the final analysis, however, narrative becomes lyric because it is reduced in the mind to *mythos*, an archetypal pattern. We don't remember the sequaciousness of the details. Thus, *Tom Jones* becomes a lyric. Is it too much to say, then, that works of literature which are most memorable (meaningful) are precisely the most *elegant*?

So here we have another fragment of our inquiry into verbal creation: the principle of elegance. And I think that a lifetime could be spent working it out. At the grubbiest level, it clearly has to do with organization; at a more esoteric level, it has to do with "universals" of the human mind.

An unpublished manuscript by Charles Pyle is floating around the department. It concerns "Pragmatics," and I think that's the title. Pyle talks about creativity in language as deviance and says that there's *good, bad,* and *ignorant* deviance. But in a corrupt society, deviance which appears bad from within may appear good from without. And that's enough to keep us thinking for a while.

Form

If you'll think about Keith Fort's powerful article, you'll realize that formal tyranny can stultify creativity. But that's only one side of the coin. Somewhere, a long time ago, I read a discussion of neoclassic versus romantic poetry, and the writer made this interesting point, which has stuck with me since, I guess, my undergraduate days: the neoclassicist sat down to write a poem, whereas the romanticist sat down to write poetry. I'm probably misinterpreting my source; nonetheless, I can decide to write a sonnet, or I can decide to write a poem about my wife. Do you see the point? Form can be heuristic—and this relates to my concept of form-oriented and content-oriented heuristics ("'Topics' and Levels in the Composing Process").

In *The Courage to Create,* May says largely these same things. And, again, I'd urge you to read Winston Weathers' essay in *Freshman English News,* discussing alternate grammars of style.

Fostering

Since a great deal of what I'm saying in this excursion has to do with the topic, I won't recap here. But I will suggest strongly that you carefully read Rogers' piece in the Anderson collection.

Hemisphericity

[The following entry interests me because it is the first words that I wrote concerning this subject, the first glimmer of interest that I had expressed. As a demonstration that the glimmer became a fire, I refer you to "Brain, Rhetoric, and Style."]

Needless to say, I'm a virtual ignoramus on this subject. But I'd like to give you one quotation that you can think about: "The words of the language, as they are written or spoken, do not seem to play any role in my mechanism of thought. The physical entities which seem to serve as elements in thought are certain signs and more or less clear images which can be 'voluntarily' reproduced and combined."—Einstein, in Ghiselin

[So dramatic has this subject become that one can hardly deal with creativity—let alone composition— if one has no introduction to the field. In my opinion, the best introduction is *The Human Brain*, ed. Wittrock. Other useful sources: Ornstein, *The Psychology of Consciousness*; Rose, *The Working Brain*; Luria, *The Conscious Brain*.]

Heuristics

As you know, I'm fascinated by this concept. A heuristic forces bisociation (Koestler). It makes a person jump from one frame into another. I don't want to extend this discussion unduly, but I would suggest two sources: Guilford, in Anderson (p. 156), where you'll find a heuristic for evaluating the creativity of your classroom; Adams, *Conceptual Blockbusting*. Let us also not forget *Rhetoric: Discovery and Change*, by Young, Becker, and Pike.

Hierarchy, Matrix, Code

Which is the basic framework of Koestler's *The Act of Creation*. Playing around with these terms is fascinating. For example, apply them to language behavior, use them as a view of sociolinguistics. The hierarchy is social organization. You are a member of that organization, and looking downward, you have freedom, whereas looking upaward, you are bound by authority (and there's that word again). The matrix is the outer possibilities of your linguistic performance, and the code is your language. I see that this is hazy, but that's all right with me if it's OK with you.

Let's take another example: the classroom. The nature of the hierarchy is obvious, and, in a sense, you're at the top. The matrix is the limits you set. The code in this case doesn't create the game, but is only the counters used to play it.

Here are some pertinent notes from Pyle:

"human interaction mediated by signs is game playing."

The concept of *frames*: "a frame is a premise about how to evaluate or identify something." "It is a mental construct that categorizes the world."

Of course, frames are evaluative, as when I won't allow an object into my frame "chair" or "polite behavior."

"Frames set up expectations or predictions and unfulfilled expectations or incorrect predictions are often met with denial and rejection of the evidence."

"This response to marginal acts or things is not the only possible one. In fact the evaluation that something is inappropriate or odd is itself the imposition of a frame. An obvious alternative frame that can be imposed on marginal or deviant things is the creative frame. In the evaluation of deviant chairs, many people impose this frame, which is equivalent in some sense to stretching their chair frame. That is, of course, the intention of people who create marginal chairs. This normative aspect of frames, the performance of marginal or deviant acts or creation of deviant things and the frames that are imposed on deviance, goes right to the heart of language use and human interaction in general."

"The present and the uniqueness of an individual in the present can only be expressed by deviance. This creative function of deviation as an expression of individuality and nowness is manifest in metaphor, poetry, and art in general, and in the spontaneous creation of unique indirect speech acts in everyday language use."

Imagic Thinking

Again and again (e.g., Einstein) we hear that creative thinking is imagic. I've said a good deal about this elsewhere and, for once, won't repeat myself. But it's a fertile field for us. [The process of thinking in images relates directly to hemisphericity.]

Infolding

Koestler's term. I've already discussed it above.

Intuition

Enough said [but it relates to hemisphericity].

Lateral thinking

This is a term coined (I think) by de Bono. Messianic and a bit nutty, but interesting, his book is well worth looking at.

In fact, haven't you noticed that creativity is almost dangerously attractive? It's so easy to think and write about (and if you don't believe that statement, look back over the pages of this piece). There's a whole category of pop creativity books:

The Universal Traveler, Psycho-Cybernetics, even *Conceptual Blockbusting.* As you'll see in a moment, I'd put Maslow in the pop category.

Life Style

Just a bit of truism here—but nonetheless, chestnuts that are meaningful to me. I honestly think that you can find people—many of them—who simply live creative lives, without turning out any particular product. This sort of person is a lot of fun to be around: his/her house is likely to be an interesting place (and, I'd contend, a serene place); his/her cooking is likely to be somewhat different from the common run; there is a whole ambience of unstartling (but not unexpected) novelty. That's why I find so many "creative" people to be such a pain: they have to work so hard to be different—not creative, but different. You know what I mean: the lifestyle in which being too-too is such work that no one enjoys the results.

And I think that here's where English teachers fall down: they don't teach literature as part of the really creative lifestyle.

I'm going to quit before I get farther behind on this one.

Motivation

A few notes.

For comedy (per Koestler) it's aggressive or self-asserting.

For Rogers and Maslow, it goes under the general name of "self-actualization." The one thing you get from Maslow is this: any theory of deficiency motivation just won't explain creativity, because in D-motivation, the moment the deficiency is removed, motivation ceases, which would mean that no one would be motivated to get more and more in any sense—more and more proficient at an art, more and more money, etc. For D-motivation, Maslow substitutes Being-motivation and Growth-motivation. I like this.

I think that you really ought to read Storr, which is a survey of motivation as neurosis. Not a debunking, but a survey, and an argument that motivation as neurosis is only part of the story. In fact, I wasn't too impressed when I read Storr early in my exploring, but in retrospect, he stands out in my mind.

Bruner (*On Knowing*) talks about motivation as an internal drama: "I would like to suggest that it is in the working out of a conflict and coalition within the set of identities that compose the person that one finds the source of many of the richest and most surprising combinations." In a way, this is a summary of Storr's point.

I guess I needn't point out that motivation is crucial in the comp class.

Neurosis

I've already mentioned Storr. Also important is Jung (reprinted in *Critical Theory Since Plato*), who argues against the Freudian notion of art as neurosis.

Apparently Adler also developed a compensatory theory of creativity, which May effectively puts down (*The Courage to Create*).

Paradox

Bruner talks about the paradox of creativity. Creative people have both detachment and commitment (notice that word; it's Bruner's). They are detached from convention and deeply attached to that which they create to replace it. Passion and decorum: passion for the project, but decorum about methods, materials, etc. Freedom to be dominated by the object. Deferral and immediacy: the final joy is the finished product, but the proximate joy is creating it.

Peak Experience

This is another Maslovian concept. Maslow loves to make lists, and his list of characteristics of the peak experience is long—but you know what he's talking about. It's that eternal moment when all is right within the world; time seems to be suspended; you undergo a wonderful sense of exhilaration and well-being. When we are undergoing a peak experience, we have "permission" to dip into primary processes: "Part of the process of integration of the person is the recovery of aspects of the unconscious and preconscious, particularly of the primary process (or poetic, metaphoric, mystic, primitive, archaic, childlike).

"Our conscious intellect is too exclusively analytic, rational, numerical, atomistic, conceptual and so it misses a great deal of reality, especially within ourselves."

An aside: The other day when I mentioned Maslow to the director of our school of religion, he said, "Stay away from that guy!" Sounds ominous, doesn't it?

Play

The idea of creativity as play is pervasive. Maybe there's a small lesson here. Since "writing with a purpose" is almost impossible in the comp class, why not writing as play?

Preparation

Everybody talks about it: incubation, immersion in a subject before the flash of insight will come, the necessity of rest and distraction before insight. Again, we can draw very practical advice for students from this.

Primary and Secondary

I think I've already discussed this. Isn't it the case that most scholarship is secondary creativity? But it need not be. Of course, I'm putting a value judgment here. The terms also imply something else, as May, I think, points out: after the first flash of primary creativity, there's all the painstaking work of secondary creativity.

Ripeness

This is analogous to preparation, but from a slightly different angle. The time must be "ripe" for certain kinds of creativity. Take all of the new programs in composition/rhetoric for instance. Most of them are unique enough to qualify as creative endeavors, but what really makes them possible is that the time is ripe. And here are some of the factors of ripeness: the literacy "crisis" in the nation; the job crisis among students in English; the turn of literary criticism away from its single-minded objectivity; the political upheavals which, in large part, caused a change in the professional associations, particularly MLA; the advent of modern linguistics. And we could extend the list greatly.

Science

Here's one that ought either to disgust you or to warm the cockles of your hearts: "If I wanted to be mischievous about it, I could go as far as to define science as a technique whereby noncreative people can create. . . . Science is a technique, social and institutionalized, whereby even unintelligent people can be useful in the advance of technology."—Maslow, *The Farther*

Self-Actualization

See here and there in these notes. See also Fromm in Anderson.

These people are gripping for the first thirty pages—but after that they become a pain. Maslow, for instance, wrote the same things over and over again: B- and G-motivation versus D-motivation. Creativity as growth. Anti-behaviorism. But it would be worth your while to take a look at what Maslow says about the self-actualizing person.

Self-Transcending Emotions

Koestler (pp. 285–86) talks about them, but they are also a big part of self-actualization.

Syntactic Fluency

In regard to this topic, let me outline Guilford's notions and the relationship of syntactic fluency to them. He discusses the primary traits related to creativity:

> generalized sensitivity to problems
> fluency of thinking
>> word fluency—ability to produce synonyms
>> *expressional fluency*—ability to produce phrases and sentences
>> ideational fluency—ability to produce ideas that fulfill certain requirements
> flexibility in thinking
> originality
> redefinition (improvising)
> elaboration

Syntactic fluency relates, of course, to expressional fluency, and note how heuristics relate to other primary traits of creativity.

Talent

May makes a commonsense observation that startled me, but that I like: creative people are not necessarily talented and vice versa. Think of the implications of this for language creativity.

Unconscious

I said all that I have to say, but take a close look at Sinnott in Anderson.

Values

Rogers in Anderson: Since the individual creates in order to actualize him- or herself, "we get nowhere by trying to differentiate 'good' and 'bad' purposes in the creative process. . . . It has been found that when the individual is 'open' to all of his experience . . . then his behavior will be creative, and this creativity may be trusted to be essentially constructive."

Bruner, *On Knowing*: The benefits of learning through discoveries that one makes oneself are (1) an increase in intellectual potency; (2) a shift from extrinsic to intrinsic rewards; (3) a knowledge of the heuristics of discovering; (4) an aid to conserving memory.

And Maslow makes a list of adjectives that describe the peak experience: truth, beauty, wholeness, etc. He says these are the same as what we have always called eternal values. So the nature of the peak experience defines *the* basic values. Of course, in saying this, he's saying everything and therefore nothing. He also says that facts have a "vectorial" nature which makes them value-laden.

Will

Rollo May: "We cannot *will* to have insights. We cannot *will* creativity. But we can *will* to give ourselves to the encounter with intensity of dedication and commitment." And I realize that I have already quoted this once before, but it's worth two readings, isn't it?

Note what a wonderful heuristic my brown box is. It's created about 10,000 words, and the process was almost painless to me.

BIBLIOGRAPHY

Adams, Hazard, Ed. *Critical Theory Since Plato*. New York: Harcourt Brace Jovanovich, 1971.

Adams, James L. *Conceptual Blockbusting: A Guide to Better Ideas*. San Francisco: W. H. Freeman, 1974.

Anderson, Harold H., Ed. *Creativity and Its Cultivation*. New York: Harper & Row, 1959.

Bruner, Jerome S. *On Knowing: Essays for the Left Hand*. Cambridge, Mass.: Harvard, 1963.

Burke, Kenneth. *A Grammar of Motives*. Berkeley and Los Angeles: University of California, 1969.

de Bono, Edward. *Lateral Thinking: Creativity Step by Step*. New York: Harper & Row, 1970.

——. *The Mechanism of Mind*. Baltimore: Penguin, 1969.

Fort, Keith. "Form, Authority, and the Critical Essay." *Contemporary Rhetoric: A Conceptual Background with Readings*. Winterowd, Ed. *College English* (March 1971).

Fromm, Erich. "The Creative Attitude." Anderson, Ed. *Creativity and Its Cultivation*.

Frye, Northrop. *Fables of Identity*. New York: Harcourt Brace Jovanovich, 1963.

Ghiselin, Brewster, Ed. *The Creative Process*. New York: New American Library, n.d.; University of California, 1952.

Guilford, J. P. "Traits of Creativity." Anderson, Ed. *Creativity and Its Cultivation*.

Hilgard, Ernest R. "Creativity and Problem Solving." Anderson, Ed. *Creativity and its Cultivation*.

Hirsch, E. D., Jr. *The Philosophy of Composition*. Chicago: University of Chicago. 1977.

Koberg, Don and Jim Bagnall. *The Universal Traveler. A Soft-Systems Guidebook To: Creativity, Problem-Solving, and the Process of Design.* Los Altos, Cal.: William Kaufman, 1974.

Koestler, Arthur. *The Act of Creation.* New York: Dell, 1967; Macmillan, 1964.

Lasswell, Harold D. "The Social Setting of Creativity." Anderson, Ed. *Creativity and Its Cultivation.*

Luria, A. R. *The Working Brain: An Introduction to Neuropsychology.* Trans. Basil Haigh. New York: Basic Books, 1973.

Maltz, Maxwell. *Psycho-cybernetics and Self-fulfillment.* New York: Bantam, 1973.

Maslow, Abraham. "Creativity in Self-Actualizing People." Anderson, Ed. *Creativity and Its Cultivation.*

———. *The Farther Reaches of Human Nature.* New York: Viking, 1972.

———. *Toward a Psychology of Being.* New York: D. Van Nostrand, 1968.

May, Rollo. *The Courage to Create.* New York: W. W. Norton, 1975.

Mead, Margaret. "Creativity in Cross-Cultural Perspective." Anderson, Ed. *Creativity and Its Cultivation.*

Murray, Henry A. "Vicissitudes of Creativity." Anderson, Ed. *Creativity and Its Cultivation.*

Ornstein, Robert E. *The Psychology of Consciousness.* New York: Penguin, 1975; W. H. Freeman, 1972; 2nd Ed., Harcourt Brace Jovanovich, 1977.

Pirsig, Robert M. *Zen and the Art of Motorcycle Maintenance.* New York: Bantam, 1975.

Rogers, Carl R. "Toward a Theory of Creativity." Anderson, Ed. *Creativity and Its Cultivation.*

Rohman, D. Gordon and Albert O. Wlecke. *Pre-Writing: The Construction and Application of Models for Concept Formation in Writing.* East Lansing, Mich.: Michigan State University, 1964.

Rose, Steven. *The Conscious Brain.* New York: Vintage, 1976.

Storr, Anthony. *The Dynamics of Creation.* New York: Atheneum, 1972.

Weathers, Winston, "Grammars of Style: New Options in Composition." *Freshman English News.* 4 (Winter 1976).

Winterowd, W. Ross. "Brain, Rhetoric, and Style." *Language and Style.* Forthcoming.

———. "The Rhetoric of Beneficence, Authority, Ethical Commitment, and the Negative." *Philosophy and Rhetoric.* 9 (Spring 1976), 65–83.

———. "The Three R's: Reading, Reading, and Rhetoric." *A Symposium in Rhetoric.* Ed. William E. Tanner, J. Dean Bishop, and Turner S. Kobler. Denton, Texas: Texas Woman's University Press, 1976.

———. "'Topics' and Levels in the Composing Process." *College English,* 5 (Feb. 1973), 701–09.

Wittrock, M. C., Ed. *The Human Brain.* Englewood Cliffs, N.J.: Prentice-Hall, 1977.

Young, Richard E., Alton L. Becker, and Kenneth Pike. *Rhetoric: Discovery and Change.* New York: Harcourt Brace Jovanovich, 1970.

Form and Style

The Grammar of Coherence

In regard to this essay, I quote from the unpublished dissertation of James Williams, University of Southern California—a work, by the way, that I directed.

Winterowd . . . equates form with coherence: "The following discussion will argue that there is a grammar of *coherence* (or *form*, for in the following, the two terms are virtually synonymous). If one perceives form in discourse, he or she also perceives coherence."

In my view, this stance is mistaken for several reasons. It seems reasonable, for example, to expect an adequate account of coherence to apply to both spoken and written language, yet Winterowd . . . ignores spoken discourse. Also, the whole question of perception is problematic. Do only decoders perceive form, or do encoders perceive it as well? Even if we limit perception of form to the sentence level, we would have to assume that decoders typically isolate function words like "and," yet we know that this is not the case; they process language for message, not for structure.

Of course, Williams is perfectly correct when he argues that readers concentrate on message, not structure, and he might have gone on to say that for a given reader a text will be perfectly coherent, but will be discoherent for another reader who "processes" it sentence by sentence.

Another problem with this essay is my failure to distinguish between *coherence* and *cohesion*. Actually, I have developed a grammar of *cohesion*, not of coherence. However, the grammar does specify the semantic relationships between T-units.

Let me advance a more modest claim than the one I make in "The Grammar of Coherence." So far as we are either reading or examining a text T-unit by T-unit, we will be able to specify relationships through the grammar developed in this essay.

"The Grammar of Coherence" has, in some ways, been an onus for me; it

This essay appeared originally in *College English* (May 1970). Reprinted with the permission of the National Council of Teachers of English.

is the most frequently reprinted of my papers, and it has typecast me as a quasilinguist interested only in form, not meaning. Overcoming the stereotype that the essay created was one of the motives behind this book.

Just at the point where it could best serve rhetoric, transformational generative grammar fails: it does not jump the double-cross mark (#) that signifies "sentence boundary" or, more accurately, "transformational unit boundary." The significance of this limitation is underscored by the inability of grammarians to write a rule for the simplest of all transformations: clause coordination.

Since the number of sentences that can be conjoined in this way is, theoretically at least, unlimited, it is not immediately obvious how to write a constituent-structure rule to permit the generation of compound sentences. . . . It is clearly unsatisfactory to have to postulate an infinity of rules.[1]

As a result, transformational generative grammar has been tremendously useful in the study of style, but it has had little application (except metaphorically) to invention and organization. That is, it has cast only dim light on concepts of form and coherence.

The following discussion will argue that there is a grammar of *coherence* (or *form*, for in the following, the two terms are virtually synonymous.) If one perceives form in discourse, he also perceives coherence, for form is the internal set of consistent relationships in any stretch of discourse, whether poem, play, essay, oration, or whatever. This set of relationships—like the relationships that rules of grammar describe—must be finite in number; otherwise: formlessness, for the very concepts of form and coherence imply a finite number of relationships that can be perceived. (A generative grammar implies a finite number of rules, some of which may be applied recursively. Following the model of grammar, one might look for some sort of "constituent structure rules" that underlie coherent utterances beyond the sentence, and then for the equivalent of "lexical rules," and finally for something approximating "transformational rules." In a very rough, loosely analogous way, the following discussion concentrates only on the "phrase structure rules" of coherence and, as a result, excludes "lexical" data which is undoubtedly significant. For instance, one reason that a paragraph "hangs together" or is a convention is that chains of equivalent words run through it. A switch in equivalence chains signals: new paragraph.[2] The present discussion will ignore everything but the abstract configurations or sets of relationships that constitute coherence. (This, of course, is not to say that any one component of the whole body of discourse is unimportant.)

Modern grammar nicely describes the first two stadia in the hierarchy of discourse relationship sets that make up coherence. The first set of relationships is those that can develop from the application of rules to S and then to all constituents that develop from S. The result (after lexical rules have been applied) will be a sentence, divided into two parts: Modality and Proposition. As Charles J. Fillmore explains:

In the basic structure of sentences . . . we find what might be called the 'proposition,' a tenseless set of relationships involving verbs and nouns (and embedded sentences, if there are any), separated from what might be called the 'modality' constituent. This latter will include such modalities on the sentence-as-a-whole as negation, tense, mood, and aspect.[3]

Each noun in the proposition stands in a *case* relationship with the verb, thus:

invariable. Thus, in 1 and 2, "Jones" is the grammatical subject of the verb; in 3, 4, and 5, "the money" is the grammatical subject; in 6, "Smith" is the subject. But "Jones" is always in the agentive case, "the money" is always in the objective case, and "Smith" is always in the dative. That is, we never lose sight of the relationships among the noun phrases or of their relationships with the verb. It is also worth noting—in

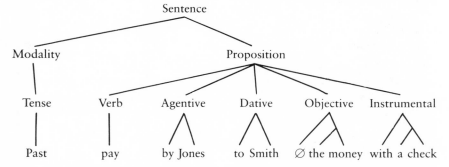

This *deep structure* can have the following surface manifestations, all of them synonymous:

(1) Jones paid Smith the money with a check.

(2) Jones paid the money to Smith with a check.

(3) The money was paid Smith by Jones with a check.

(4) The money was paid to Smith by Jones with a check.

(5) The money was paid by Jones to Smith with a check.

(6) Smith was paid the money by Jones with a check.

And with the cleft sentence transformation: *A check is what Jones paid Smith the money with.* It is worth pointing out that syntactic relationships in these sentences change, but case relationships ("who did what and with which and to whom") are

fact, crucial to this discussion—that certain "particles" which are represented in the deep structure diagram may or may not appear in the surface structure. Thus, the agentive "by" does not appear until after the passive transformation has been applied, and dative "to" disappears with application of the indirect object inversion transformation. These signals of case relationships may or may not be in the surface structure.

The first "layer" of relationships that make up coherence, then, is *cases*.

The second "layer" might well be called *syntax* (in a somewhat specialized and restricted use of the word). The relationships of syntax are described by those transformations that have to do with inserting sentences within other sentences by any means but coordination. Thus, the relationships characteristic of syntax (as I use the word) are, for instance,

complements:
    It is strange. He is here.
    It is strange that he is here.
    It is strange for him to be here.
    His being here is strange.

relatives:
    The banker owned the town.
    The banker was rich.
    The banker who was rich owned the town.
    The rich banker owned the town.

subordinates:
    He chews tobacco. He likes it.
    He chews tobacco because he likes it.

absolutes:
    The airport was fogged in. The plane circled for an hour.
    The airport being fogged in, the plane circled for an hour.

and so on.

This is the cat. The cat chased the rat. The rat ate the malt. The malt lay in the house. Jack built the house.
This is the cat that chased the rat that ate the malt that lay in the house that Jack built.

And this, of course, is just the point at which grammar ends—that very point at which *inventio* and *dispositio* really begin.

I argue that there is a set of relationships beyond case and syntax and that this set constitutes the relationships that make for coherence—among the transformational units in a paragraph, among the paragraphs in a chapter, among the chapters in a

book. I call these relationships *transitions*, and I claim that beyond the sentence marker, the double-cross, we perceive coherence only as the consistent relationships among transitions. All of this, of course, is more easily illustrated than explained, and illustration is forthcoming. For the moment, however, I should like to underscore my claim that the relationships I am about to describe constitute the grammar of coherence for *all* units of discourse beyond the level of what I have called "syntax."[4]

In another place, I will detail the method whereby I arrived at the following conclusions. But for the time being, I will concentrate on results and their applications.

Analysis of thousands of transformational units in sequences reveals that there are seven relationships that prevail among T-units and, I would argue, in any stretch of discourse that is perceived as coherent. I have called these relationships (1) coordinate, (2) obversative, (3) causative, (4) conclusive, (5) alternative, (6) inclusive, and (7) sequential. These relationships can be either *expressed* or *implied*. They are expressed in a variety of ways: through coordinating conjunctions, transitional adverbs, and a variety of other moveable modifiers. Just how they are implied remains a mystery.[5] However, the relationships are easily demonstrated.

Coordination can always be expressed by *and*. (Synonyms: *furthermore, in addition, too, also, again, etc.*)

Boswell was a Rousseau-ite, one of the first of the Romantics, an inveterate sentimentalist, *and* nothing could be more complete than the contrast between his career and Gibbon's.—*Lytton Strachey*

They almost hid from us the front, but through the dust and the spaces between running legs we could see the soldiers in the trench leap their barricade like a breaking wave. *AND* then the impenetrable dust shut down *AND* the fierce stabbing needle of the machine guns sewed the mighty jumble of sounds together.—*John Reed*

Marat is, in most of his speeches, tinsel, stage scenery, or an element in a great painting. *AGAIN*, the Brechtian songs are touching, but ironically and allusively touching; Charlotte Corday, the mad, beautiful country girl mouthing her lines, is *AGAIN* an element in a picture, an aesthetic contrivance.
—*Stuart Hampshire*

Obversativity can always be expressed by *but*. (Synonyms: *yet, however, on the other hand, etc.*)

It has been ambitious and plucky of me to attempt to describe what is indescribable, and I have failed, as I knew I would. *BUT* I have discharged my duty to society. . . .—*E. B. White*

And Johnson, as Kennedy has often acknowledged, was a man of force and decision to whom, in case anything happened, the government could responsibly be assigned.
ON THE OTHER HAND, the designation of Johnson would outrage the liberal wing of the party.
—*Arthur Schlesinger, Jr.*

Causativity can always be expressed by *for*. It is interesting to note that among the transitional adverbs commonly used (nevertheless, however, moreover, hence, consequently, nonetheless, accordingly, then, besides, likewise, indeed, therefore), none expresses the causative relationship.

Now, on that morning, I stopped still in the middle of the block, *FOR* I'd caught out of the corner of my eye a tunnel-passage, an overgrown courtyard.
—*Truman Capote*

Conclusivity can always be expressed by *so*. (Synonyms: *therefore, thus, for this reason, etc.*)

She has a rattling Corsican accent, likes Edith Piaf records, and gives me extra shrimp bits in my shrimp bit salad. *SO* some things change. Last time I heard no Edith Piaf and earned no extra forkfuls of shrimp.—*Herbert Gold*

Alternativity can always be expressed by *or*.

Now such an entity, even if it could be proved beyond dispute, would not be God: it would merely be a further piece of existence, that might conceivably not have been there—*OR* a demonstration would not have been required.
—*John A. T. Robinson*

Inclusivity is often expressed with a *colon*.

In the first century B.C., Lucretius wrote this description of the pageant of Cybele:
Adorned with emblem and crown . . . she is carried in awe-inspiring state. . . .
—*Harvey Cox*

The inclusive relationship is that of the example to the generality or the narration of the case to the statement of the case. Often, inclusivity is expressed by the transformational possibility of complementization:

He realized that their discovery [Aristotle's discovery of the statues of Daedalus] would shatter his own "natural" law: Managers would no longer need subordinates, masters could dispense with slaves.—*Michael Harrington*

With the last two clauses complementized, the sentence reads like this:

He realized that their discovery would shatter his own "natural" law, that managers would no longer need subordinates, and that masters could dispense with slaves.

The *sequential relationship* is expressed by such transitions as "first . . . second . . . third," "earlier . . . later," "on the bottom . . . in the middle . . . on top," and so on.

Three types of relationships, then, constitute coherence: cases, syntax, and transitions (with the transitions either expressed or implied). And it is, indeed, obvious that transitions can be implied, for it is common to find series of transformational units with no expressed transitions.

It is possible to love the theater and to revel in theatrically, to find the pretense and unreality of the stage wholly absorbing in its own right. It must be supposed that most actors and directors, if left to their own tastes and impulses, would strive after theatrical effects above all else. The satisfaction of any broader human interest might be quite secondary.—*Stuart Hampshire*

I read this as an "and . . . and" series, but another interpretation is possible: "and . . . for." That is, there can be ambiguity in transitions as well as in lexicon and syntax.

The interesting possibility, however, is that the seven relationships that prevail among T-units also prevail among larger elements of discourse. For instance, applied at the level of the T-unit, the seven constitute a series of topics that will automatically generate discourse, for the second T-unit must stand in one of the seven relationships to the first, and the third must stand in one of the seven relationships to the second, and so on. Therefore, transitions are topics for a generative

rhetoric. But a rhetoric that will generate only paragraphs has limited usefulness. If, however, the seven topics isolate the relationships among any segments of discourse (except those related to one another by the grammar of the T-unit), then they might well be the basis for a true generative rhetoric.

Shakespeare's sonnets have proved to be useful models for my purposes, and they will serve here to demonstrate that the seven relationships prevail in "whole works," though, of course, one might argue that a sonnet is, after all, just another kind of paragraph. Expressed transitions in the following will be in capitals; implied transitions (according to my reading) will be in bracketed capitals.

Sonnet XVII

Who will believe my verse in time to
  come,
If it were fill'd with your most high
  deserts?
THOUGH YET, heaven knows, it is but
  as a tomb
Which hides your life and shows not
  half your parts.
[BUT] If I could write the beauty of
  your eyes
And in fresh numbers number all your
  graces,
The age to come would say 'This poet
  lies;
[FOR] Such heavenly touches ne'er
  touch'd earthly faces.'
SO should my papers, yellowed with
  their age,
Be scorn'd, like old men of less truth
  than tongue,
And your true rights be term'd a poet's
  rage
And stretched metre of an antique song:
  But were some child of yours alive
    that time,
  You should live twice, in it and in my
    rhyme.

In his cycle, Shakespeare upon occasion needs two sonnets rather than one to express his complete idea. In such cases, he supplies the proper transition. The relationship between V and VI is conclusive, expressed as *then*. (*So* is the minimal transition to express conclusivity.)

Sonnet V

Those hours that with gentle work did frame
The lovely gaze where every eye doth dwell,
Will play the tyrants to the very same
And that unfair which fairly doth excel:
FOR never-resting time leads summer on
To hideous winter and confounds him there;
Sap check'd with frost and lusty leaves quite gone,
Beauty o'ersnow'd and bareness every where:
THEN, were not summer's distillation left,
A liquid prisoner pent in walls of glass,
Beauty's effect with beauty were bereft,
Nor it, nor no remembrance what it was:
  BUT flowers distill'd, though they with winter meet,
  Leese but their show; [FOR] their substance still lives sweet.

Sonnet VI

THEN let not winter's ragged hand deface
In thee thy summer, ere thou be distill'd:
[BUT] Make sweet some vial; [AND] treasure thou some place
With beauty's treasure, ere it be self-kill'd.
[FOR] That use is not forbidden usury,
Which happies those that pay the willing loan;
[FOR] That's for thyself to breed another thee,
OR ten times happier, be it ten for one;
[FOR] Ten times thyself were happier than thou art,

If ten of thine ten times refigured thee:
THEN what could death do, if thou shouldst depart,
Leaving thee living in posterity?
  [SO] Be not self-will'd, FOR thou art much too fair
  To be death's conquest and make worms thine heir.

To apply this test to a series of paragraphs that make up an essay, for instance, is too cumbersome a job for the present discussion and is, in any case, unnecessary. The reader can make his own test. "What relationships prevail among the sections—paragraphs or other—of an extended piece of discourse?" is the question. If the seven outlined here are the answer, then the system has stood the test. (By the way, the question transformation might be viewed as a transition in itself. That is, it predicts some kind of answer.)

Finally, it is necessary to clarify the exact sense in which I take these seven relationships (they might be called "topics") to constitute a generative rhetoric. The term "generative" is of itself productive, for it exactly designates the process whereby discourse—at the sentence level and beyond—comes into being. An oversimplifed explanation of the language process is to say that at any level of generality, one unit has the potential for generating other units and of combining these units in some meaningful way. Any set of topics is merely a way of triggering the process. Thus the student, say, who has difficulty with the invention of arguments, can use the seven-item list to tell him what might come next—not what content, to be sure, but what relation his next unit must take to the previous one. There are only seven possibilities.

Inability to write sentences stems

not from the writer's lack of subject matter (everyone is the repository of an infinitude of subject matter), but from his not knowing how to get the subject matter into structures. The problem at levels beyond the sentence is, I think, exactly the same. The seven relation-oriented "topics" that I have outlined name the structures that can hold the writer's ideas.

A generative rhetoric, a heuristic model, even a grammar of form— whatever it might be called, the schema of these seven relationships ought to be easily applicable in the classroom. But equally important, they should have wide ranging theoretical possibilities, for instance, in explaining the disjunction of schizoid language, in identifying "the eighth ambiguity" (that which takes place between units larger than the sentence and results from the inability to perceive transitions) and in dealing with form in literature.

NOTES

1. D. Terence Langendoen, *The Study of Syntax* (New York, 1969), 31.

2. A. L. Becker, "A Tagmemic Approach to Paragraph Analysis," *The Sentence and the Paragraph* (Champaign, Ill., 1966), 33–38.

3. "The Case for Case," *Universals in Linguistic Theory*, ed. Emmon Bach and Robert T. Harms (New York, 1968), 23.

4. The reader who is familiar with modern logic will immediately perceive the similarity between what I am about to outline and the relationships among propositions listed in logic. They are *initial, additive* (and), *adversative* (but), *alternative* (or), *explanatory* (that is), *illustrative* (for example), *illative* (therefore), *causal* (for). I would urge the reader, however, to be more conscious of the differences between the two systems than of the similarities. What I call transitions are not merely an adaptation, but, it seems to me, are manifestations of some of the most basic properties of language.

5. When I first began working on these ideas, I communicated my findings to Charles Fillmore of Ohio State. His comment on my tentative conclusions is revealing. I was talking strictly about the relationships in the paragraph, and he said, "Your ideas about paragraph structure are appealing, but it's hard to see, as you admit, how they can lead to any clarification of the problems of coherence on the paragraph level. The 'coherence' of clauses in a sentence is just as unsolved an issue as ever, but to the extent that your proposals are right you can at least claim to have demonstrated that what might have appeared to be two separate mysteries are reducible to one and the same mystery." The fact that coherence among clauses in a T-unit and coherence among T-units are reducible to the same mystery is, of course, the point here, not that coherence is mysterious. In general, I am indebted to Professor Fillmore for a great variety of insights.

Beyond Style

Two of the ideas advanced by this essay are, I think, unique and, perhaps, useful: that, in the proper circumstances, incoherence has rhetorical cogency, demanding, as it does, that readers "construct" texts; and that form protects both the poet and the reader. ("The experience of poetic craftsmanship allows both a looking away from the impulse and a handling of that impulse.")

As I hint toward the conclusion, the essay is also anti-structuralist, implying that schematics representing form do not represent poems, which are imbued with semantic intention.

It undoubtedly seems nugatory to remark that mind shapes discourse at the level of the sentence and beyond—and only slightly less so to say that, reciprocally, language shapes mind. That is, a given instrument, the brain, with its universals of "grammar" and its particularities of idiolect produces discourse, but only insofar as the system of language allows discourse to be produced, so that the process of discoursing involves the never-ending reciprocity of mind shaping message and language shaping both mind and message. Forms in discourse—forms *qua* forms, independent of meanings—must, then, have rhetorical consequences. It is not only words

This essay is reprinted from *Philosophy and Rhetoric* (Spring 1972), by permission of The Pennsylvania State University Press, University Park, PA.

put together that persuade or move, but also the abstract structures themselves. For instance, in 1897, Adams Sherman Hill wrote in *The Foundation of Rhetoric*:

To secure force in a sentence, it is necessary not only to choose the strongest words and to be as concise as is consistent with clearness, but also to arrange words, phrases and clauses in the order which gives a commanding position to what is most important, and thus fixes the attention on the central idea.

This, of course, is precisely the reasoning that underlies the periodic sentence dogma. Namely, the "important" part of the sentence is the base, and its postposition ends the sentence with a bang, not a whimper.

Much can be said for and against such dogmas as that concerning the periodic sentence, but the point is that in even the most traditional discussions, it is generally conceded that form *qua* form has rhetorical value. Nonetheless, the tendency is for rhetorical treatises to neglect form; seldom are discussions of it more than rehashings of tired dicta: save the most important point for last, use periodic rather than loose sentences, do not introduce new topics in the conclusion.

And yet, anyone who has composed anything—from personal letters to arguments for a proposition to poems—must feel that the traditional notions concerning form (of sentences and units beyond, though this discussion will focus on units beyond) somehow belie the nature of the creative act, somehow make cut and dried a process that always, the nature of the human mind being what it is, will remain tantalizingly mysterious.

The one modern rhetorician who has made tremendous contributions to our understanding of form is, of course, Kenneth Burke. "Lexicon Rhetoricae" in *Counter-Statement* is surely one of the most significant essays on "*dispositio*" that has ever been published, and Burke's definition of form has been reverberating in my mind ever since I first encountered it: "*Form* in literature is an arousing and fulfillment of desires. A work has form in so far as one part of it leads a reader to anticipate another part, to be gratified by the sequence."[1] However, in his work on form in discourse, Burke is virtually unique among contemporary rhetoricians. No "department" of rhetoric has been more neglected than *dispositio*.

The discussion to follow will be a *speculative* inquiry into the rhetoric of forms (or *dispositio*). It is obviously a companion piece to other of my essays: "Style: A Matter of Manner";[2] "The Grammar of Coherence";[3] "Dispositio: The Theory of Form in Discourse."[4] The inquiry will use as points of departure a variety of works of literature.

THE VALUE OF INCOHERENCE

It is paradoxical to start the body of an essay on the rhetoric of form by examining the power of formlessness, but such will be the *modus operandi* here.

The Waste Land is the first case in point, and that monumental poem, in the opinion of many responsible readers, is formless—a concept to which we will return.

Surely no poem of the twentieth century has been so widely influential as *The Waste Land*; its imagery has permeated the American and British consciousness; its message has become the message of our time—at least to many of those who do read poetry. In short, one can well say that *The Waste Land* is *the* poem of the twentieth century. Its impact is enormous.

Undoubtedly the importance of the poem is in large part thematic. As M. L. Rosenthal says,

one of the crucial symbols of modern poetry, in English at least, becomes Dante's pictured prisoners in the antechamber of Hell, 'wretches never born and never dead,' worthy of neither blame nor praise. These are the citizens of T. S. Eliot's Waste Land, who, lacking all moral perspective, mechanical in their motions, are trapped by their bodily selves and are incapable of meaningful commitment either to good or to evil. The modern city is their habitat.[5]

In a sense, *The Waste Land* gives a symbolic summary of the preoccupations of modern man: faithlessness, a jejune society, sterile love, the loss of tradition, mere boredom, and a hundred other contemporary maladies sensed by the poet and his readers (for literary popularity comes about only when work and audience have a meeting of the minds or of the hearts, and as poetry goes, *The Waste Land* is unbelievably popular).

However, themes are not our present concern, but rather how those themes emerge as a "coherent" totality in a poem entitled *The Waste Land*—one poem with five separate sections, a poem with "chapters," or perhaps a cycle of poems on one subject. In some way, *The Waste Land*, not simply because its pages are sequential in a black volume and not simply because five separate poems appear under one super-title, must represent for readers a coherent whole. Cleanth Brooks sees an overall pattern in the poem, a pattern that in outline looks like this:

I "The Burial of the Dead": *statement of theme*. "The first section of 'The Burial of the Dead' develops the theme of the attractiveness of death, or of the difficulty in rousing oneself from the death in life in which people of the waste land live."[6]

II "A Game of Chess": *illustration supporting the theme*. "The easiest contrast in this section—and one which may easily blind the casual reader to a continued emphasis on the contrast between the two kinds of life, or the two kinds of death already commented on—is the contrast between life in a rich and magnificent setting, and life in the low and vulgar setting of a London pub. But both scenes, however antithetical they may appear superficially, are scenes taken from the contemporary waste land."[7]

III "The Fire Sermon": *thematic restatement*. "'The Fire Sermon' makes use of several of the symbols already developed."[8]

IV "Death by Water": *contrast*. "The section forms a contrast with 'The Fire Sermon' which precedes it."[9]

V "What the Thunder Said": *restatement of theme*. "The reference to the 'torchlight red on sweaty faces' and to the 'frosty silence in the gardens' obviously associates Christ in Gethsemane with the other hanged gods. The god has now died, and in referring to this, the basic theme finds another strong restatement."[10]

At one end of the spectrum Brooks sees in *The Waste Land* a coherent, unified poem, though not, perhaps, coherent or unified in the usual sense.

At the other extreme is Graham Hough, who says that *The Waste Land* and *Four Quartets* "will survive, not assisted by their structure, but in spite of it."[11] Hough tells us that "for a poem to exist as a unity more than merely bibliographical, we need the sense of one voice speaking, as in lyric or elegiac verse; or of several voices intelligibly related to each other, as in narrative with dialogue or drama."[12] In short, Hough debunks what he considers to be the myth of unity in *The Waste Land*. The effect of the poem is "as though a painter were to employ pointilliste technique in one part of a picture and the glazes of the high renaissance in another."[13]

The interesting point here is not that Brooks views *The Waste Land* as a unified whole or that Hough views it as a series of disunified fragments. What interests us is that both of them might well be perfectly right! The poem might well be *both* a series of disunified fragments *and* a unified whole. If one looks at a schematization of Brooks' analysis of *The Waste Land*, here is what emerges: theme, illustration, restatement, contrast, restatement. While I am consciously oversimplifying Brooks' argument, in general the above five terms in sequence represent his view of the coherence of *The Waste Land*. It is interesting to note that these five terms might well describe the coherence of a paragraph, or even serve as the matrix in developing paragraphs of a certain kind. A model might look like this:

theme
Incoherence has a decided rhetorical value, for the incoherent utterance obliges the reader or listener to supply his own coherence.
illustration
It is clear, for instance, that each reader of *The Waste Land* must put the individual parts of the poem together in a way that is meaningful to him.
restatement
That is to say, where there is no "formal" coherence in discourse, the reader is quite likely to supply his own, and in the process to be engaged by the discourse that he is "putting together" or "interpreting." Thus, it is that incoherence has rhetorical value, for it engages the reader or listener.
contrast
Totally coherent discourse, on the other hand, does not demand this particular kind of engagement and, therefore, paradoxically, lacks one of the many possible kinds of rhetorical force.
restatement
To state my main point in another, simpler way: there is a definite rhetorical value in the very nebulousness and fragmentation of some discourse (and much poetry), for lack of clearcut connections (form) allows the reader or listener to participate as a "maker," conjecturally or intuitively supplying connections where none exist.

Whether or not the paragraph is a "good" one is beside the point. The fact is that the model which Brooks proposes for the coherence of *The Waste Land* is productive in generating more or less coherent stretches of discourse—and that *The Waste Land* is, for many readers, "incoherent."[14] What I am suggesting is that in discourse, there are "twilight areas," where coherence is just tantalizingly out of reach and where the reader himself must "put the work together." Of such nature is *The Waste Land*.

It seems to me that fragmentation, disunification, in a word, incoherence, is one of the major rhetorical devices of modern poetry. It is, in fact, among the really significant features that allow us to speak of modern poetry as a genre. Time and again, poet captures reader by making reader "assemble the pieces" in a way that would have seemed downright perverse had that modern reader not been prepared by such works as *The Waste Land* and Pound's *Cantos*. (It must be remembered that Pound considered the *Cantos* a *whole* epic poem on the order of *The Divine Comedy* or *The Iliad*.) This ambiguity in structure is the eighth ambiguity, the one that often brings reader and poet together as co-conspirators in the making of the poem. (Note that reader and author cannot be co-conspirators in the making of a plot which has all segments of the outline filled in, but that, for instance, a lady-or-tiger ending immediately precipitates conspiracy.)

A great many modern poems are clusters of images, symbols, and metaphors (like *The Waste Land*) awaiting the receptive mind that will assemble them in a meaningful way. Modern poetry, then, often relies upon a participatory rhetoric for its effects. Examples of such poems are legion and, in a sense, characterize modern poetry: Leroi Jones' "A Poem for Willie Best"; Lowell's "Between the Porch and the Altar" and his *Notebook, 1967–68*; Stevens' "Thirteen Ways of Looking at a Blackbird"; "Hugh Selwyn Mauberley"; Ginsberg's "Journal Night Thoughts"; Crane's *The Bridge*— and the list could go on and on. The current undergraduate favorite, *Trout Fishing in America*, is a "novel" that employs the poetic technique of incoherence for its effect.

FORMAL TENSION

Everyone knows that a kind of tension arises from the very nature of narrative. If one is interested, one asks, "And what happened next?" Insofar as the question arises and is momentarily unanswered, there is a tension in the story. In Kenneth Burke's terms, there is tension as long as the reader's appetite to know is unsatisfied. But there is another kind of tension, that which arises from the *form* of the work.

To explain what I intend here, I would like to discuss a novel that, it seems to me, deserves better than it has gotten from many critics. I mean Johnson's *Rasselas*. It is an exciting novel, the opinions of many to the contrary, but it is exciting in a particular way that is not characteristic of most fiction. Tension increases and slackens, but it is always present, even to the last sentence and beyond, for the conclusion is, as Johnson might have said, an unended ending, an unresolved resolution. And the tension which impels the reader through the novel stems from the parallelism with which it is constructed. As parallelism wanes, so does tension; the parts which are the

most perfectly parallel are the most vitally interesting.

The parallelism, of course, begins at the sentence level and pervades the whole structure of the book. Now one cannot dispute that balance in sentence structure is an inherently interesting thing; the reader is held in a state of suspense until the sentence achieves perfect balance, and then he is ready to go to the next and repeat the process. This sort of interest is, I grant, analogous to that which we give a tightrope walker; will he maintain balance from start to finish? If he does, we are relieved and normally would not want him to start the walk again. (Tension has been resolved.) And I think that we tend to admire the virtuosity of the writer's perfect equilibrium as much as we do that of the tightrope walker.

In his classic study of Johnson's prose style, Wimsatt defines the possibilities of parallelism. There can be parallelism or balance between like elements and between antithetical elements. Between like elements, there is normally a sequential relationship. "Suppose three clauses, the first of which tells the cause of an act, the second the act, and the third its consequences. These three meanings are parallel if the sequence is taken as a whole and if as a whole it is referred to a fourth meaning."[15] But this description of the parallelism at the sentence level is also a description of the parallelism of the novel as a whole. Take chapters nineteen through twenty-one as examples:

cause of act
 [Rasselas] having heard of a hermit, that lived near the lowest cataract of the Nile, and filled the whole country with the fame of his sanctity, re-

solved to visit his retreat, and inquire whether that felicity which public life could not afford was to be found in solitude.[16]

act

[After the trip to the hermit's retreat, Imlac says] We have heard at Cairo of your wisdom, and came hither to implore your direction for this young man and maiden in the *choice of life*.[17]

consequence

[Rasselas concludes, after having visited the hermit, that] The life of a solitary man will be certainly miserable, but not certainly devout.[18]

fourth meaning

The problem of the novel.

Two observations should now be made. The excitement in *Rasselas* (as a novel) comes from basically the same principle that arouses excitement at the stylistic level, that is, the tension of the novel relies upon the perfect balance and antithesis with which Johnson constructs the larger part of his tale. Furthermore, as I have repeatedly contended, the individual sentences that an author characteristically uses are a good place to begin to search for devices that will constitute, in the round, that writer's technique. That is, if balance and parallelism are characteristic of the individual sentences, one would expect larger structures to have the same characteristics.

In the case of *Rasselas*, Wimsatt's outline of the four parts of the parallel structure of sentences provides a key to understanding the structure of the novel and an explanation of the strange sort of tension that one feels as he reads the novel. The reader sees the sequential relationship and is led, as in any good story, to ask, "Then what?" The relation of *cause of act* to *act* to *consequences* to *fourth meaning* provides the structural basis for a narrative which is

apparently episodic. Herbert Read, as well as W. K. Wimsatt, recognizes the use of antithetical parallelism in Johnson's prose.[19] These antithetical parallels are another aspect of Johnson's virtuosity. They are a rhetorical adornment, but they also lie very near to the reason for tension in *Rasselas*. The astronomer, speaking of his obsession, says, "Integrity without knowledge is weak and useless, and knowledge without integrity is dangerous and dreadful."[20] Here is a perfect antithetical balance, and it is a summation of the dilemma of the astronomer. He needed someone both knowledgeable and moral to receive the mystery of his delusion of power over the elements. He found such a person in Imlac. That the dilemma existed, however, is interesting; it had two parts that exactly balanced one another. But one should note that there are two elements here which are beyond mere virtuosity; the pause that one must make to ascertain the conditions of the formula (for such it is) and the recognition of the solution and the application of that solution. This balanced sentence is, then, a problem and a statement of a dilemma in a person. As soon as the reader grasps the dilemma, he is interested in the solution.

The plan of the novel is the turning again and again from hope to disillusionment. That which presages success in the search for happiness turns out immediately to demonstrate the folly of searching for contentment in any given pursuit. Such a scheme not only fosters parallelism, but demands it: on the one hand, hope of success; on the other, recognition of failure.

Earlier, I said that *Rasselas* is an exciting novel. Now I must qualify that statement. It is exciting if one is interested in the resolution of the problem. The particular answer that Johnson gives us demands that each hope be shattered, that each tentative answer be proved false. If the plot is to have tension, incident must be balanced against incident. However, one can see immediately that this particular necessity for balance must pair the incidents and isolate the pairs. Consequently, the story is episodic. For instance, Rasselas finds that every man in Cairo is apparently happy, but actually unhappy. The scales balance. The incident has its antithetical parallelism; it is self-contained. Furthermore, the mechanics of transition from this episode to the next are rudimentary. "Rasselas rose next day, and resolved to begin his experiments upon life." [21] The mortar which joins these dual building blocks is not mechanics of plot; it is interest in the unsolved problem with which the novel begins: the futile search for perfect happiness.

THE DECISIVE MOMENT

While the money was in his hand the lock clicked. It had sprung! Did he do it? He grabbed at the knob and pulled vigorously. It had closed. Heavens! he was in for it now, sure enough.

The decisive moment in *Sister Carrie* occurs when Hurstwood, almost by inadvertence, by a stroke of malignant fate, becomes a thief. From this point on, the plot of the novel is, in general terms, predictable; the movement of the plot can be in only one direction.

This predictability can be rhetorically advantageous in much the same way that the unpredictability of "incoherent" works is. The rhetorical motive is to engage the reader, to woo or seduce or convince him to immerse himself totally in the work so that the universe of the work becomes his universe and so that he is willing to suspend disbelief or, if not disbelief, at least critical distrust. Because it gives plot a certain predictability, the decisive moment makes the reader and the author co-conspirators in constructing a work of art. (Often a "dishonest" ending is simply the result of the author's betraying the conspiracy between himself and his reader.)

There could not be a clearer example of the decisive moment than that found in *Troilus and Criseyde*, and I would like to examine that work to demonstrate in detail what happens to the reader once he is confronted with the decisive moment.

Statements such as the following are typical of commentaries on Criseyde: she is "less sentimental and more practical than either Pandarus or Troilus. . . ." [22] "The picture of the growth of her love is perfect, with a wonderful balance of feeling and good sense; a cool head and a warm heart are not inconsistent, and make a poised character." [23] I see no reason for not agreeing with the consensus that Troilus is essentially an attenuation of the courtly lover— to be sure, a courtly lover refined and made eminently human through Chaucer's artistry, but basically conventional nonetheless. Criseyde, I think, is just as conventional, but representative of another medieval tradition—Aristotelian logic.

Aristotle defines a dialectical problem as "an investigation leading either to choice and avoidance or to truth and knowledge, either by itself or as an aid to the solution of some other such problem." [24] Criseyde's whole problem is one of "choice and avoidance" and that Chaucer would provide her with Aristotelian means for ratiocination is, of course, entirely probable. Though in his works Chaucer mentions Aristotle only nine times (as compared with thirty times for Seneca),[25] medieval education took Aristotle as an entire department of the trivium. In the medieval mind, Aristotle was semi-divine, the very font and source of wisdom.

We see Criseyde the scholastic at many points in the tale, but never so clearly as in Book III, at the decisive moment, when she rationalizes her shock at Pandarus's lie concerning Troilus's jealousy over Horaste. The passage runs thus:

"O brotel wele of mannes joie unstable!
With what wight so thow be, or how thow pleye,
Either he woot that thow, joie, art muable,
Or woot it nought; it mot ben oon of tweye.
Now if he woot it nought, how may he seye
That he hath verray joie and selynesse,
That is of ignoraunce ay in derknesse?

"Now if he woot that joie is transitorie,
As every joie of worldly thyng mot flee,
Than every tyme he that hath in memorie,
The drede of lesyng maketh hym that he
May in no perfit selynesse be;
And if to lese his joie he sette a myte,
Than semeth it that joie is worth ful lite.

"Wherfore I wol diffyne in this matere,
That trewely, for aught I kan espie,
Ther is no verray weele in this world heere."[26]

When Criseyde "diffynes" her argument, she propounds a phrase that indicates the essence of life, for a definition "is a phrase indicating the essence of something."[27] In the ar-

gument leading to the definition, Criseyde proceeds via Aristotle's either-or method, the theory of contrarieties: either man knows that joy is mutable, or he knows it not.[28] And her conclusion that "there is no verray weele in this world heere" is not only logical; it is inevitable. The inevitable conclusion to the argument, it turns out, is a decisive moment that makes the rest of the plot largely predictable.

For instance, in Book V, desolate in the Trojan camp, Criseyde must resolve her situation, but since she has defined the essence of life as the impossibility of perfect felicity, the conclusion of her rationalization is predictable:

The brighte Venus folwede and ay taughte
The wey ther brode Phebus down alighte;
And Cynthea hire char-hors overraughte
To whirle out of the Leoun, if she myghte;
And Signifer his candels sheweth brighte,
Whan that Criseyde unto hire bedde wente
Inwith hire fadres faire brighte tente.

Retornyng in hire soule ay up and down
The wordes of this sodeyn Diomede,
His grete estat, and perel of the town,
And that she was allone and hadde nede
Of frendes help; and thus bygan to brede
The cause whi, the sothe for to telle,
That she took fully purpos for to dwelle.[29]

This typically Senecan conclusion, arrived at by Aristotelian dialectic, leads Criseyde to the truism that one must accept the worst with the best and attempt to fashion some kind of happiness even in the most adverse circumstances. She is stoical rather than unfaithful, and we should expect Chaucer's audience to recognize immediately and to understand the wellsprings of her motivation.

All coherent works of art rely to some extent upon what I have called "participatory rhetoric"; the reader generally is more satisfied if he is able to say, "Ah! I told you so" than if he must say, "How strange!" Insofar as we are interested in motive rather than particular outcome, we are caught up in participatory rhetoric and proceed with the author in a deductive sequence from the critical moment.

FORMAL CONTROL

The poet often feels himself caught up in the dilemma of creative cross-purposes, his sense of what he *wills* to say continually thrown off course by the demands of the form that he has chosen or that he has inadvertently let begin to develop in his poem. In his early compulsion to use rhyme in his poetry, James Dickey "felt continually carried past my subject, carried around it, sometimes close to it but never in it in the way I wished to be in it." [20] But in the same essay, Dickey tells of his development:

I began to conceive of something I called — doubtless misleadingly — the 'open' poem: a poem which would have none of the neatness of most of those poems we call 'works of art' but would have the capacity to involve the reader in it, in all its imperfections and impurities, rather than offering him a (supposedly) perfected and perfect work for contemplation, judgment, and evaluation. . . . I experimented with short lines some more and, eventually, with putting several of these together on the same physical plane to make up what I called the 'split line,' in which spaces between word groups would take the place of punctuation. . . .

Of late my interest has been mainly in the conclusionless poem, the open or ungeneralizing poem, the un-well-made poem. I hope in the future to get the reader more and more into the actions and happenings of the lines and require him less and less to stand off and draw either aesthetic or moral judgments. [31]

This is the same James Dickey who said of Allen Ginsberg that he "is the perfect inhabitant, if not the very founder of Babel, where conditions do not so much make tongues incomprehensible, but render their utterances, as poetry, meaningless." [32] And, at the risk of becoming too quotational, it was Ginsberg who said this (in a letter to John Hollander):

Back to Howl: construction. After sick and tired of shortline free verse as not expressionistic enough, not swinging enough, can't develop a powerful enough rhythm. I simply turned aside, accidentally, to writing part I of Howl, in solitude, diddling around with the form, thinking it couldn't be published anyway (queer content my parents shouldn't see, etc.) also it was out of my shortline line. But what I did taught my theory, I changed my mind about "measure" while writing it. Part one uses repeated base who, as a sort of kithera BLANG, homeric (in my imagination) to mark off each statement, with rhythmic unit. So that's experiment with longer & shorter variations on a fixed base—the principle being, that each line has to be contained within the elastic of one breath—with suitable punctuatory expressions where the rhythm has built up enough so that I have to let off steam by building a longer climactic line in which there is a jazzy ride. *All the ear I've ever developed goes into the balancing of those lines.* [33]

This letter dates back to 1958, and whether or not Ginsberg would still defend his notion of the "elastic breath" line we have no way of knowing. (The concept pretty obviously shows considerable naiveté about both physiology and grammar.) The important point, though, is that a poet who writes "verse" that is formally indistinguishable from prose (except, of course, in typography) should so vehemently protest that he does, indeed, have formal control.

Each poet, in his own way, must reason or pray himself through to a concept of form that works for him in his poetry, and it is the rare poet who does not have a theory of form, who does not wrestle with the problem of what he wants to say versus the form in which he chooses to say it.

Mere typography has an obvious but magical effect. For instance, the following passage:

If God has been good enough to give you a poet then listen. But for God's sake let him alone until he is dead; no prizes, no ceremony, they kill the man. A poet is one who listens to nature and his own heart; and if the noise of the world grows up around him, and if he is tough enough, he can shake off his enemies but not his friends. That is what withered Wordsworth and muffled Tennyson, and would have killed Keats; that is what makes Hemingway play the fool and Faulkner forget his art.

It is, as a matter of fact, a poem by Robinson Jeffers—but a poem only by virtue of its typographic form.

If God has been good enough to give
    you a poet
Then listen to him. But for God's sake
    let him alone until he is dead; no
    prizes, no ceremony.
They kill the man. A poet is one who
    listens
To nature and his own heart; and if the

noise of the world grows up around
    him, and if he is tough enough,
He can shake off his enemies but not his
    friends.
That is what withered Wordsworth and
    muffled Tennyson, and would have
    killed Keats; that is what makes
Hemingway play the fool and Faulkner
    forget his art.[34]

Visual form, typographic form, then, has the strange and yet mundane effect of "raising" prose above itself, that is, form changes a reader's expectations and emotional sets and, in this respect, heightens the experience of reading. So much is almost truistic.

But what I would like to *speculate* about is the possibility that form also serves as a means whereby the poet makes that which is unendurable—for both himself and his reader—into a controlled, and hence endurable, experience.

A startling, agonized document in support of this possibility is "The Longing," the first poem in Theodore Roethke's *The Far Field*.[35] The first part of the poem is a lament concerning the poet in the Purgatory, the modern city of night, where

The slag-heaps fume at the edge of the
    raw cities:
The gulls wheel over their singular
    garbage;
The great trees no longer shimmer;
Not even the soot dances.
And the spirit fails to move forward,
But shrinks into a half-life, less than
    itself,
Falls back, a slug, a loose worm
Ready for any crevice,
An eyeglass starer.

The second section tells us, however, that "A wretch needs his wretchedness. Yes." As if there were no way out of the maddening personal dilemma—no way, that is, except the old escape that Roethke, who literally grew up in a greenhouse, nostalgically turns to time and time again:

The rose exceeds, the rose exceeds us
    all.
Who'd think the moon could pare itself
    so thin?
A great flame rises from the sunless sea;
The light cries out, and I am there to
    hear—
I'd be beyond; I'd be beyond the moon,
Bare as a bud, and naked as a worm.

To this extent I'm a stalk.
    —How free; how all alone.
Out of these nothings
    —All beginnings come.

The final section of the poem is contradictory, or at least ambivalent, for the poet longs for both the inhuman ("I would with the fish, the blackening salmon, and the mad lemmings") and the human ("The children dancing"). The burden, however, is the yearning toward a pure simplicity, a world stripped of material complications, bone-bare, essential:

In the summer heat, I can smell the
    dead buffalo,
The stench of their damp fur drying in
    the sun,
The buffalo chips drying.

    Old men should be explorers?
    I'll be an Indian.
    Iroquois.

Thus the poem ends. The coda is perfect, for the Indian, romantically and actually, is the child of nature whose life is stripped bare of the hideous superfluities of civilization. However, the midsection of this poem to the resolution of the coda has been accomplished by a passage that bears some scrutiny—and that gets us to the point about formal control. It runs thus:

I long for the imperishable quiet at the
    heart of form;
I would be a stream, winding between
    great striated rocks in late summer;
A leaf, I would love the leaves,
    delighting in the redolent disorder of
    this mortal life,
This ambush, this silence,
Where shadow can change into flame,
And the dark be forgotten.

In this un-hip poet there are Zenist overtones, but I think that Roethke can be taken quite literally when he expresses his longing for "the imperishable quiet at the heart of form." If the poet can "form" experience to his own satisfaction, then he is able to be at rest in viewing "the redolent disorder of this mortal life." And, of course, it is the poet's task to achieve form so that both he and the reader can experience the quiet that poetry offers, a quiet that is, paradoxically, vibrant with life and sensation.

For another case in point, and there are countless, one might turn to Dylan Thomas, surely as compulsive a formalist as ever undertook the poetic task. In the "Author's Prologue" to his *Collected Poems*, he tells us,

                I hack
This rumpus of shapes
For you to know
How I, a spinning man,
Glory also this star, bird
Roared, sea born, man torn, blood
    blest.[36]

And it is no accident that his imagery again and again echoes Genesis 2–6:

And the earth was without form, and void; and darkness was upon the face of the deep. . . . And God said, Let there be light, and there was light. And God saw the light, that it was good: and God divided the light from the darkness. . . . And God said, Let there be a firmament in the midst of the waters.

John Ackerman has discussed Thomas' craftsmanship and has analyzed the intricate formal patterns of, for instance, "Fern Hill." [37] The syllable count of the poem is as follows:

Stanza	I	II	III	IV	V	VI
Line 1	14	14	14	14	14	14
2	14	14	14	14	14	14
3	9	9	9	9	9	9
4	6	6	6	6	6	6
5	9	9	9	9	9	9
6	15	14	14	14	14	14
7	14	14	14	14	14	15
8	7	7	8	8	8	7
9	9	9	6	6	6	9

Only a few comments on the intricacy of this pattern are necessary. Line 6 of Stanza I has fifteen syllables; therefore, almost inevitably one feels, Line 7 of Stanza VI has fifteen syllables. The sum total of syllables for all of the *eighth* lines in the six stanzas is forty-five, and that is also the total for all the syllables in the ninth lines.

This shaping of experience into controlled forms seems to have been an almost manic preoccupation with Thomas. J. M. Brinnin describes the poet's working methods. Regardless of how insignificant an addition or change might be, Thomas would recopy the whole poem, keeping the total form intact. "Fern Hill" went through more than two hundred revisions before Thomas was satisfied (if, indeed, he ever was satisfied). [33]

It seems to me that this ability— or need—to shape and control is one of Thomas' great successes, particularly when one compares Thomas with Ginsberg, whose failure is inability to give the raw data of experience the esthetic palliation that is the function of form in poetry.

In many ways the most original and intense of contemporary poets, Ginsberg has made a methodological decision that will eternally preclude him from coming to terms with the experiences of his own scarifying existence and that, more disastrously, will tend to keep poetic interest at arm's length. It is precisely the lack of "imperishable quiet at the heart of form" that repels the reader from much of Ginsberg's poetry. The formal requirements of art enable the poet to divert his unnerving stare from the horrors of temporality to the eternity of pure configuration and hence provide the escape that art should be, for it is certainly true that art is, in part, an escape mechanism.

The theme of one of Ginsberg's most important poems, "THE CHANGE: Kyoto-Toyko Express," [39] is that through learning to love oneself, one learns also to love the universe. What, after all, is more horrible than man's humanity?

Shit! Intestines boiling in sand fire
   creep yellow brain cold sweat
   earth unbalanced vomit thru
   tears, snot ganglia buzzing
   the Electric Snake rising hypnotic
   shuffling metal-eyed coils
   whirling rings within wheel
   from asshole up the spine
   Acid in the throat the chest
   a knot trembling Swallow back
   the great furry ball of the great
   Fear

And, the poet asks, "How can I / be sent to Hell / with my skin and blood?" But the change comes when Ginsberg can ask yet another question:

Who would deny his own shape's
    loveliness in his
    dream moment of bed
    Who sees his desire to be
    horrible instead of Him

And the resolution is the poet's acceptance of his own corporeality.

Both Roethke and Ginsberg longed, but Roethke became a shaper of experience, Ginsberg a self-idolater. The craftsman is fashioning something outside himself, is arranging parts of the universe into meaningful and bearable wholes. The experience of poetic craftsmanship allows both a looking away from the impulse and a handling of that impulse. In his preoccupation with his own unique self, Ginsberg loses much of the control that makes for art. The reader, too, it seems to me, demands that healing salvation of a double vision, both the spontaneous cry of a hyperesthetic sensibility and the tough, rational shaping of experience.

I echo Yvor Winters when I say that no critic should deal with a poet for whom that critic does not have considerable affection, and I must confess that Ginsberg always intrigues me and often moves me (I think, in spite of his method, not because of it). In any case, in a loving spirit, I would like to look at the failure, not the success, of a poem that might well have been one of the most satisfying that I have encountered. I am thinking of "This Form of Life Needs Sex" from *Planet News*. It is one of those intensely honest poems that makes us feel certain that Ginsberg puts no barrier of reticence between himself and the reader:

I will have to accept women
    if I want to continue the race,
    kiss breasts, accept
    strange hairy lips behind
        buttocks,
Look in questioning womanly eyes
    answer soft checks,
bury my loins in the hang of pearplum
    fat tissue
        I had abhorred.

Now, such total honesty is a considerable virtue in itself, and the poem becomes even more brutal in its frankness:

You can joy man to man but the Sperm
    comes back in a trickle at dawn
    in a toilet on the 45th Floor—

What is missing here is the sense that the poet is dealing with experience. To repeat, there is this difference between art and experience: art has forms and configurations that the artist imposes. And that is why we turn to art. In a world that is essentially chaotic, we gain the illusion of order.

I realize that I stand the risk of backing myself into a logical corner, for there is no way to "prove" what I contend, though perhaps a fairly convincing demonstration can be made through comparison. It is not merely, I think, Ginsberg's subject matter, his total honesty, or his vocabulary that could well put sympathetic readers off. It is his essential formlessness.

Compare three stanzas from Anne Sexton's "The Ballad of the Lonely Masturbator" with the Ginsberg poem:

The end of the affair is always death.
She's my workshop. Slippery eye,
out of the tribe of myself my breath
finds you gone. I horrify

those who stand by. I am fed.
At night, alone, I marry the bed.

Finger to finger, now she's mine.
She's not too far. She's my encounter.
I beat her like a bell. I recline
in the bower where you used to mount
    her.
You borrowed me on the flowered
    spread.
At night, alone, I marry the bed.
. . . .
The boys and girls are one tonight.
They unbutton blouses. They unzip
    flies.
They take off shoes. They turn off the
    light.
The glimmering creatures are full of
    lies.
They are eating each other. They are
    overfed.
At night, alone, I marry the bed.[40]

Granted: the subject matter of "The Ballad of the Lonely Masturbator" is probably a bit less shocking to the average sensibility than that of "This Form of Life Needs Sex," but, it seems to me, the reader inevitably will become involved with the Sexton poem because of its formal properties; the only involvement one might possibly have with the Ginsberg poem comes from the subject matter—and that is a good deal more likely to repel than to attract.

In the views of major critics, from Aristotle through Sidney to Kenneth Burke and I. A. Richards, the main function of art has been to heal (both the artist and his reader). I have suggested that the "what" of the salutary "message" is no more important than the "how." Perhaps the "what" gains significance only through the "how."

CONCLUSION

Studies of poetic form or structure as *abstract entities* are exceedingly

rare and are somewhat primitive, especially in comparison with the number and sophistication of other critical approaches. Both Kenneth Burke and Yvor Winters have made significant contributions, but one is hard put to think of other modern critics who have thought much about form *qua* form.

Although my knowledge of folklore is minimal, it appears that significant theories of form have been developing in that discipline, and an excellent article by William O. Hendricks outlines current work.[41]

The present discussion in no sense purports to be a systematic handling of the problem of form in poetry. The intent of the essay, rather, has been to demonstrate how form, conceived as abstract configuration of relationships, affects both the esthetics and the rhetoric of literature. Much of what was said is by its very nature speculative, particularly the matter of form making experience esthetically accessible to the reader.

Nonetheless, the theoretical underpinning of the discussion is valid, almost too obviously so: form has rhetorical consequences. The purpose of the essay has been to investigate some of the results that ensue from acceptance of the premise. And it bears repeating that far too little inquiry has been made into this crucial area where rhetoric and poetics overlap and become one.

Any such area is, of course, no man's land, the limbo of the faithless, for no self-respecting estheticism will vulgarize his subject by glancing, even momentarily, at rhetoric, and the rhetorician, though generally much more comprehensive in his viewpoint than the esthetician, is so busied with the "practical" discourses of history (both past and present) that he seldom has time to concern himself with poetry. It is perhaps in this neutral territory that the snobbish isolation of the esthetician and the busy practicality of the rhetorician will achieve "the imperishable quiet at the heart of form."

NOTES

1. "Lexicon Rhetoricae," *Counter-Statement* (Los Altos, Calif.: Hermes Publications, 1953), 124.

2. *Quarterly Journal of Speech*, LVI (April, 1970), 161−67.

3. *College English*, XXXI (May, 1970), 828−35.

4. *College Composition and Communication*, XXII (February, 1971), 39−45.

5. *The Modern Poets* (New York: Oxford Univ. Press, 1960), 5.

6. *Modern Poetry and the Tradition* (Chapel Hill: Univ. of North Carolina Press, 1939), 138.

7. *Ibid.*, 146.

8. *Ibid.*, 151.

9. *Ibid.*, 157−58.

10. *Ibid.*, 159.

11. *Reflections on a Literary Revolution* (Washington, D.C.: The Catholic University of America Press, 1960), 38.

12. *Ibid.*, 34.

13. *Ibid.*, 32.

14. Whether or not *The Waste Land* is, in fact, coherent is beside the point. The important fact is this: many readers, I among them, see *The Waste Land* as incoherent, that is, as a series of disunified fragments so far as the major sections are concerned. Equally important, the judgment that a poem or novel or whatever is incoherent is in itself an arhetorical, nonesthetic judgment. Coherence or incoherence can be effective for given audiences. I am only arguing that incoherence has the potentiality of being used for rhetorical effect.

15. *The Prose Style of Samuel Johnson* (New Haven: Yale Univ. Press, 1941), 16.

16. *Rasselas*, in *Shorter Novels of the Eighteenth Century*, ed. Philip Hender-

son (London: J. M. Dent & Sons, 1956), 38.

17. *Ibid.*, 41.

18. *Ibid.*, 42.

19. *English Prose Style* (Boston: Beacon Press, 1955), 41.

20. *Rasselas*, 78.

21. *Ibid.*, 35.

22. F. N. Robinson, *The Poetical Works of Chaucer* (Boston: Houghton Mifflin, 1933), 451.

23. J. S. P. Tatlock, "The People in Chaucer's *Troilus*," *PMLA*, LVI (1941), 98.

24. *Topica*, trans. E. S. Forster (Cambridge, Mass.: Harvard Univ. Press, 1960), 299.

25. George A. Plimpton, *The Education of Chaucer* (London: Oxford Univ. Press, 1935), 167−68.

26. The translation of George Philip Krapp (New York: Vintage Books, n.d.), 140−41, runs thus:

O fickle fate! O worldly joy unstable!
Of men thou makest but a sport and
    play!
All know that they to hold their joy are
    able,
Or know it not—there is no other way.
Now if one knows it not, how may he
    say
That he of perfect joy perceives the
    spark,
If ignorance still leaves him in the dark?

But if he knows that joy is transitory,
Since joy in every worldly thing must
    flee,
This troubling thought diminishes the
    glory
Of earthly joy, and so in such degree,
Imperfect must be his felicity;
If loss of joy he fears a jot or tittle,
This proves that earthly joy is worth but
    little.

And so this problem I must thus decide,
That verily, for aught that I can see,
No perfect joy can in this world abide.

27. *Topica*, 281.

28. John Peter Anton, *Aristotle's Theory of Contrariety* (London: Routledge and Paul, 1957), 95−96, explains, "The

fundamental idea which seems to underlie Aristotle's conception of affirmation-
negation opposition, especially its relation to contrariety, is that all statements
are either *affirmations*, where a predicate is affirmed of a subject, or *nega-
tions*, where a predicate is denied of a
subject. No third type is possible because of all four types of opposition the
one of 'affirmation and negation' excludes intermediates."

29. Krapp, 279:

Bright Venus soon appeared to point
  the way
Where Phoebus, wide and round,
  should down alight,
And now her chariot horses Cynthia
Whirls out of the Lion, driven by her
  might,
And Signifer displays his candles bright;
Then Cressida unto her night-rest went
Within her father's fair and shining tent,

Debating in her soul aye up and down
The words of this impetuous Diomede,
His high estate, the peril of the town,
Her loneliness and all her pressing need
Of friendly help, and thus began to
  breed
The reasons why, the simple truth to
  tell,
She thought it best among the Greeks
  to dwell.

30. "The Poet Turns on Himself,"
Babel to Byzantium (New York: Farrar,
Strauss and Giroux, 1968), 283.

31. *Ibid.*, 290–91.

32. *Babel to Byzantium*, 53.

33. Jane Kramer, *Allen Ginsberg in
America* (New York: Vintage Books,
1970), 33. Italics mine.

34. "Let Them Alone," in *Selected
Poems* (New York: Random House,
Inc.). Reprinted by permission of the
publisher.

35. (New York: Doubleday and Co.)
Reprinted by permission of the publisher.

36. Dylan Thomas, *Collected Poems*
(New York: New Directions Publishing
Corp., 1952). Reprinted by permission of
New Directions Publishing Corporation.

37. *Dylan Thomas: His Life and
Work* (London: Oxford Univ. Press,
1964), 124–126.

38. *Ibid.*, 124.

39. Copyright 1968 by Allen Ginsberg. Reprinted by permission of City
Lights Books.

40. In *Love Poems* (Boston: Houghton Mifflin Publishing Co.). Reprinted
by permission of Houghton Mifflin Publishing Co.

41. "Folklore and the Structural
Analysis of Literary Texts," *Language
and Style*, III (Spring, 1970), 83–121.

Dispositio: The Concept of Form in Discourse

This essay—in some ways, an expansion of and commentary on "The Grammar of Coherence"—makes several points that are worth considering.

First is the distinction of *matrix* and what might be called "organic form." Some years ago, in a source that I have looked for but not found, a wise person said, as I recall, "In the Renaissance, poets wrote poems; the Romantics wrote poetry." Regardless of historical accuracy, the point that my long-lost source made is this: you can decide to write a sonnet and then think of subject matter to pour into that form, or you can have a semantic intention and attempt to find a suitable form or let one grow as the work progresses. In a sense, the five-paragraph essay is a matrix, as is the classical oration strictly defined. In another essay,* I developed the thesis that form is heuristic in that it demands meaning; thus, such mundane activities as pattern practice with sentences can be generative, though I am decidedly *not* urging pattern practice.

Further, I argue that a text has a "deep structure" that can have various "surface" manifestations. To paraphrase my essay: when we see two or three manifestations of what we take to be the same work, we are experiencing a deep structure, the surface structure that the author has chosen, and other alternatives made possible by a finite structural system.

Yet further, I point out—with Robert Lowell's "Between the Porch and the Altar" as the case in point—that "The recurrence of image, symbol, idea or metaphor can serve as a kind of 'semantic' device to outline form."

Finally, I elaborate on my "grammar of coherence" and then state that the grammar of the sentence is "the most productive analogical model for exploration of 'grammar' beyond the sentence." *At this point, I emphatically repudiate that idea!*

This essay appeared originally in *College Composition and Communication* (Feb. 1971). Reprinted with the permission of the National Council of Teachers of English.

* "Style: A Matter of Manner," *Quarterly Journal of Speech*, 56:2 (April 1970), 161–67.

To grasp the shadowy and fantasmal form of a book, to hold it fast, to turn it over and survey it at leisure—that is the effort of a critic of books, and it is perpetually defeated.

—Percy Lubbock
The Craft of Fiction

One of the supreme joys of art springs from mere attentive ignorance and comes at that moment when the musically illiterate listener "makes sense" of the music that he is listening to. And the mystery is this: lacking vocabulary, the layman has no way of explaining his sense that a piece of music has a form that he can perceive. The shadowy and fantasmal form of a Mozart *divertimento* hovers in the consciousness just below the level at which it can be discussed; it is ineluctably there in the mind of the "beholder," but inexpressible, a configuration, a pattern, that constitutes its own content. Susanne Langer tells us that

There are certain aspects of the so-called "inner life"—physical or mental—which have formal properties similar to those of music—patterns of motion and rest, of tension and release, of agreement and disagreement, preparation, fulfilment, excitation, sudden change, etc.[1]

Then Miss Langer goes on to say that "Because the forms of human feelings are much more congruent with musical forms than with the forms of language, music can *reveal* the nature of feelings with a detail and truth that language cannot approach."[2] In a loose, analogical sense, music has a "grammar," but since it has no "lexicon," its effects must diverge from those of any art that depends on words. Music, that

is, is pure form while a lyric poem is both form and meaning in the usual sense.

All of this, it seems to me, is clear enough. However, it is easy to overlook the fact that form and meaning are separable entities in poetry (and I use that term in its broadest sense). I will argue this point adamantly. Milton's grandeur and the splendor of Herman Melville both depend as much on their syntax (a formal matter) as on their sublime subjects. The reader—if he reads as he ought to—must be overwhelmed by the concatenation of almost miraculous sentences as he is by the attempt to justify the ways of God to men. Only the most boorish response to literature is totally unlike the response to music, and only the most boorish literature is incapable of eliciting a "musical" response.

It is these abstract formal patterns that the following inquiry will seek out and examine. The question here is straightforward enough: How do we perceive form versus formlessness in discourse?

One of the problems in grasping the "shadowy and fantasmal form" of any discourse is the mere slipperiness of the word "form," a term with a variety of meanings that sometimes conflict with one another. In the first place, "form" and "genre" overlap and obscure one another's boundaries, even though to speak of the form "sonnet" and the form "lyric" are quite different things. Nor is the problem clarified by the semantic parallels between "organization" (Cicero and Quintilian called it *dispositio*) and "form." A bit of untangling is, then, in order.

No one, I take it, would contend that form in discourse has anything significant to do with the visual, with, for instance the shapes of "Easter Wings" or "The Altar." The form that we perceive in discourse is nonvisual, conceptual—once again, musical. Chinese may have the virtue of combining the "significant sequaciousness" of events in real life "with the density and angularity of 'things', the peculiar contribution of painting and sculpture,"[3] but Chinese ideographs and the English alphabet are two disparate systems.

The sonnet—with its fourteen lines of iambic pentameter rhyming in any one of a limited variety of ways—and the drama—with its division into acts, its prologue and epilogue, its chorus and other such conventions—are forms, certainly, in one sense of the word. However, it is paradoxically quite possible to have a perfectly formless, perfectly formed sonnet, that is, a series of fourteen lines of iambic pentameter rhyming *ababcdcdefefgg* that nonetheless seems totally amorphous in most senses of the word. The game here is not merely semantics, and the stakes in criticism and pedagogy are high, high enough to warrant a bit of sifting out and definition.

Quite unlike the form "sonnet" is the form "classical oration," with its division into *exordium* to gain the audience's attention, *narratio* to state the speaker's case, *confirmatio* to prove that case, *reprehensio* to refute the opponent's case and *peroratio* to sum up.[4] While a perfectly formed sonnet can be formless in most senses, a perfectly formed classical oration can never be formless. The reason for this apparent contradiction is that definition of the form sonnet is based on what I call *matrix*, the outward, mechanical features of that kind of poem. To define classical oration as a speech containing *exordium, narratio, confirmatio, reprehensio*, and *peroratio* is, however, quite a different sort of thing, for now the focus is not so much on matrix as on a construct, the parts of which become meaningful only in relation to each other and to two other entities which might be called the speaker's case and the opponent's case. That is, the definition of classical oration as a five-part entity implies an internal consistency of meaning and an "outside referent." Consider the sequence *narratio, confirmatio*, and *peroratio*. The concept *narratio* implies some kind of case involving judgment, choice or avoidance, praise or blame, and *confirmatio* implies exactly the same subject while *reprehensio* implies its obverse. In other words, there is an internal consistency; a "syntax" that is both unavoidable and apparent. In this sense, the definition of classical oration is generative. Applied again and again to different cases, the definitive schema for the classical oration will generate an infinity of classical orations. Of course, a definition of sonnet might be generative in roughly the same way:

it can be seen that the Italian sonnet will regularly divide between the eighth and ninth lines—between, that is, the octave and the sestet—while the Shakespearean sonnet, though there may be slight breaks after any one of the quatrains, will have a major break between the third quatrain and the final couplet. This means that the Italian sonnet tends to divide into two more or less coordinate considerations (whether complementary or opposed) of its topic, while the Shakespearean tends to arrive at a forceful, epigrammatic affirmation or denial, in the brief couplet, of the topic developed through the three quatrains.[5]

It is necessary, then, to differentiate between "form" and "form," between *matrix* and what I refer to when I speak of "form." Form might be defined as *the internal set of consistent relationships perceived in any stretch of discourse, whether poem, play, essay, oration, or whatever.* (As a corollary, it might be added that no discourse can be totally formless and still be discourse.)

Modern grammar leads me to believe that our perception of form in discourse comes about through the apprehension of an underlying set of relationships that, for each work, are invariable and basic, but that are "played off" against a variety of possible surface realizations. Grammar, of course, deals with the sentence, but it provides an analogy on which to build a theory of form for stretches of discourse beyond the sentence. The very notion *in medias res* implies that a work has an underlying configuration, a chronological dimension, that can achieve a variety of surface realizations. But chronology is only one, and normally the most simple, of the sets of relationships that go to make up form.

Between the grammar of the sentence and a grammar of form there is undoubtedly a long leap, but perhaps an analogical bridge can be built. Chomsky has said,

The principles that determine the form of grammar and that select a grammar of the appropriate form on the basis of certain data constitute a subject that might, following traditional usage, be termed "universal grammar." The study of universal grammar, so understood, is a study of the nature of human intellectual capacities.[6]

Sentence grammar indicates more and more forcefully that perception of meaning comes about through the interoperation of two concepts: deep structures and grammatical transformations that bring about surface structures. To repeat, then: it is not unreasonable to posit that our perception of form is contingent upon recognition—intuitive or otherwise—of a set of relationships (i.e., a proposition) in the deep structure of units of discourse, relationships that can gain a variety of surface realizations. In this case, the form is not merely the surface structure—and certainly not the matrix—but the result of the interplay between (1) the invariable deep structure, (2) the surface structure that the author has chosen, and (3) the other alternatives made available by a finite system of "organizing" that the "proposition" itself makes possible. The classical oration can serve as a paradigm here. It is a classical oration because its segments are arranged *exordium*, *narratio*, *confirmatio*, *reprehensio*, and *peroratio*, but that is not the only arrangement possible. Obviously, *narratio* might come first, followed by *exordium*, and *reprehensio* can precede *confirmatio*. However, *peroratio* cannot precede *narratio* without causing formlessness. That is, the simple "proposition" of the classical oration has a variety of ways in which it can come into being, though only one of those ways will result in what can be termed "classical oration," which will be, in this sense, a matrix.

It is not to be assumed that the relationship between segments of discourse longer than the sentence are necessarily the same as those within the sentence: that is most definitely not the point. The point is, to reiterate, that an analogous situation must prevail whenever we can say that this poem or that essay has form or is well formed.

To explore another aspect of the sentence analogy: the language has built into it a tremendously complex system that dictates both syntax and the conjoining of semantic features.[7] We should expect then that forms beyond the sentence would have "semantic features" as well as "syntax." Lacking a syntax (as, supposedly, some modern poetry does), the poem would nonetheless be held together, would gain form, through a meaningful repetition of ideas, very much like what Donald Davie means when he says,

The dislocated syntax of Ezra Pound in the *Cantos* may look like the dislocated syntax of William Carlos Williams, but in fact of course the *Cantos* are, or are meant to be, articulated most closely. They are articulated, however, by a syntax that is musical, not linguistic, by "the unifying, all-embracing artifice of rhythm," understood in its widest sense, to mean not only the rhythm that rides through tempo and metre in the verse-paragraph, but also the rhythmical recurrence of ideas hinted at in one canto, picked up in another much later, suspended for many more, and so on.[8]

The recurrence of image, symbol, idea, or metaphor can serve as a kind of "semantic" device to outline form. An example that occurs to me is Robert Lowell's "Between the Porch and the Altar." It may be recalled that this work is a series of four loosely related poems which symbolically tell the story of a man's break with his maternal past and his subsequent entry into a sordid adulterous affair with "Katherine." "Mother and Son," the first poem, tells of the narrator's uncomfortable relationship with a domineering mother who "makes him lose ten years, / Or is it twenty?" every time he meets her. The poem ends with a pseudo-benediction from the mother's hand, "Dangling its watch-chain on the Holy Book— / A little golden snake that mouths a hook." The second poem of the quartet, "Adam and Eve," tells, among other things, of the beginning of the affair with Katherine and how the narrator is torn between her and his wife and children: "I taste my wife/ And children while I hold your hands. I knife / Their names into this elm." But later: "When we try to kiss, / Our eyes are slits and cringing, and we hiss; / Scales glitter on our bodies as we fall." The third poem, "Katherine's Dream," contains more of the reptilian imagery. However, the final poem, "At the Altar," is apocalyptic: both the narrator and Katherine know the enormity of what they have done. After a mad dash through the city at night, the pair end up in a church, where the priest "mumbles through his Mass." As day breaks, the narrator discovers that "Here the Lord / Is Lucifer in harness." The symbolic serpent of evil becomes the Evil One himself, and the poem ends. The recurrent imagery with its attendant ideas has created a "syntax" of sorts and has outlined, though vaguely, a kind of form—or has created one of the integuments whereby the reader perceives form.

There are other "semantic" elements that contribute to the sense of form versus formlessness—pronouns and their antecedents, for instance, and what tagmemicists call "equivalence classes" (i.e., words that have the same referent or that stand for the same thing in a stretch of coherent discourse).[9] And the list could be expanded greatly.

Strangely enough, however, the sense of form versus formlessness hovers just slightly above the sense of meaning versus meaninglessness. It is quite possible to sense form without understanding meaning—at least in relatively short stretches of discourse. In fact, metaphor is an excellent example here, for that figure springs into being at the point where the cup of meaning runneth over, but formal requirements are ignored. Emily Dickinson, for instance:

After great pain a formal feeling
  comes—
    The Nerves sit ceremonious like
    tombs;
The stiff Heart questions—was it He
  that bore?
And yesterday—or centuries before?

The sequence of words in this stanza has its own internal formal requirements that prevail regardless of meanings in the real world or the world of the poet's imagination. The word "formal" (in the first line of the poem), like any other word in the language, functions according to a double set of meanings. There is first the referential, existential kind of meaning that a dictionary tries to capture and that might run something like this: pertaining to form; regular; ceremonial; done according to the rules.

But there is also a set of "metameanings" that are not referential in nature. The first metaphor in the poem comes to life when "formal" and "feeling" are coupled syntactically, because feelings are simply not formal in any literal sense. That is, the word "formal" has built into its total meaning certain restrictions that preclude it from functioning as an attributive adjective with "feeling," except in the metaphorical sense. The sequence "Nerves sit" is of exactly the same order.[10]

The most convenient unit of discourse to analyze for form and on which to test theories of form is the paragraph. The paragraph, of course, is not merely a collection of sentences, but a concatenation of transformational units.[11] Since this is the case, the first inquiry about the form ought to concern the way in which the sparks of coherence jump the gaps between T-units. In order to begin the investigation, I examined forty-seven paragraphs from expository prose written during the 1960s.[12] This investigation made it apparent that there must be two sorts of transitions between T-units: those that are marked and those that are not. In other words, we perceive the coherence of both of these utterances:

I would like to fly to Europe. I can't
  afford it.
I would like to fly to Europe. But I can't
  afford it.

The first transition is *implied*; the second is *expressed*. A survey of the forty-seven paragraphs revealed these totals for expressed transitions:

and	30	or	1
and so	1	parentheses	2
but	21	question	5
for	6	repetition	1
however	1	so	2
indeed	2	so that	3
in other words	1	though	3
instead	1	then	1
meantime	1	thus	1
moreover	1	yet	3
of course	1		

Most of these transitions need no illustration or explanation, but three of them do. *Parentheses, questions,* and *repetitions* are special cases that warrant brief discussion. We are dealing here with "quantitative" transitions—transitions in which an "and" is really an "and" and a "so" is really a "so." In this sense, parentheses, questions, and repetitions are expressed transitions. For instance:

Parentheses. The disaster which Muller fears is a result of gene mutations. These are small structural changes in the genes (he calls them "submicroscopic accidents") which are usually harmful to the organism. Because Muller believes that mutations are accumulating, he concludes that the human race is beginning to decline. In the end, the whole world will become a hospital, "and even the best of us will only be ambulatory patients in it."[13]

Parentheses obviously serve to insert one T-unit within another *sans* transformations. They also serve to insert other material that has no grammatical link with the T-unit as well as material that does; for parentheses, quite arbitrarily, can substitute for commas. They are listed as expressed transitions because they do indeed bridge the gap between T-units.

Question. We are assured that more jobs will be created by new industry, that higher skills will be required, that economic stability will be guaranteed by automation. There are pitifully few facts available to support these euphoric hopes. More likely a vast trauma awaits us all, to use Irving Howe's phrase. Then why automate? The underlying motives were exposed with unaccustomed bluntness in one of the trade journals recently when an automation advocate wrote: "[Machines] don't call in sick; they don't talk back; they work early and late and without overtime; they don't get tired; and last, but far from least, they don't line up at the cashier's window every week for a slice of the operating funds."[14]

The question transformation is classed as an expressed transition because questions can be recognized on the basis of their form. And, simply, a question normally calls for an answer.

Repetition. And when she told me about exploitation and economic forces I believed her. I believed her, but I was still afraid of Negroes.[15]

The mere fact of repetition creates form, as in the case of "Between the Porch and the Altar." When repetition occurs in adjacent T-units, the effect is to bridge the gap.

The other transitions are pretty much of the garden variety (on the surface, at least; investigation will reveal layers of complexity as, for instance, in the meanings of "and"). The data in my counts reveal clearly that modern prose relies heavily on "and" and "but" to get from T-unit to T-unit. The data also reveal that expressed transitions fall into four categories: (1) coordinating conjunctions; (2) moveable interrupters like "however," "then," "thus," and "in other words"; (3) parentheses (which may indeed not be transitions at all); and (4) sentence devices such as the question transformation or repetition.

Much remains to be said about form or coherence in discourse. But this much is clear: discourse at all levels has as its "meanings" a "deep structure" that has the possibility of various surface realizations. Part of one's appreciation and understanding of any "message" should be cognizance, subconscious or not, that any given surface structure is only one among a variety of choices and that the actual utterance must be played off against the unchosen possibilities. Sometimes the transitions that bridge the gap between units of discourse longer than the T-unit are easily recognizable, for they appear in the surface structure, but just as often they do not appear and are merely implied. They are *particles* that may or may not come to the surface. But above all, in the discussion of form or coherence, it is well to keep in mind the grammar of the sentence as the most productive analogical model for exploration of "grammar" beyond the sentence.

NOTES

1. *Philosophy in a New Key* (New York: n.d.), 193.

2. Ibid., 199.

3. Donald Davie, *Articulate Energy: An Inquiry into the Syntax of English Poetry* (London, 1955), 34.

4. Cicero, *De Partitione Oratorio* Vol. II, *De Oratore*, trans. H. Rackham (2 vols.; Cambridge, Mass., 1942), 27.

5. Jerome Beaty and William H. Matchett, *Poetry, from Statement to Meaning* (New York, 1965), 326.

6. *Language and Mind* (New York, 1968), 24.

7. For an excellent introduction to the problem of semantics, see D. Terence Langendoen, "The Nature of Semantics," *The Study of Syntax* (New York, 1969), 34–51.

8. *Articulate Energy*, 19–20.

9. A. L. Becker, "A Tagmemic Approach to Paragraph Analysis," *The Sentence and the Paragraph* (Champaign, Ill., 1966), 33–38.

10. I realize that my use of the term "formal" has been fast and loose in the foregoing, but not inadvertent. In two senses, lexical features are formal. In the first place, they are a regular set of rules and hence are formal in the same way that mathematical formulae are. In the second place, their formality often shows up in the forms that words take. Consider the following (for which I take dubious credit): "The glib runs through the mountains, / Over hill and dale./Splashing in the fountains, / It guzzles beer and ale." Only with the appearance of the pronoun "it" with its feature *nonhuman* does the possibility of metaphor emerge, a sort of formal metaphor, the exact meaning of which can never be determined. All we can say is that "glib" must be nonhuman (or, just possibly, a baby) and that nonhuman subjects normally do not "guzzle" anything, let alone beer and ale.

11. It will be remembered that a T-unit is the shortest stretch of discourse that can be set off, legitimately, with sentence punctuation. Thus, for instance, each of the coordinate clauses in a compound sentence is a T-unit.

12. The paragraphs are from *The Sense of the 60's*, ed. Edward Quinn and Paul J. Dolan (New York, 1968). This collection contains forty-eight essays. I examined the first paragraph in the first essay, the second paragraph in the second essay, and so on through the tenth; I examined the last paragraph in the eleventh essay, and with the twelfth, I started the process over again. I skipped one author, Thomas Merton, because of the brevity of his essay. Among the authors whose paragraphs I did examine are Paul Goodman, Staughton Lynd, John F. Kennedy, Susan Sontag, Tom Wolfe, Jimmy Breslin, Martin Luther King, Jr., John Updike, Robert Lowell, Bruce Jay Friedman, John Barth, and Marshall McLuhan.

13. Lucy Eisenberg, "Genetics and the Survival of the Unfit," *The Sense of the 60's*, 372.

14. Ben B. Seligman, "Man, Work, and the Automated Feast," *The Sense of the 60's*, 417.

15. Norman Podhoretz, "My Negro Problem—and Ours," *The Sense of the 60's*, 242.

Reading

The Three R's: Reading, Reading, and Rhetoric

"For the past few years, we have been witnessing . . . a [revolutionary] change in the field of literary theory and criticism. The words *reader* and *audience*, once relegated to the status of the unproblematic and obvious, have acceded to a starring role."*

How, after all, does one react to such a statement? With a demoralized sigh of despair, perhaps? Or, in another mood, a not-at-all charitable chuckle? A sneer of cold command? Amazement?

Nonetheless, literary theory is becoming more rhetorical, narrowing the gap between "our" concerns and "theirs." One panjandrum of the MLA has even said, "Rhetoric is the only game in town." (Another recently called me a "wrongheaded bigot" when I advanced arguments something like this one and those that appear in my essays on the profession, but, said this eminent humanist later, he was, of course, speaking ironically.) This development must inevitably be good for us, as it will be enormously salubrious for them.

In my essay, I argue that psycholinguistic theory of reading illuminates literary theory and that an adequate theory of literature will be virtually identical with a theory of rhetoric—or, appositely, that literary theory and rhetorical theory should be by and large identical.

Any theory of literary criticism states or at the very least (and more usually) implies a theory of reading. It should be illuminating, then, to examine prominent movements in criticism from the standpoint of what we have learned, in roughly the last ten years, about the phenome- non of reading. Freed from the limitations of structuralist-behaviorist theory, psycholinguistics of the "mentalistic" transformational-generative school has made a quantum leap in explaining what happens when a visual system mediates between strange black squiggles and a recep-

This essay appeared originally in *Rhetoric and Change*, ed. William E. Tanner and J. Dean Bishop (Mesquite, Tex.: Ide House, 1982). Reprinted by permission.

* Susan R. Suleiman, "Introduction: Varieties of Audience-Oriented Criticism," *The Reader in the Text*, Ed. S. R. Suleiman and I. Crossman (Princeton: Princeton University, 1980), p. 3.

tor mind in the process of deriving meanings. Insofar as a theory of criticism contradicts what we know to be the case in reading, that theory must be faulty; on the other hand, reading theory can verify some of criticism's hermeneutic, exegetical techniques and procedures. In general, it turns out to be the case that reading theory almost always illuminates critical theory, and often critical theory illuminates reading theory. (In order to cut down on awkward verbiage, I will henceforth use *criticism* to mean *critical theory* and *psycholinguistics* to denote *reading theory*.)

Before I undertake to map out the correspondence between criticism and psycholinguistics and before I elaborate the second premise of this discussion (that critical theory is usually nothing more than fragmented rhetorical theory), I would like to pause long enough to illustrate what I mean concerning the relationship between criticism and psycholinguistics.

It is virtually a dogma of modern criticism that all literature is ironic, must be ironic to qualify as literature. And part of the irony arises from texture, which is, in effect, the intractability that arises from the conflict of matter with manner, the tension between what is being said and the way in which that content is expressed. As Robert Penn Warren (only one among a great number that could be cited) puts it: "Can we make any generalizations about the nature of the poetric structure? First, it involves resistances, at various levels. There is the tension between the rhythm of the poem and the rhythm of speech . . . between the formality of the rhythm and the informality of the language; between the particular and the general, the concrete and the

abstract; between the elements of even the simplest metaphor . . . the poet is like the jiujitsu expert; he wins by utilizing the resistance of his opponent—the materials of the poem. In other words, a poem, to be good, must earn itself. It is a motion toward a point of rest, but if it is not resisted motion, it is motion of no consequence."[1] In effect, a poem has *texture*, which arises from the various resistances inherent in the nature of the art.

Psycholinguistics is extremely useful in clarifying the irony of poetic structure.

It is axiomatic that the reader employs three cue systems in the process of deriving meaning; in the jargon, these are the *graphophonic*, *syntactic*, and *semantic systems*.[2] Each of the cue systems demands brief explanation.

To be sure, there is a correspondence between the graphic system of the poem as written and the phonic system of the reader's spoken dialect. So much goes without saying. It is obvious, however, that there is not a letter-by-letter correspondence, for a word such as *phthisic* contains only five phonemes: roughly, /tizik/. Not so obvious, but hardly astounding, is the fact that proficient readers derive meanings from graphemes, not phonemes. That is, meaning is derived from the configuration on the page without the mediation of sound. This is a well-established principle of psycholinguistics.[3] Even though there is a graphophonic correspondence between the written and the spoken versions of a text, in nonesthetic reading that correspondence is ignored, and the reader proceeds directly from the graphemic system to meaning. And here I will stress the difference between what I call *nonesthetic* and *esthetic* reading, a point that I will clarify in a moment.

The function of the syntactic cue system is obvious. There is all the difference in the world between *Man bites dog* and *Dog bites man*. Furthermore, the syntactic system determines the parts of speech that can fill various slots in a sentence. In the sequence DOG BITES —, the empty slot can be filled only by a nominal or an adverbial. This much is obvious. Equally obvious is the principle of accessibility, that is, the relative difficulty or ease with which meaning can be derived from a sentence. Both

(1) The child tossed up the ball which its father put down.

and

(2) The child tossed the ball which its father put down up.

are perfectly grammatical, but 1 is clearly more accessible than 2. It goes without saying that the less accessible version of any sentence is more *visible* than the more accessible version. Grammatical distortions, as in Cummings, are maximally *visible*, call attention to themselves as structures. In nonesthetic reading, the optimal condition is invisibility of syntax.

Meaning in a sentence is not, of course, a mere 1 plus 1 plus 1 sum of its parts, a principle that is easily illustrated by the fact that no one is really uncertain about the meaning of the following: Last month we flew to New York in a ____. (I think there are only two words that will fill the slot, *plane* and *jet*, and they are virtually semantic equivalents.) But, in fact, the semantic systems of nonpoetic and poetic writings differ in

radical and significant ways. Perhaps the best discussion of this difference is by Philip Wheelwright.[4] In literal language, symbols are discrete, univocal, invariant; in expressive language, symbols have iconic significance, are characterized by plurisignation, are given soft focus, are semantic variables which shift their meaning (to some extent) in context. In literal language, the significance of utterances as speech acts is normally definite; utterances are commands, requests, promises, and so on. But in expressive language, *assertorial tone* is softened.[5]

In sum, for maximum efficiency in nonesthetic reading, the graphophonic system must be invisible, sentences must be maximally accessible syntactically, and semantics must be *logical* rather than *translogical*, to use Wheelwright's terms.

Much poetry—perhaps most— seems particularly designed to make reading (in the sense of the efficient processing of black squiggles on a page to derive meaning) difficult, if not impossible. Consider what happens in the reading of this stanza from a relatively easy poem:

There is a Garden in her face,
Where Rose and White Lillies grow;
A heav'nly paradice is that place,
Wherein all pleasant fruits doe flow.
There Cherries grow which none may
   buy
Till Cherry ripe themselves doe cry.

The insistence of rhythm and rhyme makes the grapho-phonic system highly visible; the reader inevitably finds it more or less difficult to keep the phonics of the poem from coming between himself or herself and the meaning, which, as we have said, should emerge without the mediation of sound. Reading a metered and rhymed poem, then, is in a real sense a primitive activity, taking one back in time to the halting period of childhood, when reading was indeed the tortuous process of making enigmatic black squiggles correspond to meaningful sounds. (In the jargon, the reading model GRAPHEME—PHONEME—MEANING is called mediated word identification.)[6]

As to syntax and accessibility, the structure here is relatively straightforward, but clearly the following is more easily read than its original version: "There cherries grow which none may buy until they themselves do cry Cherry ripe." If syntax calls attention to itself, it does not function with maximum efficiency in the unmediated acquisition of meaning through use of the cue system. In other words, once again, the cue system becomes an object, not an instrument.

The translogicality of the semantic system in the stanza is pervasive, and I will comment on it briefly. *Garden* and *cherries* are both metaphoric and iconic. It is almost impossible to assign an exact meaning to *pleasant fruits*. And so on.

Here, then, is a great irony: the expressive language of poetry is not efficient language. A Coleridgean metaphor comes to mind: the language of poetry is like a pane of glass textured by frost which partially blocks the vision and which calls attention to itself as an object worth contemplating. This irony of texture is precisely—though not completely—explicable in terms of how the cue system works in the psycholinguistic process called reading.

The purpose of the foregoing was to give immediate demonstration of a principle: that it is productive to consider criticism from the view-point of psycholinguistics. Now I would like to become more general in my survey and to introduce the notion of rhetorical criticism.

In the first chapter of *The Mirror and the Lamp*, M. H. Abrams gives a concise and brilliant outline of critical viewpoints, which, as everyone recalls, fall into four categories: mimetic, expressive, pragmatic, and objective. Mimetic theory, viewing the poem as a mirror of reality, stresses the ratio between the poem and *reality* or *truth*. Expressive theory, viewing the poem as an expression of the poet, stresses the ratio between the poem and the poet. Pragmatic theory, viewing the poem as it affects a reader, stresses the ratio between the poem and the reader. And objective theory, viewing the poem as a unique artifact with its own ontological status, solipsistically implies a ratio between the poem and itself. Singleminded focus and close attention to the text bring the poem into being and create its value.

Schematically, then, we have the *mimetic ratio*: poem-reality; the *expressive ratio*: poem-poet; the *pragmatic ratio*: poem-reader; and the *objective ratio*: poem-poem. It must be said emphatically that seldom does an individual critic or school remain *pure*. Nonetheless, the four categories are a roughly accurate way of placing critics and schools; more important, the categories are a productive heuristic, as will be seen.

Out of context, statements that purely represent all of the viewpoints are easy to come by.

Mimetic

Tragedy, then, is an imitation of an action that is serious, complete, and of a certain magnitude.—Aristotle

Expressive

Poetry, in a general sense, may be defined to be "the expression of the imagination"; and poetry is connate with the origin of man. Man is an instrument over which a series of external and internal impressions are driven, like the alterations of an ever-changing wind over an Aeolian lyre, which move it by their motion to ever-changing melody. But there is a principle within the human being, and perhaps within all sentient beings, which acts otherwise than in the lyre, and produces not melody alone, but harmony, by an internal adjustment of the sounds or motions thus excited to the impressions which excite them.—Shelley

Pragmatic

As virtue is the most excellent resting place for all worldly learning to make his end of, so poetry, being the most familiar to teach it, and most princely to move towards it, in the most excellent work is the most excellent workman.—Sidney

Objective

Most of the distempers of criticism come about from yielding to the temptation to

Critical Viewpoint	Ratio	Correspondence to Rhetoric
Mimetic	poem-reality	logos
Expressive	poem-poet	ethos
Pragmatic	poem-reader	pathos
Objective	poem-poem	arrangement, style

take certain remarks which we make *about* the poem—statements about what it says or about what truth it gives or about the formulations it illustrates—for the essential core of the poem itself.—Cleanth Brooks

Granted that these out-of-context statements quite unfairly represent the extremes of the four viewpoints, nonetheless there is a tendency for critics and criticism to emphasize one or the other and thus to become reductive. To demonstrate this re-

ductiveness—and to make an essay toward a different kind of criticism— I would like now to turn back to psycholinguistics and to introduce the concept of discourse that is traditional in rhetoric. In other words, I want to survey critical theory in the light of psycholinguistics and rhetoric. In order to do this, I will construct two bare-bones schemata, one of rhetoric and one of the psycholinguistic phenomenon of reading.

Ignoring memory and delivery, we can say that the traditional body of rhetoric consists of three departments: invention, arrangement, and style. In turn, invention consists of three elements: *logos* (or reasonableness), *ethos* (or the character of the speaker), and *pathos* (or the nature of the audience). This age-old scheme is not to be written off lightly, and perhaps its usefulness is no better illustrated than by demonstrating how it, in its totality, fits with the fragmented view of discourse presented by critical theory.

This chart is, of course, simple enough, but it is also dramatic. It demonstrates the holistic, synthetic nature of rhetoric and the fragmented nature of literary criticism. Hereafter we will discuss the implications of the chart more thoroughly.

The axioms of psycholinguistic theory are a productive heuristic for thinking about critical theory. First, one hardly needs proof that by far the most important factor in the phenomenon of reading is the perceiving mind with all its limitations, its emotional sets, its reservoir of past experience. In fact, it is empirically demonstrable that the amount of information a skilled reader derives from a text is amazingly small. In general, "There is a limited-capacity short-term memory that creates a bottleneck in the transmission of visual information to the comprehension processes of the brain; therefore, it is essential that the brain provide more information from its side of the eyeballs than the eyes pick up from the page."[7] Psycholinguists talk about the magic number seven plus or minus two: short-term memory is capable of holding only between five and nine bits of information. A *bit* is a piece of information that reduces uncertainty by one-half. For instance, if I am holding a card from an ordinary deck and ask you to name the suit, you will need two bits of information to do so. First bit: "Is the card black?" (I answer, "No." You are now certain that the card is red.) Second bit: "Is the card a heart?" (I answer, "No." You are now certain that the card is a diamond.)

Second, we obviously derive meanings that are somehow independent of the words that originally carried them. If I were to ask you to tell me what I have said so far, I would think you mad—and be convinced you are an idiot savant—if you quoted what I have so far written word-for-word. Obviously, whole texts—poems, articles, novels—have deep and surface structures, just as sentences do.

Third, reading is a process of *scanning, predicting, testing,* and *confirming.*[8] It is simply demonstrable that close reading during initial contact with the text reduces one's ability to derive meaning. During the first contact, the closer the reading, the less the meaning derived.

(I am not arguing against ultimate close reading.) Or another perspective: "the perception of serial displays has three stages: *scanning,* to form a schema; *ordering* of the schematic elements; and *impleting* or filling in of the schematized but ordered items."[9] And if you have now picked up my cues and have begun to think about the New Criticism as a theory of impletion, you are on the right track.

All of the foregoing has, in fact, been prefatory to the main thrust of this paper. The preface having been gracefully danced through, we can now begin to saw wood.

Mimetic theory implies that the meaning *in here* in the poem somehow corresponds to a truth or a reality *out there* in the universe beyond the poem. The mimetic critic typically asks, "Is the poem true? Is it verisimilar?" In these questions is implied a system of values. If the answer is yes, the poem is *good.* In other words, as the schema that was developed some pages back would indicate, mimetic theory is concerned with what rhetoricians call *logos.* Here is Yvor Winters: "The theory of literature which I defend in these essays is absolutist. I believe that a work of literature, in so far as it is valuable, approximates a real apprehension and communication of a particular kind of objective truth . . . . The poem is good in so far as it makes a defensible rational statement about a given human experience (the experience need not be real but must be in some sense possible) and at the same time communicates the emotion which ought to be motivated by the rational understanding of that experience."[10]

In regard to *logos,* it turns out that poetics and psycholinguistics are of great help to rhetoric. We are dealing essentially with the question, "What is the meaning of meaning?" In the essay "Myth, Fiction, and Displacement" from *Fables of Identity*, Northrop Frye argues that as we are reading fiction, we are directly concerned with continuity, but after we have read, we lose sight of and interest in sequaciousness. Our knowledge is of what is generally called *theme*, and theme consists of *subject*, *allegory* (Hamlet personifies indecision, for instance), and *mythos*, which is the work "as a simultaneous unity, when the entire shape of it is clear in our minds." It is *dianoia*. (One might say that *dianoia* is the deep structure, and Frye does argue that the same *mythos* can have various surface realizations.) Frye says, "because myths are stories, what they 'mean' is inside them, in the implications of their incidents. No rendering of any myth into conceptual language can serve as a full equivalent of its meaning. . . . its life is always the poetic life of a story, not the homiletic life of some illustrated truism." Naturalism and realism are just indirect mythologizing, to which Frye applies the term *displacement*. "Literary shape cannot come from life; it comes only from literary tradition, and so ultimately from myth."[11]

The mystique of contextualism, as in Eliseo Vivas and Murray Krieger, deals interestingly and productively with meaning in a way not too far removed from Northrop Frye. In summary, the contextualists argue something like this: In the world *out there* are unformed, inchoate ideas floating in and forming the stream of experience. These can become the materials of poetry—the *substance*. The poet shapes these materials through the form of the poem, gives them *insistence* and hence more than merely inchoate being. Through the insistence of the poem, these materials gain *existence* and become cultural artifacts.[12] The poem itself *means* as what Krieger calls a *reductive metaphor*. As he explains,

The repetitive patterns of a work, which give stillness to the movement by freezing freedom, must be read by the critic into his hypothesis of the work's form, as he makes it a reductive metaphor—an emblem, a constitutive symbol—for all the moving life and liveliness of the work. The metaphor, while excluding so much of the middle in its reductive, extremist purity, is in its emblematic fullness at the same time all-inclusive.[13]

So far, so good. Both Frye and Krieger are telling us in their own ways that meaning has an independence of the text, and this only makes sense: you and I can meaningfully talk about the meaning of *Hamlet*, but we certainly could not recite the text, beyond a few of the soliloquies which have become set pieces. But in their discussions of meaning, Frye and Krieger, like most critics, keep their eyes too firmly focused on the poem-reality ratio which characterizes mimetic statements. (I am not necessarily saying that Frye and Krieger are mimetic critics.) For Frye, the ultimate reality is myth, while for Krieger, interestingly enough, the ultimate reality is the poem.

As a rhetorical-psycholinguistic corrective to critical discussions of meaning, I propose the following:

All perception might be regarded as a process of decision-making based on significant differences detected in the environment. The actual nature of the significant differences is not determined by the physical events themselves, but by the perceiver's rules for distinguishing those events that he wishes to treat as functionally equivalent from those that he wishes to treat as different. Events to be treated as equivalent will be allocated to the same cognitive category, which is specified by the rules that are represented in its feature lists. In other words, the perceiver brings a highly structured knowledge of the world into every perceptual situation. Rather than saying that he discovers order and regularities that are properties of the environment, it is more appropriate to say that the perceiver imposes his own organization upon the information that reaches his receptor systems. The organization of his knowledge of the world lies in the structure of his cognitive categories and the manner in which they are related—in the way the perceiver *partitions* his knowledge of the world.[14]

An account of meaning, then, that does not take the perceiving mind into consideration is only a partial account. In this respect, we are more satisfied with Frye's conception of the rockbottom mythic nature of literary knowledge than we are with structuralist or contextualist theories of meaning as a function of the text exclusively.

In surveying mimetic criticism as a source for an account of *logos*, we have now argued, on the basis of psycholinguistics and rhetoric, that the mimetic ratio of poem-reality must be expanded to include *pathos*, and our ratio becomes poem-reality-reader. Obviously this expanded ratio is highly rhetorical in nature, for the concept of audience has entered.

In its various manifestations, objective criticism, particularly New Criticism, is deeply anti-expressivist. Wimsatt and Beardsley's classic essay "The Intentional Fallacy" comes to mind here, and it is so widely known that it need not be quoted. Expressive criticism, however, is undergoing a renaissance in a variety of

quarters, some of which I would like to survey briefly. In their work, J. L. Austin and John Searle have begun to work out a grammar of expressivism, in effect arguing that without intention, any language is meaningless.[15] I am reluctant to explore even the peripheries of speech act theory here, but perhaps some brief illustrations will nail the concept down sufficiently. If you think about a sentence such as "Could you raise the window?" you will realize that, even though it is interrogative in form, it is ambiguous until you can supply an intention. The sentence is either a yes/no question or a request. In other words, your supplying an intention is not a fallacy at all, but a necessity.

Walter Ong argues movingly that "all words projected from a speaker remain, as has been seen, somehow interior to him, being an invitation to another person, another interior, to share the speaker's interior, an invitation to enter in, not to regard from the outside."[16] And, of course, Wayne Booth's fascinating *A Rhetoric of Irony* is largely an argument in behalf of the intentional fallacy.

In dealing with mimetic theory, we argued that the ratio had to be expanded from poem-reality to poem-reality-reader, else the criticism would fall short of its pretensions to explain and evaluate works of literature. Expressive criticism, from the Romantics onward (indeed, from Plotinus onward), has stressed the poem-poet ratio. Can we not productively combine mimetic and expressive theory to arrive at a poem-reality-reader-poet ratio? If we do this, we are coming even nearer to what might be called rhetorical criticism, for we have introduced the concept of *ethos*. In fact, however, our own intuition as well as tradition tells us that rhetorical criticism and literary criticism are different sorts of activities. The nature of the difference becomes clear when we take the pragmatic and the objective viewpoints toward texts.

Blatantly Marxist, gay, or feminist criticism is often representative of pragmatism at its most raucous and least interesting, but to claim that there is not a pragmatics of literature is to deny that literature has an effect. Once again, Northrop Frye can help us. In his terms, the imaginative world of literature is virtually the shortstopping of action, of strictly pragmatic results: "So we begin to see where the imagination belongs in the scheme of human affairs. It's the power of constructing possible models of human experience. In the world of imagination, anything goes that's imaginatively possible, but nothing really happens. If it did happen, it would move out of the world of imagination and into the world of action."[17] Thus the use of literature is to construct a vision of the possible, not to effect the actual.

One of the great shortcomings of modern psycholinguistic theory in reading is its pragmatic nature, viewing reading as the processing of information to bring about understanding, which is defined as the reduction of uncertainty: "Reading is an act of communication in which information is transferred from a transmitter to a receiver, whether the reader is a scholar deciphering a medieval text or a child identifying a single letter on a blackboard. Because of this basic nature of reading, there are insights to be gained from the study of theories of communication and information; there are concepts that are particularly useful for the construction of a theory of read-

ing, and a terminology that can be employed to increase the clarity of its expression."[18] This language, which represents the thrust of reading theory and the mental sets of the theorists, can be significantly influenced by a corrective from literary criticism. What the critics realize and describe again and again is an experience that I call *esthetic immersion*. What I mean by esthetic immersion has been stated again and again by critic after critic, for anyone who reads imaginative literature passionately has had the experience. This experience of reading has never, I think, been more beautifully described than by Sartre, and I will quote him in lieu of compiling a chrestomathy or of compounding words: "the characteristic of aesthetic consciousness is to be a belief by means of commitment, by oath, a belief sustained by fidelity to one's self and to the author, a perpetually renewed choice to believe. I can awaken at every moment, and I know it; but I do not want to; reading is a free dream . . . reading is an exercise in generosity; and what the writer requires of the reader is not the application of an abstract freedom but the gift of his whole person, with his passions, his prepossessions, his sympathies, his sexual temperament, and his scale of values."[19] In other words, esthetic reading is a passionate exchange in freedom between an author and a reader. Freedom being mankind's greatest good, the value of reading lies in the exchange of freedom.

Whether or not we are moved by Sartre's dithyramb, we must admit that in some sense esthetic reading is less purposeful than nonesthetic reading. The pragmatics of esthetic reading involve immersion; the pragmatics of nonesthetic reading stress the acquisition of information *for some use.*

Meaning is, of course, independent of reference, but purpose in nonesthetic reading is closely tied to reference; that is, we do frequently read to gain mastery over Reality. Teleologically, then, esthetic reading is radically different from nonesthetic reading, and, as we all know, the experiences themselves differ. The pragmatics of esthetic reading are anti-pragmatic.

The anti-pragmatic nature of esthetic reading has been dealt with most extensively by objective critics. You will recall that at the beginning of this discussion we developed a long digression concerning the cue system in reading and the nature of poetic texture. The concept of texture is, of course, one of the major ideas in objective criticism. In general the objectivists explore the ontological status of the poem. Of particular significance are structure and style.

In nonesthetic reading, structure and style achieve, as I have pointed out, a certain invisibility that they do not have in esthetic reading. The objective critic—in his attempt at purity—views the poem as an esthetic structure, but the interpretation of *structure* here must be broad enough to allow for the totality of the imaginative construct, from the prosody of a sonnet to what Percy Lubbock called (as I paraphrase him) "the shadowy and phantasmal form of the novel."

As far as they go, the great objectivists—Brooks, Warren, Tate, Ransom—are perfectly right. Structure, texture, irony, tension, ambiguity—these do constitute a good deal of what we point to when we differentiate poetry from rhetoric. The objectivists, however, as psycholinguists

might point out to them, have a strange notion of that highly personal idiosyncratic receptor, the brain, which cannot lobotomize itself at will and exclude its intuition that someone did have a motive for writing this poem, that this novel does bear on the facts of American history, that that play is uncannily near to the viewer's actual experience.

In other words, criticism must be rhetorical criticism in that it takes account of *logos, pathos, ethos,* structure, and style. In fact, critical logomachies are largely the result of the failure to place the study of literature within a holistic framework such as that provided by rhetoric.

In this paper, there are many problems that I have not dealt with—the persona of the narrator, for instance. What I have tried to suggest is simple enough. Literary criticism deals with reading, either implicitly or explicitly, and reading is the process of deriving meaning from written discourse. It should be the case, then, that literary criticism would shed light on reading theory and vice versa. I hope that I have demonstrated as much. Furthermore, I have argued that rhetoric—transformed at crucial points—is a vital corrective for the fragmentation of literary criticism. It seems to me that literary studies are vital to rhetoric, but even more so, rhetoric is vital to literature, for the field has a robustness that can be a healthy corrective for the effeteness of some—perhaps most—literary studies.

NOTES

1. Robert Penn Warren, "Pure and Impure Poetry," *Critical Theory Since Plato,* ed. Hazard Adams (New York: Harcourt Brace Jovanovich, 1971), 991.

2. Kenneth S. Goodman, "Psycholinguistic Universals in the Reading Process," in *Psycholinguistics and Reading*, ed. Frank Smith (New York: Holt, Rinehart and Winston, 1973), 25.

3. See, for instance, Frank Smith, "Decoding: The Great Fallacy," *Psycholinguistics and Reading*, 70–83.

4. Philip Wheelwright, "The Logical and the Translogical," in *Critical Theory Since Plato*, 1103–12. (This is Chapter 4 of *The Burning Fountain: A Study in the Language of Symbolism*.)

5. Wheelwright does not use the term *speech acts*, but he is clearly talking about the principle that Austin and Searle, among others, have explored in detail.

6. Frank Smith, *Understanding Reading* (New York: Holt, Rinehart and Winston, 1971), 159–84.

7. Ibid., 69.

8. Goodman, "Psycholinguistic Universals in the Reading Process," 23–24.

9. Paul A. Kolers, "Three Stages of Reading," in *Psycholinguistics and Reading*, 32.

10. Yvor Winters, *In Defense of Reason* (Denver: Alan Swallow, 1947), 11.

11. Northrop Frye, "Myth, Fiction, and Displacement," *Fables of Identity* (New York: Harcourt Brace Jovanovich, 1963), 21–38 passim.

12. Eliseo Vivas, "The Objective of the Poem," in *Critical Theory Since Plato*, 1069–77.

13. Murray Krieger, "Mediation, Language, and Vision in the Reading of Literature," in *Critical Theory Since Plato*, 1244.

14. Smith, *Understanding Reading*, 187.

15. J. L. Austin, *How to Do Things with Words* (Cambridge, Mass.: Harvard University Press, 1962); John R. Searle, *Speech Acts: An Essay in the Philosophy of Language* (Cambridge: Cambridge University Press, 1970).

16. Walter J. Ong, S. J., "A Dialectic of Aural and Objective Correlatives," in *Critical Theory Since Plato*, 1162.

17. Northrop Frye, "The Motives of Metaphor," *The Educated Imagination* (Bloomington: Indiana University Press, 1964), 22.

18. Smith, *Understanding Reading*, 12.

19. Jean-Paul Sartre, "Why Write?" in *Critical Theory Since Plato*, 1062.

The Rhetorical Transaction of Reading

In "The Three R's: Reading, Reading, and Rhetoric," I argued that literary theory becomes more adequate as it approaches and then becomes virtually identical with rhetorical theory. In "The Rhetorical Transaction of Reading," I carry my argument one step further, suggesting that meaning-making through reading is not essentially different in kind from meaning-making through dialectic.

I would also stress the concept of *transaction*. The current model of composition/rhetoric takes "process" as its key term, but I would substitute "transaction," for both the rhetor and his or her audience are, in complex ways, involved with the meaning-making.

The writer projects his meanings, intentions, and so forth onto the page in the form of raw information, black squiggles against a white background. The reader processes this information to reconstruct the writer's meanings, intentions, and so forth. To concentrate on the page and what can be found there, however, will inevitably bring about a serious misunderstanding of the rhetorical transaction of reading.

It goes without saying that all composition teachers are, *ipso facto*, reading teachers; therefore, it should be useful to understand the relationship between reading and rhetoric. Indeed, such an understanding will have practical consequences in the classroom.

To explore this relationship, we will merely survey rhetoric from the standpoint of reading theory. Our question will be, simply, how does reading theory bear on the concepts of *logos* (logical arguments), *ethos* (arguments based on the character of the speaker), and *pathos* (arguments based on the nature of the audience), which constitute the classical department of invention, on arrangement or form (*dispositio*), and on style? We will use these categories loosely, as a method of organization and as a heuristic.

This essay appeared originally in *College Composition and Communication* (May 1976). Reprinted with the permission of the National Council of Teachers of English.

THE MEANING OF "MEANING"

We will equate *logos* with what might be called "pure" meaning, which includes information (a term that will be defined hereafter), logical consistency, and reference. Indeed, this extension does not seriously warp Aristotle's intention but merely expands it. From the standpoint of reading theory, what is the meaning of "pure meaning"?

The page itself, with its black squiggles against a white background, contains no meaning, only information from which meaning can be derived. The information on the page is arranged in a series of interrelated *cue systems*: graphophonic, syntactic, and semantic.[1] Take the following example:

(1) We flew to New York in a _____.

If we are beginning or inefficient readers we can "sound the sentences out" to make the correspondence between the printed marks (graphemes) and the meaningful sounds which they represent (phonemes). Of course, efficient readers go directly from grapheme to meaning, without the mediation of sound,[2] like this:

GRAPHEME → MEANING

Only the inefficient or beginning readers need the mediation of sound, like this:

GRAPHEME → PHONEME → MEANING

Furthermore, the syntactic system of the language determines that the blank can be filled only by a Noun Phrase, just as the syntactic system of the language determines the contrast in meaning between

(2) Man bites dog.

and

(3) Dog bites man.

Finally, the semantics of the language and the semantic "field" of the sentence (as well as our knowledge of the world) allow us to predict with some certainty that the blank will be filled by either *plane* or *jet*. Notice the increasing improbability and strangeness of the following:

(4) We flew to New York in a plane/jet.
(5) We flew to New York in a balloon.
(6) We flew to New York in a carrot.

Information, of course, is not meaning, but we can use information to construct meaning; in fact, that is precisely what we do in the reading process.

In regard to *pathos*, the reader is the audience for written discourse, and meaning is not "down there" on the page, but "up here" in the reader's mind. In processing the information on the page to derive meaning, the reader employs three "systems": eyesight, short-term memory, and long-term memory. The short-term memory is a screening device which keeps the long-term memory from being continually flooded with information to process. It is axiomatic that the short-term memory can process only *seven-plus-or-minus-two* bits of information at one time. A bit of information is a "chunk" of some kind that reduces uncertainty by one-half. If I am holding a playing card from an ordinary deck and ask you to guess the suit, you might ask me, "Is it black?" When I answer, "No," you have received one bit of information. You now ask, "Is it a heart?" I answer, "No," and you are certain that the card is a diamond. Two bits of information were all that you needed to achieve certainty.[3]

How many bits of information are there in the sentence *Man bites dog*? That question is, of course, impossible to answer, for we can view every horizontal and vertical line, every curve and every serif as a bit of information. Obviously, if we used all of the information there is in the sentence, we could never derive meaning, for our short-term memories impose the seven-plus-or-minus-two limit on us. Somehow, we obviously chunk our information, and under no circumstances do we use all of the plethora of information that is available on the printed page.

The construction of meaning, then, takes place in the mind of the reader. The meaning constructed is curiously independent of the information from which it is derived; at this point, you can probably explain to me or to someone else the meaning of what I have written so far, but in doing so you will probably use none of the exact sentences or even phrases that I have written. You will translate the meaning you have derived into information that can be reprocessed for meaning.

If I *write* the sentence

(7) I stopped the auto, shut off the engine, and opened the bonnet.

and you *tell* me that the sentence means

(8) /I stopped the *car*, shut off the *motor*, and opened the *hood*./

you have obviously not misread, for you have gained meaning and have

translated that meaning into another information system.

The importance of this concept is obvious. If, for instance, a speaker of the urban black dialect reads

(9) My father is at home.

and *says*

(10) /My father be at home./

he or she has not misread but has gained the meaning from the sentence and has translated that meaning into his or her own dialect.

Consider that the graphophonic correspondence is tenuous at best, as the following demonstrates: *tough, through, though*. Consider, further, the following renditions of *Cuba is rather close*:

(11) /Cuber is rathuh close./
(12) /Cuba is rahther close./
(13) /Cuba's rather close./

Even though these examples are only loose attempts to give written approximations of some American dialects, it should become apparent that dialect *per se* has nothing to do with reading ability.

In the construction of meaning from the information provided by print, the mind of the reader is obviously all-important. This is embarrassingly self-evident. If I had trouble in reading *Principia Mathematica*, I would certainly not go to Evelyn Wood to improve my reading ability but would go to the math department for a few courses. The reader brings his or her totality of experience and knowledge to bear in the reading process; thus, reading is partly a mechanical skill—the ability to use the cue system efficiently. But, even more important, it is a rhetorical transaction in which the pathetic factor is supreme.

We have drawn a correspondence between *logos* and the information on the page and between *pathos* and the use of that information by the reader. (Perhaps the correspondence is too rough, but I think not.) However, we have still not totally accounted for meaning—as the following sentence makes clear:

(14) Could you raise the window?

As it stands, it is ambiguous. Namely, we wonder if it is an inquiry or a request. In other words, does (15) or does (16) capture the intention

(15) I *inquire* of you, "Could you raise the window?"
(16) I *request* of you, "Could you raise the window?"

Presumably, (15) would result in an answer of "yes" or "no," but (16) would result, probably, in the hearer's raising the window. Sentences, in other words, are *intended*—as statements, warnings, exhortations, requests, and so on. Intention implies a writer. In other words, the concept of *ethos* enters our account of meaning.

Reading theory has almost nothing to say that bears on *ethos*. In fact, at this point, rhetoric can fill out a gap in reading theory. Equally important to the function of *ethos* in meaning is speech-act theory.[4] To develop an adequate account of speech-act theory in regard to reading would demand a separate essay, but a brief sketch will provide a hint of the connections.

The speech act is composed of *utterance act*, making speech sounds or writing graphemes; *propositional act*, in which reference and predication take place, as when I predi-

cate "yawn" of "Norma" in *Norma yawns;*[5] *illocutionary act*, which is actually the speaker's intention to state, warn, promise, dare, etc.; *perlocutionary act*, which is the effect of the sentence, as when I utter *Norma yawns*, you may take the sentence as a statement, a warning that you'd better liven up the party, an insult that implies your conversation is dull, and so on.[6]

Clearly, you cannot interpret a sentence until you know how it is intended. Intention (or motive) suggests a writer, and the intentional fallacy is not a fallacy but a necessity.

In the foregoing, of course, I have not done justice to reading or speech-act theory. Both are rich bodies of thought—and data—that I feel composition teachers should be thoroughly familiar with. But what I would like to do now is to construct a rough model of reading as a rhetorical transaction—simply, a writer influencing the beliefs, actions, attitudes, etc. of an audience through the medium of the printed page.

The page itself is a meaningless bit of opacity covered by not particularly attractive designs. The reader comes to the page with the ability to process these designs for meaning— that is, with the mechanical ability to read—and with a whole world of ideas, attitudes, cultural sets, and so on—with everything, in short, that constitutes the human mind. If the page is from, say, *PMLA* and the reader has made a lifelong career of literary scholarship, the reading task will probably be fairly simple, as it would not be for a Ph.D. in mathematics who had very little experience in the world of literature. It is a fact, however, that in one sense the reading of all texts is equally easy (or equally difficult), provided that the reader is familiar with all of the vocabularies used; namely, the process of reading as the use of the cue system is constant throughout all materials. But reading is the derivation of meanings; therefore, a number of factors make reading more or less difficult for the "good" reader: familiarity with the concepts developed in the text; the accessibility of the syntax employed by the author;[7] cultural biases in the text; the clarity of the print; and so on.

In the process of reading, the reader must construct, more or less clearly, a concept of intention and hence supply a writer. Take the following example. These lines

(17) Lift receiver.
Deposit coin.
Listen for dial tone.
Dial number.

are found in (1) a phone booth and (2), with the title "AT&T," in a paperback volume entitled *Now Poetry*. In the first instance, they are a set of instructions; in the second instance, they are an esthetic object, perhaps a satire or a spoof. To translate this concept into the jargon of speech-act theory, the perlocutionary act is the reader's discovery of the illocutionary act. In irony, of course, intention is the fulcrum upon which the weight of the work can be swung.

There is, then, a correspondence between current theories of reading and classical notions of invention. The rhetorician is quite at home as a teacher of composition or as a teacher of reading.

ARRANGEMENT: ATTACK SKILLS AND DISPOSITIO

Though I seriously doubt that there is any such thing as speed reading in the popular sense of that term, there certainly are (1) different reading purposes and (2) more or less efficient ways to process the information on the page to derive meaning.

The most efficient way to derive meaning from a text is to get a general idea of what "it's all about" through scanning, after which the general outline can be "impleted" with details. This would imply that the most efficient way to read a book or an article is to scan two or three times and then to return for close reading. Kenneth Goodman says that efficient readers *sample*, to get a notion of the meaning of a text; then they *predict* what the meaning will be; next they *test* this prediction; and then they *confirm* or *disconfirm* it.[8] The sampling-predicting-testing-confirming process can operate at the sentence level or beyond.

This principle is richly suggestive about organization in writing. Suppose that the intention of the writer is to facilitate the reader's understanding of the piece. In that case, the organization will demand a very general statemental outline of the essay, chapter, or whatever, followed by paragraphs or sections that systematically "implete" the general concepts in the outline; paragraphs will start with a clearcut topic sentence, and subsequent sentences will fill in the details, as in the subordinate-sequence paragraphs that Francis Christensen describes.[9] (You will notice that I have not followed my own advice in this essay.)

Of course, it is not the purpose of all writing to be optimally readable. The desire for a given rhetorical effect might well dictate a "surprise ending" or an inverted order, in which the essay proceeds from details to more and more broad generalities.

Nor should all reading be "efficient." In my engagement with a novel, I seldom want to lose the sequacious richness of the development in order to read efficiently.

I would like, however, to suggest a pedagogical gimmick. I think that we are seldom very helpful in our attempts to teach students how to organize. If we point out that efficient reading demands an inexorable movement from the general to the specific, in the whole essay and in the individual paragraphs, we will have set up a formal principle which is coherent and simple. Once the essay has been written according to this plan, what are the permutations that rearrangements can bring about, and what will be their rhetorical effects? Explorations of this kind can demonstrate that form has consequences.

STYLE AS ACCESSIBILITY

It is axiomatic that some sentences are easier to read than others. For instance, the grammar of the language allows us to place the particle either before or after the Noun Phrase object of the verb, thus:

(18) She turned *off* the light.
(19) She turned the light *off*.

Notice what happens with the following, however:

(20) She tore down the shed which he put up.
(21) She tore the shed which he put up down.

Or even more horrendously:

(22) She tore down the shed which fouled up the view when the sun came down.

(23) She tore the shed which fouled the view when the sun came down up down.

Clearly, some structures are easier to process for meaning than others. (That is just one of the points regarding heavy nominalization.) This is a facile statement which can be taken too broadly; for instance, evidence indicates that passive is as easy to process as active, depending on the context.[10] Nonetheless, it is a fact that syntax can stand in the way of efficient reading.

We have seen that efficient readers process meaning from graphemes, without the intervention of phonemes. In other words, efficient reading demands that we *not* make the grapheme-phoneme correspondence. However, it is a fact that some writings virtually force this correspondence upon us. I refer, of course, to poetry, in which rhyme, meter, alliteration, assonance, and so on, reify the graphophonic correspondence that, as efficient readers, we have been able to ignore. Even in everyday expository prose, sound patterns tend to make the graphophonic system visible, whereas in efficient reading it should be invisible or transparent. In the last sentence, the alliteration of "everyday expository" turns those words into phonic phenomena.

Just as syntax and the graphophonic system should be "invisible" or "transparent" for efficient reading, so should the semantic system. This is merely a truism in one sense; the moment we stop to ask "I wonder what that word means?" efficiency in reading ceases, and, in a sense, the semantic cue system is reified. Or to state the point another way: in reading, we are merely processing language; when we must ask for a definition, we have shifted our concern to metalanguage, that is, to language about language.

In regard to the semantics of non-literary and literary discourse, I can think of no better discussion than Philip Wheelwright's "The Logical and the Translogical."[11] Wheelwright's point in general is that non-literary discourse uses a relatively firm semantic base. That is, the terms do not tend to shift their meanings, and they have little or no iconographic quality. In literary language, a term is quite likely to have the nature of a variable, taking the value that the reader assigns it in his or her attempt to get at the meaning of a work. And the literary term is likely to have both an imagistic and a strictly semantic value: "the marriage of true minds," "time's winged chariot," "bare ruined choirs," "a woman lovely in her bones." The nonliterary term is also, of course, frequently an image, but the imagistic quality is normally subordinate to what might be called the cognitive or referential quality.

In regard to the cue system, we can think of the Coleridgean image of a frost-covered window pane. We can see through the pane to the outside world, but we can also contemplate the frost patterns as objects of delight.

This is the point regarding style as accessibility. In efficient reading, the graphophonic, syntactic, and semantic cue systems have no visibility; they are clear panes of glass that allow us to see meaning through them.

LITERATURE AS "MERE" RHETORIC

But, of course, a pane of glass, regardless of how Windexed, is none-theless a pane of glass. It reflects and diffuses. Even when not frost-covered, it presents a visual experience for anyone who is interested in looking. Whether the pane of glass is "there" or not depends on the intention (and attention) of the viewer. Under any and all circumstances, you can look either through it or at it. You can contemplate the designs of the frost or the shadowy forms that reveal themselves beyond the frost.

"Pure" literature—and, of course, there is no such thing—is an object of contemplation. It is the frost-covered window, and we are interested in the frost.

The moments when we can contemplate frost with intensity and satisfaction, however, are rare and fleeting. Suddenly the frost patterns become mountains or faces or snow-scapes, and suddenly we become aware of the shapes in the world beyond the windowpane. We are out of the realm of purity and into the realm of experience, memory, hope, desire.

When we read, we are also in the realm of experience, memory, hope, desire. We are human beings reading, not reading machines. Which means that "pure" literature exists only at the imaginary interface between contemplation and the act of reading.

For when we read, we continually try to grasp intention; in so doing, we supply an author. We cannot escape from the rhetorical, pathetic, intentional fallacy.

The meaning is meaningful only in terms of our own beings. We are caught inexorably in the affective fallacy, and there is no escape. Across the cryptic neatness of the page, a writer is contacting a reader.

A poem can never be an artifact,

for in language, an artifact is merely data, information; and information is meaningless. Surely no one would argue that a true poem is meaningless.

But there is a supreme irony about literature. The poem invites us to contemplate it *as if it were* an artifact. This we can never do, for poems are to be read.

Reading theory leads me to conclude that literature is "mere" rhetoric.

NOTES

1. Kenneth S. Goodman, "Psycholinguistic Universals in the Reading Process," *Psycholinguistics and Reading*, ed. Frank Smith (New York: Holt, Rinehart and Winston, 1973).

2. Frank Smith, *Understanding Reading* (New York: Holt, Rinehart and Winston, 1971), 204−10; Frank Smith, "Decoding: The Great Fallacy," *Psycholinguistics and Reading*.

3. Smith, *Understanding Reading*, 12−26.

4. J. L. Austin, *How to Do Things with Words* (New York: Oxford University Press, 1962); John Searle, *Speech Acts* (Cambridge: Cambridge University Press, 1969).

5. Searle, 22−26.

6. As Searle (p. 25) explains: "Correlated with the notion of illocutionary acts is the notion of the consequences or *effects* such acts have on the actions, thoughts, or beliefs, etc. of hearers. For example, by arguing I may *persuade* or *convince* someone, by warning him I may *scare* or *alarm* him, by making a request I may *get him to do something*, by informing him I may *convince him* (*enlighten, edify, inspire him, get him to realize*)." The italicized expressions above denote perlocutionary acts.

7. More about this later.

8. Goodman, "Psycholinguistic Universals in the Reading Process."

9. "A Generative Rhetoric of the Paragraph," *Notes Toward a New Rhetoric* (New York: Harper & Row, 1967).

10. Dan I. Slobin, *Psycholinguistics* (Glenview, Ill.: Scott, Foresman 1971), 33−38.

11. *Critical Theory Since Plato*, ed. Hazard Adams (New York: Harcourt Brace Jovanovich, 1971). The essay is Chapter 4 of *The Burning Fountain: A Study in the Language of Symbolism* (Bloomington: Indiana University Press, 1954).

The Realms of Meaning: Text-Centered Criticism

In the first place, this essay is a counter-statement, reflecting what was at the time of its publication my growing dissatisfaction with rhetoric as represented by the *Quarterly Journal of Speech* and, to a certain extent, by *Philosophy and Rhetoric*.

As I survey the hypotheses in the essay, I find particular resonance in the explanation of meanings which it is the critic's duty to understand: formal, a meaning without meaning, which is Burke's point; referential, the author's view of the world, to be captured by the critic (which is very nearly what Hirsch means by "horizon of meaning"); extrinsic, which Hirsch would call "significance," for a certain age and audience.

Of course, these meanings are not inscribed in the text, but every text has the potential for generating them for the reader.

Historically and by its very nature, rhetorical criticism has tended to move around the text, not into it as has the best of literary criticism. The reason for this tendency lies in the philosophical premises of the two arts, literary criticism ultimately being concerned with the text and how it operates, rhetorical criticism being concerned with how the text operates on an audience. Almost every statement of a "philosophy of rhetoric" has built toward an audience. George Campbell, for instance, is typical:

This essay appeared originally in *College Composition and Communication* (Dec. 1972). Reprinted with the permission of the National Council of Teachers of English.

Pure logic regards only the subject, which is examined solely for the sake of information. Truth, as such, is the proper aim of the examiner. Eloquence not only considers the subject, but also the speaker and hearers, and both the subject and the speaker for the sake of the hearers, or rather for the sake of the effect intended to be produced in them.[1]

Indeed, I would argue that the proper goal of *all* criticism is to find out how the text achieves its effects; that is, I would resist the separation of rhetorical and literary criticism. But I would insist that criticism be text-centered and meaning-oriented, that its effort should be to penetrate the jungle of the work in question, not to measure the perimeters and estimate the effect that miasmal mists emanating from the dense undergrowth will have on the subdivision that is being built nearby.

Once the critic begins to discover—by penetrating deeply—how the text itself works, he will also begin to discover how the text works existentially on an audience. So I am not advocating that the traditional methodology be junked, rather that emphases be realigned. The simple question that the critic must ask is "What does this text mean?"

Every text—springing to new life in the light of varying sensibilities that examine it—has, first of all, a "meaning" without meaning, a purely formal, musical dimension that is "contentless" but all important. In one of his most fascinating hints, Marshall McLuhan says, "The form of any game is of first importance. . . . For . . . it is the *pattern* of a game that gives it relevance to our inner lives. . . ."[22] Formal meaning, which is the entire meaning of music, occurs at all levels in works of fiction (and I will confine my examples to fiction, though I believe that what I have to say is applicable to the criticism of any discourse), from the atomic segments called phonemes (alliteration, for instance) to macrocosmic world-views configured in the pattern of a work.

The search for the formal coherence of a work of fiction is oftentimes an interesting process. In a novel such as *Tom Jones*, a mere plot outline will often delineate the almost mystic thing that we mean when we speak of "pure form." But *Steppenwolf* or *Moby Dick* or *Towards a Better Life* are different matters altogether. Kenneth Burke gives a dramatic instance of an author frustrated in the search for *a priori* form and finally letting form

emerge from purpose. Of his composition of *Towards a Better Life*, he says,

Originally I had intended to handle this story in the customary manner of the objective, realistic novel. To this end I made a working outline of plot, settings, incidental characters, and the like, before attempting to write any of the chapters in detail.[3]

But his repeated efforts to proceed in the traditional manner ended in frustration. In the following longish quotation, Burke explains the resolution of his dilemma:

Lamentation, rejoicing, beseechment, admonition, sayings, and invective— these seemed to me central matters, while a plot in which they might occur seemed peripheral, little more than a pretext, justifiable not as "a good story," but only insofar as it could bring these six characteristics to the fore. These mark, these six mark, in a heightened manner, the significant features of each day in our secular, yet somewhat biblical, lives—and what I most wanted to do was to lament, rejoice, beseech, admonish, aphorize, and inveigh. Yet I found that the technique of the realistic, objective novel enabled one at best to bring in such things "by the ears." . . . So I reversed the process, emphasizing the essayistic rather than the narrative, the emotional predicaments of my hero rather than the details by which he arrived at them—the ceremonious, formalized, "declamatory." In form the resultant chapters are somewhat like a sonnet sequence, a progression by stages, by a series of halts; or they might be compared to an old-style opera in which the stress is laid upon the arias whereas the transition from one aria to the next is secondary. . . .

I have described my changing of the framework as a decision reached by logical steps, but the process was really much more confused.[4]

If the reader comes to *Towards a Better Life* with traditional expectations, the novel is certain to be unsatisfying. To understand the true accomplishment of the work, it is necessary to begin to appreciate a form in which themes get stated, modulated, transmuted, and restated. *Towards a Better Life* is indeed a series of declamations with an internal structure of its own, a structure that the critic must follow in a "musical" way. Burke's analogy of his novel with a sonnet sequence is completely to the point. Shakespeare's sonnets can be read—probably should be read—as constituting a "novel" that handles various themes contrapuntally.

As Burke's description of his attempts to forge a novel makes clear, the process of "forming" a work of fiction is generative. When he sits, pen in hand or paws poised over the typewriter, the writer is about to start an exploratory journey, the terminus of which he realizes at best vaguely. What he comes up with ought to surprise him—as well as his readers. In any act of creation there is something of the wonder that E. M. Forster felt when he said that his characters came to life and gained a volition of their own. One of the joys in writing a novel, then, is to wonder what those damn fool characters will do next. Under the artist's fingers, the construct comes to life, "preprogramming" its own intricate workings out and adjusting those programs every page—every line—of the way. But the final triumph of any work of literature is the sense that it gives of a unified view of life.

Steppenwolf—a novel deserving popularity on other grounds than its current "propagandistic" worth—is an example of how "pure" form transcends localized meaning and of how important the explication of form is in arriving at an understanding of the effectiveness of the work. In his *modus operandi*, Hesse seems unwilling to break the continuity of a spectrum by segmenting his narrative (which is, to be sure, fairly straightforward) into chapters. The novel flows inexorably from a worldvision dominated by the prudential and rational toward the primeval sea of feeling, illusion, and imagination, from the bourgeois order of a well-scrubbed vestibule toward the apocalypse in which a Latin Mozart performing in a magic theater gives Steppenwolf a joint. Says Mozart,

"Enough of pathos and death-dealing. It is time to come to your senses. You are to live and to learn to laugh. You are to learn to listen to the cursed radio music of life and to reverence the spirit behind it and to laugh at its distortions. So there you are. More will not be asked of you."

Gently from behind clenched teeth I asked: "And if I do not submit? And if I deny your right, Mozart, to interfere with the Steppenwolf, and to meddle in his destiny?"

"Then," said Mozart calmly, "I should invite you to smoke another of my charming cigarettes." And as he spoke and offered it to me, he was suddenly Mozart no longer. It was my friend Pablo looking warmly at me out of his dark exotic eyes.

The disadvantage in talking about formal meaning in the context of a paper that must, by its nature, cover much territory is that the study of form demands minute analysis: at the stylistic level, at the plateau where shapes of sentences become meaningful in relation to larger configurations, from the viewpoint of a whole concept "poured" into a certain matrix. Thus an essay on the "form" of *Towards a Better Life* or

Steppenwolf is a project of considerable dimensions.

Which brings me to a by-path that I must follow since part of my intent here is a polemic against current practice in rhetorical criticism. Namely, the rhetorical critic—as witness the journals that all of us read more or less dutifully, and, I must admit, as this paper witnesses—the rhetorical critic, I say, is committed to the macrocosmic view of things, to formulating and then using the super-rubric that will define all, categorize all, and, most often, anesthetize all. We rhetoricians traditionally have felt at home with the "big view." A case in point is the very first article in the very first issue of *Philosophy and Rhetoric*. This article sets out, with a kind of classic modesty (one thinks of *edle Einfalt und stille Grösse*) to define the rhetorical situation. "What characteristics, then," asks the author, "are implied when one refers to 'the rhetorical situation'—the context in which speakers or writers create rhetorical discourse?" The question prepares one for a calculus of context that might, computerized and given infinite time, produce at least "The Gettysburg Address." But it turns out that "there are three constituents of any rhetorical situation: the first is *exigence*; the second and third are elements of the complex, namely the *audience* to be constrained in decision and action, and the *constraints* which influence the rhetor and can be brought to bear upon the audience."[6] One eagerly awaits the next issue of the journal so that other philosophical questions can be disposed of. And disposed of they are. In the next issue— or the one after that or the one after that—we find, for instance, that "it would seem there is a finiteness

characterizing man's ability to categorize which, largely transcending the barriers of time, space, and cultural influence, renders a kind of stability and predictability to the patterns of human conceptual behavior."[7] We have now rediscovered the wheel and ought to be ready to construct a simple cart to carry our equipment along the path into the jungle of the text.

End of digression.

Formal meaning, it seems to me, carries much of the pure esthetic delight of the text. Sublimity might well reside in noble thoughts, but I suspect that it resides also in ignoble thoughts well expressed. Style and larger form—these are important factors in differentiating logic and rhetoric. The pure musical joy of perceived form is the "art" in the art of rhetoric.

But there is meaning in yet another sense, a subjective, internal, personal sense. Now the focus of inquiry changes from the meaning of form to *referential* meaning. At last, it seems, the discussion is becoming *genuinely* rhetorical, for *referential* implies something in the text that refers to something outside the text in the real world, an equation of stimulus and response. However, we are not out of the jungle yet; we are still moiling around in the text. Suppose, for instance, that I say of my Uncle Albert, "He is an old maid." The "he" has a referent in the traditional, general-semantic sense, a "Bessie the Cow." But what about "old maid"? It refers, certainly, to Uncle Albert, but in a strange way. Grammatically, it violates the rules of selectional restrictions, which would demand that a masculine pronoun take a masculine complement. There is, however, a difference between my internal, mental world and the logical, external world. It is the function of metaphor to bridge that gap, and all works of fiction—probably all instances of discourse—are metaphorical in that they mediate between the author's view of the world and the reader's view of the world. It is the function of the critic to capture, as nearly as he can, the author's view of the world. (This, after all, is the rhetorical motive: to bring about understanding, to bridge the gap between the island of you and the island of me.)

One problem of grammar is to build a system that will not allow the generation of such sequences as *Meat loves company*, except in the metaphorical sense. That is, somehow the grammar must specify that ordinarily the inanimate noun *meat* will not act as subject to a verb such as *love*. This seems like a simple problem, but, indeed, its solution entails great difficulties, difficulties not yet surmounted. A grammar must be able to specify the grammaticality of such strings as *The world is flat* and *I will be reincarnated as a racehorse*, one of which is *flatly* a wrong statement and the other of which is empirically unverifiable. When the rhetorician attacks the grammatical problem, the question becomes not "How should I make a semantic specification?" but "How should I explain the false and the fictive?" Both false and fictive meanings are a part of discourse, and they must be understood if one is to understand the text. In fact, there are two worlds: that in the author's mind—the referential—and that in which the tigers leap and the alligators slosh, that in which Tarzan was conceived, and that in which he might swing on a vine. The solution to the grammarian's problem here is also the solution to that of the rheto-rician. If, in grammatical notation, one ignores the real world and concentrates on the world of the "speaker's" mind, and if one makes notation from the mentalistic viewpoint, the problems of fictive meaning disappear.[8] The rhetorical situation lies somewhere between the real world in the author's mind and a very real world out there, or between "his" reality, "my" reality, and ultimate reality—which is just as far as I intend to carry the idea of existence.

But in this second pass in the attempt to determine the meaning of the text, the critic must come, *tabula rasa* insofar as possible, with the intention of finding that reality in the text that corresponds with the reality in the author's mind, his referential meaning. The object in this phase of the game is empathy, identification, understanding. The critic who would criticize Hitler must become Hitler. Now the critic of Steppenwolf must become a wolf of the steppes. At this moment, the critic, like Harry Haller, "vereint in sich alle Gegensätze von der Bestialität bis zum Heiligen; er sucht qualvoll sein Ich, ohne von sich selbst und durch sich selbst erlösen zu können. 'Der Gott, an den wir glauben müssen, kann zu Gott nicht ja sagen.'"[9] Something like Coleridge's willing suspension of disbelief must prevail. The world of the novel must become temporarily the real world.

John Neal in *Towards a Better Life* is a reprehensible sort of fellow, both in Kenneth Burke's theory and in the working out of the novel. "He is a very frank, a very earnest, a very conscientious man, in whom one should place slight confidence."[10] He leaves his family, he degrades an innocent woman, and he allows himself the foolishness of canonizing another. He is a monstrous parable of all that is human, but, because monstrous, unadmitted. The rhetorical critic—hacking through the jungle of meaning—must admit all. The Marquis de Sade and the author of *My Secret Life* must become tragic heroes. For the very reason that the critic sees the world "out there" only through their eyes. Thus, the debauching of a little girl becomes a cunning experiment in the satisfaction of that primal human condition, enunciated by Henderson the Rain King as "I want." The existential act of enunciation here becomes transcendent in its importance. In *Towards a Better Life* John Neal says,

I am aware . . . that many of life's questions have found unseemly answers through being of such importance that they were prematurely asked, while art, by the greater clarity it brings to any subject, may seem to magnify the indecencies which it is enlightening. People who have focused their purposes upon other matters than speech, allowing their familiarity with it to grow by hazard, can condone in practice what would alienate them if harshly spoken. Not considering the breach between thought and action, they can brook no great speculative latitude, and will restrict the possible more jealously than the real. Thus, at least part of the blame must be shifted to my auditors.[11]

The rhetorical critic, as auditor, should not lay himself open to blame.

And so a work of fiction has both formal and referential meaning, both of which are inward, text-oriented, demanding empathy as well as analysis. Where lies the traditionally rhetorical element? What is the path out of the jungle toward the suburban development?

The path is what I shall call *ex-*

trinsic meaning, the kind of meaning that has resurrected *Steppenwolf* and *Towards a Better Life* at this moment and place in history. (But a disclaimer is in order: I think that both of these novels transcend time and place in their formal and referential meanings. Like Henry Roth's *Call It Sleep*, they are sleepers whose time has come within history. There is a kind of poetic justice here. The rhetorical situation alone will not rocket a work into posterity. If the rhetorical critic is concerned with the eternal, he must concentrate on the first two kinds of meaning, the kind that the literary and scholarly establishments cultivate in their hermetically sealed hothouses. The magical thing is this: sometimes—as I believe is the case with *Steppenwolf* and *Towards a Better Life*— the eternal coincides recurrently with the temporal.)

In any case, the question that one asks about extrinsic meaning is not so much what the text says as what it says to an audience in a given time and place. But strangely enough, unless one delights in saying the obvious, there is normally less that can be said about extrinsic meaning than about formal or referential meaning. In most instances, explication of the text from the inside leads outward, and the comments that one can make on extrinsic meaning are limited. For instance, does one need more explication of the rhetorical situation that produced *Towards a Better Life* than the following?

The first ten chapters of this novel . . . were written and published as "work in progress" during the fatal months that were urgently on the way towards the "traumatic" market crash of 1929. The book was completed in the "traumatic" months immediately following that national crisis. And it was published in 1931, when the outlook was exceptionally bleak.[12]

No doubt, with certain works, one needs more knowledge of the context. For the modern reader, *The Dunciad* needs copious footnoting.

But there is a subtler sense of extrinsic meaning. I assume that no work can have real meaning outside the living, breathing society in which man functions; hence, there must, finally, be a ratio between the author's world view and that of the reader. Here all sorts of chimeras dart. And for the critic, truth is a good deal less than fiction, the fiction constructed by the author and the fiction constructed by the reader as his world view. When these two mystic entities come together, they constitute the new thing that is known as perception.

In the fall of the year, a susceptible reader picks up a novel. Quite by chance, it is *Towards a Better Life*, with a stylized picture of an almost denuded tree, leaves fluttering downward, on the front of the dust jacket, and with a picture of the author in his springtime and one of him in his autumn on the back. The work itself is much concerned with seasons and what Gloucester termed "ripeness," a theme that carries over in the reader's experience from an intense encounter with *King Lear*. And roughly half way through the book, this occurs:

If we must have a slogan, let that slogan be the present. To move vigorously through chill water, and stretch like a snake in the sun—to do this actually, and to do the equivalent as regards the subtler pleasures of the mind—such is gratitude to Makers. If I built a house, I should want the house to stand self-assertively, at peace with its placing. Let

us then be as though builded. Let man take each brilliant day as one dropped from an eternity of silence. Let him enjoy the unique organization of his hulk. Let him be rained upon, wind driven, sunned, firm-footed—living first among the elements and shaping his other experiences by this immediacy. Surely no flower protests at withering in the autumn; even subsidence can be a purpose—and days of gentle ecstasy might bring us to welcome our decline.[13]

The miracle is that the crotchety, egomaniacal, one-sided world view of the novel and the equally eccentric perception that the reader brings to it click together to produce something unique, a new view of the work. And now strictly rhetorical evaluation is possible. The book will make an audience better or worse—and, regardless of what it said, it would dissuade some from voting Republican. Such is the nature of the rhetorical act.

In an illuminating article, Richard L. Lanigan quotes Maurice Merleau-Ponty:

What we *mean* is not before us, outside all speech, as sheer signification. It is only the excess of what we live over what has already been said. With our apparatus of expression we set ourselves up in a situation the apparatus is sensitive to, we confront it with the situation, and our statements are only the final balance of these exchanges. Political thought itself is of this order. It is always the elucidation of an historical perception in which all our understandings, all our experiences, and all our values simultaneously come into play—and of which our theses are only the schematic formulation.[14]

Extrinsic meaning—which is situation-oriented—is exactly this "excess of what we live over what has already been said." Interpretation, during this third pass, involves making the intrinsic extrinsic: judgment and understanding of the work as it functions at *the* moment or during any moments.

Here, then, is another little rubric to add to the vast storehouse of rhetorical rubrics—both great and small—that have accrued since Aristotle. And yet I should like to think of the realms of meaning—formal, referential, extrinsic—as ratios that function in a three-dimensional scheme of discourse to bring about effect. But, more important, I should like to consider the quest for meaning to be the primary function of the rhetorical critic—meaning that goes from the text outward and that is interpreted by the reader.

NOTES

1. *The Rhetoric of Blair, Campbell, and Whately*, ed. James L. Golden and Edward P. J. Corbett (New York: 1968), 172.

2. *Understanding Media.* (New York: 1965), 242.

3. "Preface to the First Edition," *Towards a Better Life* (Berkeley and Los Angeles: 1966), xi.

4. Ibid., xiii–xiv.

5. Hermann Hesse, *Steppenwolf*, trans. Basil Creighton (New York: 1963), 216–17.

6. Lloyd F. Bitzer, "The Rhetorical Situation," *Philosophy and Rhetoric*, I (January, 1968), 1–14.

7. William F. Nelson, "Topoi: Evidence of Human Conceptual Behavior," *Philosophy and Rhetoric*, II (Winter, 1969), 1–11.

8. James D. McCawley, "The Role of Semantics in a Grammar," *Universals in Linguistic Theory* (New York: 1968), 138.

9. Fritz Martini, *Deutsche Literaturgeschichte* (Stuttgart: 1959), 504.

10. *Towards a Better Life*, xvii.

11. Ibid., 35–36.

12. Ibid., v.

13. Ibid., 90.

14. "Rhetorical Criticism: An Interpretation of Maurice Merleau-Ponty," *Philosophy and Rhetoric*, II (Spring, 1969), 65.

Teaching Composition

Developing a Composition Program

After consultation and deliberation, I have resolved to preserve the churlish tone of the following remarks.

We know that we can develop effective composition programs and that our model is elegant.

Through reading, students gain a substratum of competence—in the "code" of edited standard English, in stylistic variations, in genre expectations, and in countless other aspects of written communication. On the basis of this *acquired* competence, they can begin to produce texts themselves. The function of teaching is to provide rich response to *semantic intention*, not to form at any level. This response can take place in one-on-one conferences, in group read-arounds, in whole-class discussions. And that, in a nutshell, is the basis for a composition program.

Why, then, is it so difficult to develop effective programs?

First, faculties are diverse in many respects. I have, as a matter of fact, an infallible staff development formula. One-third of the typical faculty needs only *cooperation*, the necessary time and logistical support to function, plus a bit of sympathy and recognition. A second third needs *inspiration*. These souls have potential which, for various reasons, they are not living up to. Perhaps they need to believe that they can be successful, or possibly merit pay is the needed carrot. Thus, with two-thirds of the typical faculty, cooperation and inspiration will work wonders. How about the final third? They need, I am convinced, *assassination*. They are beyond hope, and in their sullen lassitude they subvert the efforts of their colleagues to be professionally alive.

In the public schools, administrators are usually a problem. Typically they hold Ed.D.'s, those quick and dirty credentials which often pay off so lucratively; they are highly political, serving as they do at the pleasures of boards; they have tremendous power over teachers, dictating not only edu-

This essay is reprinted from *Reinventing the Rhetorical Tradition* edited by Aviva Freedman and Ian Pringle (Conway, AR, for the CCTE, 1980), copyright by the Canadian Council of Teachers of English, and reprinted by permission.

cational goals, but curricula, materials, and methods. If public school administrators were willing to relinquish professional authority to teachers, decent composition programs would be far easier to develop.

Finally, every parent knows precisely how reading and writing should be taught, and this homespun, dogmatic expertise is most often not only wrongheaded, but destructive.

In spite of these and many other adversities, that marvelous top third of the faculties does accomplish a very great deal. For which the reward is certain, but unlikely to be gained in this life.

Like smog in the Los Angeles Basin, the "literacy crisis" besmirches the atmosphere of public education, creating all of the unpleasant symptoms of distrust and outrage. It is tempting for me—almost irresistibly so—to present my views on the crisis and on the people and factions engaged in the current logomachy (among others, John Simon, *Newsweek*, and CBS), but since the purpose of this essay is to report on a composition project that gives evidence of great success and, more important, to outline the rationale and procedures for such a project, I will sacrifice eloquence for utility, wit for pragmatism, and get on with this report, which will have the following sections: "Results," the data which indicates the program discussed has real-world effectiveness; "Values," a discussion of why value systems have influenced literacy, kindergarten through graduate school; "Knowledge," an argument that teachers involved with literacy (i.e., reading and writing, "higher" and "lower") need special kinds of preparation that the academy is unprepared to give and an outline of that training; "Knowhow," a look at what constitutes pedagogical methodology for a teacher of composition; "Scenes," an explanation of how the English class can be abol-

ished or transformed into two effective scenes for learning and instruction, the workshop and the laboratory; "Developing a Program," the problems and possibilities, plus some practical tips based on experience.

It can be taken for granted that there is a literacy crisis—precisely because a large segment of the concerned citizenry believes that there is. For the purposes of this discussion, the plethora of data pro and con is irrelevant. What I say will bear upon both of the skills of literacy—reading and writing—but my emphasis will be upon writing.

In October of 1976, the Huntington Beach (California) Union High School District commissioned me to establish a literacy project in six high schools. Working with my colleague and student, Professor Dorothy Augustine of Chapman College, I proposed an intricate plan to the District, and Superintendent Frank Abbott, Assistant Superintendent John Gyves, and the Board gave us the go-ahead.

Much of the present essay will be based on our experiences with and evaluations of the Huntington Beach Project. Currently the Huntington Beach model has been adapted for and adopted at the University of Southern California. The results of this freshman writing program will not start to come in until the end of the current academic year (1978–79), but as Mark Twain said somewhere, you gain worlds of knowledge by picking a cat up by the tail. Professors Sylvia Manning and Stephen Krashen and I have begun to get some of this useful knowledge from the program (which Professor Manning directs), and not all of it, fortunately, is scratching and clawing.

I would like, then, to give a fairly complete report on a secondary composition program which has been successful and which is now ready to be adopted, *mutatis mutandis*, by other secondary schools or by colleges and universities (and which is currently in operation at the University of Southern California).

RESULTS

The complete 1977–78 evaluation report of the Huntington Beach Union High School district Ninth Grade Writing Program is too long to reproduce here in its entirety. In the body of this paper, however, I want to call attention to four paragraphs from "Summary and Conclusions" and these only, for the report itself does not need interpretation. The key passages are the following:

The data presented in this report show that, on the average, posttest writing scores were substantially higher than pretest writing scores. The gains were much higher among the students showing low pretest performance. This may, in part, be accounted for by normal regression effects. However, the 1977–78 gains for this group are considerably higher than those for the 1976–77 comparable group suggesting a greater program impact. The same conclusion holds for the total ninth grade population.

The performance of the students at W(estminster) H(igh) S(chool) is most encouraging. This performance is contradictory to what is generally seen in test results in the district (WHS is normally the lowest scoring school), but repeats the 1976–77 finding of WHS scoring at the top. These two years of consistent data would certainly suggest a program strength at WHS.

The dramatic turnaround of student performance at O(cean) V(iew) H(igh) S(chool) is also very encouraging, particularly for the total ninth grade. This change would suggest that OVHS found or developed instructional techniques that are highly effective.

The strength of performance at WHS and OVHS would indicate that the remaining schools could benefit by reviewing their programs in terms of those at WHS and OVHS.

The total Huntington Beach Union High School District program was closely monitored—by Professor Augustine and myself, by District administration, and by an outside consultant. Particularly during 1977–78, it became clear to everyone concerned that WHS and OVHS were using the model that I had developed (i.e., were deeply into the program), whereas the other four high schools had developed their own procedures.

It would be possible, but cumbersome, to give detailed descriptions of the programs at all six high schools; however, in this document, I will delineate only the programs (and the preparation) that are characteristic of WHS and OVHS. I am hypothesizing, then, that the success of these two high schools in their writing programs is based on their having adopted the model that I am about to outline.

VALUES

There is a powerful "technology" of literacy, virtually all of it software; there are theory and application; there are effective administrative strategies. All of which are meaningless outside a system of values which will provide the critical mass, the fuel, to make the technology work. When I talk about values, then, I am dealing with what experience has taught me is the single most important factor in a successful literacy program—a factor that is not readily amenable to empirical testing, an uncontrollable, but that is so pervasive as to be invisible, like the air we breathe or the background noise that we shut from our consciousness merely by not paying attention to it.

The values that I am speaking of—and which are an integral part of our efforts on the secondary and college levels—are authority, commitment, and what I choose to call beneficence.[1] The report itself would be meaningless—its details, its facts and figures, its explanations of procedures—if the whole were not put in the context of the value system which provided my impetus and, subsequently, the very practical motivation for the teachers and administrators involved.

Authority then. A faculty needs a sense of authority, not conferred by a dean, a superintendent, or a board, but arising from the members' sense that they know their field, that they understand what they're doing, that they are genuinely professionals.

It is paradoxical that the academy—universities which train teachers of reading and writing—typically bestow authority *in the wrong field*. By and large, the secondary and college teachers of reading and writing have gained authority in the study of literature, in interpretation, history of ideas, biography, and so on. Here, for example, is Ian Watt:

I would like my own activities as a student and teacher of *English* to be as simple and yet comprehensive as that act [of Ponge, who at one time embraced a table and explained, "You see, if I love it, it's because there's absolutely nothing in it which allows one to believe that it takes itself for a piano"]. It should contain the same four necessary constituents: an intellectual recognition of just what I am modestly but directly attending to; an aesthetic appreciation of the object of my attention for what it exactly is; a direct commitment of my feelings to that object; and lastly, perhaps incidentally, an attempt to express all of the first three things in words.

Our teaching, then, should make its major objective the reading of literature which really is literature. What that reading process should be like seems to me to be easy enough to envision, though impossible fully to achieve; it is only, as Arnold put it, to see the object as it really, in itself, is.

A few words about the most difficult task of all, teaching writing. *Personally, I find the basic issue quite simple; there's very little knowledge about writing required beyond that which comes with attentive reading.*

English Department classes should be classes for the reading—and the real reading—of literature that is really literature, and then for writing about it in a way that, in its own appropriately humble manner, attempts to be literature, or at least not to demean it (1978, pp. 13–15, emphasis added).

I have cited Watt at some length because his own work in literature is so admirable and because his attitude toward literacy is so typical, his value system is so characteristic.

The authority that teachers have is a paradox precisely because teachers of reading and writing are not so much concerned with the text as with the *processes* whereby a text is constructed by a writer and subsequently reconstructed by a reader. It might be said that knowledge of literature is mainly knowledge of texts and that knowledge of literacy is mainly knowledge of processes. I am *not* claiming that these two bodies of knowledge are mutually exclusive, but they are quite obviously not identical.

And now the problem for the writing and reading teacher becomes poignant. There is no place—no *single* place—in the academy which deals with this knowledge of process, no home base, no department, no major. And that statement can be demonstrated rather easily: if one were to assemble the group of scholars in the United States—indeed the world—who are doing the most interesting work in literacy, they would come from, among other fields, cognitive psychology, linguistics, anthropology, sociology, education, philosophy, cybernetics. (In recent years, a handful of scholars in English departments have begun to do significant work.)

Let me give one homely example. Learning to write is the acquisition of a language skill. To have authority, a teacher of writing, then, must know about language acquisition, and that takes one, at least, to linguistics, psychology, and anthropology. And let me make this example even more homely:

SECONDARY SUPERINTENDENT: In your writing class, Mr. Harumph, you are, I assume, teaching a language skill—at least in part.
SECONDARY ENGLISH TEACHER: I'd

never thought of it that way, but I guess you're right.
SUPER: Where could I find out about current work in language learning?
TEACHER: Beats me!
SUPER: But with the literacy crisis, Proposition 13, and a skittish board, we've got to speak with authority about what we're doing.
TEACHER: Maybe you ought to call USC to see if anyone up there can help us. Frankly, I'm so busy correcting themes that I don't have time to get into that ivory tower stuff.
SUPER: Good idea! We'll hire a consultant. I should have thought of that in the first place. After all, it's unreasonable for me to expect an English teacher to have any knowledge about language processes and literacy.

And one more example, for the point is crucial. There is, of course, extensive literature on the relationship between students' knowledge of grammar and their ability to write (e.g., Petrosky, 1977). In my work with new teaching assistants at USC (probably more than 250 of them) and with high school teachers (more than I could count), I have not encountered one teacher who was aware that the literature existed. In fact, they had no really sound reasons for either teaching or not teaching grammar in their writing classes. And that issue is certainly one of the great logomachies in the profession.

A teacher without authority is always a victim. A teacher with spurious authority victimizes. Obviously one effort of any literacy program must be to confer genuine authority on teachers.

I will say less about commitment and beneficence, though I believe that they are crucial values for a teacher. Commitment is disinterested allegiance to a field. Beneficence is humane concern for the relationship between the field and students. The authority without commitment is likely to be an authoritarian cynic whose self-confidence in the field of endeavor translates into browbeating and clever showmanship. The teacher with commitment and beneficence, but without authority, is quite likely to be extremely effective with most students, with the easy cases, but will be ineffective with students who need to be taught (who, unlike the easy cases, do not simply learn) and disastrously inept at planning or supervision, activities that often involve the spending of large sums of money for textbooks, equipment, inservice training, and so on.

The preservice and inservice training in the high school district and at USC have as their rationale the conferring of authority upon teachers. This authority, of course, comes from knowledge, and the knowledge itself results in knowhow or methodology. Knowledge is strategic, providing a coherent framework for a set of extremely complex activities that extend over a semester, a year, four years, and that vary from student to student. Knowhow is tactical; it is the application of knowledge in a scene, to solve a given problem with a certain student at some time. Knowledge confers authority. Without knowledge, knowhow is an incoherent set of gimmicks that may or may not work most of the time, but which can never serve as the basis for a program. And reasonable, coherent programs are absolutely essential for literacy.

KNOWLEDGE

What sorts of knowledge do teachers of literacy, and particularly of writ-

ing, need? How do they best gain that knowledge?

To answer that question, it will perhaps be useful to outline the inservice training program which Professor Augustine and I developed for the Huntington Beach Union High School District and which in substance is very much like the preservice and inservice training program at USC. (At USC, I have collaborated with Professor Stephen Krashen of linguistics and Professor Sylvia Manning, who directs the freshman writing program.)

Many teacher-training programs in literacy attempt to fill in lacunae in the teachers' knowledge of their subject, but in the work that my colleagues and I have been doing, we assume that there are no lacunae, for there can be no gaps in a void. It is a brutal fact that most teachers of writing in particular, especially beginners fresh from university English departments, simply have *no* knowledge and hence cannot begin asking even the most rudimentary questions. (And here I am not criticizing teachers or English departments; the departments are the result and hence the victims of history, and the teachers are the unintentional victims of those departments.) In any case, the preparation begins with the most basic considerations of written composition as a *rhetorical act*, as a writer with a semantic intention to convey to an audience that is always more or less hypothetical in some more or less specific scene. According to my definition, any discourse act, written or spoken, is *the projection of a SEMANTIC INTENTION through a STRUCTURE to an AUDIENCE in a SCENE.*

It might well be that a whole semester of work could be spent on the rhetorical and pedagogical implications of intention, structure, audience, and scene. Though in our training we do not introduce classical rhetoric, except by the way, in fact the concepts that I have just mentioned are part of the tradition from Aristotle onward (except that English departments for reasons which I will not develop here have pared rhetoric down virtually to a narrowly conceived view of stylistics and some relatively unilluminating concepts of form). But writing teachers need to know and think about *ethical* (writer-centered), *pathetic* (audience-centered), and *logical* arguments; about style; about form or arrangement; and particularly about the ratios among these factors in the discourse act.

It happens that ordinary language philosophy (with its explorations of illocutionary and perlocutionary force), literary theory (with its recent emphasis on literature in the reader rather than on the page), psychology, linguistics, and other fields (not to mention real rhetoric, such as that of Burke, Booth, and others, as opposed to the pseudo-rhetoric of the composition handbook) all bear on and clarify this elegant set of concerns with audience, stance, style, form, and deduction and induction that pretty much define what the field of rhetoric has been in the past and is to a large extent at present.

To summarize, our teacher preparation gives a clear picture of the questions that rhetoric can ask and some of the answers to those questions, without presenting a history of rhetoric or even asking necessarily that trainees read in the traditional sources. I frankly cannot understand how really effective and ethical instruction in the art of discourse, written or spoken, can proceed if teachers are completely ignorant of

the very questions that can bring understanding of the process whereby a discourse says what the writer intends it to say effectively for a given audience. And as backup for this point, I merely refer my readers to the many writing classes (typical classes?) in which there is no audience but the teacher-evaluator and in which scenic considerations arise only by accident if at all. One excellent document bearing on this strange situation is the important book *The Development of Writing Ability, Ages 11–18* (1975) by Britton, Burgess, Martin, McLeod and Rosen.

I recommend my own *Contemporary Rhetoric: A Conceptual Background with Readings* (1975b) as a reasonable source to put trainees in touch with the field of rhetoric and the questions that it asks.

Once this framework of rhetoric has been established, other components of the preparation fit nicely.

As I said earlier, writing teachers need—and invariably find useful!—something more than a layperson's knowledge of language: sociolinguistics, psycholinguistics (particularly language acquisition and split-brain theory), and some syntax and grammatical theory. In Huntington Beach, for instance, teachers worked their way through Nancy Ainsworth Johnson, *Current Topics in Language: Introductory Readings* (Winthrop 1976); William Labov's now classic *The Study of Nonstandard English* (1970); and Frank O'Hare, *Sentence-Combining: Improving Student Writing Without Formal Grammar Instruction* (1973); plus some other pieces [such as an unpublished paper on cerebral hemisphericity and Walter Loban's *Language Development, K-12* (1976)]. As I will explain, Krashen's monitor theory of second language learning is important in our work, and trainees read two of Krashen's papers on the theory.

Of course, front-line teachers do not have unlimited time, and assuredly they are in one of the most energy-draining of all professions; therefore, in Huntington Beach Professor Augustine and I did not hesitate to summarize important works and to suggest that, for instance, Kenneth Burke would be worth reading in the future and that Chaim Perelman has important things to say, even to ninth-grade teachers. In short, Augustine and I attempted to provide a broad background, a context, for the specific readings that the trainees did.

Furthermore, we attempted to give the sense that the work we were doing was at the cutting edge of knowledge in the field. We discussed the Loban monograph shortly after it was published; we discussed the monitor theory and hemisphericity papers before they were published. And all of us, I think, gained the sense that we are in a developing field and that, as a consequence, any knowledge we acquire will be forever just a beginning. No longer, then, can the professional who needs a sense of authority stop being a learner (i.e., a scholar) upon graduation and entry into the profession.

KNOWHOW

All of the knowhow in our composition programs at Huntington Beach and USC relates to one of the following categories: (1) prewriting, (2) composing, (3) reformulation, and (4) editing. Prewriting includes all of the activities that go into formulating a preliminary semantic intention

(in terms of classical rhetoric, "invention"); composing is the expression of that intention in structures (sentences, paragraphs, etc.); reformulation is the process of changing structures in order to express the semantic intention more cogently or to change that intention; and editing is the process of adjusting the "surface" of the text so that it approximates, more or less nearly, the only universal written "dialect," Edited Standard English. (Editing has to do with spelling, punctuation, verb agreement, reference, and so on.) It may not be necessary to mention that these processes are always contingent, to a greater or lesser degree, upon *audience* and *scene*, but mention it we do, again and again.

It is necessary, then, that teachers have effective techniques to intervene in and facilitate the subprocesses of the composing process. The writing teacher needs specific knowhow.

Another homely example. Suppose that student X appears to have trouble with sentences. The instructor Y must have the knowhow to help the student overcome that problem. Such a statement may seem embarrassingly obvious, but my experience has shown me that teachers most often comment on the ineptness of sentence structure ("Your sentences are choppy"; "Your sentences sprawl"; "Your prose is hard to read") without the knowhow to make suggestions for solving the problem. The advice that students should read George Orwell and E. B. White in order to develop an effective style is simply turning away from the process and back to the text. The teacher must have the knowhow (and the "technology") to teach syntactic fluency and accessibility. (In our programs, it is axiomatic that each criticism of a piece of writing must be followed by "And I'll show you at least one way to do it better.")

In regard to *prewriting*, our know-how relies heavily on heuristics and the journal. Among other sources, we have drawn our techniques from James Adams (1974); Rohman and Wlecke (1964); Kenneth Burke (1945); Young, Becker, and Pike (1970); Edward de Bono (1970); and Roman Jakobson (1960). These heuristics (techniques of invention, of problem definition and problem solving) range from the simple to the complex, and they are adaptable to individual students or to given populations of students. In our programs, they are effective with ninth- and tenth-graders and with college freshmen. So far, our widest experience is at the secondary level, but we do have evidence for the effectiveness of heuristics in colleges (Young and Koen, 1973).

Prewriting is the formulation and refinement of a semantic intention, and *composing* is the mapping of that intention into structures, most basically sentences and paragraphs. Knowhow in the area of teaching composing involves (among other concerns) syntactic fluency and to a lesser extent paragraph form. The *knowledge* concerning syntactic fluency comes from psycholinguistic studies that demonstrate the nature of languaging and its basis in the simple proposition and the combining of propositions into multi-level sentences,[2] and from studies of the effect of gains in fluency on student writing.[3] The knowhow is in sets of materials that teachers have available: Strong's *Sentence Combining* (1973), O'Hare's *Sentencecraft* (1975), *The Christensen Rhetoric Program* (1968), and Winterowd

and Murray's unpublished syntactic fluency program.

Knowhow regarding the paragraph is more nebulous and less varied and rich. For "basic writing" students, we use techniques drawn largely from concepts developed by Alton Becker (1966) and Francis Christensen (1966). Most of the materials which either are or will be in use are currently in manuscript and are being tested for effectiveness.

Both the sentence and the paragraph are necessary forms with psychological reality.[4] To compose effectively, students must be versatile in using them. But I do not mean to imply that the whole process of teaching the composing process is encompassed by work with the sentence and the paragraph—or that all students need such work, though a great many of them do.

Beyond the sentence, knowhow becomes less and less specific and merges with knowledge. For instance, in dealing with the coherence of whole essays, we have just begun to apply the principles of discourse analysis, but that is an emerging field that has not yet been shaken down into specific techniques and materials. In fact, I personally feel that here is one place where training in literary analysis can be especially valuable to teachers of writing, for people who have dealt with texts in detail have gained tacit knowledge of how they hang together, knowledge which can be translated into knowhow on the spot.

Reformulation is clearly an important process, and to teach it effectively the instructor must have knowledge of how texts work in general. In our programs, that knowledge translates into some fairly simple knowhow. Any act of reformulation must be one of the following: deletion, addition, rearrangement, or substitution of words, phrases, sentences, paragraphs, sections. . . . With that much background, plus a sensitivity to the complexities of texts, teachers can give students a powerful skill.

As to *editing*: writers must, when the occasion (i.e., audience and scene) demands, be able to approximate the surface structure of Edited Standard English. Knowhow, then, is nothing more than the ability to give students the necessary skills—at the proper time and in the proper place. In a later section, we will discuss the proper place, but for the moment, it is important to stress that the features of Edited Standard English (e.g., punctuation) are coherent systems, and that being the case, it is most effective to teach them as systems, not randomly. In other words, if a student cannot punctuate, he or she needs to grasp the system of punctuation as a whole, not to correct random errors on this paper and that.

The knowhow here has great strategic advantages, for it frees the writing teacher from the odium of making all those red squiggles— those futile, demoralizing, and frustrating wounds—in the margins of papers. In Post-Einsteinian physics, what the teacher saves in energy, the student makes up in the acquisition of the desired skill.

It is important to understand that the *skills* of editing are independent of audience and scene. They gain value for certain audiences in a given scene. And the import of this remark will become obvious when we turn to a discussion of the writing workshop and the language skills laboratory.

It has been our experience that editing skills programs are easily and economically developed and readily "borrowed" from existing sources. We have seen demonstrably effective sets of programs in a number of settings, the nature of which will be clarified hereafter.

Common sense should have told us long ago that it is impossible to edit a blank page; therefore, prewriting, composing, and reformulation must take precedence over editing. It is also axiomatic and has been amply demonstrated that attention to editing can effectively impede or stop the composing process.[5] The writing class that places heavy weight on editing will likely create many compositional stutterers who are afraid to compose a paragraph because in the process they will generate errors that can be censured. Which is *not* to say that editing is not tremendously important in many completed texts!

SCENES

In the Huntington Beach High Schools, we have created two scenes for instruction in writing: the writing workshop and the language skills laboratory. Roughly characterized, the writing workshop is rhetorically charged with values and with the concerns of audience and scene; unsystematic; "messy"; unpredictable. The laboratory is *a*rhetorical, systematic, neat.

In general, the workshop teaches prewriting, composing, and reformulation, whereas the laboratory teaches editing. This way of distributing instructional tasks and goals makes good sense, but in practice the cut is not quite so clean as one might assume. Hereafter I will attempt to give clear pictures of the workshop and the lab.

The workshop-lab arrangement of instructional scenes results from the influence of various theories and bodies of knowledge. For example, we believe that discourse takes place and is learned most effectively in a rhetorical situation or scene, the necessary elements for which are at least exigency (a need, a situation which can be changed through discourse), audience, and constraints which approximate those of the real world (as opposed to the classroom world) as nearly as possible (Bitzer, 1960). Furthermore, it is axiomatic with us that any language instruction which runs contrary to the known processes of language learning must be undertaken with caution and viewed with suspicion.

We have tried to create in the workshops, then, a scene or situation in which learning to write would approximate as nearly as possible, and as frequently as possible, a real-world, out-of-school situation. The laboratory—with its programs and drills—obviously resembles nothing in the real world of language use, and that is one good reason for keeping it separate from the workshop.

In fact, a great deal of theory and a growing body of empirical evidence lies behind our decision to create these two learning scenes. In this paper, I will discuss only monitor theory, for while it does not account for what goes on in the workshop, it does give justification for our workshop-lab split.

The term "learning" is inadequate when one discusses the acquisition of a second language (and we view learning to compose as, in many ways, like learning a second language), for in that acquisition two quite different processes go on (in the case of most learners, at least).

On the one hand, the learner listens and reads and begins to talk and write; *input* provides the basis for *output*. Whether in a classroom or on the street of a foreign city, this kind of learning is necessarily rhetorically charged and value-laden. Often there is an audience and a controlling scene to which the learner must try to adjust his or her purpose. In other words, we have all the elements of natural language learning; exigence, audience, constraints, scene. The attempt is to project a semantic intention through a structure to an audience in a scene.

But, of course, we can also turn to paradigms and rule systems which we consciously master. Thus, we memorize the system of German definite articles and, at times, consciously use that knowledge to produce the correct forms in written or spoken German.

In fact, a great deal of theory and a growing body of empirical evidence lies behind our decision to create these two learning scenes. In this paper, I will discuss only monitor theory, for while it does not account for what goes on in the workshop, it does give justification for our workshop-lab split.

The term "learning" is inadequate when one discusses the acquisition of a second language (and we view learning to compose as, in many ways, like learning a second language), for in that acquisition two quite different processes go on (in the case of most learners, at least). On the one hand, the learner listens and reads and begins to talk and write; *input* provides the basis for *output*. Whether in a classroom or on the street of a foreign city, this kind of learning is necessarily rhetorically charged and value-laden. Often there is an audience and a controlling scene to which the learner must try to adjust his or her purpose. In other words, we have all the elements of natural language learning; exigence, audience, constraints, scene. The attempt is to project a semantic intention through a structure to an audience in a scene.

But, of course, we can also turn to paradigms and rule systems which we consciously master. Thus, we memorize the system of German definite articles and, at times, consciously use that knowledge to produce the correct forms in written or spoken German.

In second language learning, then, there are two related processes: the "naturalistic" one which often takes place in (results from) a rhetorical

ing situation or a self-study program. Formal learning situations are characterized by the process of feedback or error correction, absent in acquisition environments, and "rule isolation," the presentation of artificial linguistic environments that introduce just one new aspect of grammar at a time (1976).

In order to avoid terminological difficulties, I will adopt the typographic convention of using capital letters for LEARNING in the broad sense that includes both acquisition and Krashen's sense of learning. Thus, a language LEARNER acquires and learns.

The result of learning is the construction of a *monitor* which allows the user consciously to regularize or correct output. Thus:

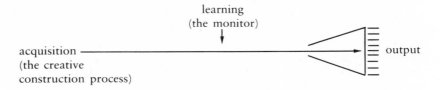

situation; and the "artificial" one which results from the desire to learn certain skills of language. The first sort of learning is called by Krashen *acquisition*, and the second he terms *learning*.

The technical term language *acquisition* is here used to refer to the way linguistic abilities are internalized "naturally," that is, without conscious focussing on linguistic form. It appears to require, minimally, participation in natural communication situations, and is the way children gain knowledge of first and second languages. . . .

Language acquisition is a subconscious process. Language *learning*, on the other hand, is a conscious process, and is the result of either a formal language learn-

In a sense, the monitor is a low-level device; one cannot consciously learn extremely complex rules of language, but one internalizes them through acquisition. (Indeed, not all rules of language can be stated, for example, those concerning audience and scene.) One can, however, learn such rules and paradigms as those which make up the system of articles in German or which constitute standard punctuation in English. In fact, it is my hypothesis—not necessarily Krashen's—that all of the skills of editing can be learned.

Now we can redefine workshop as a place where compositional skills (prewriting, composing, reformulation) are acquired and the laboratory as a place where editing skills are learned. In practice, the division is not quite so neat, but the processes, materials, and ambience of the workshop are quite different from those of the lab, as, of course, are the goals.

One other aspect of Krashen's work is important here, and it gives credence to the intuition that successful writing teachers have had all along. He has identified three types of monitor users: overusers, who are ineffective at producing meaningful output because so much attention is devoted to conscious monitoring (the student writer who will not launch forth because he or she is afraid of making an error); underusers, who place no value on the skills of monitoring and thus produce quantities of error-ridden output (the student writer who will not edit); and the optimum user, who employs the monitor to regularize output, but does not let attention to monitor skills clog up the stream of discourse. The laboratory should be the best scene for producing optimum users, and, in fact, that has been our experience. Heavy emphasis on the skills of editing in the workshop is quite likely to produce overusers who will never be effective composers.

As to the physical scenes themselves—the places where workshop and editing skills are taught. The laboratory, as we stress again and again, is not a place, but a concept. It is a given kind of instruction for certain goals. In fact, two of the most effective labs in Huntington Beach look like this.

Lab 1 is a file cabinet on wheels, which the teacher can move from room to room throughout the day. In this cabinet are exercises on dittoed sheets—some of them adapted from existing sources, some of them

devised by the teacher herself, all of them fitting a general framework or inventory of monitor skills that was compiled when the Huntington Beach Project first got under way. Lab 1 is literally wheeled into the space where the workshop is being held.

Lab 2 is a separate room. (In this lab, a good deal of individual conferencing goes on, much of which concerns prewriting, composing, and reformulation, none of which are amenable to the systematic neatness of the monitor.) For observers who expect to find an electronic wonderland in a good lab, Lab 2 must be a terrible disappointment, for its "equipment" is nothing but a couple of dozen cardboard boxes, filled with dittoed exercises and arranged according to an inventory of monitor skills. Offhand, I cannot say how much was spent on materials and equipment, but obviously the sum was insignificant.

In the case of Lab 1, the workshop teacher is also the lab teacher; in Lab 2, the teacher does primarily lab work, the students having been referred by a group of workshop teachers in the school.

Every writing teacher knows that editing skills are a variable among students in a class; some appear to need everything, while others have problems in limited areas. The separation of the lab from the workshop allows—indeed demands—the individualization of instruction. The English class model of grammar drill on Monday, discussion of a poem Tuesday, theme assignment on Wednesday, library activities Thursday, and time for elective reading on Friday breaks down. For the lab and the workshop are interactive, flexibly so.

To characterize the workshop and

how it interacts with the lab could best be accomplished with a video tape that would demonstrate, not tell about. However, a picture of the workshop can be presented. Here is a montage of the kinds of things that go on there:

(1) Discussion of and practice with prewriting techniques by the whole class.

(2) Small group activities of two or three students, e.g., two students reacting to and making suggestions regarding a paper (perhaps a rough draft) produced by a third student.

(3) Composing - on - the - board, with volunteers making attempts to solve a given writing problem, e.g., getting a paper by one member of the class under way effectively.

(4) Whole class discussion of one, two, or three dittoed papers produced by class members.

(5) Conferencing, the teacher circulating about the class to help individual students with writing problems while the other members of the class work on their papers.

(6) Some editing lessons for the whole class, dealing with a limited problem that all have in common.

(7) Reformulation exercises, in which all of the class members make suggestions for improving one of their fellows' papers.

(8) Class discussion of audience, the adjustment of a given paper for a certain audience.

(9) Freewriting.

(10) Journal writing.

(11) Language games, such as the round-robin sentence, in which students successively add modifiers to a base, perhaps (depending on the class's level of sophistication) in the attempt to parody some author such as Faulkner.

(12) Publishing activities, in which groups of students or the whole class participate in getting a collection ready for the "press" and distribution.

(13) Class development of writing assignments, during which students devise topics, define audiences, and delineate situations.

The workshop is a messy place, highly charged, purposive in terms of writing something for someone for some reason. When it becomes obvious that the student's semantic intention must have a given surface structure to "reach" a certain audience in a scene, the lab assignment becomes meaningful. Because editing skills are put into a context, students grasp their importance.

I believe that the skills of composition are either transferable or local and that the purpose of both the workshop and the lab is primarily to teach transferable skills. A transferable skill is one that prevails in many, most, or even all writing situations (e.g., rhetorical stance or syntactic fluency), and a local skill is specific to a given writing task. For example, I have at least the basic transferable skills, but I lack certain of the local skills that would make me an effective writer of, say, a paper in the social sciences. In a laboratory, working with a "unit," I could easily attain those local skills as an overlay to the transferable skills which are a necessary first condition for any composing. An effective laboratory can develop units to teach these local skills when they are required by students. The lab, then, in its ideal form teaches editing and local skills.

Syntactic fluency should be a lab activity. Students who are not syntactically fluent are stopped from composing, and we have ample evidence that syntactic fluency can be taught to virtually every student, certainly from the ninth grade on. But syntactic fluency boils down to style, and style spills over from the neatness of the lab to the meaningful disarray of the workshop. In practice, we have found that syntactic fluency bridges the gap between lab and workshop. Language games, sentence building, reformulation, exercises in readability—these activities take place in the workshop, and they demonstrate the purpose behind fluency. Students who need extensive work then turn to the lab.

If my pictures of the lab and the workshop have been at all clear, then it should be apparent that knowledge translates itself into knowhow in these two learning scenes, and it should be equally apparent that intricate syllabi are mere hindrances to the goal of teaching students the power of writing and how to be powerful writers. The workshop is much nearer to an art studio in spirit and operation than it is to a traditional English class. Within the framework of goals and strategies, the students are working on their individual projects under the guidance of a skilled teacher and with the cooperation of their classmates.

DEVELOPING A PROGRAM

It is axiomatic that new programs in literacy must come from the faculty with the support of the administration. The analogy that I use again and again is this: in a hospital, the medical staff develops plans and procedures and identifies needed equipment; the administrator and board of trustees find ways to finance and administer. If reading and writing teachers have authority, then the administration can turn to them for problem solving, and this, of course, takes us right back to the proposition that knowledge and the authority it confers will translate into knowhow.

There is a special problem in secondary schools, however—undoubtedly in most public schools. English teachers are isolated from the contacts, activities, and rewards that energize a faculty. It is a sad fact that teachers (especially English teachers) rank low on the scale of prestige. The problem of demoralization must be overcome if any educational program is to be successful. There must be rewards, and even though salary is important, professional rewards always transcend dollars, and they provide the stimulus which creates a good faculty.

A first necessity, then, is to give teachers professional stature, and this comes about from engaging in professional activities that go beyond teaching. Publication, research, attending professional meetings, consulting within or outside of the district—these are just some of the opportunities that raise teachers' images of themselves and that engage them totally in their profession. (Recently a teacher friend of mine spoke of a trend within her district. Many of her colleagues were taking real estate licenses in order to run a business after school hours, on weekends, and during the summer. One who is totally engaged in a profession simply does not have time for other major concerns.)

However, these opportunities are

hard to create if a faculty is isolated from the scholarly community at large, and, therefore, a university connection is essential. Simply: a school district should establish a close relationship with a college or university which shares professional interests with the schools' faculties. And I cannot stress this point enough.

If such ties are established, the university has a readily accessible base for research, and the schools have the resources of university faculty members. There is established a collegiality which perforce brings teachers into the professional circle.

The changes which I've talked about in this document do not come easily or overnight. They cannot be brought about by administrative fiat from above. Furthermore, teachers are understandably cynical: a consultant comes into the district, gives a rousing Saturday workshop, and then disappears; the superintendent issues a mandate concerning accountability or declining test scores, and then, in effect, he too disappears; the state spends millions of dollars on new textbooks, and in classrooms north to south, the books disappear under the dust on shelves; a teacher has a serendipitous breakthrough and the urge to share it with colleagues, but he or she seldom has the opportunity to appear.

A nucleus of professionals do not disappear, and month by month teacher after teacher becomes more and more attracted to the project.

Finally, here is some practical advice about establishing a literacy project:

(1) Find someone in authority who is sympathetic: an administrator, a board member, a city council-person. Talk to that person to gain access to the decision-maker or makers.

(2) Once access is gained, present a clearcut and relatively simple proposal.

(3) Make it clear that not much money is involved. There is nothing to buy except the time of the people involved.

(4) When you get the mandate to proceed, carefully identify a relatively small group of faculty members who will work with you to get the project under way.

(5) Make a realistic one-year plan, and in that plan, make projections about the continuation of the project in the second year. (In the second year, project toward the third, and so on.) Insofar as the project is successful, it will eventually cease to be a project and will become a way of life, but until that happens it takes conscious effort and planning to keep the momentum up.

(6) If you do not have a university connection, establish one if at all possible.

In Huntington Beach, we have just concluded our third year of the Project and, in fact, are beginning to plan activities for 1979–80. We will initiate some research projects, will schedule meetings to discuss what is happening in the field of literacy, and will begin to organize and plan our fourth semester-long intensive in-service training seminar.

We are preparing to present in-service workshops throughout the United States, and we are revising our comprehensive *Project Manual* that will serve as a guide to other districts and to colleges and universities which adopt or adapt the Huntington Beach model. Now that hard data are coming in, and after three years' experience, we are more than willing to help with replication.

Perhaps the single most happy result of the Huntington Beach Project is that all of us enjoy it enormously—because we are seeing results, because we have become colleagues and friends, and because we have gained self-respect.

NOTES

1. See W. Ross Winterowd, "The Rhetoric of Beneficence, Authority, Ethical Commitment, and the Negative" (1976).

2. An excellent discussion of this principle is to be found in Herbert H. Clark and Eve V. Clark, *Psychology and Language* (1977).

3. The principal study is Frank O'Hare, *Sentence Combining: Improving Student Writing Without Formal Grammar Instruction* (1971). Since O'Hare's study, a substantial literature concerning sentence combining has developed. Also, we are developing a great deal of data in Huntington Beach.

4. In other words, experienced readers will be able to mark sentence and paragraph boundaries in a text from which all punctuation and paragraph indentations have been removed. This experiment is easily replicable.

5. This is one of the points in Krashen's monitor theory.

From Classroom Practice into Psycholinguistic Theory

Knitting in some of the loose threads from "Developing a Composition Program," this essay is actually a plea that theory should result from practice just as surely as practice should result from theory.

In 1975, one of my students (now Dr. Dorothy Augustine of the University of Houston) and I set out to design a composition program for the Huntington Beach (California) Union High School District. This program, now in its fourth year, has been successful as judged by most criteria: District evaluations have indicated that we are getting more than satisfactory results, teachers have become increasingly enthusiastic, and from 1975 to 1978, the District leaped from the 73rd to the 86th percentile on the verbal portion of the California Assessment.[1]

Going into the project, Dr. Augustine and I had some fairly clear-cut notions or theories, in mind.

1 INSERVICE PREPARATION: UNDERSTANDING

Teachers need a conceptual-theoretical background in which to work, or else all of their pedagogy is *ad hoc*.

Further, this background must be shared knowledge, i.e. teachers in a school or a district need to know the rationale behind the 'official' policy, but the policy itself is not a set of laws, merely a conceptual framework that gives coherence to what goes on within and among individual classrooms. It is important to stress that I am *not* talking about a syllabus mandated by the District. Furthermore, this framework should square with what we know about how language actually works, i.e. should take account of linguistic, psycholinguistic, learning, and rhetorical theory.

An example: we felt that work in syntactic fluency would be a crucial part of the program, as indeed it has demonstrated itself to be, but we chose not to mandate that teachers should devote X amount of time to fluency exercises with Y students. Rather, we hoped that teachers would grasp the linguistic and psy-

This essay appeared originally in *Learning to Write: First Language/Second Language*, edited by Aviva Freedman, Ian Pringle, and Janice Yalden (London and New York: Longman, 1983). Reprinted by permission.

cholinguistic underpinnings of sentence combining and use it when appropriate. (More about appropriateness and syntactic fluency later.)

In setting forth concept and theory, we were not demanding or even asking that teachers abandon their own practices—only that they understand the what and the why of the program that we were setting forth.

Therefore, it was essential that we organize and conduct extensive inservice preparation, for, as I have argued elsewhere, very few composition teachers have any preservice preparation, though the situation is gradually changing.

2 INSERVICE PREPARATION: KNOWHOW

Composition teachers need techniques for intervening in the *process* of writing, and many 'old hands' have an array of effective methodology, but many teachers, old and new, concentrate on the written product, 'correcting' and grading without paying attention to how the present text can be reformulated or how the next one might be more successfully written. We adopted the following maxim: when you levy a criticism against a student paper, you must always add, 'And I'll show you at least one way to do it better'.

Again, an example: it is futile to admonish students to reformulate (revise) and leave them to it. We demonstrate to them in general and specifically that reformulation involves the *addition*, the *deletion*, the *rearrangement*, and the *substitution* of words, phrases, sentences, paragraphs. . . .

We have made an arbitrary divi-

sion of the composing process into *prewriting*, *writing*, *rewriting*, and *editing*, and teachers need the knowhow to intervene in every stage of the process. (We realize that our segmenting of the composing process is artificial, but it is strategic.)

SCENES: WORKSHOP AND LABORATORY

Following a hint by Mellon (1969), we felt that the kinds of learning necessary for successful writing could be roughly divided into two categories, the rhetorical and the arhetorical. Rhetorical skills would be learned in the workshop and arhetorical in the laboratory. (In fact, the theories of both Kenneth Burke and Roman Jakobson were very much in our minds.)

In 'Developing a Composition Program (in Freedman and Pringle 1980a), I give the following characterization of the workshop and the lab:

To characterize the workshop and how it interacts with the lab could best be accomplished with a video tape that would demonstrate, not tell about. However, a picture of the workshop can be presented.

Here is a montage of the kinds of things that go on there:

1. Discussion of and practice with prewriting techniques by the whole class.

2. Small group activities of two or three students, e.g. two students reacting to and making suggestions regarding a paper (perhaps a rough draft) produced by a third student.

3. Composing-on-the-board, with volunteers making attempts to solve a given writing problem, e.g. getting a paper by one member of the class under way effectively.

4. Whole class discussions of one, two, or three dittoed papers produced by class members.

5. Conferencing, the teacher circulating about the class to help individual students with writing problems while the other members of the class work on their papers.

6. Some editing lessons for the whole class, dealing with a limited problem that all have in common.

7. Reformulation exercises, in which all of the class members make suggestions for improving one of their fellows' papers.

8. Class discussion of audience, the adjustment of a given paper for a certain audience.

9. Freewriting.

10. Journal writing.

11. Language games, such as the round-robin sentence, in which students successively add modifiers to a base. . . .

12. Publishing activities. . . .

13. Class development of writing assignments. . . .

The workshop is a messy place, highly charged, purposive in terms of writing something for someone for some reason. (Pp. 168–69)

The laboratory should be the best scene for producing optimum users [of editing skills], and, in fact, that has been our experience. . . . The laboratory, as we stress again and again, is not a place, but a concept. It is a given kind of instruction for certain goals. (P. 167)

The laboratory, then, teaches primarily the skills of editing: punctuation, verb agreement, pronoun reference, and so on.

Our conception of the program— which I have outlined in its barest bones—was soon given a sharper definition by the work of my colleague Stephen Krashen. In August of 1976, Professor Krashen issued his important paper 'Second Lan-

guage Acquisition' (Krashen 1977), the explanation of his 'monitor theory' of language learning. Subsequently, he published 'On the Acquisition of Planned Discourse: Written English as Second Dialect.' (Krashen 1978). In the following pages, I would like to outline Krashen's monitor model, to show how it influenced our practice, and to demonstrate how our practice leads to an enriched version of the monitor model—from practice into theory. I quote from 'Developing a Composition Program':

The term 'learning' is inadequate when one discusses the acquisition of a second language (and we view learning to compose as, in many ways, like learning a second language), for in that acquisition, two quite different processes go on (in the case of most learners, at least). On the one hand, the learner listens and reads and begins to talk and write; *input* provides the basis for *output*. Whether in a classroom or on the street of a foreign city, this kind of learning is necessarily rhetorically charged and value-laden. Often there is an audience and a controlling scene to which the learner must try to adjust his or her purpose. In other words, we have all the elements of natural language learning. . . .

But, of course, we can also turn to paradigms and rule systems which we consciously master. Thus, we memorize the system of German definite articles and, at times, consciously use that knowledge to produce the correct forms in written or spoken German.

In second-language learning, then, there are two related processes: the 'naturalistic' one which often takes place in (results from) a rhetorical situation; and the 'artificial' one which results from the desire to learn certain skills of language. The first sort of learning is called by Krashen *acquisition*, and the second he terms *learning*. . . . The result of learning is the construction of a *monitor* which allows the user consciously to regularize or correct output. Thus:

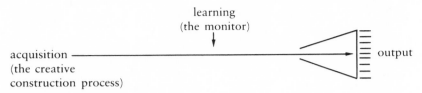

learning
(the monitor)

acquisition ——————————————————→ output
(the creative
construction process)

In a sense, the monitor is a low-level device; one cannot consciously learn extremely complex rules of language, but internalizes them through acquisition. (Indeed, not all the 'rules' of language can be stated, for example, those concerning audience and scene.) One can, however, learn such rules and paradigms as those which make up the system of articles in German or which constitute standard punctuation in English. . . .

Now we can redefine workshop as a place where compositional skills (prewriting, writing, rewriting) are acquired and the laboratory as a place where editing skills are learned [if they have not already been acquired]. (Pp. 166–67)

When we learned of monitor theory, we were able to schematize simply and usefully thus:

editing skills—the skills necessary to make the surface of a text conform to the features of what we call Edited Standard English—are learnable, and I base this conclusion on extensive reports by teachers, on the results of the California Assessment, on the basis of gains on the District's own *Test of English Writing Skills* (which is almost exclusively editing), and on our observation of the pre- and post-tests of writing which we administer each year.[2] Admittedly I am on shaky ground here, for no compelling evidence indicates that students have not *acquired* these skills in the general process of their educational maturation, but we can demonstrate that virtually all students show gains in the pre- and posttests of laboratory skills. What we cannot demonstrate—and this is

PROCESS	*Prewriting—Writing—Rewriting*	*Editing*
'LEARNING'	Acquisition	Learning
SCENES	Workshop	Laboratory

We often say, not totally in jest, that the line between acquisition workshop and learning laboratory is the most important line in the profession.

In spite of this neat formulation, however, important questions have arisen. (Or because of this neat formulation!) (1) What can be learned? (2) What *must* be acquired?

Krashen and I are at odds in regard to learning, but the evidence, I think, is on my side. I believe that

the rub—is that the laboratory learning has carry-over into the writing situation, though we feel strongly that it does.

Of more theoretical interest than editing is the learning of global skills such as paragraph development. If students can *learn* such skills, then it must be the case that the elements of these skills are precisely specifiable. That is, we must be able to present algorithms—and I use that term somewhat loosely—the application of which will result in the desired written product. The infamous five-paragraph essay is just such an algorithm, as is the tagmemic concept of the paragraph (Becker 1966), which we are using with remedial students. In its barest form, this algorithm asks students to supply a 'topic' sentence and to illustrate it two or more times, thus:

Topic	Living near the beach has many advantages.
Illustration	You can go surfing every weekend.
Illustration	The air is not smoggy on the coast.
Illustration	Beach cities are cooler than downtown.

The enriched monitor theory, then, would include not only the learning of specific rules ('capitalize the first letter in a sentence'), but also of paradigms (such as a chart of the forms of the present tense of *be*), and of algorithms that apply to paragraphs and whole essays.

The greatest potential for development of the monitor theory lies in the concept of acquisition. In our continual fascinating and friendly go-arounds, Krashen and I meet head-on at one point. He implies in his published work and states flatly in his conversations that acquisition of the ability to write is through 'input', i.e. reading. I believe that position to be untenable. Sticking to the communication jargon, I believe that *feedback* is as essential as input.

In 'On the Acquisition of Planned Discourse', Krashen states:

It is useful to posit that the well-educated adult native speaker of English has several 'dialects' available to him: an *unplanned* style, which is used primarily in spontaneous conversation, a *planned* dialect (Pl_1), used for certain kinds of writing (such as narratives and descriptions), and a third code, *well-planned* discourse (Pl_2), used for written essays of the expository kind. . . .

The freshman English situation is exactly what the [monitor] model predicts. There seem to be at least two kinds of students in freshman English. There is the mature writer at one extreme, the student who has done some reading and has at least acquired Pl_1. Instructions from the teacher on how to write, rules on the use of topic sentences, transitions, etc. are in a sense old information for such students, as they have already acquired them subconsciously. This student, at best, may gain learning where acquisition was already present, a kind of composition appreciation. More commonly, he will wonder why the teacher is explaining the obvious. At the other extreme is what Shaughnessy . . . calls the 'severely unprepared freshman', the student who has not acquired Pl_1. . . . For these cases, such instructions are new information, and rules are to be taken as definite orders as to how to perform. When such students do carry out these instructions, the result is often a wooden, awkward paper, a product of the fact that instructions given in the writing class represent only a small portion of the rules for planned discourse. Discovering and teaching all the rules for Pl_1 and Pl_2 in the classroom are not the answer. The work of Keenan, Loban, Crystal and Davy, and others shows that many of these rules (lexical, structural, pragmatic, semantic, etc.) are extremely complex; their conscious control is beyond the capacity of even our best students.

Krashen does not characteristically become muddled; in fact, he is one of the clearest thinkers I know. But in this instance, he has tripped himself up and in so doing has partially eviscerated his own monitor theory. To explain what I am getting at, I would like to outline some work that is now being undertaken by myself,

Krashen, and our colleague Betty Bamberg. We might term this 'The Bamberg-Krashen-Winterowd Theory of Freshman Populations.'

The data is not yet in, but we posit that at the University of Southern California, as at other colleges and universities, freshman composition students will fall into three groups upon entry: (1) those who test out of the course, or would be able to test out if given the opportunity; (2) those who can produce Pl$_1$ and halting versions of Pl$_2$; (3) 'basic writers', 'target students', 'remedial students', or whatever term seems least scarifying. The second group can be subdivided into two populations: those who have done extensive pleasure reading during the ages ten to fifteen and those who have not. (Members of group 1 will invariably have been readers, and members of group 3 almost invariably will not have been.) For economy, we will refer to the subcategories of group 2 as R (readers) and NR (non-readers), but it is important to realize that the NR students can read well enough to matriculate and are not 'hardcore' cases. The NR students are not typically admitted to the university under special dispensations, as are members of the third category, nor is their lack of experience in reading apparent to their instructors in most of their courses.

We predict that the R students will very quickly—perhaps in as little as one semester—begin to produce Pl$_2$, and we also predict that follow-up studies will reveal that they did not have extensive writing instruction in high school, if any at all.[3] What they brought with them to the university was 'input,' what they had never attempted was 'output,' and what they had never received was 'feedback.' To be sure,

the R students do not need to 'learn' rules, for they have acquired these through their reading. What they need to do, however, is to activate this acquired knowledge in a rhetorical situation, in a workshop.

With a certain amount of impish glee, then, I take Krashen to task for his failure to differentiate between the kind of acquisition provided by a writing workshop and the kind of learning that some writing classes try to set forth. In fact, the NR students need more learning than do the R students, but as Krashen points out, most of what must be 'learned' about composition is far too complex to be stated specifically as a set of rules.

One might say that the R students are primed for the acquisition of rhetorical skills while the NR are not. What, then, are these rhetorical skills that must be acquired—not necessarily in a writing workshop, but through some kind of intense feedback? I would enrich monitor theory by bringing rhetorical theory to bear upon it.

The modification of Krashen's work through rhetorical theory is, I think, necessary, but it would be the subject of a much longer paper than this one, which is already extending itself pages beyond what I had originally envisioned. One microcosmic example (drawn from work that I am doing with Dr. Dorothy Augustine) must suffice.

From the standpoint of my enriched monitor theory, we would say that a student who has not *acquired* the ability to produce a sentence like the following may *learn* to do so, perhaps through exercises in syntactic fluency or pattern practice.

(1) I claim that the fuel shortage is a capitalist conspiracy.

From the standpoint of rhetoric, however, we might say that the sentence (in context) might involve problems of *ethos*, *pathos*, and *logos*. If Hearer (H) does not accept the authority of Speaker (S), an argument *ad hominem* may ensue:

(2) H: You've always been a lousy communist.
 S: I have not! I'm just a socialist.

The problem here regards *ethos*, the character of the speaker. If it turns out that S misjudges the nature of H, nothing will result from the opening statement:

(3) H: So what are you telling me for? I've been making that same claim to you for six months.
 S: Yeh, I guess I wasn't thinking.

The opening statement has misfired on the basis of *pathos*. The argument *ad rem*—the only real argument—comes about when there is the *possibility* of negating a proposition (*pace* Kenneth Burke), that is, when the focus is on *logos*. Thus,

(4) S: I claim that the fuel shortage is a capitalist conspiracy.
 H: It is not a capitalist conspiracy, for Atlantic-Richfield is spending millions of dollars to promote fuel economy.

And the dialectic has begun.

The rhetorical force of the performative verb is also worth considering, for rhetorical force—as opposed to intention—seems to constitute what Kenneth Burke calls 'attitude'[4] and certainly contributes to the hearer's sense of rhetorical stance and tone. A 'claim' is stronger than a 'statement' and not so strong as an 'avowal'.

Though *ethos*, *pathos*, and *logos* (with all that they imply, which is a very great deal) are 'messy' concepts, not amenable to tidy formulation, they are nonetheless real. The skills that could be characterized as 'ethical', 'pathetic', and 'logical' can only be *acquired*—which means attempt and response, in other words, a writing workshop or its equivalent.

Finally, a concern which for some time I called Sentence Combining (SC); growing tired of that term (and of the whole subject, for that matter), I changed to Syntactic Fluency (SF). Being bored to death at this point, I have chosen the term Sentence Manipulation (SM). Though SC/SF/SM is not a conceptually rich aspect of our field, it is enormously important, and from our practice with it in Huntington Beach, we have developed one further modification of the monitor model.

In our original plans for the Huntington Beach composition program, Dr. Augustine and I firmly planted sentence combining in the laboratory. It was programmatic and arhetorical, we thought; it was a skill to be learned by those students with a deficit. Very soon, we discovered that in practice, our best teachers were bringing sentence combining into the workshops, in the form of language games, the writing of parodies, and so on. What we began to realize is that with some students (perhaps those whom we would characterize as readers), the fluency exercises very quickly activated a competence which must have been there all along, for the rapidity with which these youngsters increased their stylistic options and hence sophistication could not be attributed to the painfully slow processes that learning such complexities must entail.

On the other hand, we find that some students need extensive, carefully planned work in sentence combining in the laboratory. We propose that these students are learning—not via rules or any kind of descriptive statements, but by doing, though not in the 'natural', 'holistic', 'unconscious' way that characterizes Krashen's acquisition. There seems to be a middle ground between acquisition and learning and between workshop and laboratory, and sentence combining, we have discovered, is one bridge.

A revised monitor theory—the result of experience and rhetorical theory—might, in brief, look like this:

Acquisition: the 'learning' of the skills of *ethos*, *pathos*, and *logos* through input and feedback.
Learning: the 'learning' of arhetorical skills through rules, algorithms, paradigms, and programmed exercises.

Put more simply, acquisition takes place rhetorically, and learning takes place arhetorically. That, I think, is a significant contribution to the work that Krashen began so ably and that has been so valuable to me and my colleagues.

NOTES

1. The program was not designed specifically to raise scores on grammar-usage tests; hence our gains on the California Assessment were a bonus of sorts—but very impressive to the District's administration and board. The following quotation from the *1978–79 Ninth-Grade Writing Programme* evaluation report shows something of the results of in-house monitoring:

> The data presented in this report show that, on the average, posttest writing scores were substantially higher than pre-test writing scores. The gains were much higher among the students showing low pretest performance. This may, in part, be accounted for by normal regression effects. However, the 1978–79 gains for this group are considerably higher than those for 1976–77 comparable group, suggesting a greater programme impact. The same conclusion holds for the total ninth-grade population.

2. The writing tests are holistically scored essays, in general like those administered by the California State University and Colleges system. Scoring is guided by a rubric, and each paper is read at least twice.

3. Our predictions have been partially verified by a study that a graduate student, Ronald Kimberling, carried out.

4. In a discussion with graduate students at the University of Southern California, Burke said that attitude—with which he would now expand his Pentad into a hexad—encompasses illocutionary force.

Black Holes, Indeterminacy, and Paulo Freire

Are Kenneth Burke and Paulo Freire, like Jacques Derrida, deconstructionists? The question is, in a way, irrelevant and should be replaced by another: "Once the deconstructionists have robbed readers of blissful ignorance, is any thinker encountered by such readers *not* a deconstructionist?" The apple is a crab, bitter and woody, but its consequences are certain, expelling one from the old world of books, definiteness, logos, summarizing enthymemes, conclusive argument—into the new world, the nature of which I try to capture in this paper.

ON THE GOOD SHIP "DECONSTRUCTION"

When you're sucked into the indeterminacy hole, it's a mighty black hole indeed, and down and down you go, round and round you go, like a leaf. . . . (How does one shoot through space in a Buck Rogers ship that spits sparks like a fizzling firework? Zipping? Gliding? Soaring?) *Sputtering* through space toward Alpha Centauri, the ship begins to drift off course.

"Wilma, light the auxiliary giant sparkler. We need more power!"

But to no avail. The ship has entered an inexplicable force field, a funnel of gravity leading to the black tunnel, which empties its contents into an alternative universe.

"Good lord, Wilma, look at that

This essay appeared originally in *Rhetoric Review* (Sept. 1983). Reprinted by permission.

creature! 'A toothless humanity . . . in a prone position . . . using . . . limbs . . . to push buttons with [Derrida, *Of Grammatology*, p. 85].

"Buck! Buck! Oh heavens, Buck! You . . . you . . . and I look just like it!"

When you go through the funnel to the tunnel and out into the alternate universe, strange things happen to you. The familiar world of determinate meanings (and *logos* and presence) becomes a strange, unstable world. What once was open-and-shut becomes open-and-open.

One would not, for instance, expect a prone, adontic Louise Rosenblatt, and yet when *Literature as Exploration* (1938) goes through the time warp of post-structuralism it becomes in large part a treatise on the indeterminacy of literature, as radical a statement in many ways as anything one could find in current reader-response criticism (Tompkins, 1980). "Every time a reader experiences a work of art, it is in a sense created anew. . . . The import of any work will remain thoroughly personal, since it is re-created by a specific personality with its own sense of values" (Rosenblatt, pp. 113–14).

Unsurprisingly, Kenneth Burke was saying it all as early as 1930—had flashed through the black hole and has been zipping around the alternate universe during virtually his whole career.

For compositionists and rhetoricians, the black hole and the alternate universe are inevitable, as I argue in "Post-Structuralism and Composition." And now I shall drop my black hole-alternate universe metaphor, which, though extended perilously, has pleased me mightily. The post-structuralist debacle, represented most dramatically by Derrida, is changing and will change the way we perceive and teach the universe of discourse. To develop this point and to advance some notions about an important theoretician and practitioner, I will discuss Paulo Freire as a post-structuralist, realizing that he does not view himself as such.

A BIBULOUS INTERLUDE

What a marvelous conversation it would be, in a bar, a salon, or a barrio, that inconclusive and hence unending talk among Kenneth Burke, Jacques Derrida, and Paulo Freire. Like all good dialecticians, they would cherish their differences as much as their agreements, one of them songfully playful, another wittily sardonic, the third completely (though lovingly) serious, all three, we should hope, committed to the

purpose of the dialogue, which would be nothing less than exploring the proposition that language created not only the edifices in Century City (Los Angeles, Cal.), but also that other edifice, *The City of God*, but that, regardless of monuments of unaging intellect, the dialogue must go on to the end of time. As Kenneth Burke (in a passage that I quote repeatedly) has put it:

Where does the drama get its materials? From the "unending conversation" that is going on at the point in history when we are born. Imagine that you enter a parlor. You come late. When you arrive, others have long preceded you, and they are engaged in a heated discussion, a discussion too heated for them to pause and tell you exactly what it is about. In fact, the discussion had already begun long before any of them got there, so that no one present is qualified to retrace for you all the steps that had gone before. You listen for a while, until you decide that you have caught the tenor of the argument; then you put in your oar. Someone answers; you answer him; another comes to your defense; another aligns himself against you, to either the embarrassment or gratification of your opponent, depending upon the quality of your ally's assistance. However, the discussion is interminable. The hour grows late, and you must depart. And you do depart, with the discussion still vigorously in progress. (*The Philosophy of Literary Form*, pp. 95–96)

Suppose the clutch of pages before you to be a book—an extremely short book, but amenable to printing on vellum, calfskin binding, and a Library of Congress call number—and then ask what you have received and where it came from. In an ostensibly felicitous speech act, "I hereby declare this to be the definitive book on the epistemology of Paulo Freire." Then you might respond, "Whence the definitiveness?" To which I would answer, "From the books of Paulo Freire and others." You see the abyss—you are *in* the abyss: books about books about books. . . . In a rare moment of poignancy, the witty, sardonic Derrida tells us that

The idea of the book is the idea of a totality, finite or infinite, of the signifier; this totality of the signifier cannot be a totality, unless a totality constituted by the signified preexists it, supervises its inscriptions and its signs, and is independent of it in its ideality. The idea of the book, which always refers to a natural totality, is profoundly alien to the sense of writing. (*Of Grammatology*, p. 18)

Burke, Derrida, and Freire reach one of those rare halcyon moments of agreement; as the sun sinks in the west, casting a burnished path on the calm sea—for the bar overlooks the ocean—they sip contentedly, nod pensively, and say, one after another, "Yep!" "Oui!" "Sí!"

Then Burke says, "We are concerned with the analogy between 'words' (lower case) and The Word (*Logos*, Verbum) as it were in caps. 'Words' in the first sense have wholly naturalistic, empirical reference. But they may be used analogically, to designate a further dimension, the 'supernatural.' Whether or not there is a realm of the 'supernatural,' there are *words* for it. And in this state of linguistic affairs there is a paradox. For whereas the words for the 'supernatural' realm are necessarily borrowed from the realm of our everyday experiences, out of which our familiarity with language arises, once a terminology has been developed for special theological purposes the order can become reversed. We can borrow back the terms from the borrower, again sec-

ularizing to varying degrees the originally secular terms that had been given 'supernatural' connotations" (*The Rhetoric of Religion*, p. 7).

To which Derrida responds, "Sin has been defined often . . . as the inversion of the natural relationship between the soul and the body through passion. Saussure . . . points at the inversion of the natural relationship between speech and writing. It is not a simple analogy: writing, the letter, the sensible inscription, has always been considered by Western tradition as the body and matter external to the spirit, to breath, to speech, and to the *logos*. And the problem of soul and body is no doubt derived from the problem of writing from which it seems—conversely—to borrow its metaphors" (*Of Grammatology*, pp. 34–35).

After a pause, Freire adds, "To exist, humanly, is to *name* the world, to change it. Once named, the world in its turn reappears to the namers as a problem and requires of them a new *naming*. Men are not built in silence, but in word, in work, in action-reflection" (*Pedagogy of the Oppressed*, p. 76).

Momentary consubstantiality, the ultimate goal of all talk, the one many, the many one. In heaven the moment is eternity, but time-doomed creatures live in the illusory Now between Then and Then, stopping psychological time briefly until someone utters the inevitable observative: "But. . . ." And the loom of discourse clacks on, warp and woof of statement and counterstatement.

SCENES AND INTERPRETATIONS

Freire uses "representative anecdotes" often and tellingly. (See Kenneth Burke, *A Grammar of Motives*, pp. 59–61, and Winterowd, "Dramatism in Themes and Poems.") One of these is very much to our point:

In Santiago . . . a group of tenement residents discussed a scene showing a drunken man walking on the street and three young men conversing on the corner. The group participants commented that "the only one there who is productive and useful to his country is the souse who is returning home after working all day for low wages and who is worried about his family because he can't take care of their needs. He is the only worker. He is a decent worker and souse like us." (*Pedagogy of the Oppressed*, p. 111)

Reality is objective enough, Freire tells us, but is meaningless without interpretation and is thus multiple, not single; to translate Freire's viewpoint into Burkean language, we can say that one's attitude toward history results from the dialectic of an agent-scene ratio (*Pedagogy of the Oppressed*, p. 85). The starting point for any educational program must be the existential situation, not only because attitude and scene are in some ways synonymous, but because meaning is scene-bound, context-oriented: ". . . neither language nor thought can exist without a structure to which they refer. In order to communicate effectively, educator and politician must understand the structural conditions in which the thought and language of the people are dialectically framed" (*Pedagogy of the Oppressed*, pp. 85–86).

One lives in a "thematic universe," a web of interlocking concerns that make up what Burke would call attitude, and it is these "generative themes" that form the basis for Freire's pedagogical method, which I will now briefly outline.

The literacy teacher begins with a *generative word*, such as *favela* (slum) and breaks it into syllables: *fa-ve-la*. These syllables in turn generate phonemic groups: *fa-fe-fi-fo-fu*, *va-ve-vi-vo-vu*, *la-le-li-lo-lu*. However, the word *favela* is not presented visually until the group "discusses the problems of housing, food, clothing, health, and education in a slum and . . . further perceives the slum as a problem situation. . . ." Other generative words are presented, and ultimately the group is using its newly acquired knowledge of phonemic combinations to read and then write other words (*Education for Critical Consciousness*, p. 82).

The method involves what might be called *technic* (that is, phonemic instruction) and *rhetoric* (that is, the relationships of words to the thematic universe in which the subjects live), and of the two elements, rhetoric is by far the most important. Technic makes words, but rhetoric makes meanings.

The literacy method leads both to *conscientization* and to *problematization*. Conscientization is the awakening of critical awareness, enabling one to enter into the "eternal dialogue between man and man, between man and the world, between man and his Creator. It is this dialogue which makes of man an historical being" (*Education for Critical Consciousness*, pp. 17–18).

Problematization is basically a theory of education and is opposed to the "'banking' concept of education, in which the scope of action allowed to the students extends only as far as receiving, filing, and storing the deposits" (*Education for Critical Consciousness*, p. 58).

In problem-posing education, the students are not passive recipients of information—or of solutions to already discovered problems—but are active participants in the dialogue through which their own visions of the world change along with those of their teachers.

Underlying banking-education, of course, are the consoling certainties of presence and *logos*, but problem-posing education sucks us into the vortex of indeterminacy. Freire uses even those resonant terms "permanence and change" to characterize the two sorts of education (*Pedagogy of the Oppressed*, p. 72).

Often as I jet here and there, I look below me at the clouds and have the strange, irrational illusion that they are solid stuff; falling out of the plane, I would land on the billowy mass and be saved. But then comes the alternate vision of a terrified plunger clawing at vapor as he passes through the cloud mass toward annihilation. In the last sentence of the following passage—which nicely characterizes problem-posing education—one sees the plummeting Paulo clawing at the milky billows of *logos*.

The problem-posing method does not dichotomize the activity of the teacher-student: he is not "cognitive" at one point and "narrative" at another. He is always "cognitive," whether preparing a project or engaging in dialogue with the students. He does not regard cognizable objects as his private property, but as the object of reflection by himself and the students. In this way, the problem-posing educator constantly re-forms his reflections in the reflection of the students. The students—no longer docile listeners—are now critical co-investigators in dialogue with the teacher. The teacher presents the material to the students for their consideration, and re-considers his earlier considerations as the students express their own. The role of the problem-posing educator is to create, together

with the students, the conditions under which knowledge at the level of the *doxa* is superseded by true knowledge, at the level of the *logos* (*Pedagogy of the Oppressed*, p. 68).

PAULO FREIRE AS KENNETH BURKE

It is fair to say that Freire is a tacitly dramatistic thinker, but that would probably be the case with any social philosopher-theorist who was not adamantly scientistic, since drama is not accidentally related to the human situation and hence provides a rich analytic terminology. In one sense, then, we could make a dramatistic translation of everyone from Malainowski through Margaret Mead to Irving Goffman (and would undoubtedly be rewarded for having done so). On the other hand, such a translation is only to say that we take dramatism to be the optimum terminological screen.

Freire is, however, more than "generally" Burkean, though his dramatism is, to be sure, tacit. For example, the Pentadic ratios in Freire's work are so obvious as to seem derivative. Here, for example, we see the agent-scene dialectic:

The point of departure of the movement [problem-posing education] lies in men themselves. But since men do not exist apart from the world, apart from reality, the movement must begin with the men-world relationship. Accordingly, the point of departure must always be with men in the "here and now," which constitutes the situation in which they intervene. Only by starting from this situation—which determines their perception of it—can they begin to move. (*Pedagogy of the Oppressed*, pp. 72–73)

And, of course, the agent-agency ratio is a motif throughout the works.

Anyone who has read Freire must surely perceive the dramatistic bent, but Freire is unwittingly Burkean in other, more specific ways.

Burke draws his marvelously paradoxical formulation of "trained incapacity" from Thorstein Veblen (*Permanence and Change*, pp. 7–9). Whatever his source, Freire develops the notion, positing that "massification" through mass production "while simplifying man's sphere of participation . . . simultaneously distorts this amplification by reducing man's critical capacity through exaggerated specialization" (*Education for Critical Consciousness*, p. 34). In a sense, then, we have Burke, Freire, and Derrida at a point of agreement: specialization as opposed to *bricolage* is incapacitating (*Of Grammatology*, pp. 74–93). And this viewpoint leads directly to the anti-scientism which runs throughout the thinking of Burke and Freire. Denis Goulet delineates the case when he says that

> Problematization is the antithesis of the technocrat's "problem-solving" stance. In the latter approach, an expert takes some distance [*sic*] from reality, analyzes it into component parts, devises means for solving difficulties in the most efficient way, and then dictates a strategy or policy. (*Education for Critical Consciousness*, p. ix)

But problem-posing is a group endeavor, calling on the skills of bricoleurs to change the relationship with society and nature.

In the Freirian philosophy and methodology, of course, persuasion gives way to identification, with the ultimate goal of consubstantiality, which is the essence of dramatistic argument. Conversion brings about rebirth and comradeship, through which "the converts understand their [the oppressed's] characteristic ways of living and behaving . . ." (*Pedagogy of the Oppressed*, p. 47).

In short, Burke and Freire are very near one another in their philosophy and theory; in spirit and attitude, they are nearly consubstantial. You and I would enjoy the companionship of both, as I have, upon occasion, enjoyed the companionship of Burke.

ADIEU, JACQUES

In this paper, I have attempted to show that Jacques, Kenneth, and Paulo share certain crucial views toward knowledge and knowing. I have also argued (perhaps too feebly) that knowing post-structuralist doctrine is like original sin: it forever bans you from the innocent garden in which a book could be definitive and text could say what it had to say, so many things in an almost equal number of words.

The signal difference among Burke, Freire, and Derrida is just this: Burke and Freire are overwhelmingly concerned with consequences in the real world, where literature can be equipment for living and literacy can be revolutionary— where rhetoric is the best hope for peace and understanding. Derrida is unsoiled by rhetoric of this demotic sort; he is more concerned, one thinks, with elegant argumentation than with effective persuasion, and as a result, one senses that he would be taken as the fool outside extraordinarily precious learned circles. Perhaps I'm being unfair to Derrida and overly charitable to Burke and Freire, but I think that the latter two have that fatal touch of humanity which always makes them think of consequences in and relationships with the world of everyday life. Derrida, one senses, plays the game for the fun of it, out of competitive spirit, but without enormous commitment to others—and I base this judgment on his mode of presentation, not on his substance.

Let's go back to the bar, then. But not a fancy bar in the lobby of a Westin hotel, mind you, rather one around the corner, on a side street, where fellowship prevails and pool is played and the music is largely country and western. I'm quite at home, and hope that you are. But notice: Jacques hasn't joined us.

REFERENCES

Burke, Kenneth. *A Grammar of Motives*. Berkeley: University of California Press, 1969 [1945].

———. *Permanence and Change*. Los Altos, Calif.: Hermes Publications, 1954 [1935].

———. *The Philosophy of Literary Form*. New York: Random House, 1961 [1941].

———. *The Rhetoric of Religion*. Boston: Beacon Press, 1961.

Derrida, Jacques. *Of Grammatology*. Trans. Gayatri Chakravorty Spivak. Baltimore: The Johns Hopkins University Press, 1974.

Freire, Paulo. *Education for Critical Consciousness*. Trans. Myra Bergman Ramos. New York: Continuum, 1981 [1973].

———. *Pedagogy of the Oppressed*. Trans. Myra Bergman Ramos. New York: Continuum, 1982 [1970].

Rosenblatt, Louise M. *Literature as Exploration*. New York: Noble and Noble Publishers, 1976 [1938].

Tompkins, Jane P., ed. *Reader-Response Criticism*. Baltimore: The Johns Hopkins University Press, 1980.

Winterowd, W. Ross. "Post-Structuralism and Composition." *Pre/Text* 4:1 (Spring 1983), 79–92.

———. "Dramatism in Themes and Poems." *College English*, 45:6 (Oct. 1983), 581–88.

Teaching Composing across the Curriculum

This paper is aimed at writing teachers who are not specialists in composition/rhetoric, and yet the discussion systematically lays out basic principles that are worth the consideration of "our gang"—all in one place and all at once. Insofar as the paper is for compositionists, then, it is a distillation (an "alembication," to use one of Kenneth Burke's favorite terms) of basic principles, some of which are so fundamental as, perhaps, to have escaped our awareness. For example, the essay starts with the statement that *inscribing* and *writing* are different activities and that one can write without inscribing.

A major problem with writing across the curriculum is the belief held by our colleagues in other disciplines that they need some kind of arcane knowledge to teach writing and that, anyway, to get involved is to commit oneself to tedious hours of paper "correction." The essay makes the point that an intelligent, literate person can become an effective writing teacher without extensive training and that to do so does not commit one to weekends hunched over a pile of themes, red pencil firmly in hand.

INSCRIBING AND WRITING

We *inscribe* with our fists and fingers, but we *write* with our minds. Milton *wrote Paradise Lost*; his daughters *inscribed* it for him. We view writing as a means of communication, but it is just as surely an instrument of thought; not only the "wordy" fields such as history and philosophy, but also the "exact" sciences, mathematics and physics, for example, use written natural language, as well as specialized metalanguages, in their development and dissemination.

Metalanguages such as calculus and PL/I are enormously useful, even essential, in dealing with problems that can be well defined (e.g., desired rocket trajectories), but are useless, except to provide evidence and example, when questions cannot be well defined (e.g., an investigation of the writing process) or when the issue involves "ought" or "ought not."

This essay appeared originally in *The Writing Instructor* (Winter/Spring 1982). Reprinted by permission.

TRANSFERABLE AND LOCAL
ABILITIES

Since all fields deal with questions that cannot be defined precisely enough for a metalanguage to provide answers, and since "ought" and "ought not"—in Kenneth Burke's terms, "the hortatory negative"—pervade all actions, the problem of composition is transdisciplinary: writing as a means of communication and as an instrument of thought.

Writing abilities are either "transferable" or "local" as I claim in the article *Transferable and Local Writing Skills* in the Spring 1980 *Journal of Advanced Composition*. This is an obvious proposition that has enormous importance for composition.

A transferable ability is a "universal," a skill that can be useful or essential in any writing situation. For example, the ability to write maximally readable or "accessible" prose is one of those universals. And we can take accessibility as *one* case in point for a responsibility of composition across the curriculum, only *one* case among many, but especially appropriate as an example.

Depending on the situation, we want our students to be able to write either a maximally accessible version of a sentence or a minimally accessible version or something in between. In other words, we want to teach our students stylistic virtuosity. "Sentence combining" texts such as Donald Daiker's *The Writer's Options* (NY: Harper and Row, 1979) and Rippon and Meyers' *Combining Sentences* (NY: Harcourt Brace Jovanovich, 1979) are intended to aid the stylistic virtuosity of students. Here are examples of a less readable and then a more readable version of a sentence:

1. That Bill claimed that Bert said that Bob is insane is odd.
2. It is odd that Bill claimed that Bert said that Bob is insane.

If 2 is indeed more readable than 1, why should we want students to be able to produce 1? In context, the motive for a relatively opaque sentence—the "semantic intention" behind it—may well be completely justified. We know, for instance, that "noise" demands increased concentration and attention; thus, a "noisy" sentence within a "quiet" passage will force the reader to focus attention. Relative unreadability, then, is a rhetorical device that can help readers grasp the saliency of points. (If most of a text is noisy, then a lucid sentence becomes cognitively italicized.)

In any case, this kind of stylistic versatility applies to writing not just in one field, but in most. To be sure, our main obligation is to help students develop the skill of expressing their ideas in lucid prose.

Like accessibility, the other transferable skills that we want our students to acquire are also context-sensitive, i.e., dependent on purpose and audience.

As for local skills, good examples are the jargon and format requirements of specific fields. A sociologist knows the expectations of readers in sociology much better than the English department compositionist, and thus the sociologist-as-writing-teacher must assume the responsibility for conferring the appropriate local skills on his or her students as the situation demands.

Local skills are seldom much of a problem for writers who have command of the universal, transferable abilities: defining topics, developing ideas, putting these ideas into the structural matrices of sentences and paragraphs, using effective revision strategies, eliminating grammatical/mechanical and punctuation errors—according to audience and purpose.

The act of writing involves expressing *semantic intentions* through a hierarchy of *structures* for an *audience* in a *scene*. As writing teachers, we are concerned with semantic intentions, structures, audiences, scenes.

KNOWING ABOUT AND KNOWING HOW TO

It was a remarkable experience to watch Gregor Piatagorsky, that great lovable bear of a musical genius, teach one of his master classes. So much happened, and so little was said. An aspiring young cellist—gifted and obviously temperamental—suddenly stopped in despair as he was demonstrating a passage: "Maestro, Maestro! I don't know what's wrong. This passage always moves too fast."

Piatagorsky looked at him with the utmost patience and said, "Vell den, play slower."

The student, heartened by this profound advice, reapplied his bow and, apparently to everyone's satisfaction, played the selection through to its conclusion.

No one doubts that Piatagorsky knew *how to* play the cello very well, indeed miraculously, but how much did he know *about* how to play the cello? And how much of that knowing about could he put into words?

It is an enormous mistake to overestimate the sort of conscious knowledge that we can explain in words. In fact, in *The Origin of Consciousness in the Breakdown of the Bicameral Mind* (Boston: Houghton Mifflin, 1976), Julian Jaynes has demonstrated that consciousness is not necessary for many kinds of learning, and in particular he says that when you learn complex skills

Consciousness takes you into the task, giving you the goal to be reached. But from then on, apart perhaps from fleeting neurotic concerns about your abilities at such tasks, it is as if the learning is done for you. (P. 33)

Granted, Jaynes is talking about such skills as typewriting, but the general point holds for writing ability: if we were conscious that we were learning, our acquisition of the great transferable skills would be impeded.

The how-to knowledge of good writers is overwhelmingly, to use Polanyi's term, *tacit*, that is, knowledge that we don't know we have: some of it can be brought to the conscious level, some can't.

"LEARNING" LANGUAGE SKILLS

The following story is true in essence. In Plato's sense, it is not "boorish wisdom," sticking to the facts merely for the sake of the facts, but it is artfully contrived to get at a real truth. (No less an authority than Aristotle tells us that fiction is truer than history, for the poet can deal with general verities, whereas the historian must stick with the idiosyncratic particulars of events.)

A bride—call her Norma—arrives in Vienna for a first year of connubial life. Her husband and she, both small-town Westerners, must cope: find the railroad station (and the proper WC within the station), shop for food, carry on at least minimal social dialogue (*Guten Tag,. Wie geht's? Danke schön. Auf Wiedersehen*), complete everyday language transactions. The husband

the definite article *the* works with all genders and cases of the noun, but in German the article varies according to gender, number, and case. Thus, to use the definite article properly, you must learn the following paradigm:

	Masc.	Fem.	Neut.	Plur.
Subjective	der	die	das	die
Genitive	des	der	des	der
Dative	dem	der	dem	den
Objective	den	die	das	die

has studied German in college, but the bride is monolingual.

Within the first few days of her advent in Vienna, Norma is functioning admirably: she can order *Wurst, Kaše,* and *Brötchen* at the *Delikatessen*; with supreme confidence (and some gestures) she can ask for directions to the *Postamt.* She has picked up a good deal of *competence* in German, in much the same way that a young child gains competence in its native language: through listening and then attempting to communicate. (I need not, I think, draw the analogy between reading and listening and writing and talking.)

Very soon, Norma has a magical breakthrough, discovering that German *der* is equivalent to English *the.* What power! Now she can talk about *DER Mann, DER Frau,* and *DER Brot.* But as we all know, pride goeth before a fall, and the sublime moment of hubris is dashed when a helpful Viennese tells her, "*Nein, nein, gnädige Frau: DER Mann, DIE Frau, DAS Brot!*"

In consternation she bursts in upon her all-knowing husband to report the tragedy. Wisely he smiles, carefully lights a Donau cigarette, and patiently explains: "In English,

Then you will be able to say,

DER Mann ist höflich.
Ich kenne die Frâu DES Mannes.
Ich gab DEM Mann einen Küss.
Ich sah DEN Mann.

If you'll memorize this paradigm, and if you know the gender of the noun, then you will be able to use the correct definite article."

Two cups of tea, a wedge of Sacher Torte, a good deal of mumbling— and after an hour, Norma has memorized the paradigm; it is part of her *conscious* knowledge of the German language. Now, if she takes the time and energy to think about the rules, and if she knows the gender of the noun, she can use the definite article correctly.

In a sense, she knows the system of definite articles better than most native speakers of German; she can rattle off the system more readily than they can. However, they can use the proper form without investing conscious attention; they use the language without paying attention to the surface form.

As my colleague Steven Krashen has demonstrated, there are two radically different processes of language "learning." (See "On the Acquisition of Planned Discourses: Written English as a Second Dialect," *Proceedings of the Claremont Reading Conference* [Claremont Calif.: 1978].) By the first process, we *acquire* tacit knowledge that amounts to a competence. By the other, we consciously learn rules and systems that allow us to monitor our usage.

The importance of Krashen's "monitor theory" for teachers of writing will become clear in the next two sections of this paper.

TEACHING "METHODS"

It should be obvious that a writing teacher must know *how to* write, just as a drawing teacher must know how to draw and a violining teacher must know how to violin. The problem is the transfer of this "know-how"—the teaching methods that allow the master to be maximally useful to students, enabling them to acquire without conscious attention to the acquiring and to learn rules and paradigms where necessary (but only where necessary).

The primary teaching method is elegantly simple in theory, but extraordinarily difficult and subtle in application: the teacher must, at appropriate times, give useful responses to the student's writing. ("Maestro, Maestro, this paragraph just doesn't convey my idea!" "Vell den, put in more detail.") And these responses will address the following concerns:

Semantic intention—the writer's purpose; tone (serious, ironic, sarcastic, etc.)

Content—the information in the paper; the validity of the argument's logic

Structure—organization and coherence

Medium—the design of the text (appropriate subheads, helpful italics, listings, and so on)

Style—sentence structure, diction, figurative language; grammar and mechanics

All of these controlled by the writer's sense of audience.

AUDIENCE

A paper that is ideal for one group of readers—or one reader—may be inappropriate or ineffective for another audience; hence, we might say that response to students' texts must always be in terms of ratios—semantic intention: audience, content: audience, and so on.

One learns to respond to texts by watching others do it; through practice, one develops the ability to respond usefully.

"Methods" training sessions would, then, be demonstrations: one-on-one conferences, class discussions led by a Maestro, peer-group discussions, and so on. (For peer discussion to be maximally effective, classes need a bit of training in reader-response methods.)

HANDLING THE PAPER WORK

My sons' grandpa had a sign—hanging in guess which room of his apartment—that read, "The job's not finished until the paper work's done." I introduce the scatological overtones here because, of course, the paper load in composition is the least attractive part of the writing teacher's mission. All of those weekends with all of those papers awaiting the red (green is more traumatic for the student!) squiggles in the margins.

Another group of methods useful to writing teachers is more up-front, amenable to fairly concise formulation and hence directly teachable. For example, students often need help with the problem of problems: how to recognize and formulate them, how to develop ideas concerning them. Heuristics—which are learnable and teachable in the traditional senses—give writers power in those activities that are termed, variously, rhetorical invention or prewriting. Kenneth Burke's Pentad is only one example. (See *A Grammar of Motives* [Berkeley: Univ. of California, 1968]. Winterowd's *The Contemporary Writer*, 2 ed. [NY: Harcourt Brace Jovanovich, 1981] contains many heuristics for writers.) There is also an extremely effective array of methods for teaching style, both fluency and accessibility.

In other words, writing teachers must largely acquire certain methods (for example, the ability to respond productively to student texts), but can learn others (e.g., the "software" of modern stylistics).

In a paper, a student of mine coined a particularly felicitous metaphor: you can't make a cow's purse out of a pig's ear! Granted. But you *can* make a good writing teacher out of a psychologist or a mathematician or even a philosopher, provided that he or she (1) is a competent writer and (2) wants to become a competent writing teacher. How long does this training take? Offhand, I usually say two weeks of intensive preservice and a semester or two of continued inservice. And what is the exact nature of that preservice and inservice? Ah, you'll never know, for

my editors have limited this piece to ten typewritten pages! (But if you're really interested, you might see my essay "Developing a Composition Program," in *Reinventing the Rhetorical Tradition*, eds. Aviva Freedman and Ian Pringle [Conway AR: L&S Books for the Canadian Council of Teachers of English, 1980].)

After all, though, marking papers—catching every lapse, every undotted *i*—has much to recommend it: it keeps writing teachers occupied, it doesn't cost money, and it doesn't cause obesity, cancer, or cirrhosis of the liver as do other, less salubrious after-hour activities. On the other hand, the squiggles don't do students much good.

First, think about the learning theory discussed in this paper. Ideally, writers *acquire* their abilities, including the skill of editing to eliminate mechanical/grammatical errors.

If they have not achieved this acquisition by the time they reach us at the freshman level, then they need to *learn* systematically.

This, it seems to me, is a supremely important, though pretty obvious, point: the features of Edited Standard English—punctuation, verb agreement, pronoun reference, and so on—are systematic, and that being the case, it is more effective to learn the system and then apply it than to correct individual errors and try to build systematic knowledge on this hit-or-miss basis.

Therefore, the writing teacher from whatever department is wasting time as error-hunter and is undoubtedly demoralizing the student in the process. Suppose, for example, that Mr. Jinx uses the comma erratically or not at all. The best cure for the malady is to suggest that he go to the writing lab and learn the *system* of comma punctuation in modern American English.

The writing teacher should deal with semantic intention, structures, style, the concept of audience—not with correcting the final version of the text. In other words, a writing teacher is dealing with writing as the expression of thought, not writing as the subskill of eliminating "surface" errors. Hence, the sociologist and biologist cannot cop out of their responsibility by claiming that they know nothing about "grammar." In the first place, you don't have to be a chicken to recognize an egg, and, in the second place, we are asking them to teach writing, not editing; our writing laboratories will take care of grammar/mechanics and punctuation for the writing teachers.

ADVICE FOR THE NEWLY ENLISTED COMPOSITIONIST

Convince your students that *editing* should be the last process in completing a text.

Here is the logic behind that statement.

We have limited mental capacity for paying attention, just as our visual attention is necessarily circumscribed. If a writer attempts to attend simultaneously to the surface of a text and to the semantic intention that he or she is trying to express, one or the other must get slighted. A student who has learned rather than acquired the system of editing must, of course, invest conscious attention in getting the surface right, with the frequent result that the whole enterprise goes awry: neither the editing nor the content is satisfactory.

Of course, many writers have acquired editing skills and make corrections as they go, using the final pass at the text merely to proofread, catching oversights and lapses.

L'ENVOI

It's pretty grim to be McFidditch, the name that James Sledd applies to those English teachers who spend their lives hunting for errors, struggling eternally through the gritty surface details of texts, never dealing with writing as thinking.

It's a heady business, however, to be a writing teacher, concerned with semantic intention . . . and so on.

ENDPAPER

With a bit of special training, *any* literate faculty member can become an effective teacher of composition.

Knowing How to Write

Simply, a writing teacher must be a writer and should demonstrate this ability to his or her students.

1. "Give-a-Topic": Tell your students that periodically you will give them a topic on which to write in class for fifteen minutes. Conversely, they must be prepared to give you a writing topic. As they compose at their desks, you compose at the blackboard. The result is that students see you as a writer—and you can discuss your successes and failures with them, referring to sentences and paragraphs that you have inscribed on the blackboard.

2. Give your students samples of your writing.

Knowing About Writing

If you know *how* to write, then you know *about* writing, but this "knowing about" is *tacit* knowledge that must be brought into focus before you can use it in teaching. For instance, though your own prose is brilliantly clear, you don't know how you might instruct students to produce equally lucid writing; or you have a sure control of tone without knowing precisely how you create it or even exactly what it is.

Furthermore, as a writing teacher, you are attempting to confer an ability, not a body of knowledge. You are concerned more with process than with product.

Methods

Therefore, the methods that you need will enable you to intervene in the composing process, not merely to judge the finished text. You need effective methods to help students with:

PREWRITING (gathering information, solving problems and even identifying the problematic, getting unique angles of vision on subjects . . .)

WRITING (the process of expressing a *semantic intention* through *structures* to an *audience* in a *scene*—involving sentences, paragraphs, style, tone, organization . . .)

REWRITING (*adding, deleting, rearranging,* or *substituting* words, phrases, sentences, paragraphs . . .)

EDITING (bringing the surface of the text into conformity with Standard Written English: matters such as spelling, verb agreement, punctuation, pronoun reference . . .)

Handling Papers

Both common sense and research indicate that red squiggles in the margins of papers are largely a waste of your time—the kinds of red squiggles that indicate mechanical errors, that is. Students who need to can learn the skills of editing systematically in the writing laboratory.

I recommend the following kinds of responses to papers: single-comment reaction, conference, peer discussion.

The Profession

The Paradox of the Humanities

Since 1975, I have been working with the Huntington Beach Union High School District in the development of a "language-arts" program. During the past four years, my colleagues from Huntington Beach and I have had our share of triumphs— for example, from 1975 to 1977, the district leaped from the seventy-third to the eighty-sixth percentile on the written-expression section of the California Assessment—and a disheartening array of tragedies. Anyway, I want you to know that I have descended from my ivory tower (not a long descent in my case) to mix it up in the real world of public education. My years with the Huntington Beach District have been most rewarding—and most instructive.

While I will spare you the litany in regard to declining SAT scores and John Simon's herculean efforts to purify the corrupted language, I will concede that we are in the midst of a literacy crisis, caused not by the dereliction of MLA types or the ineptitude of public school teachers but by times and tides that perhaps

defy analysis and that are, at any rate, too complex to be handled in a brief paper.

What I would like to talk about is the strange relationship between, on the one hand, the humanities and, on the other, theory, research, and pedagogy in literacy. Since I have much territory to cover, I will be blunt and sketchy, but I hope that my remarks will stimulate thought and discussion.

THE QUESTIONS OF LITERACY

Any field is defined by the questions that it asks and the methods that it uses in the attempt to answer those questions. The central questions of literacy concern process: how it comes about that brain and mind generate intentions and meanings that can result in a BIC's leaving traces on a page (can result, but not necessarily so, for the marks themselves are incidental to the process of writing), and how it comes about that another mind and brain can make sense of those marks. Perhaps

from *ADE Bulletin* (May 1980), copyright 1977 by the Association of Departments of English.

the following is an adequate general statement of the problems of literacy:

Any act of discourse, written or spoken, is the projection of a *semantic intention* through *structures* to an *audience* in a *scene*. Reading is the audience's interpretation of those scene-bound structures to arrive at semantic intention.

Just a bit of exegesis will fill out the problems of literacy from my perspective. The act of writing itself is both mental and (usually) kinesthetic, reflecting cognitive style, (sometimes) neurological problems, and (not so trivially) manual dexterity. The structures are those made possible by language and convention. The audience is always more or less an unknown. And scene involves the immediate circumstances of writing, the possible circumstances of reading, and such factors as the cultural and socioeconomic backgrounds of writer and reader.

Where in academia is the staff that addresses these central questions of literacy? Certainly not in the English department. And not in psychology, linguistics, sociology, or anthropology—though these departments are doing work that is of great interest to students of literacy. In the school of education? In spite of the "humanistic" reflex bias against "educationists," this school might in some ways be the best in an array of not very good bets. Literacy is, in fact, a discipline without a home. And I will restate the obvious: literacy includes *both* reading *and* writing. (I will weaken my case slightly, and reluctantly, by suggesting that you might write the English departments at Michigan State, University of Virginia, and University of Southern California about their literacy programs.)

THE HUMANITIES AND LITERACY

Of all disciplines, the humanities are the most book-bound, and since books are written by writers and read by readers, the humanities should have a deep involvement with literacy. One humanistic question, but only one, concerns the meanings of texts. Other basic questions concern the generation of texts by writers (both the freshman English student and Coleridge) and their reconstruction by readers (both the second grader and Stanley Fish). To limit humanistic questions to those concerning products is to impoverish the humanities.

Another angle of attack. Any critical theory is by definition a theory of reading. Since many critics have not conceived of their work thus, they (1) have either overlooked or ignored a great body of scholarship and theory that could be of immense value to them and (2) have tended to spin out reading after reading of given texts, on the tacit assumption that finally one reading (theirs) would be definitive and thus "correct" and "true." Furthermore, any question regarding a reading of a text can be dealt with in one or both of two ways: rationalistically and empirically. To ignore the psychology of reading is to foreclose the possibility of dealing empirically with questions that demand empirical answers.

One brief example. The work of literature is not the marks on the page but the mental representation that those marks enable. Once a reader has gained a meaning, the marks are things of the past—recoverable, but only to be lost once again in the refinement of meaning. In other words, meaning lives in memory, not on the page. The literary critic, then, should be interested in one of the most basic questions of literacy, the representation of meaning in memory. As a matter of fact, both the literary critic Northrop Frye (e.g., "Myth, Fiction, and Displacement," in his *Fables of Identity* [New York: Harcourt, 1963]) and the psychologist Walter Kintsch (*The Representation of Meaning in Memory* [New York: Wiley, 1974]) have addressed that problem. Frye's approach was rationalistic, Kintsch's was empirical. No law should force us to choose one method over the other, but common sense tells us that we should look at both.

Continuing in my simple vein, I think that most of you would agree that the rock-bottom value of the humanities is what they do for people; otherwise, the massive effort of the humanities—so well represented by the MLA—is crewelwork, an elegant pastime that allows faculties to earn a living and indulge themselves in . . . nothingness. But then, if my assumption is correct, humanists are constrained to pay attention to literacy and pedagogy; books are for people, else they are for nothing. Literary studies, literacy, pedagogy—I ask that you determine the ratios among them in your departments and in the MLA. And I further ask: Are questions about literacy and pedagogy inherently less complex and challenging than questions concerning the literary text? (Of course, different strokes for different folks, but I should come clean: I personally find the current issue of *Research in the Teaching of English* much more interesting than the cur-

rent issue of *PMLA*. No invidiousness intended here.)

Paradoxically, English departments are the custodians *and* the beneficiaries of literacy; freshman writing courses and undergraduate introductions to literature support the whole mighty enterprise. English departments train English teachers. English teachers teach reading and writing.

And I can assure you of this: regardless of how skilled English teachers may be in explicating texts or introducing high school sophomores to literature, with a few notable exceptions they know absolutely nothing about literacy.

I ask that you discount the following statement—chalk it up to the smugly righteous fervor of a man whose career went awry (from literature to literacy) and who has been suffering the consequent scorn during most of his professional life. The MLA has discovered literacy (and no one should carp about such serendipity). The association stirs its massive thighs and gives birth to a hydrocephalic runt, the Division on the Teaching of Writing. My gripe here has to do with perspective and priority. As the MLA itself knows, philosophy, theory, and research must precede, or be concurrent with (in both the temporal and logical senses), application, and that is precisely the accomplishment of the organization in the field of literature: the viewing of literature as a subject matter worthy of rigorous study, amenable to theoretical formulation, subject to the tests of scholarship. Suppose that the MLA were the ATL, the Association for the Teaching of Literature: almost certainly an MLA would have been an offspring or a splintering off.

For historical reasons, the humanities have placed a high value on literary scholarship and a low value on any work in literacy.

RESULTS

The strange and lugubrious situation that I have been outlining has resulted in numerous disasters, minor and major, the most obvious being humanities graduates' inability to get jobs. (In my opinion, taking a Ph.D. is the world's worst hobby!) No jobs, falling enrollments. Falling enrollments—and my God! no one shows up for the seminar that I have spent all these years preparing, and I'm forced to teach one or two or more freshman sections, thus displacing a graduate assistant who might, next year, have elected to take my seminar had we not deprived that student of the financial means to continue in graduate school. And this *is* a vicious circle. (One hears various reactions to the situation. One chairperson was elated, for now, he said, students would pursue degrees for the right reason: sheer love of knowledge. Another told me that the quality of graduate students in his department had risen; bright middle-aged faculty wives are being accepted as doctoral students, and they really don't need to sweat the job market.)

But another, less obvious result intrigues me.

Scholars in education, psychology, linguistics, anthropology, and other fields outside the humanities are doing much of the work in composition, the vast bulk of the work in reading, and a significant portion of the work in pedagogy. As a result, and quite naturally, theoretical and practical work in these fields does not strongly reflect those values that

humanists cherish most dearly. For example, if one looks at a book such as Gibson and Levin's *The Psychology of Reading*—a very good book indeed, one that any humanist would find interesting and valuable—one comes away with the feeling that poems and stories are somehow outside the scope of literacy, that the purpose of reading is the gathering of information and the reduction of uncertainty and nothing more.

By default, then, the humanists are undermining those values that they subscribe to: imaginative experience, the freedom implied in the ambiguous text, and—if you'll forgive me—beauty. Not to mention literature as an important kind of knowledge. I would strongly argue that the more powerful the work in literacy becomes, the more it will tend to undermine the humanities simply by its failure to proceed within the frame of reference and value system of that field.

If I were a major publisher with two or three million dollars to spend on the development of a literature program for slow readers (and there are major publishers with millions of dollars), hoping that the books would sell tens of millions of copies (and such books do rather frequently sell in such quantities), and if my major, if not my only, concern were receiving the maximum return on my investment (and I understand that commercial publishers do hanker to make money), I would, I am afraid, not go to the most renowned English department in the greatest university in America (choose whichever you like) for guidance but would turn to the reading experts, virtually none of whom is in an English department (Alan Hollingsworth being a noble and notable exception), and let them guide my construction of the books. The result would, I assure you (for I am privy to certain developments in the publishing world), make you wince. I am convinced that there is good and great literature that is accessible to the slowest reader—for example, the traditional stories in a newly found book from my childhood, *New Found Tales*, drawn from all nations and tribes. But reading these "simple" tales demands skills that the reading experts seem to ignore and other skills that the literary establishment chooses to ignore. (In its crudest terms, the problem involves both decoding and interpretation. While the reading experts are big on decoding and the humanists are high on interpretation, Johnny and Joan in central Los Angeles gain their introduction to the world of literature through excerpts from *Boy's Life* and *Miss Teen America*.)

Oh boy! What a mess. And in the meantime the humanities and the MLA rattle on their way in a cloud of literary logomachy.

But you see, I had resolved when I first began to write this piece that I would be rational, cool, reasonable, calm, collected. Well, I have become unreasonable, perturbed, discombobulated, but every reader must admit certainly that I have brilliantly maintained my rationality.

RECOMMENDATIONS

So what should we be doing? What is our responsibility to public education? Simply this: We should concern ourselves with reading and writing (and the pedagogy thereof)—a principle that gets us out where we began, for, as I said, stories and poems and plays, like textbooks and newspapers and sets of instructions, are written by writers and read by readers.

Getting It Together in the English Department

Until very recently, the English department rhetorician has lived in the ghetto. The teacher of writing was:

- a graduate student supporting him- or herself by teaching a couple of sections of comp
- a young Ph.D. who somewhat reluctantly went through the purgatory of composition as a necessary purification for the Paradise of upper-division and graduate literature courses

The director of composition was most often:

- again a young Ph.D. willing to do *any* service for the department in order to get tenure and, thus, move toward his or her real commitment and real love, the literature class
- the tenured faculty member gone slightly to seed who had to do something—anything—to earn his or her keep in the department

The state of rhetorical scholarship was lugubrious. Even though some-

This essay is reprinted by permission of the Modern Language Association of America from *ADE Bulletin* (Nov. 1977), copyright 1977 by the Association of Departments of English.

times dull and trivial, the articles in *PMLA* were normally intelligent and respectable in a scholarly sense. The rhetoric-composition journals, such as *CCC*, were filled with:

- essays about how best to teach poem X to a bunch of recalcitrant freshmen on Monday morning
- endless logomachy about concerns of the surface features of Edited Standard English
- inspirational pieces about the humanistic mission of the expository essay, the research paper, etc.
- an endless string of pedagogical tips: teaching without teachers; teaching with tape recorders; teaching with or without writing; teaching writing through immersion in TV game shows; teaching games through immersion in writing; infinite variations on the touchy-smelly-looky-listeny-writey model
- a whole bunch of fascinating pieces on plagiarism

In other words, the state of the rhetoric side of the profession was dismal.

Think of two values: commitment and authority. The English department commitment was to literature.

The authority of the English department was in literature. The English departments that I have known (until very recently) have not been departments of English, but departments of literature. As I hope to point out, the consequences of this singlemindedness have been bad for the departments *and* for literature.

Now think about this paradox, for which I will use my own institution as the specific example. We have a massive composition program—not, certainly, as large as some, but huge nevertheless. We run about 180 sections of freshman composition, serving something like 3,600 students (each of whom currently pays $432 to take the class). We employ 75 or 80 graduate teaching assistants to teach these classes, and our total *active* graduate enrollment is something over 100. In other words, any way you look at it, the freshman program is the foundation for the department.

Teaching assistants support the undergraduate major and the graduate programs in literature. That is a fact at USC and at a great many institutions. The graduate faculty, pursuing literary studies with commitment, authority, and excellence, needs freshman English—much more, I am afraid, than freshman English needs the graduate faculty.

Suppose that Professor X, having lived his life to teach that seminar in Skelton, were to confront an empty room at the beginning of the semester! A lifetime's preparation and nobody shows up. But graduate teaching assistants will show up. They will also, I might add, cling to their assistantships year after year, through poverty and degradation, realizing that their chances of finishing the degree are not very good and

realizing even more paradoxically that if they do finish the degree, their chances of landing a job aren't good at all. Well, that's a subject for another paper, or for a melancholy conversation over sherry some afternoon. (If no one showed up for *my* English 612, *I* would not be destroyed. But ah! how much poorer the world would be.)

It is obvious that I do not understand the particular madness of the English department: composition is our sustenance, but virtually all of our commitment and authority are devoted to literature.

Commitment and authority. Those words are resonant for me. If a person is committed to a job or to a discipline, he will pursue it with intense passion. Authority is gained by knowing the field. The people we admire in English departments do their jobs in literature with commitment and authority. As I have pointed out, the *departmental* commitment to composition is secondary, expedient, subservient. And I don't want to be monomaniacal on this point, but I must ask, "Who in the profession speaks with authority about composition-rhetoric?"

The situation—which, as I shall point out, is changing—was brought about largely by the isolation that the English department willfully imposed upon itself and that history imposed on the department.

I am going to drop the term "composition" and speak of "rhetoric," the discipline underlying composition, the discipline of which composition is a branch.

There were no bad guys, I suppose. There were the objectivists—the New Critics—to whom we owe so much and whom we must admire since they taught most of us how to read literature. However, objective criticism is particularly antirhetorical in its thrust, a point which is of great interest to me.

In the first chapter of *The Mirror and the Lamp*, Abrams briefly and brilliantly outlines the major "schools" of criticism. Since our presuppositions for the study of literature largely determine how departments of English will develop in their commitment and in their authority, I would like to review Abrams' schema, and for the sake of brevity, I will do it in shorthand form:

1. Mimetic
Typical questions: What is the truth value of the work? How does the work square with reality?
The mimetic ratio: poem-reality.
2. Expressive
Typical questions: What sort of

ontological status of the poem?
Objective ratio: poem-poem.

What I am doing here—somewhat unfairly, to be sure—is illustrating that the "schools" as Abrams outlines them are reductive, in that no single school views the poem as a language transaction involving poet-meaning-structure-language-reader. Note particularly the ratios I have invented. Of course, my poem-poem ratio for objectivism borders on the invidious. Nonetheless, I will stick with my model, qualifying it by stating that it is a model to be used for whatever value it might have and then discarded.

One more gimmicky but nonetheless useful point. Note that rhetoric, as opposed to the "schools" of criticism, is holistic and, in effect, embraces them all. Again, I can make my point diagrammatically:

Schools *of* *Criticism*		*Corresponding* *Departments* *of Rhetoric*
	Invention	
Mimetic	Logos (appeals to reason)	
Expressive	Ethos (arguments based on character of speaker)	
Pragmatic	Pathos (arguments based on nature of audience)	
Objective	*Arrangement and style*	

person is the poet? How does the poet illuminate reality?
The expressive ratio: poem-poet.
3. Pragmatic
Typical questions: What is the effect of the poem on the reader? What results does the poem have in the world?
Pragmatic ratio: poem-reader.
4. Objective
Typical questions: What is the structure of the poem? What is the

My point is simple enough. Rhetorical criticism, which is in no sense merely pragmatic criticism, is more likely to bring us to an understanding of a literary text than is "pure" criticism based on any of the "schools." And this is a point that Kenneth Burke, I. A. Richards, and Wayne Booth, among others, have been making for some years now.

But what I'd like to get at is the point that, for historical reasons which are interesting but complex, rhetoric was banished from the English department and supplanted by composition, thus bringing about the major schism between the two camps, the literature people and the comp people, and devaluing rhetoric, taking from it departmental commitment and authority. As all of us are well aware, rhetoric escaped to the speech department, and that's another unhappy story.

Of course, in our solipsistic single-mindedness, we gave up not only rhetoric; linguistics first moved to a suite of offices down in the basement and then, as a separate department, into clean, pleasant offices in a building across the street.

And reading—that, in my opinion, is a real tragedy. Someone donated five million dollars to build an edifice for the school of education, and the whole seventh floor was given to reading, hovered over paternalistically by the spirit of B. F. Skinner. (A true story: A young man taking a Ph.D. in reading was experimenting to determine if money would serve as an efficient proximate reward for remedial reading students. When I asked him how his experiment was coming along, he told me that he had encountered a major problem: his wife had lost her job, and thus he was having trouble raising money to carry on his dissertation research.)

If the English department were *only* a department of literature all of this would not constitute such a grim situation.

Let me go on to discuss a bit further the madness of turning reading over to—well, to anyone but the English department. We believe, sincerely and I hope justly, that literature is the central experience in the humanities, the humanizer *par excellence*. Of course, we are more than a little elitist in this belief, but justifiably so I think. Now, literature comes in books, and books must be read; therefore, it is the business of the English department to teach reading. What happens when reading escapes the English department is this: reading is viewed *only* as the efficient processing of a text for information; it becomes only a skill (which, to be sure, it is in part), not an imaginative, fundamentally humane experience. In other words, I sincerely believe that the teaching of reading—the best of it and the worst of it, and some of it is very good indeed—tends to undermine the exact values that we in English departments cherish. Anyone who is skeptical about my passion should simply turn to the best work in reading, that by Frank Smith, Kenneth Goodman, George Miller, for instance. I find this body of work infinitely fascinating and useful, but I also find a lopsidedness to it, a distinct bias toward information theory and away from the values that make reading important for us.

By giving up our commitment to reading as a skill, we are undermining those values which give us the moral authority to pursue our lives in our departments.

It seems to me that we have two alternatives, the first of which appalls me. We can begin honestly to advertise ourselves as departments of English literature, letting composition escape into its own divisional status, or we can start to advertise ourselves as departments of reading and writing.

I'd like to play around with the second alternative a bit. Notice that it is not exclusionary. A department of reading and writing would encompass all of the activities that go on currently in English departments, everything that appears in our journals, for everything concerning literature by definition concerns reading. In fact, I think it is crucial that we preserve our successes, and they, by and large, are in the areas of literary scholarship, theory, and interpretation.

Our departments of English—which are actually departments of literature—are, as I have been arguing tangentially, destructively exclusionary. Think, for example, of the genuinely excellent scholarship which never receives the validation of departmental esteem: Janet Emig's monograph on the composing process, Frank O'Hare's study of syntactic fluency, Richard Young and Frank Coen's exciting work with heuristics, Alan Purves's studies of response to literature, Frank Smith's and Kenneth Goodman's revolutionary work in regard to reading, Chaim Perelman's theories of good reasons, Charles Fillmore's case grammar, James Kinneavy's monumental theory of discourse, Frank D'Angelo's speculations concerning the nature of form, and I could go on and on. Paradoxically, all of the studies that I have mentioned have either a direct or a tangential bearing on the study of literature as literature. And why not? I view all of them as parts of rhetoric.

It is a fact, I think, that most departments of English would not value any of this work as highly as a competent but run-of-the-mill essay that found its way into *PMLA*. But that's what I've been saying all along. We are as singleminded in our values as we are in our work—necessarily so.

The department of reading and writing—that title has a ring to it that I like. I think, for instance, of the freshmen I encounter; all of them are alienated from poetry, if not from literature in general. Naturally. The English department is not organized to deal with the concerns of the student who wants to gain skills and perhaps—just perhaps—to receive a bit of guidance toward the good life, which you and I know must include the experience of literature. That is anti-elitist. It implies that the business of the department is doing important things for real people in the real world.

Just a word more about reading. In a rough and ready way, I classify the reading experience as either "ordinary" or "aesthetic." Ordinary reading is efficient, cool, practical, rational; its thrust is to get meaning in the sense of information. Aesthetic reading is something quite different; it is the experience that all of us want to get out of literature and that we want students to learn to get out of literature. A department of literature is quite likely to concentrate on the literary edifice, but a department of reading and writing should concern itself with the experience of reading, both ordinary and aesthetic, for if you're not first an "ordinary" reader, you can never become an aesthetic reader.

As to writing: In the literature department, we stress the literary essay, the junior *PMLA* piece, the atypical response to literature, for *real* readers do not respond to a poem by dashing off an essay concerning it. Not that our newly aligned department would not teach the *PMLA* essay, both junior and senior, not to mention the doctoral dissertation. We would, however, make writing relate more nearly to the real world concerns of real world people. After all, the "uses" of writing are many and varied: simply to "get it out"; to explore, explain, or verify ideas; to construct imaginative worlds; to persuade. How many departments that you know of encourage the exploration of the whole world of writing?

I find having gone this far, that my typewriter is hot. The words seem to spill out effortlessly. This being the case, let me go one (dangerous) step further. Why don't we simply advertise ourselves as departments of *rhetoric*?

The bush that I have been beating around is not so impenetrable after all. I have simply been implying that we need a unifying theoretical basis for activities, because our present theoretical basis has fragmented us. I would like to suggest that rhetoric—as a long intellectual tradition and as a subject renewed in the last couple of decades—provides the unifying theory that we need. It seems to me that history is on our side for such a shift.

Our monolithic professional organization, the MLA, is opening itself up to concerns broader than those it concentrated on in the past. And even *PMLA* is struggling to change. In other words, insofar as English departments take their definition from the MLA, it seems to me that reading and writing will become more prominent because of the credence given them by the association.

And the general public is alarmed. The literacy crisis is a hot issue. Perhaps irrationally, school boards and politicians are looking to English departments for solutions. We have our opportunity if we will take it. And we must take it, for . . .

Our traditional graduates are un-employable. The world can absorb only so many literary scholars. If we become departments of reading and writing, we will be able to survive. We will be providing a valuable, tangible service to the world.

In fact, the doctor of arts movement was doomed, for it provided simply *less* of the same. But we are now seeing major departments realign themselves so that they square better with reality. Graduate programs in rhetoric are running full force at Iowa, Virginia, and USC, and such programs are being instituted at Wayne State and Ohio State. (When it comes to survival, we fuzzy-headed elitist literary gents know where it's at.)

Literary studies have become palpably boring. I see this ennui in the graduate students at USC, and I suspect it is not atypical at other institutions. To write one more paper for one more seminar on one more British or American author. To read one more issue of *PMLA*. To write one more dissertation. When I walk down the hall in the English department I smell it—not smog, but boredom. As a matter of fact, I don't perceive that stifling mustiness when I visit my friends in linguistics. There is, I think, a difference. Consider this image: the monthly meeting of the English Conference, mandatory for graduate students and attended dutifully by most faculty. The guest reads her or his paper in more or less of a drone. Some heads nod dutifully. The paper ends. Two or three or four dutiful questions are asked. And then there is a universal sigh of relief as everyone escapes to the wine and cheese that is the reward.

Rhetorical studies at present are simply more interesting than literary studies.

So how about this? If you haven't bought all of my somber (and I suppose, pompous) moralizing about commitment, authority, and service to humanity—well, just for fun, try rhetoric.

You'll like it.

The Politics of Meaning: Scientism, Literarism, and the New Humanism

So, then, the problem: Deeper realizations were accorded only to the sciences, and there within strict limits. The same methods, the same energies, could not be applied to the deeper questions of existence. It was conceivable, even, that science had drawn all the capacity for deeper realization out of the rest of mankind and monopolized it. This left everyone in a condition of great weakness. In this weakness people did poetry, painting, humanism, fiddle-faddle—idiocy.

—Saul Bellow,
The Dean's December

The meaning of meaning has been a concern of the humanities throughout Western history, and it is currently a preoccupation of social scientists. In effect, two attitudes toward meaning—implying different value systems, goals, and scholarly methods—compete for status in the learned community: as I call them, the "scientismic" and the "literarist." And this competition is not merely a disinterested search for an adequate account of meaning, but is, in fact, like all matters concerning

This essay appeared originally in *Written Communication*, 2:3 (July 1985). Reprinted by permission of Sage Publications, Inc.

language, a political contest, which the humanities are losing.

The question "How do poems mean?" seems benign enough, the sort of problem that literary ladies and gentlemen could discuss among themselves, thus occupying their time harmlessly with an essentially interesting, though inconsequential, pursuit. As I shall argue, however, the methods used to arrive at an answer and the nature of that answer have enormous consequences for the humanities, for education in general, and especially for literacy.

I shall not start at the beginning and work my way through Plato and Aristotle to the New Critics via Sir Philip Sidney, but to set the scene will quote that brilliant poet and irascible critic Yvor Winters (1943):

The theory of literature which I defend . . . is absolutist. I believe that the work of literature, in so far as it is valuable, approximates a real apprehension and communication of a particular kind of objective truth. . . . *The poem is good in so far as it makes a defensible rational statement about a given human experience . . . and at the same time communicates the emotion which ought to be motivated by that rational understanding of that experience.* (P. 11) [Emphasis added.]

Gerald Graff's *Poetic Statement and Critical Dogma* (1970) nicely defines a central issue in the politics of meaning: the position that poetry does not convey what Graff calls "propositional meaning"

tends to reduce poetry to a form of mythotherapy. The typical opposition between propositional and presentational meaning renders the theorist's well-intentioned appeals to the world of objective reality illegitimate and induces him to obscure the distinction between what is true and what is desirable. The separation of poetry and ideas tends to destroy the unity of humanistic knowledge, intensifying the fragmentation which the theory originally set out to repair. (P. 24)

Graff's argument relies on what might now be called the principle of "exophoric reference." The poem, in effect, is a set of instructions "pointing" toward what Kenneth Burke calls "scene," and in following those instructions, the reader constructs a meaning that is partially derived from and hence relates to reality.

Anticipating the current psychological notion that knowledge is dual (some of it "semantic" and some of it "episodic," an important concept that we will discuss in detail hereafter), Graff (p. 27) says that poetry both asserts propositions and dramatizes states of mind; it is meaningful both propositionally and presentationally. It is common, then, to argue that literature conveys two kinds of knowledge.

The "Scientismic" Approach

From the "scientismic" viewpoint, meaning is quantifiable. Work in linguistics and cognitive psychology

has concerned itself with what Graff would call "propositional meaning," and it is this historical fact that constitutes the first part of the argument that I am developing.

Of course, it would be impossible for me to recapitulate all recent work in the psychology of language and cognition, but two prominent and influential researchers and theorists will serve as cases in point.

More than a decade ago, Endel Tulving (1972) proposed that memory has two components, the *semantic* (or "verbal") and the *episodic*. Semantic memory

is a mental thesaurus, organized knowledge a person possesses about words and other verbal symbols, their meaning and referents, about relations among them, and about rules, formulas, and algorithms for the manipulation of these symbols, concepts, and relations. (P. 386)

Episodic memory

a. "receives and stores information about temporally dated episodes or events";

b. also receives and stores temporal-spatial relationships among these events;

c. can store events solely in terms of perceptible properties or attributes;

d. always stores in terms of the event's "autobiographical reference to the already existing contents" of episodic memory. (Pp. 385−86)

For example,

Semantic Knowledge

a. I remember that the chemical formula for common table salt is NaCl.

b. I know that summers are usually quite hot in Katmandu.

c. I know that the name of the month that follows June is July, if we consider them in the order in which they occur in the calendar, or March, if we consider them in alphabetical order.

Episodic Knowledge

a. I remember seeing a flash of light a short while ago, followed by a loud sound a few seconds later.

b. Last year, while on my summer vacation, I met a retired sea captain who knew more jokes than any other person I have ever met.

c. I remember that I have an appointment with a student at 9:30 tomorrow morning. (Tulving, pp. 386–87)

If we do not insist on an absolute binary opposition, the distinction between semantic and episodic knowledge holds up pretty well, it seems to me. The verbal is depersonalized, whereas the episodic is essentially autobiographical and hence personal.

Using Tulving's semantic-episodic distinction, Walter Kintsch (1974) advanced "a propositional theory for the representation of meaning and knowledge in memory," the two bases for which are *word concepts* and *propositions*.

Word concepts are nothing more, in fact, than personal (as opposed to dictionary) definitions of words. These definitions may include sensory information (e.g., as part of the "lexical" entries for colors) or motor programs (e.g., "walk"); however, in the work under discussion Kintsch chooses to ignore all but the semantic component of definitions. Nor are those definitions agglomerations of semantic primitives; they are words, each of which "is thus defined by reference to other words" (p. 10). (Semantic memory also includes categories for which there is no single term—e.g., the cities of Baja California.)

Kintsch argues that semantic knowledge is "much more broadly useful than specific, personal, context-bound experiences" (p. 4). After all, we associate semantic knowledge with "referential" discourse, that mode which explains, explores, and demonstrates ideas, and with persuasion. Semantic memory can generate new knowledge; it is an instrument of conceptualization.

In the semantic base of a text, the word concepts (i.e., lexical items) are ordered in propositions, and a proposition is a predicate with its arguments. Since the general concept, not its details, concerns us, Kintsch's first six examples (p. 13) will suffice to explain the principle. In the parenthetical analyses, the first terms are the predicates; the others are the arguments.

1. John sleeps. (SLEEP, John)
2. Mary bakes a cake. (BAKE, Mary, cake)
3. A robin is a bird. (BIRD, robin)
4. A bird has feathers. (HAVE, bird, feathers)
5. The man is sick. (SICK, man)
6. If Mary trusts John, she is a fool.
   (IF (TRUST, Mary, John), (FOOL, Mary))

To boil Kintsch's argument down to its essence, we understand a text by apprehending the word concepts and their propositional interrelationships.

A subtle transformation has taken place here: the equivocation of the terms "semantic" and "propositional," which have become virtually synonymous though, in fact, a text expressing episodic knowledge (for example, an autobiographical narrative in a diary) could be represented via the schematics of propositional analysis. In effect, Kintsch's move is to view all texts as purveyors only of semantic knowledge. (If your sole tool is a hammer, then you treat everything as if it were a nail.) This gambit, which seems as

much attitudinal as it does methodological, is the obverse of the literary
theory which argues that poetry
does not, to use Graff's term, convey
"propositional" knowledge, that is,
knowledge of the world "out there,"
referential knowledge. (I am completely aware of the terminological
snarl which has unavoidably developed, and hereafter I will do some
untangling. For the moment, I will
simply remind that the basic distinction we are dealing with is that
between "general" and "personal"
knowledge.)

Specifically, Kintsch says, "How is
an idea to be represented? It is suggested here that propositions represent ideas, and that language (or imagery) expresses propositions, and
hence ideas" (p. 5). It is difficult to
imagine how imagery might *express*
propositions though images in
poems must be expressed in language, the *structure* of which is basically propositional. However, the
parentheses are, in effect, a shrug of
the shoulders, and Kintsch thereafter ignores the problem of imagery
(as well as figurative language—
metaphor, irony, and so on).

This discussion of the scientismic
slant on meaning could go on indefi-
nitely—for instance, to the standard
works on reading, such as the admirable bringing together by Gibson
and Levin (1975) of psychological
and linguistic research into the processes of *"extracting information
from text"* (p. 5; emphasis in original) and on to a more recent and excellent mapping of the same territory, *The Psychology of Reading*, by
Taylor and Taylor (1983). (And note
well the language which Gibson and
Levin used in their definition of
"reading.")

In the tradition of Tulving and
Kintsch is a widely criticized and

frequently misunderstood work, *The
Philosophy of Composition* (1977),
by E. D. Hirsch, Jr.

I do not want to appear ungrateful
for a courageous, provocative book,
one that defined important issues
and that developed its argument
with Hirsch's characteristic lucidity
and grace. However, *The Philosophy
of Composition* does exemplify the
scientismic attitude as taken up by
an eminent humanist. In order that
I not misrepresent Hirsch's point, I
shall let him speak for himself:

I infer that there are universal stylistic
features in all good prose of every kind
and that these features of good style are
all reducible to a single principle: One
prose style is better than another when it
communicates the same meanings as the
other does but requires less effort from
the reader. Since this stylistic principle is
tolerant of every conceivable semantic
intention in prose, it does not favor any
single prose style. Intentional elegance,
intentional obscurity, and intentional lucidity are equally governed by the principle. Moreover, the principle itself is
grounded in linguistic history and in
universals of human psychology. (P. 9)

Hirsch calls this unexceptionable
principle "relative readability"—
unexceptionable because a writer
could not possibly *intentionally* be
more obscure, lucid, elegant, or
whatever than he or she intended to
be. Thus, the deliberate choice of,
say, a Faulknerian style is the concern of ethics and rhetoric (if the two
are separable), not of technique. (If
the writer blunders into a given style
because of ineptness or lack of attention, the concern is in the area of
technique.)

In defining the principles of readability, Hirsch sounds very much like
Kintsch—and, in fact, relies to a
great extent on the Kintschian analy-

sis of texts. Hirsch's sophisticated discussion of readability goes back to the two principles of semantic closure and unity. "The clause, then," he says, "is the primary perceptual unit of all languages because it is the minimal unit that has semantic determinacy" (p. 109). For clause, read "proposition," and you have the essence of the principle of semantic closure: because readers can more easily derive propositional content, some versions of sentences are absolutely less difficult to read than other versions of those same sentences. For example, of the following, 1 is more readable than 2:

1. A secretary who is severe, cool, extraordinary, beautiful, pleasant.
2. A severe, cool, extraordinary, beautiful, pleasant secretary. (Hirsch, p. 116)

The reader achieves semantic closure after each adjective in 1, but must hold all of the predicates in short term memory until the final word (the argument) in 2. Schematically, this idea can be represented as follows:

1a. (SEVERE, secretary) (COOL, secretary) (EXTRAORDINARY, secretary) (BEAUTIFUL, secretary) (PLEASANT, secretary)
2a. (SEVERE, ?) (COOL, ?) (EXTRAORDINARY, ?) (BEAUTIFUL, ?) (PLEASANT, secretary)

In the second version, the reader cannot determine who is severe, cool, extraordinary, beautiful, and pleasant until the word "secretary"; this presumably puts a burden on short-term memory.

In order to explain the principle of "unity," Hirsch relies on work by Walter Kintsch, Kozminsky, Streby, McKoon, and Keenan (1975). The main point is this: the more "thematic tags" in a passage, the more difficult it is to read.

Thus, even though the two passages below each contain eight propositions and are virtually identical in length, the "Greek" passage is easier to read because it contains only three thematic tags (Greek, art, and Roman), whereas the "Babylonian" passage contains eight (Babylonian, hill, garden, flower, fountain, pavilion, queen, pleasure)

1. The Greeks loved beautiful art. When the Romans conquered the Greeks, they copied them, and thus learned to create beautiful art. (21 words, 8 propositions)
2. The Babylonians built a beautiful garden on a hill. They planted lovely flowers, constructed fountains and designed a pavilion for the queen's pleasure. (23 words, 8 propositions) (Pp. 126–27)

In order to show that the two passages do indeed express the same number of propositions, Kintsch provided a schematic analysis which it is unnecessary to reproduce here.

Though Hirsch reminds us that his title is ironic, his purpose is deadly serious: to improve the teaching of composition. Hirsch, then, used scientism in the cause of literacy.

In the foregoing discussion, I have not meant to imply that all—or even most—work in cognitive psychology and linguistics relies upon propositional analysis or that all researchers and theorists uncritically accept Tulving's bifurcation of knowledge into semantic and episodic. What I do claim is that the concatenation I have traced—from Tulving to Kintsch to Hirsch—is, to appropriate a term from Kenneth Burke, a valid and productive *representative anecdote*, a way to comprehend the "scientismic" attitude toward meaning and to trace its consequences.

Frank Smith (1983) can sum up for us:

Our perceptions of literacy are narrowed if not distorted by the pervasive tendency, in education as well as in language theory and research, to regard language solely as the means by which information is shunted from one person to another. The model from which I want to escape perceives language as synonymous with communication and communication as the transmission of information, the exchanging of messages like sums of money or bags of oranges. What you get is what you are given. (P. 117)

A CRITIQUE OF "VERBAL KNOWLEDGE"

I would now like to suggest three criticisms of the sharp distinctions between semantic and episodic knowledge. First, episodic knowledge can be and frequently is a tool of conceptualization. Second, language use is always an event, is never abstracted from episodes. Third, the purposes for which discourse modes are employed overlap and are not separate and discrete.

A long rhetorical and linguistic tradition has pointed out, accurately enough, that writing must be more highly contextualized than face-to-face speech. First, a speaker can refer or point to his or her immediate surroundings. Second, speakers can be less specific than writers, for hearers can request more information or ask for clarification. Third, speakers usually share cultural backgrounds with their hearers. But as Tannen (1983) points out, these features characterize spontaneous face-to-face conversation, not planned spoken discourse such as orations or lectures. In such conversations,

the fact of speaking is relatively more important than the content of the message conveyed. That is, what Malinowski calls "phatic communion" is relatively more important than the content of the message conveyed. It is almost a form of talk for talk's sake. In fact, most of what is said in social settings is not new information. (Tannen, p. 81)

On the other hand, expository prose is clearly the model for what linguists and psychologists take to be writing. If the purpose of much spoken discourse is *phatic*—talk for the sake of establishing and maintaining human contact—then certainly the purpose of all exposition is *referential*, as Kinneavy (1971) puts it, "explanatory," "exploratory," and "scientific" discourse to explain, explore, and demonstrate.

The phatic-referential dichotomy is much like that of verbal-episodic knowledge: a convenient fiction that makes some analyses possible. All discourses obviously, however, are both phatic and referential in varying degrees, for no discourse that could be seen or heard would be totally uninformative, and for the discourse to be attended to, it must have some phatic element.

The problem with Tulving's distinction of verbal and episodic knowledge is that the cut is along the wrong biases, causing multiple strands to fray. The stark verbal-episodic distinction discounts *purpose* and *mode* in favor of content, creating (or implying) dichotomies that are untenable.

Exposition is the *mode* most frequently employed for referential purposes, but *narrative* often carries the point.

A man explains his fondness for the island of Saint Martin by recounting a typical day there.

A woman explores her own attitude toward abortion by recounting the experiences of women she knows who have had abortions.

Peter Drucker (1980) recounts a fascinating story that is very much to our point. As a prologue to his tale, Drucker tells us that

There are lots of people with grasshopper minds who can only go from one specific to another—from stockings to buttons, for instance, or from one experiment to another—and never get to the generalization and the concept. They are to be found among scientists as often as among merchants. But I have learned that the mind of the good merchant, as also of good artist or good scientist, works the way [my] Uncle Henry's mind worked. It starts out with the most specific, the most concrete, and then reaches for the generalization. (P. 201)

Such a good mind was that of Charles Kellstadt, retired head of Sears Roebuck, who chaired a U.S. Defense Department advisory board on which Drucker served during Robert McNamara's tenure as Secretary of Defense.

At one meeting, the board was discussing a radical new method of pricing, which impressed everyone—except Kellstadt, who began a seemingly irrelevant tale about problems with the cup sizes of brassieres in the first store he had managed, in Chillicothe, Ohio. Becoming irked at the seemingly irrelevant narrative, an assistant secretary said, "You don't understand, Mr. Kellstadt; I'm talking about concepts." "So am I," replied an indignant Charlie, and he continued.

Ultimately the panelists realized that Kellstadt had demolished the proposal (actually, for pricing the C5-A, one of the sorrier chapters in Defense Department history), showing that the whole scheme was too complex and depended on too many variables.

Leaving the meeting, a fellow member of the board said to Kellstadt, "Charlie, that was a virtuoso performance. But why did you have to drag in the cup sizes of the bras in your bargain basement forty years ago?" A surprised Kellstadt replied, "How else can I see a problem in my mind's eye?"

The sequel is, of course, that the Department of Defense went ahead with the pricing scheme for the Lockheed jumbo jet. Perhaps if Mr. Kellstadt had kept his means of conceptualization to himself, pretending to work by rigorous "logic," propositionally, the taxpayers would have been saved the hundreds of millions that were wasted in producing the C5-A.

The point here is, of course, that what appeared to be "episodic" knowledge to the Whiz Kids was, from another point of view, "verbal" knowledge. Kellstadt, like many writers and thinkers, was using an "episode" as a conceptual pivot, a way of getting at his subject matter. (See Winterowd, 1983.)

The distinctions are not at all easy to draw, and, after all, if you can express Tulving's "episodic" knowledge in prose or poetry, is it not, by very definition, "verbal"? In fact, of the criteria for episodic knowledge (temporal dating, spatial relationships, autobiographical reference, and perceptible properties or attributes), only the last seems to hold up as an absolute differentium. We acquire gustatory, olfactory, tactile, auditory, and visual knowledge without the intervention of words, and this knowledge is extremely difficult to express directly.

Sondra Perl (1983) talks about a writer's "felt sense," a term that she appropriates from the philosopher Eugene Gendlin (1978). As he explains, the felt sense is

the soft underbelly of thought . . . a kind of bodily awareness that . . . can be used as a tool . . . a bodily awareness that . . . encompasses everything you feel and know about a given subject at a given time. . . . It is felt in the body, yet it has meanings. It is body and mind before they are split apart. (Pp. 35, 165)

Perl, who has examined the composing processes of young writers, says that writing topics evoke this felt sense: "What is elicited, then, is not solely the product of a mind but of a mind alive in a living, sensing body" (1979, p. 45).

Another perspective: that of Ricoeur's (1974) distinction between *structure* and *event*. Ricoeur argues that structuralism has been successful in describing its own kind of intelligibility when one can "work on a corpus already constituted, finished, closed, and, in that sense, dead" (p. 79). This very success, however, entails eliminating the texture of events, the dramatistic give-and-take that constitutes language as communication rather than language as structure.

If we think about "pure" verbal knowledge—"The formula for table salt is NaCl"—we realize that an adequate semantic theory will find the underlying "corruption" in words, phrases, and sentences. An account of meaning must, of course, deal with reference, but also with the situation of use and the relationship of the word, sentence, or text to the "larger system of knowledge and belief" of which it is a part. (Miller and Johnson-Laird, 1976, p. 696)

James Boyd White (1983), for example, argues that the difficulty of legal discourse for laypersons is not so much the vocabulary as the "invisible" assumptions that operate in the larger system known as "the law." "Behind the words, that is, are expectations about the ways in which they will be used, expectations that do not find explicit expression anywhere but are part of the legal culture that the surface language simply assumes" (p. 139).

For example, legal rules are often stated as descriptions: "Burglary consists of breaking and entering a dwelling house in the nighttime with intent to commit a felony therein." As soon as the rule enters the discourse of a given case, however, its descriptive nature is replaced by judgment: Is a one-room apartment in the loft of a garage a "dwelling house"? Is the gloaming "nighttime"?

It appears that the legal rule calls for deductive reasoning, much like a rule in geometry; however, such is not the case, for much of the reasoning about the rule involves dialectic and stipulative definition. Furthermore, the result of the complex reasoning that takes place in the law is always a simple binary statement: either such and such is or is not a dwelling house; either such and such an act is breach of contract or it is not. In ordinary discourse, the either-or situations do not prevail, but they are essential in law.

The law provides just one example of "invisible" semantics in a realm of discourse; any domain, class, sect, lodge, calling—in short, any group who are bound by customs, rules, laws, and purposes—

has its own system of invisible semantics.

Verbal knowledge, as viewed by psychologists and linguists, is associated with exposition as a class, reference as a purpose, essay as a genre, structure as a subject for analysis, and denotation as definition.[1]

THE "LITERARIST" APPROACH

The term "scientismic," as opposed to "scientific," is, of course, pejorative, and such is the case with my neologism "literarist" as opposed to "literary." As I have implied, the "scientismic" attitude toward meaning is almost Gradgrindian, or, at the least, "pragmatic," slanted radically toward language as an agency for getting things done and against language as play. After following the scientismic arguments—most of them interesting and informative— one becomes aware that the scientismic consciousness has no place for poems and stories, but is concerned overwhelmingly with *information* and the reduction of uncertainty.

On the other hand, the literarist view privileges "play" and "pure" knowledge while denigrating the "useful" and "applied."

Perhaps the main task of poetics is and always has been to answer the schoolchild question regarding the knowledge conveyed in poetry. ("Well, if Marvell was trying to tell us that life is short and we should enjoy it while we can, why didn't he just come right out and say so?") After all, the *Encyclopedia Americana* is a richer store of certain knowledge than all the literature ever written.

Some years ago, my son, then nine or ten, appealed to my fatherliness and conned me into taking him to a drag race—an experience that I am happy to have had and equally happy to know that I shall not have ever again.

The fragile tubing of the frames, the hulk of the engines in the rear, the oversized tires—those machines, so obviously useless for anything but the sizzling sprints down the track, were mightily impressive to both of us: their drivers in silver asbestos, the roar palpable, almost intolerable, the blue flames spurting from the manifolds.

Tony's teacher had assigned an essay, due the following Monday, and he chose to write on something like "At the Drag Races with Father." However, the piece simply would not come, regardless of how hard he labored. Finally, he asked me for help, and I immediately knew that he didn't want to write an essay at all; he needed to write a poem to convey the meaning that the race had for him. He and I collaborated on he poem, and he found another topic for his essay, a subject about which he could develop a thesis ("topic sentence") to support with evidence and reasoning. His problem could be stated thus: Tony was attempting to convey episodic knowledge with the presentational strategies of the verbal. His experience at the race was not "rational" (or irrational, for that matter); he didn't want to explain or argue in favor of anything. To borrow Graf's terminology, he wanted to use language "presentationally."

Whereas scientismic studies of language are biased in favor of verbal knowledge, literarist studies are heavily slanted toward episodic knowledge of the kind that my son attempted to capture in his poem or that any "poet" attempts to convey. The methods of study tend not to be quantitative—in fact, are biased against this kind of empiricism.

This point seems so obvious that I will not linger over it, but will give an example that underscores the truism that I am advancing.

In *The Act of Reading*, a most worthwhile book, Wolfgang Iser (1978) characterizes what might be called "coherence" thus:

Each sentence correlate contains what one might call a hollow section, which looks forward to the next correlate, and a retrospective section, which answers the expectations of the preceding sentence (now part of the remembered background). Thus every moment of reading is a dialectic of protension and retention, conveying a future horizon yet to be occupied, along with a past (and continually fading) horizon already filled; the wandering viewpoint carves its passage through both at the same time and leaves them to merge together in its wake. (P. 112)

On the other hand, here, adapted from Clark and Clark (1977, pp. 97–98), is a psycholinguistic account of roughly the same phenomena that Iser discusses:

In reading, the given-new strategy allows one to determine what the speaker is referring to. For example,

1. Norma cooked dinner. The dinner was delicious.

It is hardly amazing that readers instantaneously determine the antecedent of "the dinner" in the second sentence, perceiving coherence between the two sentences. On the other hand, the coherence of the following two sentences is not so easily explained:

2. Norma cooked dinner. The turkey was delicious.

Since there was no mention of "turkey" in the first sentence, readers must use their world knowledge to build "bridging assumptions."

Most statements involve this sort of implicature, for speakers or writers could not possibly spell out every detail of their intention.

The formation of bridging assumptions, however, takes time. Haviland and H. Clark (1974) had people read pairs of sentences, one after the other, as in 17 and 18:

17. Mary got some beer out of the car. The beer was warm.
18. Mary got some picnic supplies out of the car. The beer was warm.
In 17, the beer referred to by *the beer* is explicitly mentioned in the first sentence. In 18, however, it must be inferred to be among the picnic supplies. The listener has to draw the implicature in 18:
18. The picnic supplies include some beer.
Building this bridging assumption ought to take time, and it did. People took more time to read and comprehend *The beer was warm* in sequence 18 than in sequence 17. (p. 98)

In order to capture both the tone and the method of scientism, I have quoted from my source, a standard work in psycholinguistics. The differences between the literarist and scientismic works are significant. Iser proceeds rationalistically, developing his ideas metaphorically: the "hollow section" of the sentence correlate; the "future horizon" and a "past (and continually fading) horizon"; "the wandering viewpoint carves its passage through both at the same time and leaves them to merge together in its wake." Iser cites no statistics and refers to no controlled "scientific" studies. Clark and Clark, on the other hand, build on the data of controlled experiments and eschew metaphor; theirs is the dry lucidity of the scientific style.

Literarist studies of meaning, then, have their own style; their object is, of course, literature; and their method is rationalistic, literary, if you will.

LITERARISM IN ACTION

As Hirsch's *The Philosophy of Composition* is an example of scientism in action, so Richard Lanham's *Literacy and the Survival of Humanism* (1983) represents the literarist stance.

The interesting point about these works is that they reach the same conclusion via their different routes: composition, that territory of the literacy enterprise claimed by English departments, boils down to stylistics.

Paradoxically, Lanham bases his argument on sociobiology: the notion that humans are genetically "programmed" for certain kinds of activities—one of which, preeminently, is play and game.

Primates are status animals. Their society is based on it. Emulous striving is at the heart of the leftover evolutionary baggage. People, then, like to play at all kinds of games. And there it was—the *techne* of rhetoric, the range of motive to which Sophists pointed as fundamental to man's nature, the reason why the rhetorical curriculum lasted so long. (P. 7)

The motive for rhetoric, then, is sociobiological and as unavoidable as other drives that humans have inherited from their distant ancestors.

So far, one is willing to live with

the premise even if not overwhelmingly convinced by it—just until we discover Lanham's definition of "rhetoric": "Rhetoric was, had been all along, a genuinely *evolutionary* theory of style—in the last analysis, a theory of behavior" (pp. 7–8).

Lanham's conclusion: *composition is style.*

It is characteristic of a genre—scientismic or literarist—that the premises can be revolutionary if they are developed with the methods and usages of that genre. Thus, Lanham's "post-Darwinian humanism" is less shocking than Hirsch's scientism, for Lanham argues his premises via literary analysis ("The Choice of Utopias: More or Castiglione," "The Chaucerian Biogrammar and the Takeover of Culture"), and when he deals with style, it is in the manner of Iser, not of Kintsch; he is not quantitative or schematically analytical. When humanists read Lanham, they must feel, I think, quite at home.

However, rhetoricians find *Literacy and the Survival of Humanism* disquieting. Stylistics cannot proceed arhetorically, and rhetoric brings with it—to use accepted terminology—all of the problems of invention (logos, ethos, and pathos) and arrangement, as well as style.

In *The Philosophy of Composition*, Hirsch argues that composition "is a craft which cannot properly be subsumed under any conventional subject matter. It is not a branch of literary study, or logic, or even of rhetoric" (140–41). Certainly composition as a practical skill or art is not a branch of rhetorical theory and history; no one, however, would deny that, like all other acts of communication, it is a *use* of rhetoric, and if it is not that, I have no idea what it might be. Thus, to limit composition to stylistics is to deny what we know to be the case, namely, that writing, like other acts of discourse, is the projection of a semantic intention through structures to an audience in a scene and calls upon all of the skills that have been defined since classical times as "rhetoric."

The composition teacher is a rhetorician in just the sense that the cardiologist is a physician. The patent absurdity of these two statements reinforces my point: "I'm a cardiologist, but I'm not a physician." "I teach written communication (i.e., composition), but I know nothing about rhetoric."

When the study of literacy proceeds under the aegis of either scientism or literarism, it is quite likely to get pared down to matters of "code"—that is, stylistics, in one manifestation or another.

THE NEW HUMANISM AND LITERACY

It should be obvious that scientism has a great deal of power and that literarism does not. That is to say, scientism is the more powerful rhetoric for government grants, for school reform, for editorializing, and perhaps even for private fund raising. Just one example of the disparity between scientism and the whole range of the humanities, including literarism: in its 1985 budget, the Reagan administration proposed $125,000,000 for the National Endowment for the Humanities (down from $140 million in 1984) and 15.5 billion dollars for the Department of Education, the most scientismic of all government agencies.

For its 1984 meeting, the American Educational Research Association scheduled 46 sessions dealing with writing alone. A total of 107 papers and other presentations were listed for written composition. AERA is overwhelmingly scientistic and, of course, much more influential in matters of literacy than MLA or NCTE. A representative session from the 1984 meeting concerns "Development of Writing Skill" and includes the following papers: "The Development of Knowledge-dependent and Knowledge-independent Writing Skills"; "Control of the Cohesive Devices in Writing, Grades Two through Six"; "Developmental Contributions of Identity and Similarity Relations to Text Coherence in Children's Written Narratives"; "Information Processing Demand of Plot Construction in Story Writing"; "The Use of Reference in Discourse Tasks: The Role of Language Knowledge in Comprehension, Production, and Revision."

My point certainly is not that such work is "bad"—only that it, like literarism, is lopsided and univocal. AERA is a strange land to literarists, but MLA is just as alien to scientismists.

One more example of the destructive schism that creates scientism on the one hand and literarism on the other. In 1982, Frank Smith organized a conference on preschool children and literacy. Fourteen researchers "with extensive and overlapping backgrounds in anthropology, linguistics, psychology, sociology, and education" (Goelman, Oberg, and Smith, 1984) attended. If these researchers had been discussing merely the "technic" of literacy, perhaps the conference would have been irrelevant to humanists; it is the case, however, that "technic" is less a concern in literacy than the ethical and dramatistic implications of rhetoric. That humanists should have had much to say to their scientismic colleagues is made apparent by Smith's reaction to the conference:

Before the University of Victoria Symposium, I probably would have written that literacy was a universal concern. I probably would also have said that literacy was a universal good and that it was to the advantage of every child to be taught to read and to write. Whatever I might still feel about the value of literacy personally, I can no longer regard the benefit of its acquisition as axiomatic. Rather, the proposition that literacy is desirable and worth the effort of learning has to be argued and defended—especially, perhaps, with the children we so egocentrically expect to follow our example (or our precept) in the development of literate skills and interests. (P. v)

A final quotation from *Awakening to Literacy*, the collection of papers from the University of Victoria conference, is a poignant example of the scientismic attitude toward literacy and its threat to humanism:

Few people would argue with the assertion that the United States is a literate society. Writing and its associated technologies are central to scientific discourse and the organization of industry, government, and education. "Get it in writing" is not merely an adage; it is the accepted legal practice. Literacy also is used extensively by businesses in their dealings with the public. Advertising, product labels, billing systems, directions, and receiving and distributing the family income all make use of written language. In the United States, literacy is an integral part of food gathering, the acquisition and maintenance of shelter and clothing, transportation, entertainment, and other recreational activities. Literacy seems to be involved in many of the essential domains of human activity as they are organized in this society. (Anderson and Stokes, 1984, p. 24)

Iser's *The Act of Reading*, Derrida's *Of Grammatology*, Fish's *Is There a Text in This Class?*—these and other literarist works have had no apparent influence on the course of literacy studies, which have been and remain overwhelmingly scientismic,[2] with the obvious result that exposition takes precedence over poetry, "semantic" knowledge over "episodic," the "useful" over the "esthetic," the straightforward over the eloquent; instructions, reports, arguments—these have greater presence (and hence greater value) in scientistic literacy studies than do poems and stories. Since scientism controls public education, children are learning and will learn to value instructions, reports, arguments—at the expense of poems and stories.

The more powerful scientismic studies of literacy become, the more they will undermine the values ostensibly held by literarists, and this undermining will be reflected in public education, for it is scientismists, not literarists, who influence curriculum, instructional materials, and teacher training; in effect, the success of scientism and the failure of literarism in the study and promulgation of literacy devalues literary literacy.

I have attempted to demonstrate that both scientism and literarism are limited as methods of studying literacy. In fact, I see no epistemic reason for their sharp separation, but trace the schism to the structure of the academy, in which there is no real "place" for the study of literacy. It is puzzling—and, to me, disheartening—that a graduate student entering the American University (Slippery Rock State or Johns Hopkins, University of Utah or Yale) cannot, with rare exceptions such as my own university, undertake a course of study in literacy, i.e., reading and writing and all that those intellectual skills and cultural accomplishments entail.

In the modern university, the English department, and others in the Humanities, do their kind of literarist theorizing about the nature of reading and, to a much lesser extent, about the nature of writing while the linguists, educationists, psychologists, and anthropologists go about their powerful scientism, but in none of the departments is literacy a field of study; it has no home in either the social sciences or the humanities, though one begins to notice that halfway houses are springing up in departments of education and linguistics.

English departments, which are home base for most literarists, have begun to make considerable noise about composition and have even started "composition" strands in their graduate curricula. Symptomatic of the strange situation is the MLA's discovery of composition. "The association stirs its massive thighs and gives birth to a hydrocephalic runt, the Division on the Teaching of Writing" (Winterowd, 1980, p. 2).

The fallacies of departmental and MLA efforts to "get into" composition (from whatever motives) are three.

First, teaching, one application of knowledge, should result from theory and philosophy. As I said in the essay quoted above,

As the MLA itself knows, philosophy, theory, and research must precede, or be concurrent with (in both the temporal and logical senses), application and that is precisely the accomplishment of the organization in the field of literature: the

viewing of literature as a subject matter worthy of rigorous study, amenable to theoretical formulation, subject to the tests of scholarship. Suppose that the MLA were ATL, the Association for the Teaching of Literature: almost certainly an MLA would have been an offspring or a splintering off. (P. 2)

Second, it is unreasonable to deal with writing without also taking reading into account. Reading and writing are not, of course, mirror images of one another, but it is truistic to say that they are interdependent. Thus, one wishes that departments of English and the MLA had turned their attention to literacy, rather than to composition exclusively.

Third, literacy studies demand the methods of both the social sciences and the humanities, depending on the questions to be answered; thus, humanistic scholarship must expand, but in the expansion, it will gain the political power that it now so sadly lacks.

The shape of the new humanities, at least in English departments, is fairly clear to me. In the first place, we should teach literature as a component—in my opinion, the most important component—of a liberal education: not literature for specialists, but literature as what Kenneth Burke calls "equipment for living." Second, we should teach writing, both "creative" and the other, more utilitarian varieties.

These first two components of the new humanities are, of course, already pretty standard in most departments. It is the next alignment that I consider both revolutionary and necessary.

Rhetoric would be reestablished as a guiding discipline for humanities studies, and the major components of rhetoric are literary theory and literacy, since every literary theory is at least tacitly a theory of how texts mean and assume value for communities of readers and since literacy theory and research cannot limit themselves to technique, "the mechanics" of reading and writing, but must deal with exactly the same questions as literary theory, namely, how texts mean and assume value for communities of readers and also with the processes whereby texts are generated by writers and interpreted by readers (texts, that is, as "sets of instructions" through which meanings can be derived).

Times are propitious for a rapprochement of scientism and literarism under the aegis of rhetoric, forming, thus, a new humanism. Via their own routes, scientismists and literarists are reaching the same conclusions about the nature of texts (and indeed logos and "presence," though the scientismists do not use those terms). For example, in the following, Kintsch (1974) is downright "post-structuralist," a psychologist-Derrida:

In principle, a text T may be derived from a base structure S (for speaker) and may yield as a result of comprehension by two listeners the base structures L_1 and L_2 with $S \neq L_1 \neq L_2$. The differences may be due to omissions on the part of the listeners or misinterpretations, but there may also be more subtle differences: The tokens in L_1 and L_2 may be alike, but the word concepts to which they refer may differ in significant ways. Finally, the possibility must be considered that the text itself is an incomplete or misleading expression of the speaker's base S. The speaker may have deleted part of the text base S in constructing T (because it was obvious to him from context, or for stylistic reasons, or perhaps merely because he wanted to be ob-

scure). Obviously, such discrepancies must be limited; otherwise communication breaks down. (P. 11)

Schematically, then, the newly humanistic English department would look like this:

Literature
  periods
  genres
  . . .
Writing
  "creative"
  expository
  technical
  . . .
Rhetoric
  literary theory
  literacy
    reading
    writing

The new department—and perhaps the new Modern Language Association—would have all of the political power and modernist panache of scientism and thereby would be able to influence the course of literacy and the values inherent in materials, curricula, instructional methods, teacher training, educational administration, government programs, legislative acts—in short, would have the political clout necessary to put faith into action, for does not every English department humanist believe that literature is essential to the good life? Does not every humanist believe that there are, indeed, two kinds of knowledge, and that they are equally valuable?

The problems, of course, are massive. Changing the academy by proposals such as the one I advance is as difficult as changing the course of the Mississippi with a pick and shovel. Changing the attitudes of humanists might be even more difficult, for obviously, the new humanism places great value on application, views the humanities as "applied" arts, somewhat like medicine or architecture, which are "good" and valid only when they result in action in the real world. If the new humanism is to succeed, humanists must give status to teaching and to all of the kinds of research that are necessary to unravel the problems of literacy.

Nothing less than the future of the humanities is at stake.

NOTES

1. Flower and Hayes (1984), whose work falls into the scientismic category, develop a richly provocative critique of the Kintschian text model.

We believe that the plan a writer uses to produce text is not like the Kintschian text base . . . consisting of information in a uniform propositional representation. Rather, it is a mixture of at least three general classes of information:

1. Pointers to information that may be stored in many different forms, such as schemas, episodes, or images (e.g., "tell them about the first day of class last year," "explain the rules of Rugby"). By a pointer we mean a name or cue that can be used to retrieve a body of related information from long-term memory.

2. Word images, perhaps in auditory form, of particular words or phrases to be included in the essay. . . .

3. Goals that include such things as objectives for influencing the audience and content free directions to the writer, such as "add introduction" or "make a transition here."

2. An exception is Robert Pattison's *On Literacy* (1982). This volume, directly in the literarist tradition, has achieved popular success, but it has not,

I think, been influential among linguists, psychologists, and anthropologists.

REFERENCES

Anderson, A. B. and Stokes, S. J. (1984). "Social and Institutional Influences on the Development and Practice of Literacy." In H. Goelman, A. Oberg, and F. Smith, Eds. *Awakening to Literacy*. Exeter, NH: Heinemann Educational Books.

Clark, H. H. and Clark, E. V. (1977). *Psychology and Language: An Introduction to Psycholinguistics.* New York: Harcourt Brace Jovanovich.

Drucker, P. F. (1980). "Ernest Freedberg's World." In P. Drucker, *Adventures of a Bystander*, New York: Harper & Row.

Flower, L. and Hayes, J. R. (1984, January). "Images, Plans, and Prose." *Written Communication*, 1, 120–60.

Gendlin, E. (1978). *Focusing*. New York: Everest House.

Gibson, E. J. and Levin, H. (1975). *The Psychology of Reading.* Cambridge, MA: MIT.

Goelman, H., Oberg, A., and Smith, Frank, Eds. (1984). *Awakening to Literacy.* Exeter, NH: Heinemann Educational Books.

Graff, G. (1970). *Poetic Statement and Critical Dogma.* Chicago: University of Chicago.

Haviland, S. E. and Clark H. H. 1974. "What's New? Acquiring New Information as a Process in Comprehension." *Journal of Verbal Learning and Verbal Behavior*, 13, 512–21.

Hirsch, E. D., Jr. (1977). *The Philosophy of Composition.* Chicago: University of Chicago.

Iser, W. (1978). *The Act of Reading.* Baltimore: Johns Hopkins.

Kinneavy, J. L. (1971). *A Theory of Discourse.* Englewood Cliffs: Prentice-Hall.

Kintsch, W. (1974). *The Representation of Meaning in Memory.* Hillsdale, NJ: Lawrence Erlbaum Associates.

Kintsch, W., Kozminsky, E., Streby, W. J., McKoon, G., and Keenan, M. J. (1975, April). "Comprehension and Recall of Text as a Function of Content Variables." *Journal of Verbal Learning and Verbal Behavior,* 14, 196–214.

Lanham, R. (1983). *Literacy and the Survival of Humanism.* New Haven: Yale University.

Miller, G. A. and Johnson-Laird, P. N. (1976). *Language and Perception.* Cambridge, MA: Harvard University.

Pattison, R. (1982). *On Literacy.* New York: Oxford University.

Perl, S. (1979, December). "The Composing Processes of Unskilled College Writers." *Research in the Teaching of English,* 13, 317–36.

Perl, S. (1983). "Understanding Composing." In J. H. Hays, P. A. Roth, J. R. Ramsey, and R. D. Foulke, Eds. *The Writer's Mind: Writing as a Mode of Thinking.* Urbana: NCTE.

Ricoeur, P. (1974). "Structure, Word, Event." R. Sweeney, Trans. In Don Ihde, Ed. *Conflict of Interpretations: Essays in Hermeneutics.* Evanston: Northwestern University.

Smith, F. (1983). *Essays into Literacy.* Exeter, NH: Heinemann Educational Books.

Tannen, D. (1983). "Oral and Literate Strategies in Spoken and Written Discourse." In R. W. Bailey and R. M. Fosheim, Eds. *Literacy for Life: the Demand for Reading and Writing.* New York: MLA.

Taylor, I. and Taylor, M. M. (1983). *The Psychology of Reading.* New York: Academic Press.

Tulving, E. (1972). "Episodic and Semantic Memory." In E. Tulving and W. Donaldson, Eds. *Organization of Memory.* New York: Academic Press.

White, J. B. (1983). In R. W. Bailey and R. M. Fosheim, Eds. *Literacy for Life: the Demand for Reading and Writing.* New York: MLA.

Winterowd, W. R. (1980, May). "The Paradox of the Humanities." *ADE Bulletin,* 64, 2.

Winterowd, W. R. (1983, October). "Dramatism in Themes and Poems." *College English,* 45, 581–88.

Winters, Y. (1943). *In Defense of Reason.* Denver: Alan Swallow.

Index

Works cited in part 1 of this book appear in the index under the last name of the author and the date of the work in parentheses, thus: Cain (1981). Full bibliographic information appears in the references, beginning on page 113.